THE BRITISH FIGHTER SINCE 1912

Royal Air Force fighter power displayed by the English Electric Lightning F.Mk.1s of No. 74 Squadron. (Rolls-Royce Photo.)

THE
BRITISH FIGHTER
SINCE 1912

SIXTY-SEVEN YEARS OF DESIGN
AND DEVELOPMENT

Peter Lewis

F.I.B.A., Associate R.Ae.S.

PUTNAM
LONDON

By the same author

BRITISH RACING AND RECORD-BREAKING AIRCRAFT

THE BRITISH BOMBER SINCE 1914

BRITISH AIRCRAFT
1809–1914

SQUADRON HISTORIES
R.F.C., R.N.A.S. & R.A.F. SINCE 1912

ISBN 0 370 10049 2

Printed in Great Britain for
Putnam & Company Limited
9 Bow Street, London WC2E 7AL
by Fletcher & Son Ltd, Norwich
Set in Monotype Plantin
First published 1965
Second edition 1967
Third edition 1974
Fourth edition 1979

To the test pilots
– past and present –
whose skill, courage and sacrifice have
advanced the British fighter.

CONTENTS

PREFACE

Among the weapons in Great Britain's arsenal the fighter has, since its inception as the scout of the Army and the Navy, an unbroken history of continuous and intensive development, allied to a magnificent record of service established over fifty years by those types selected for production as squadron equipment.

The evolution of British fighters has been dictated to a considerable degree by the requirements issued by the Services demanding the aircraft and these needs have resulted across half a century in a relatively diverse selection of types in pursuit of the ideal machine called for at the time.

So as to place this evolution in perspective *The British Fighter Since 1912* outlines the birth of military and naval flying in the United Kingdom, together with the early acceptance of the scout and its subsequent arming to quickly become a fighter in the 1914–18 War. A number of the most illustrious types established their reputations in the inferno of two great wars when they were flown on their intended duties with great bravery by Service pilots. Their stirring exploits have been deservedly recorded at length many times and *The British Fighter Since 1912* has been written to encompass solely the development of the aircraft by the designers, constructors and test pilots concerned.

To attempt to chronicle the whole complex story would result in a work of such inordinate length as to remove it from the bounds of a commercial venture but it is hoped that, within the prescribed commercial and security limits, *The British Fighter Since 1912* has recorded to a worthwhile degree the evolution of one of the greatest of British engineering products.

Throughout the whole of the period devoted to the preparation of this work the following organizations have rendered untiringly every possible assistance and I am greatly indebted to them:—A.B.C. Motors Ltd.; Airscrew-Weyroc Ltd.; Sir W. G. Armstrong Whitworth Ltd.; Austin Motor Co. Ltd.; Wm. Beardmore and Co. Ltd.; Blackburn Aircraft Ltd.; Boulton Paul Aircraft Ltd.; Bristol Aircraft Ltd.; Bristol Siddeley Engines Ltd.; de Havilland Aircraft Ltd.; de Havilland Engine Co. Ltd.; Dowty Group Services Ltd.; Dunlop Rubber Co. Ltd.; English Electric Aviation Ltd.; Firestone Tyre and Rubber Co. Ltd.; Flight Refuelling Ltd.; Folland Aircraft Ltd.; General Precision Systems Ltd.; Gloster Aircraft Co. Ltd.; Goodyear Tyre and Rubber Co. Ltd.; Handley Page Ltd.; Hawker Aircraft Ltd.; Irving Air Chute of Great Britain Ltd.; Lockheed Precision Products Ltd.; Mann Egerton and Co. Ltd.; Martin-Baker Aircraft Co. Ltd.; Napier Aero Engines Ltd.; Palmer Aero Products Ltd.; A. V. Roe and Co. Ltd.; Rolls-Royce Ltd.; Rover Co. Ltd.; Fredk. Sage and Co. Ltd.; Saunders-Roe Ltd.; Short Brothers and Harland Ltd.; Triplex Safety Glass Co. Ltd.; Vickers-Armstrongs (Aircraft) Ltd.; Westland Aircraft Ltd.

Of the greatest value also was the willing contribution made by a number of members of the staff of the Ministry of Aviation.

In addition, I am very grateful for the kindness of Mr. H. F. King, then Editor of *Flight International*, in granting me additional facilities for research, and for the very competent and ready assistance received from Miss Ann C. Tilbury, the Photographic Librarian of *Flight International*.

The help rendered by Mr. J. F. Golding of the Photographic Section of the Imperial War Museum, Mr. S. H. Handasyde, Mr. E. C. H. Hine of the Photographic Section of the Imperial War Museum, Mr. G. H. Miles, Mr. Richard T. Riding and Wg.Cdr. N. H. F. Unwin was deeply appreciated.

Finally, a word of thanks is due to my wife for her assistance in numerous ways throughout the entire time spent in preparing the book.

P.M.H.L.

Benfleet,
Essex.
February, 1965.

PREFACE TO FOURTH EDITION

Research prior to publication of the third edition of *The British Fighter Since 1912* in 1974 disclosed the drastic—and, consequently, exceedingly disturbing —reduction in the customary prodigious activity displayed in British fighter design, a sphere responsible formerly for the creditable and stimulating diversity of aircraft types, many of which—during half a century of intensive development—had acquired universal renown and had contributed immeasurably to the United Kingdom's survival.

The progression of this extremely grave situation has been confirmed in the course of the ensuing five years, the solitary example of continued development of a British-conceived first-line fighter for the Royal Air Force and the Fleet Air Arm being that of the Hawker Siddeley Harrier, the evolution of which—together with that of the derivative Sea Harrier F.R.S.Mk.1—is recounted in this fourth edition. Recorded also is the conception of the Hawker Siddeley HS.1182 Hawk as a fighter for export.

Although *The British Fighter Since 1912* was conceived to narrate the history of exclusively indigenous British fighter aircraft, as use as a fighter is included among the specific rôles of the collaborative-venture S.E.P.E.C.A.T. Jaguar G.R.Mk.1 and Panavia 200 Tornado F.Mk.2 details have been included of both of these aircraft to bring this survey of British fighter evolution up to date.

P.M.H.L.

Benfleet,
Essex.
July, 1979.

Grahame-White Type 11 Warplane at Hendon in 1914.

CHAPTER ONE

PRELUDE TO POWER

Every field of activity has, in each era of History, been blessed with its share of visionaries and men of intelligence and initiative who, by their endeavours, have made profound contributions to progress. In numerous instances, their efforts and foresight have subscribed greatly to the defence and the ultimate survival of their homelands.

Great Britain, no less than any other country, owes a debt of the greatest magnitude to those of her sons who saved her in the times of peril when her traditional freedom was challenged by those who, in their enmity, sought to destroy her. The time is long since past when inborn courage coupled with primitive weapons was sufficient to ensure the Nation's continued well-being. The inexorable, relentless progress of science extends its influence either dramatically or insidiously, with methods of waging warfare always a particularly receptive objective.

With the advent of the free balloon in the middle of the 18th Century and the arrival of the mechanical revolution at the beginning of the 19th Century, the start of the demise of the old traditional weapons, which had been firmly entrenched with comparatively little change over many decades, was discernible. The art of ballooning gradually gathered momentum, with several scientists, research workers and chemists using it as a convenient means of transporting themselves and their instruments aloft to broaden their knowledge of the Earth and its surrounding atmosphere. These earliest aeronauts were civilians but the invention began to attract the notice of the Army as a useful way of organizing observation of the enemy's disposition in time of war.

In 1862 a British army officer, Lt. George Edward Grover of the Royal Engineers, conducted with vigour a series of experiments in the lighter-than-air field, committing the conclusions he reached in his investigations to two papers entitled *On the Employment of Balloons in Warfare* and *On the Uses of Balloons in Military Operations*. For several years afterwards conferences were held with the authorities in quest of a grant to enable the officer to continue his balloon work but, following a decision made in 1868 by the Secretary of State for War that the proposal "may wait", Lt. Grover was forced through lack of finance to discontinue his experiments. At least, however, in view of his scientific approach to the subject and his recording in his two papers of the results, Lt. Grover earned himself the honour of the title of "Father of British Military Aeronautics".

Official reluctance to take a progressive step towards allowing aeronautics to play a part in assisting the Army was overcome to a small degree a few years later when, early in 1878, Capt. J. L. B. Templer of the 2nd Middlesex Militia was successful in obtaining an allocation of £150 to construct a balloon for the use of the Army. This small sum is a matter of importance in British military history as it constitutes the first example of official allotment of funds for the purpose—in short, it was the first Air Estimate.

Through the use of his private means Capt. Templer had become a balloonist of some aptitude and possessed his own balloon, the *Crusader*. Out of the grant of £150, £71 was put into constructing at Woolwich Arsenal another, the *Pioneer* of 10,000 cu.ft. capacity. The new balloon, with a varnish-impregnated cambric envelope was completed in August, 1878. Its tests, following a first ascent on 23rd August, were successful and, as a result, Capt. Templer was delegated by the War Office to undertake the training of a group of Royal Engineer officers as balloonists. In the same year, the Balloon Equipment Store, comprising the Balloon Factory and later the Balloon School, was established at Woolwich to provide quarters. To expedite his work, Capt. Templer employed his *Crusader* in conjunction with the *Pioneer*.

In this way was laid the very foundation upon which has since been built, step by step, the vast organization of British military and naval flying services and their associated experimental establishments.

During the Summer of 1882, the Balloon Section of the Royal Engineers participated in the army manœuvres at Aldershot and exhibited such promise that the Balloon Equipment Store was transferred to Chatham to become part of the School of Military Engineering which was based there. The War Office ordered the move in October, 1882, and the following year saw the construction, with the assistance of Lt. J. E. Capper, R.E., of the *Sapper*, a smaller balloon of 5,600 cu.ft. made with a silk envelope impregnated with linseed oil.

Hearing of these activities a private balloonist, Walter Powell, called on Capt. Templer for help in completing his own balloon which was being constructed of goldbeater's skin. Together with the Weinlings, a Swiss family who were helping him to construct his 10,000 cu.ft. envelope, Powell had run into trouble in its manufacture. The War Office sanctioned the use of the Balloon

The F.E.3, known also as the A.E.1, carried its tail on a single boom and mounted a 1·5-pounder C.O.W. gun in the nacelle. (Imperial War Museum Photo.)

Section's facilities and Powell's balloon was finished in a roofed-over ball-court at St. Mary's Barracks in Chatham. The new balloon, christened *Heron*, turned out to be very successful in its tests and was directly instrumental in the War Office's decision that goldbeater's skin should be used for the envelopes of all future lighter-than-air products of the Balloon Factory.

During the same period, 1883–84, balloon capacity categories were established as F class of 5,000 cu.ft., S class of 7,000 cu.ft. and T class of 10,000 cu.ft.

In the immediate ensuing years a number of other balloons were constructed by the Balloon Factory for the expanding Balloon School until, in 1886, larger premises than those at the Chatham Barracks were found to be essential. To a man of Capt. Templer's drive and initiative, the slowness of the War Office grants was a great handicap and he bought out of his own funds some land adjacent to his home at Lidsing, some five miles outside Chatham, to provide extra accommodation. Until 1887, Capt. Templer had met from his own pocket a considerable portion of the cost of running the Balloon Equipment Store, but eventually, as Major Templer, he was gazetted on 1st April, 1887, as Instructor in Ballooning.

Sir Evelyn Wood's report on the 1889 army manœuvres held at Aldershot emphasized the value of the accuracy of the observations made from Major Templer's balloons and recommended that the Balloon Factory and School should be moved from Chatham to Aldershot to improve liaison with other Army formations. The War Office approved of the suggestion and in 1890 allocated a site for the Balloon Section, Royal Engineers, within the Royal Engineers' Lines in the South Camp at Aldershot. Increased recognition by the War Office of the scouting value of balloons was shown in the Army Estimates for 1890 which, in addition to the Instructor in Ballooning's salary of £600, allocated over £3,000 for stores and another £1,000 to provide a new depôt and school. All of this was expected to repay the Army with improved observation facilities and marked the Service's growing appreciation of the possibilities of the new science.

In 1892 the School of Ballooning, together with the Factory, was set up in Balloon Square, Aldershot, and experimental work continued, resulting in larger balloons being constructed under V class of 11,500 cu.ft. and A class of 13,000 cu.ft.

The scope of the Royal Engineers' aeronautical activities was broadened in June, 1894, with the setting up of a man-lifting kite section at the Balloon School. This new indulgence was approved as a consequence of successful tests with large kites carried out at Farnborough and Pirbright by Capt. B. F. S. Baden-Powell of the Scots Guards. By this time the Balloon Factory was firmly ensconced at Aldershot under Lt.Col. Templer's efficient direction so that, in 1897, he was appointed Superintendent. The instructional work was the responsibility of the Officer in Charge of the Balloon Section.

Two years later the Boer War of 1899 saw balloon detachments being sent to South Africa to assist the Army in observation, and this called for a doubling of the Factory's normal production rate of one a month to meet the demand.

In 1902, as a result of reports of the experiments made by Santos Dumont and Count von Zeppelin, the Balloon Factory started to take an interest in airships. Permission was sought and granted for two non-rigid, elongated, goldbeater's skin envelopes, each of 50,000 cu.ft. capacity, to be made and they were ready in 1904 but work then came to a halt owing to insufficient money being available.

1904 brought the colourful S. F. Cody on the scene to demonstrate his system of man-lifting kites to the War Office, which was impressed to the extent of appointing him as Chief Kiting Instructor at the Balloon School in 1906.

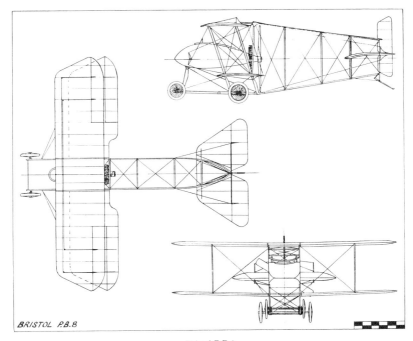

Bristol P.B.8

14

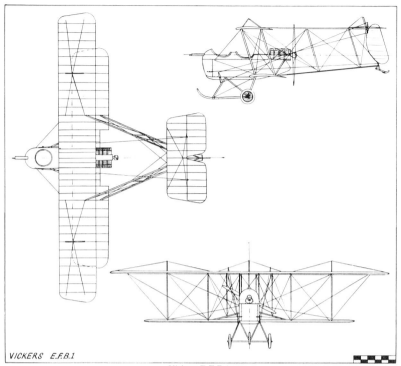

VICKERS E.F.B.1

Vickers E.F.B.1

Yet another move was in prospect for the Balloon Factory which, in 1905, found itself in a better position at South Farnborough. During the Spring of 1906, Col. J. E. Capper, R.E., took over as Superintendent from Col. Templer who was made Consulting Engineer. Cody then became associated with Col. Templer in a project to complete an airship from one of the pair of 1904 non-rigid envelopes, and the finished product, *Nulli Secundus 1*, flew in September, 1907. Its performance was not particularly spectacular but the airship had at least given the Factory its start in powered flight.

Coincident with the Factory's lighter-than-air work were the first tentative steps taken within its boundaries towards the construction of a heavier-than-air machine. Since the turn of the century Lt. J. W. Dunne, encouraged by his friends the inventor Sir Hiram Maxim and the visionary H. G. Wells, had been experimenting privately with models as a prelude to an inherently stable design of aeroplane. During 1905 he was introduced to Col. Capper by Col. J. Winn, R.E., a member of the Royal Engineer Committee, with the result that in the following year, under conditions of the strictest secrecy, work was started in No. 3 Building on the Balloon Factory's first full-size aeroplane, the Dunne D.1. On its completion in 1907 it was taken to the seclusion of Blair Atholl in Scotland for flying trials, initially as a glider and then powered with a pair of small Buchet engines.

Cody was not slow in seeking permission to emulate Dunne and his first machine, flown pilotless in 1907, consisted of one of his kites equipped with a 15 h.p. Buchet for power. The final failure of the *Nulli Secundus 2* airship presented Cody with the opportunity to use its 50 h.p. Antoinette engine, around which his British Army Aeroplane No. 1 was constructed. Despite the backing given to Dunne, both the D.1 and the D.4 were unsuccessful in accomplishing anything more than very short hops, but Cody was somewhat luckier. His triumphant moment came on 16th October, 1908, when he covered 1,390 ft. in the air to establish the first official powered and sustained flight in Great Britain. At long last the deed had been accomplished but the aspirations of Cody and Dunne, as far as His Majesty's Balloon Factory was concerned, were brought to a halt during the Spring of 1909 with the War Office's conclusion that the limited results achieved, after an expenditure of £2,500, did not warrant further grants to the two experimenters. This unfortunate decision was announced at a time when Germany's current expenditure on military aviation was £400,000. Cody and Dunne thereupon severed their connections with the Factory and, over the ensuing few years, went on independently to turn their widely-differing concepts into successful flying machines. Their stay at the Factory, however, had not been without general benefit and they left behind them a legacy of innovations which their work had brought to the establishment. As well as having gained some practical experience in aeroplane structures, the design side had, in 1907, acquired its first wind tunnel which was operated by Capt. A. D. Carden, R.E., to provide data for Lt. Dunne's work. This wood and canvas tunnel of similar layout to that already in use at the National Physical Laboratory, had a working section of about five feet square and was twenty feet long.

Under Col. Capper's energetic guidance and his enthusiasm for the new science, with its adventure and boundless scope for investigation, experiments had been initiated and conducted into wireless signalling, aerial photography, aero-engine design and the production of the accessories associated with aeronautical construction and operations. In short, the Factory derived considerable and far-reaching benefits through the stimulus created by the needs of the early aeronauts working under its wing.

During Col. Capper's period as Superintendent he was confronted with the usual problem met by anyone employed under a higher authority and striving for success in a new field. General scepticism of the value of such new-fangled devices as flying machines, and a lack of appreciation of the immediate difficulties and needs of those actually engaged in the work at first hand, were instrumental in encouraging the Treasury to keep a tight grip on the purse-strings, despite Col. Capper's recommendations, on his return from his visit in 1904 to the Wright brothers at Dayton to obtain details of their experiments, that development of the aeroplane should be fostered in the interests of maintaining the superiority of the British Army over any rivals. The War Office was not prepared yet to demonstrate a virile attitude of out-and-out encouragement towards the establishment of British military aviation on a firm footing, but condescended to keep in touch with progress abroad.

The shapely S.E.2 of 1913 with monocoque fuselage. (Imperial War Museum Photo.)

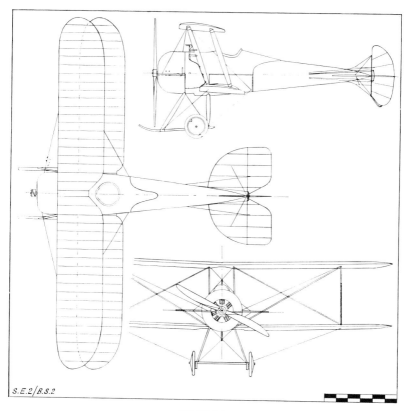

S.E.2/B.S.2

S.E.2/B.S.2

17

This complacent and irresolute behaviour—to be seen to the misfortune of the country on countless occasions to the present day, owing to the inexperience and incompetence of those in whose hands it has been unfortunate to place the decisions for its defence policy—was brought to a stop in 1909. In the previous year Wilbur Wright's demonstrations in France, coupled with the growing successes of the French flyers, had made it clear to even the most obtuse that the aeroplane was gathering irresistibly in its wake a rapidly growing following of experimenters, a force which was bound to establish itself and forge ahead with increasing momentum. Louis Blériot's traversing of the English Channel on 25th July, 1909, was the final blow at the barrier to the advance of military aviation in the United Kingdom. These events, together with the successful development of the airship by Count von Zeppelin in a visibly militant Germany, brought home to the British people the scandalous state of unpreparedness to counter attack from the sky, and the fact that the time had arrived when, without further disastrous vacillation, aeronautics must form an integral portion of the Nation's armed forces.

The first result of this realization was that instructions were issued in the early part of 1909 for the reorganization of H.M. Balloon Factory to ensure increased production of airships, and for the setting up of an Advisory Committee for Aeronautics. At the end of 1909 the Balloon Section of the Royal Engineers broke away from the Factory and was put under Col. Capper's command. A prominent consulting engineer, Mervyn O'Gorman, was ap-

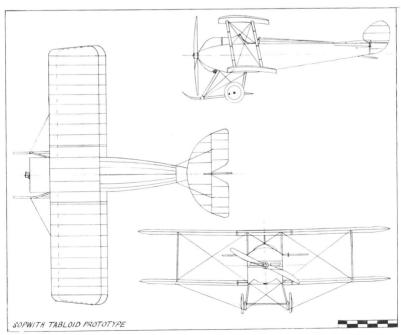

SOPWITH TABLOID PROTOTYPE

Sopwith Tabloid

Sopwith Tabloid prototype at Brooklands. (Flight International Photo.)

pointed Superintendent of H.M. Balloon Factory. The Factory thus at last gained the status due to it as a specialist scientific establishment. F. M. Green joined the organization to fill the newly-created position of Assistant Engineer of Designs and expansion took place in departments for Chemistry, Engines, Metallurgy, Physics and Wireless, so that facilities were available within call to resolve problems as they were met. And so the Factory was set up on a rational, organized basis to make its contribution to the defence of the country. The field of design, which had hitherto been treated somewhat as an art, now advanced into the realm of calculated science, with mathematics taking over in the stressing of structures and in the assessment of control and stability characteristics.

During this first decade of practical flight in Great Britain while the Army engineers were at least, albeit slowly, acquiring improved facilities, the picture was a vastly different one for the private individual experimenter. The Army aeronauts were lucky enough to be shielded from public derision and were able to carry out their aerial activities as their paid work, even though the funds at their disposal were meagre. On the other side of the fence, the civilian enthusiast had to bear the entire cost of his experiments himself and hardship was the lot of a number of the pioneer constructors with little or no likelihood of financial reward to reimburse them even should their machines be successful. In spite of these poor prospects numerous aeroplanes were appearing from civilian sheds up and down the country and March, 1909, saw the first Aero Show at Olympia presenting some of the pioneer creations, fantastic and otherwise, for the public's appraisal.

Over a period of some forty years since Lt. Grover's early investigations into what aeronautics could offer, the War Office had very slowly and reluctantly begun to recognize that there might be some advantages to be gained by the employment of balloons and dirigibles and, finally, even of aeroplanes for scouting. This realization, aided and abetted by the personnel of the Balloon Factory and the Balloon Section of the Royal Engineers, had by the end of 1910 brought the Army to the point where, under official approval, it possessed its own facilities for the production, maintenance and employment of its aeronautical equipment.

Parallel with the stirrings of the birth of military aviation in the country were the attempts being made to fly by private individuals in widely-scattered parts. Ballooning had been practised and popular since the latter part of the 18th Century but, as the free balloon could not be induced to transport its passengers where and when they wished, the idea took hold of the navigable, powered airship. Several were built by private constructors during the decade from 1902, notably those by Dr. F. A. Barton, Spencer Brothers and E. T. Willows. The Willows non-rigid airships, five of which were produced at Cardiff, were outstandingly successful; Nos. 4 and 5 were bought by the Admiralty for training and Willows's idea of swivelling propellers to endow vertical movement was adopted by the Army Balloon Factory for use on its 2a, *Gamma* and *Delta*. Those whose approach to the problem of flight followed the path of the balloon or the airship, with built-in lift in a gas-filled envelope, could hardly fail to leave the ground.

The heavier-than-air machine, however, presented a far more formidable obstacle to overcome. There was a dearth of collated knowledge of any form of aerodynamics or control and any suitable power plant was non-existent. Gradually, throughout the 19th Century, interest increased as more experimenters joined in the quest for a man-carrying flying vehicle.

Head and shoulders above the early researchers was Sir George Cayley, whose investigations were carried out on remarkably sound lines and who left behind him such magnificent records of his work. By the end of the 18th Century, Cayley had arrived at, and recorded, the basic layout of the heavier-than-air machine and was to develop the form through experiments, models and three full-size gliders until his death in 1857. No other inventor of the period was able to make such an outstanding contribution to the advancement of the science, but little subsequent progress ensued until the approach of the 20th Century. New investigators, among them Horatio Phillips, Sir Hiram Maxim and Percy Pilcher, had taken up the challenge and, but for Pilcher's sudden death during 1899 in his glider, the Hawk, it is indeed likely that his would have been the honour of making the World's first powered flight as, at the time of his demise, he had already constructed an aero engine of his own design specially for the purpose.

During the ensuing ten years, while the War Office-sponsored experimenters were busy in their various ways, a succession of new names appeared on the civilian scene, all of them intent on grappling with the problem and solving it, despite the lack of prospect of any monetary return for their labours and the risks to their very lives that their self-taught flying entailed. Spurred on by reports of success following success on the Continent, particularly in France, the British pioneers strove to be the equals of the foreigners. Through sheer tenacity and endurance, their efforts eventually bore fruit.

Of the numerous designers and constructors who indulged their fancy in constructing aeroplanes, a hard core won through to have their names perpetuated as the founders of the British aircraft industry. Among the survivors of the uncertainties of the early gruelling and dangerous days were Robert Blackburn, the British and Colonial Aeroplane Company, Geoffrey de Havilland, Claude Grahame-White, Frederick Handley Page, Martin-Handasyde, Noel Pemberton Billing, Alliott Verdon Roe, the Short brothers, T. O. M. Sopwith and Vickers. Many among the pioneer constructors and flyers could not afford to continue to jeopardize their livelihoods in such a risky venture and gave up but others teamed up in the small firms being formed to design and manufacture aeroplanes, subsequently achieving fame as designers or pilots.

During 1910 there occurred one of those chance meetings which may sometimes have such far-reaching effects. F. M. Green engaged in conversation with Geoffrey de Havilland who, after having crashed his first aeroplane early in its tests, had constructed another and taught himself to fly on it. De Havilland told Green that, as the financial resources which he had had for pursuing his flying experiments were all but exhausted, it looked as though he might have to terminate such work. At Green's suggestion, de Havilland applied to the Balloon Factory for a post as designer and test pilot. The outcome was that in December, 1910, he and his friend and assistant, F. T. Hearle, joined the staff of the Factory, taking with them to Farnborough the biplane for which the War Office paid £400. Although at the time it was evident neither to the authorities nor to de Havilland, in this way was the pioneer constructor enabled to carry on his work to such outstanding advantage in later years to the country, and to give immediate impetus to heavier-than-air development at the Factory by delivering to it a reasonably practical aeroplane. The Factory was so enamoured of its new acquisition that it bestowed on it the honour of the first official designation F.E.1.

In design and execution de Havilland's machine was, without exception, typical of the aeroplanes of the period. The layout was that of the successful Farman-style two-bay biplane with stabilizing and control surfaces carried on four booms fore and aft of the wings. The pilot's position was the logical one on the leading edge of the lower wings, with the engine and its pusher propeller mounted behind him. Two main wheels and a tailskid formed the landing-gear and ailerons gave the machine its lateral control. The engine was the 45 h.p. unit which had been made to de Havilland's design by the Iris Motor Company at Willesden. The entire framework of the biplane was of wood, the material resorted to by most of the constructors at the time. Its great virtue was that it was easily worked, without the necessity on the part of the impecunious flyers for any outlay on expensive tools or machines. Besides, wood was strong and cheap and easily repaired after the all-too-frequent mishaps which attended the attempts to stagger off the ground. The structure was braced with tensioned wire and covered with fabric.

During the first few months of the F.E.1's life at H.M. Balloon Factory, the advent of the aeroplane as a practical and serious entity was recognized by the renaming of the establishment on 26th April, 1911, as the Army Aircraft Factory.

An Army Order of 28th February, 1911, gave similar recognition in announcing that, on 1st April, 1911, the Balloon Section of the Royal Engineers would be reorganized as the Air Battalion of the Royal Engineers. The headquarters were to be at South Farnborough alongside No. 1 (Airship) Company, while No. 2 (Aeroplane) Company was to be formed at Larkhill for the express purpose of creating a trained nucleus of aeroplane pilots.

In the face of obstinate refusal to wake up and exploit with vigour the great advantages that it could give to both the Army and the Navy, the military potential of the aeroplane had belatedly been given the chance to prove itself. In addition to its duties of training aeroplane pilots, the Air Battalion was to include in its scope the kite and balloon handling instruction hitherto carried on by the Balloon School. The Air Battalion soon got down to work under the overall command of Major Sir Alexander Bannerman; the Airship Company was in the charge of Capt. E. M. Maitland and Capt. J. D. B. Fulton administered the Aeroplane Company. By August, 1911, nine aeroplanes of assorted type were in use by the unit but none could be looked upon as being able to perform in an offensive rôle.

The general picture in the Navy was hardly more favourable. Comfortably ensconced in a long tradition of the unbeatable might of the Royal Navy, the Admiralty showed little desire to bestir itself to add these featherweight wood and canvas contraptions to complement the bulk and strength of its fleet of iron dreadnoughts with their massive guns and heavy firepower. Its sole sign of interest so far had been the placing of an order with Vickers, Son and Maxim for the Naval Rigid R.1, popularly known as the Mayfly, an airship which eventually broke its back without flying.

The spark which finally moved their Lordships to action early in 1911 came from a prominent member of the Royal Aero Club, F. K. McClean. In February, on temporarily suspending his flying activities at the Club's aerodrome at Eastchurch on the Isle of Sheppey owing to making a trip to Fiji with an expedition, he offered to lend his pair of Short biplanes to the Admiralty so that naval personnel could be given instruction in piloting. Another of the earliest flyers, G. B. Cockburn, volunteered to act as instructor without reimbursement. Such magnanimity melted any remaining opposition in the Admiralty and a call for volunteers for the course was quickly sent out. Four officers—three naval and one marine—were selected from more than two hundred applicants and on 2nd March, 1911, started on the venture which included technical instruction by Short Brothers in their Leysdown works. Although the course was scheduled to last for six months, the enthusiasm of the trainees was so great that it was completed successfully in a quarter of the intended time. Such progress was instrumental in influencing the Admiralty to purchase both of McClean's Shorts and to set up at the end of 1911 at Eastchurch the first naval school of flying by acquiring ten acres of land alongside the Club's ground. The staff consisted of the four members of the original course, together with twelve ratings, and the establishment constituted the groundwork upon which arose the Royal Naval Air Service and its successor, the Fleet Air Arm.

Although the Army now had its Air Battalion and the Navy its flying school, neither service could claim that it yet possessed any air power of usable proportions. Obviously, the whole position of aeronautics in the defence of the country would have to be reviewed without delay and put on a positive footing for the best use of the money being spent and, at the same time, to maintain at least parity with the Continental powers who were forging ahead strongly in their determination to exploit the new militant force to their own advantage.

Accordingly, a Technical Sub-Committee of the Committee of Imperial Defence was convened on 18th December, 1911, to make its recommendations for the formation of an effective third Service with the air as its medium of operations. Compared with the inordinate period taken by various committees in later decades to reach any conclusions, useful or otherwise, the Technical Sub-Committee under Lord Haldane, then Secretary for War, performed their difficult task in a remarkably short time, setting an example of which later generations might well have taken note with advantage. But three years had passed since the first faltering flight had been made in Great Britain and there were few of experience on whom the members of the Sub-Committee could draw for guidance and advice. Even so, their understanding of the problem was such that their work was complete in ten weeks and two months later, on 25th April, the Committee of Imperial Defence accepted their recommendations.

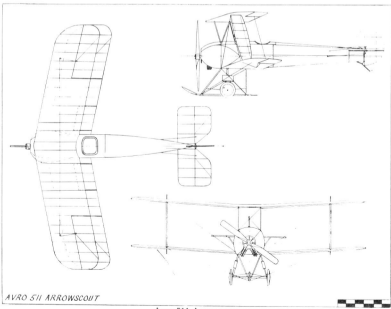

Avro 511 Arrowscout

23

These proposed the formation of a new service, to be known as the Royal Flying Corps, within the framework of which were to be a Military and a Naval Wing, a Central Flying School, a Reserve and the Royal Aircraft Factory. 13th May, 1912, was selected as the date for this important addition to the country's armed forces.

Acceptance of the aeroplane and the setting up of the facilities for its employment as a weapon did not mean, however, that suitable machines were available as operational equipment. This was far from being the case as was obvious from the heterogeneous collection of types which had until then been at the disposal of the Air Battalion of the Royal Engineers for initiation into flying. There had been no attempts on the part of the few struggling civilian aircraft constructors to produce any machine designed specifically for military operations. What was the point of building an aeroplane for use by a non-existent service? Financially, survival was still too precarious a business to risk money and effort on development of a class of aircraft for which there was no foreseeable demand. Again, too short a time had elapsed for the machines then flying to be reliable enough to withstand the rigours of regular military use without further intensive and steady development.

Another obstacle was the lack of a reasonably broad range of aero engines of the requisite light weight and performance. As early as 1904, the Balloon Factory had been conscious of the dearth of suitable engines for its needs and 35 h.p. upright four- and six-cylinder experimental aero engines, designed by F. McWade, were constructed but not developed into production units. This awkward position was eased somewhat by the appearance of the Green, E.N.V., N.E.C. and one or two other British engines but the main drawback continued to be the poor power/weight ratio.

Then, suddenly, the entire picture changed with the advent at the first Olympia Aero Show in March, 1909, of the French 50 h.p. Gnome seven-cylinder rotary. Here, at last, was sufficient power coupled with reasonably acceptable reliability and the low weight of 165 lb. Little time elapsed before Mons. Séguin's engine was proclaiming itself on the British flying scene with its now often nostalgically recalled odour of burnt castor oil. The appearance of the Gnome was the signal for an immediate advance in aircraft performance and brought forth in the next few years a galaxy of new designs using its power.

The immediate use seen for the aeroplane by its advocates in the armed services was that of reconnaissance in which it could replace the traditional cavalry as a scouting force. Increased speed in reporting the enemy's disposition and far greater range of vision were two of the new arrival's great attributes.

Since the days when it had been the Balloon Factory, the Army Aircraft Factory had naturally, in its daily association with the military aspect of aeronautics at Farnborough, been conscious of some degree of war potential in the aeroplane and had experimented accordingly with wireless and photography. Eventually, it was realized that an aeroplane reconnoitring enemy positions might need to carry its own defensive armament, and to test such

Two-seat Vickers Scout of 1914. (Vickers Photo.)

an installation a Maxim free-firing machine-gun was fitted on a simple mounting in the nose of the nacelle of the F.E.2 biplane during 1912. The F.E.2 was originally the F.E.1 which had been reconstructed in 1911 with modifications following its crash during the Summer of the same year while being flown by Lt. T. J. Ridge, then the Factory's Assistant Superintendent. The Iris engine had been replaced by the popular 50 h.p. Gnome and crew comfort was improved by the addition of a two-seat covered nacelle projecting in front of the lower wings.

The way ahead to the evolution of the armed scout was clearly opening up. Successful tests throughout the year prompted yet another rebuilding of the long-suffering F.E.2, and early in 1913 the machine was completely re-designed and reconstructed as a two-seat gun-carrier of greatly refined aspect compared with its earlier appearance. The former crude, slab-sided nacelle had given way to a new structure of far cleaner and pleasanter aerodynamic form with good protection for the tandem-seated crew. Behind them was the increased power of a 70 h.p. Renault engine driving a four-blade propeller. The well-rounded plan-form of the B.E.2a was evident in the new outer wing panels and the entire tail unit had been revised, attention being paid also to cleaning up the landing gear. The gun mounting in the nose had been improved and, altogether, the new F.E.2 presented an extremely workmanlike appearance. The alterations had brought the span up to 42 ft. and increased the loaded weight by 50%. The top speed also had been improved to 67 m.p.h. The machine continued to be flown for the rest of the year but its end came abruptly on 23rd February, 1914, when it crashed near Wittering while being flown by Ronald Kemp, with fatal consequences to the other occupant, E. T. Haynes. The cause of the accident was ascertained to have been lack of fin area to balance the forward side area which had increased when the new enlarged nacelle had been fitted. Nevertheless, the F.E.2. had served the Factory well and had proved to be very good value at the £400 which the War Office had paid originally for it. In its final metamorphosis the machine played the part of the progenitor of the Fighting Experimental series of pusher biplanes the first of which, the F.E.2a, had been designed at the Factory during August, 1913, some six months before the F.E.2's demise.

Although, in the straightforward two-bay pusher biplane layout of the F.E.2, the Factory's designers had played safe by following a formula which was by then well proven, the next machine to be built within the Fighting Experimental category, the F.E.3, displayed an innovation which was a startling departure from the conventional. Designed primarily as a gun-carrier with a crew of two, it appeared at Farnborough in 1913. With a span of 48 ft. and a loaded weight of 2,100 lb., the machine was larger and heavier than its predecessor, the F.E.2. Stagger had been introduced in the wing cellules and the nacelle enclosed the 80 h.p. Chenu engine which received its supply of cooling air by way of the circular nose orifice. The four-blade propeller was mounted at the rear end of the nacelle and was remarkable in that it revolved around the single metal tubular boom which carried the tail

Vickers E.F.B.2 Gunbus of 1913. (Imperial War Museum Photo.)

surfaces and which replaced the structure of a quartette of braced wooden booms normally utilized for the purpose. The wheel and skid undercarriage was quite conventional. The F.E.3's alternative designation was A.E.1, a title which is likely to have indicated Armed Experimental in view of the aircraft's intended purpose. The Coventry Ordnance Works 1·5-pounder quick-firing gun was mounted inside the nacelle to fire its shells through the nose opening, trials of the installation being carried out during the Summer of 1913 in the single example built of the F.E.3.

Despite the fact that the abortive Military Trials staged at Larkhill in August, 1912, had failed completely to satisfy the War Office's avowed intention of procuring suitable aeroplanes for the equipment of the Royal Flying Corps, and had deprived the constructors of anticipated orders, the embryo British aircraft industry continued to expand and consolidate itself. Several firms were now set well on their feet, particularly those companies which had been formed as aviation departments of already soundly established parent organizations.

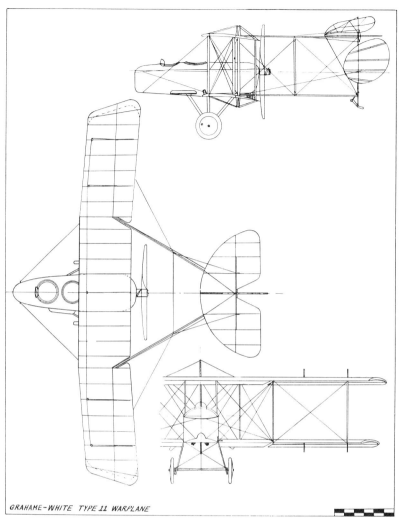

GRAHAME-WHITE TYPE 11 WARPLANE

Grahame-White Type 11 Warplane

The British and Colonial Aeroplane Company, backed by shrewd management, financial security and with a galaxy of designing and flying talent at its disposal, was in this happy position. The Bristol Boxkite had been an instant success from its flying début at the end of July, 1910, and continued in production until the Autumn of 1914. Its ascendancy as a trainer turned it into a good business proposition for the Company and settled once and for all any doubts that the firm might have had about expanding in the new field of aviation.

The design team working at Bristol included G. H. Challenger, Mons.

27

Pierre Prier, E. C. Gordon England, F. S. Barnwell, C. W. Tinson and the volatile Mons. Henri Coanda. This versatile Roumanian, a striking personality with his flowing black hair, puttees and a very large bow-tie, was responsible for the design of the Coanda Military Monoplane which crashed on 10th September, 1912, near Wolvercote, Oxford, killing the crew Lts. C. A. Bettington and E. Hotchkiss. The cause of the accident was wing failure attributed to the length of the inner bay of the spars to effect their attachment to the cabane pylons and also to the shallow, ineffective angle of the inner bracing wires. Coming after instances of mishaps in flight with other types of monoplane, the Wolvercote crash was instrumental in bringing forth the following month the War Office ban on monoplanes for use by the R.F.C. Military Wing. This hasty and arbitrary edict remained in force until February, 1913, and so reduced confidence in the monoplane that resulting prejudice against it retarded its development in Britain for many years afterwards to the detriment of all-round performance which the Nation had a right to expect in the aircraft for which it was paying.

By 1913 the civilian aircraft constructors were also aware of the inherent offensive military potential in their machines and awakening interest led several manufacturers to experiment with gun-carriers. Coanda's first serious attempt at a fast single-seat scout manifested itself in his design in 1913 for a tractor monoplane powered by an 80 h.p. Gnome and designated S.B.5. Work was started at Bristol on the machine under works number 183 but was stopped after a short time as there was little hope of any order for it in the face of the ill-feeling against monoplanes in official quarters.

Although his S.B.5 had become a victim of the ban, Coanda still retained his enthusiasm for a military design and transferred his ideas to a two-seat gun-carrying pusher biplane layout which was constructed during 1913 as the Bristol P.B.8, works number 199. A compact machine of 27 ft. 6 in. span and length, it was powered by an 80 h.p. Gnome with the propeller revolving between the closely-set pairs of tail booms. The usual Coanda-style four-wheel landing-gear supported the P.B.8 but, although it was completed at Brooklands, it was not flown and had never been a popular project with the drawing-office from the start. Coanda indulged in several other unusual designs for all-steel pushers in the midst of the general enthusiasm aroused for fitting a gun to an aeroplane but none of them progressed to the construction stage. In his search for a satisfactory layout to incorporate a gun, Coanda was forced to adhere to the pusher type of machine by the lack of any gear to ensure safe firing through a tractor propeller's path.

J. D. North, designer to Claude Grahame-White's concern at Hendon, tried his hand at a gun-carrier with the Type 6 Military Biplane which was ready in time for display at the 1913 Aero Show at Olympia. Designed on comparatively unorthodox lines, the machine was fitted with an Austro-Daimler engine mounted in the nose of the deep nacelle. The crankshaft was extended rearwards the length of the nacelle, where it was connected to the two-blade propeller by a chain drive. The propeller itself revolved around the upper tubular tail-boom which acted also as its bearing. This feature was reminiscent

Vickers E.F.B.3. (Vickers Photo.)

of the arrangement adopted in the Royal Aircraft Factory's F.E.3 but the
Type 6's tail had the benefit of additional support from a pair of lower booms
making in all a rigidly-braced triangular framework. The bore of the uppermost boom was used to carry the control wires to the rudder and elevators.
Centre-section struts were omitted, the upper wings being carried across the
nacelle by the inner interplane struts. Twin pairs of main wheels were suspended in slots in ski-shaped skids, and the nacelle carried two passengers on
the sprung tops of the tool boxes on each side of the engine, the pilot being
accommodated behind them. The Type 6's single machine-gun was a Colt
installed in the nose with 50˚ vertical and 180˚ horizontal field of fire.

A more conventional approach to the same type of aircraft was visible in
the Vickers E.F.B.1 which was displayed on the Company's stand at the same
1913 Olympia Aero Show. The Vickers machine had been designed by A. R.

Vickers E.F.B.4, with gun mounting on nose.

Low and G. H. Challenger to meet the requirements of an Admiralty contract, which the firm had received on 19th November of the previous year, calling for an experimental biplane armed with a machine-gun for offensive use. Equipped also with the bellicose name Destroyer, the first example of the Gunbus series followed, too, the pusher style forcibly dictated by circumstances at the time for any gun-carrier. Constructed under Vickers number 18, the E.F.B.1 was given two-bay, staggered wing cellules of unequal span. Composite construction was employed, with wood being used mainly but with tubular steel forming the tail booms and duralumin the covering of the two-seat nacelle. No. 18's engine was an eight-cylinder V, air-cooled Wolseley developing 80 h.p. with water-cooled valves. The Destroyer's all-important armament consisted of a Vickers-Maxim machine-gun installed in the nose coaming and capable of being aimed through a slot with 60° vertical and horizontal movement. This form of mount was not particularly satisfactory with its restriction on speed and in freedom of movement of the gun. Belt-feeding of the cartridges proved particularly awkward, both in following the gun as it was swung and in storing satisfactorily in the limited space in the nose. The E.F.B.1 is thought to have crashed the first time that it left the ground but was believed to hold such prospects of ultimate success that a revised version was put in hand. The E.F.B.1's important distinction is that it represented the first serious attempt at designing from the start a true fighting aeroplane for the British services without being compromised by being simply a modification of an existing airframe.

The second Experimental Fighting Biplane, the E.F.B.2, abandoned the staggered wings, surfaces and struts featured in its predecessor and received the extra power of a nine-cylinder 100 h.p. Monosoupape Gnome engine mounted at the rear of a shorter nacelle. At the forward end, the Vickers gun swivelled in a ball-and-socket type of mounting and the crew's vision was given the added benefit of large transparent celluloid panels on each side of the nacelle. The tailplane was modified to have a curved leading-edge and twin skids in the undercarriage replaced the single one fitted to the E.F.B.1. Brooklands was the scene of the testing of the E.F.B.2 by R. H. Barnwell in October, 1913.

By the same year, Short Brothers had become a firmly-established company with a number of extremely successful practical designs to their credit and had already begun to specialize in floatplanes, a type of machine in which they rapidly excelled and for which they were justifiably widely known. Among their products for 1913 was the S.81 Gun-carrier, designed for them by A. Camden Pratt specifically to carry out tests of armament. The machine was destined to be the final pusher Short floatplane and was a three-bay biplane, the wings of which folded. No.126 was a fairly large machine and was supported on the water by twin main and tail floats, augmented by one under each lower wingtip. A 160 h.p. Gnome provided the power at the rear of a nacelle which had to be particularly strong to stand up against the tremendous recoil of the quick-firing Vickers 1·5-pounder gun, for the thorough testing of which the S.81 had been ordered from Short Brothers.

These trials had been instituted by the Naval Wing of the R.F.C. on 29th July, 1913, when Lt. R. H. Clark-Hall, a naval gunnery officer, had been given the job of supervising the assessment of suitable armament for naval aeroplanes. First intentions were that the Vickers 1·5-pounder received by the Navy was to be installed in the *Astra Torres* airship and then in a Sopwith Gunbus but the big gun finally found a home in the S.81, only one of which was built. The Gun-carrier carried out its allotted task for some two years, being used in early 1915 as a vehicle for the testing of the recoilless 6-pounder Davis gun.

By 1913 it was obvious that both the Army and the Navy had reached a firm appreciation of the value of being able to mount guns, either large or small, on their aircraft for dealing with an enemy.

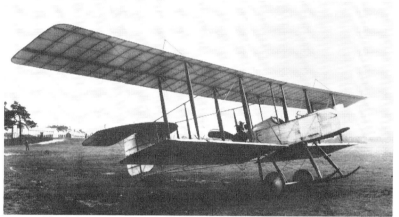

The single experimental Vickers F.B.6 of 1914. (Imperial War Museum Photo.)

The pusher biplane, the only type of machine capable of deploying such weapons with any effect, in its two-seat form was not endowed with a particularly sparkling performance. Indeed, compared with the vastly cleaner tractor layout, it was hardly in the running, and the pusher's main virtue was simply that it was a very convenient means of getting a gun into the air and being able to use it there. The use envisaged both by the Army and the Navy for the aeroplane, that of a scout to reconnoitre an enemy's disposition, meant emphatically that speed was of prime importance to make the intelligence obtained in reconnaissance worthwhile to the officers responsible for planning strategy and tactics. The tractor machine may not have been able to bring a gun to bear but at least it could operate at considerably greater speed and, as far as could be judged, should be able to complete its mission without needing the use of any armament.

With this concept in mind development began in 1913 of the high-speed single-seat scout and nowhere, in the immediate future, was better progress visible in this new sphere than at Farnborough.

Bristol Scout A prototype in original form. (Bristol Photo.)

Although the primary duty laid down for the Factory was that of ministering to the needs of the Air Battalion originally and then to those of the Royal Flying Corps, the temptation to indulge in designing and constructing some aeroplanes of its own fancy had finally been simply too strong to resist. Both the S.E.1 and the B.E.1 had been created as original designs by "reconstructing" two machines sent for repair and, once the pleasures of doing this type of work had been tasted, the habit had formed and was hard to break. Wasn't this far greater fun than just repairing the broken aeroplanes produced by some private constructor? In their enthusiasm for this newly-found outlet for their talents, the Factory staff thought so. The struggling members of the embryo British aircraft industry, however, felt just the exact opposite. They were barely established in business and could foresee the orders for military aeroplanes, which they had hoped to supply to the Corps, being met instead by a factory growing up inside the Service. This could not be allowed to happen and a period of general recrimination began which was not settled for several acrimonious years.

Meanwhile, the Royal Aircraft Factory had been extremely fortunate in attracting to its staff some of the best brains in the new science. The scope of technical investigation had increased steadily with the improvement in facilities for research, and sufficient practical experience had been accumulated to enable the staff to undertake the design and construction of a small but, for the era, remarkably advanced series of scouts.

The first outcome of this new line of investigation was the B.S.1, designed by Geoffrey de Havilland during 1912 and completed early in 1913. Considering that the machine was drawn up such a short time after consistent and reasonably reliable flying had become commonplace in Britain, it was an extraordinary and brilliant example of swift progress and advanced applied aerodynamics. Gone was the simple rectangular-section fuselage which had so far been the accepted thing. In its place was a finely-contoured, wooden monocoque structure with the engine cleanly blended into the circular section under a neat metal cowling. Originally the fourteen-cylinder, two-row 140 h.p. Gnome was chosen but substituted was the less-powerful ten-cylinder two-row 100 h.p. Gnome. The B.S.1's elegant form was that of a tractor biplane with well-staggered single-bay wings, this last feature—in company with cut-outs at the upper and lower centre-sections—being incorporated to give the pilot the best possible view from his well-shielded cockpit. Streamlined bracing-wires, known as Raf-wires, were Factory developments and were used on the scout. The shape of the wingtips and the tail unit showed that the B.S.1 had its ancestry in the B.E.2 and B.E.3.

The machine, the first in line of all single-seat scouts, was tested by de Havilland during March, 1913, but, in his hands, crashed in the same month. Before the accident, however, tests revealed an excellent performance, including a top speed of 91·4 m.p.h. over a measured course, a climb of 900 ft./min. and an endurance of 3 hours. The mishap, which gave the pilot a broken jaw, was the result of faulty side area balancing, a part of the art of design which was then still rather a mystery.

The B.S.1's flat spin had damaged it but rebuilding was put in hand with particular attention to the tail unit. This was given small fins above and below the fuselage, a larger rudder of entirely new design and divided elevators in place of the former one-piece type. The engine was altered to a nine-cylinder 80 h.p. Gnome matched by a propeller of smaller diameter and finer pitch. On leaving the workshops the machine was redesignated B.S.2 for a short while but this was then changed to S.E.2. to signify Scouting Experimental in keeping with the aircraft's avowed duty, and was in line with the revision of S.E. from the old Santos Experimental used solely for the ill-fated tail-first S.E.1.

Despite a lower speed of 85 m.p.h., the S.E.2 was found to be a superior flyer in its new form and its sprightly performance, unmatched by any of its contemporaries, earned it the soubriquet of the Bullet.

Continued flying of the machine encouraged further development and once again, during 1913, the S.E.2 went under cover to be brought into the open after its metamorphosis as the S.E.2a. The after portion of the fuselage monocoque had been replaced by a fabric-covered former and stringer structure terminating at the rear in a revised tail unit with larger fin and rudder, the alterations being accompanied by a slight reduction in weight.

In retrospect, 1913 is seen now as a year of great importance for British military aviation. Although the country, during the 19th Century, had been well ahead in the quest for a practical aeroplane, it had been slow in pressing forward during the first decade of the present century when flying had become a reality. By the middle of 1913, however, most of the lost time had been made up in quality although not in quantity, and Great Britain was pioneering the concept of what was to become one of the most important types, the fast scout, rapidly approaching its rôle as a fully-fledged fighter.

In particular, as far as the breed of British fighters is concerned, the year was of note as marking the début of the Tabloid, the progenitor of the outstanding, unbroken line of Sopwith and Hawker fighters for the next half-century. The prototype Tabloid was designed by T. O. M. Sopwith and F. Sigrist, with the Sopwith test pilot, H. G. Hawker, contributing some of his own ideas.

The work continued through the Summer of 1913 under a shroud of secrecy until the machine was ready for flying at Brooklands in the Autumn. Hawker flew the Tabloid to Farnborough on 29th November for its official trials. These disclosed a highly satisfactory top speed of 92 m.p.h., coupled with a speed range of 55·1 m.p.h. This performance was obtained with the 80 h.p. Gnome in a machine which had been built as a side-by-side two-seater. Exhilarated by the success of the new machine, Hawker flew it from Farnborough to Hendon later in the same day and, as one of the very popular Saturday flying meetings was in full swing, arrived to find a ready-made, appreciative audience of 50,000 people to whom to display the Tabloid's wonderful turn of speed by flashing around the bustling field twice at 90 m.p.h.

The machine which so delighted the crowd was a small tractor biplane of simple and compact layout, with a conventional fabric-covered wooden structure. Hawker then took the prototype to his native Australia for demonstration in an attempt to generate interest there and, while he was away, the Tabloid was put into production early in 1914 at Kingston as a single-seat scout for the Military and Naval Wings of the R.F.C.

While interest in the single-seat tractor scout had been rising steadily during 1913, the two-seat pusher was still being promoted as a gun-carrier and, on 27th November, a Grahame-White Boxkite piloted by Marcus D. Manton, flew over Bisley with a Lewis-gunner, suspended between the undercarriage, who fired at the ground targets.

The fifth Olympia Aero Show in March, 1914, brought forth further examples of the armed two-seat pusher biplane in the Avro 508 with an 80 h.p. Gnome and the pleasingly-proportioned Type 11 Warplane, designed for Grahame-White by J. D. North and powered by a 100 h.p. Monosoupape Gnome. Louis Noel tested the Warplane at Hendon in May but the machine displayed poor longitudinal stability and neither it nor the Avro reached production status.

Tempted also by the idea of the small scout, A. V. Roe showed their conception in the Type 511 Arrowscout, in reality a scaled-down 504 with single-bay sweptback wings and an 80 h.p. Gnome. The machine was tested by F. P. Raynham and turned in a top speed of 100 m.p.h. but made no further progress. One of its advanced features was the incorporation of airbrakes in the lower wing roots, an early example of their use.

At the same Aero Show Vickers exhibited their two-seat tractor Scout with a 100 h.p. Monosoupape Gnome but this was another which failed to be anything but a single prototype.

With their E.F.B.3 No. 18B revised Gunbus, also at the Show, Vickers were more successful in that it was part of the developing series which finally went into production as the F.B.5. The E.F.B.3 still carried the single nose gun in a nacelle which was now without the side windows. Minor modifica-

Henry Folland's remarkably advanced design of 1914, the S.E.4, on 4th August, 1914. (Imperial War Museum Photo.)

tions compared with its predecessor, the E.F.B.2, were strut-connected ailerons, equal-span wings and no cut-out in the upper centre-section trailing-edge as the engine and propeller had been moved slightly further rearwards.

Immediately following the E.F.B.3 came the E.F.B.4 which had fabric sides to the nacelle, cable-connected ailerons and wooden interplane, centre section and upright struts between the tail booms in place of metal used so far. The undercarriage was enlarged but perhaps the most significant difference was that the gun had been raised from its trunnion form of mounting onto a pillar to give completely free movement in aiming.

The next Gunbus, the E.F.B.5, was the final prototype for the production F.B.5 and reverted to steel struts, combined with equal-span wings and curved tailplane. An official order had still not been received for the Gunbus but Vickers, sensing that war was but a short time away, took the step of putting a batch of fifty of the type into production on their own responsibility as the F.B.5. Once again the design was altered before it was ready for its tests at Farnborough in July, 1914. To simplify production a rectangular tailplane was substituted; wooden struts were fitted again and the vertical tail was of well-rounded outline. The Vickers-Maxim gun had not proved to be the handiest of weapons for such an installation and was replaced by the lighter and more flexible Lewis with its drum cartridge feed.

Also in July, Vickers produced another single experimental version of the Gunbus series, the F.B.6. This used, too, the 100 h.p. Monosoupape Gnome and was basically a modified F.B.5 with extended upper wingtips braced by kingposts and wire. At the same time the shape of the rudder was revised.

In the West Country, at Bristol, Henri Coanda turned his hand to a design for the Breguet firm for a small biplane single-seat scout, the S.S.A. No. 219 which Harry Busteed flew and crashed at Filton early in 1914. The entire front portion of the machine's fuselage was armoured by constructing it as a riveted sheet steel monocoque, automatically bringing forth the nickname of the Bath. A large spinner with an annular cooling slot faired the propeller into the engine cowling and skids extending to the rear of the wheels took the place of the usual single tailskid. Another advanced feature was the castoring of the wheels as an aid to crosswind landings. When the almost complete lack of ground clearance for the large propeller, then rather an obsession with Coanda, was pointed out to him by the drawing office staff, back came his usual answer "I don't care, I make so!".

Meanwhile, also at Bristol, another single-seat scout had taken shape. During the previous year, Frank Barnwell, one of Coanda's prominent fellow-designers, started on a new design under works number 206 using parts of Coanda's defunct monoplane S.B.5. Harry Busteed contributed to the design which evolved as a trim single-bay biplane with staggered wings and powered by a semi-cowled 80 h.p. Gnome. After its initial flight by Busteed at Larkhill on 23rd February, 1914, the Scout A was put on display at that year's Olympia Aero Show. Immediately afterwards larger wings of 24 ft. 7 in. span were substituted for the original ones of 22 ft. During its A.I.D. tests with Busteed, on 14th May, the machine showed a top speed of 97 m.p.h. and a climb rate of 800 ft./min. but the prototype was lost in the English Channel on 11th July, 1914, while Lord Carbery was competing in the London–Paris–London race.

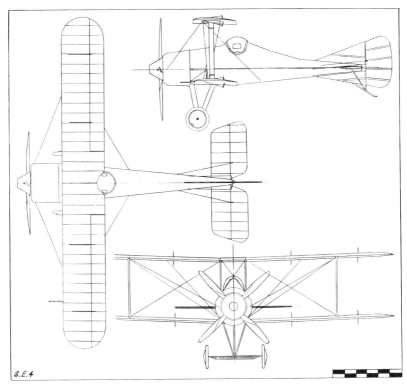

S.E.4

The Scout A had shown such promise that two modified versions were produced as Scouts B for the R.F.C. and were numbered 633 and 634. The Bristol Scouts A and B had been constructed on completely conventional lines with wire-braced box-girder fuselage, wooden structure throughout and fabric covering.

However, the Royal Aircraft Factory's staff had not been idle and in June, 1914, revealed a successor to the S.E.2a. A projected modification of the S.E.2a, the S.E.3, was dropped and the Factory went ahead to construct the S.E.4 designed by H. P. Folland, a man destined to play an ever-increasingly important part in British fighter design for many years afterwards.

In the S.E.4 he produced a fast, unarmed scout embodying the very latest advances in aerodynamic practice. To reduce drag to the absolute minimum the fourteen-cylinder, two-row 160 h.p. Gnome was closely cowled and faired into the circular section, wooden monocoque fuselage. Single centre-section and interplane struts were used and both upper and lower wings had full-span ailerons which could be brought into play as landing flaps. The undercarriage was reduced to three struts and a leaf-spring axle, but uncontrollable swaying on the ground brought a reversion to the conventional vee-type structure. Another very advanced feature was the moulded celluloid cockpit canopy which was so distrusted by the pilots that it was soon discarded. With its original engine the S.E.4 No. 628 achieved a top speed of 135 m.p.h., making it the World's fastest aircraft of its time. The 160 h.p. Gnome gave trouble with cooling, however, and was replaced by a 100 h.p. Monosoupape Gnome with an attendant drop in speed to 92 m.p.h.

Although it was a brilliantly-conceived design, and was liked by its test pilots Norman Spratt and Major J. M. Salmond, the S.E.4's landing speed of 52 m.p.h. was thought excessive for general use and, after damage in a landing accident, it faded from the scene. During its brief career, the S.E.4 had shown just what could be achieved at such an early stage in scout and fighter development and the machine remains a masterpiece of early aeroplane design.

One other early scout design was the Grahame-White Type 13 two-seat tractor biplane which was abandoned as the firm's entry in the cancelled 1914 Circuit of Britain contest and was revised for reconnaissance. Again it was found unsuitable for its intended purpose and ended its days as a trainer at Hendon.

During the months immediately prior to the 1914–18 War an event took place the significance of which was at the time completely unsuspected. Great Britain did not enter for the inaugural Schneider Trophy race held in 1913 but, the following year, C. Howard Pixton won a sweeping victory at Monaco for Sopwith in a Tabloid on floats at 86·75 m.p.h.

Unbeknown to all, this initial participation and win by Britain was to act as the catalyst for a line in development of engines and airframes for later contests which was to build up a store of engineering knowledge and experience on which, to a great extent, the country's survival was to depend decades later.

By 1914 the sunny atmosphere of Edwardian well-being was becoming misty and chilled. For the last year or two, unrest and talk of war had become commonplace and on the Continent of Europe, Germany was openly growing increasingly militant, spending sums on arms which were far in excess of normal defence needs. In Britain apprehension was widespread with strident warnings being sounded time and time again in an effort to rouse the Government from its lethargy and complacency and to imbue it with a sense of urgency.

By mid-1914 the rate of expansion of the Naval Wing of the R.F.C. made reorganization essential and the date of 1st July, 1914, was set for the Navy to take over entirely its air arm as the Royal Naval Air Service. The Navy's completely different attitude towards the aeroplane and its development, one of freedom and encouragement, had resulted in excellent progress being made by the nautical flyers.

Despite the various attempts on the part of those constructors and designers who had the well-being of the Nation at heart and the sagacity to develop the aeroplane into a fighting machine as it was inevitable that it must finally become, the R.F.C. and R.N.A.S. went into the raging conflict pitifully ill-prepared.

When the final pressing, unavoidable need arose, the money necessary for development was released in a flood and the orders were placed but that could not make up overnight for the appalling loss of time engendered by the total lack of a well-conceived, forward-thinking policy laid down and energetically supported, adhered-to and decisively put into action for the good of the R.F.C. and R.N.A.S. and their gallant pilots.

As far as scouts and gun-carriers were concerned, the few Sopwith Tabloids, Bristol Scouts and Vickers Gunbuses were all that we possessed, each of them with the standard wire-braced, wooden fabric-covered type of structure. In the absence of any suitable British engines, reliance was placed mainly on the range of Gnome or le Rhône rotaries as power units.

Two-seat Grahame-White Scout of 1914.

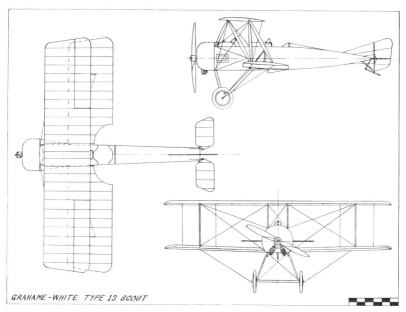

GRAHAME-WHITE TYPE 13 SCOUT

Grahame-White Type 13 Scout

In retrospect, disappointment could be felt at the mysterious reluctance to put either the Royal Aircraft Factory S.E.2 or S.E.4 scouts into production. Their performance was, for the period, of a very advanced order and their availability in quantity would have given both the R.F.C. and the R.N.A.S. absolute superiority in fast scouting facilities from the very first contact with enemy forces. Maintenance would not appear to have raised any particular problems as the S.E.s' structures were of simple and uncluttered design. At the beginning of 1914, in January, the sole S.E.2a joined No. 5 Squadron, R.F.C., as No. 609 but, even with this imposing machine at its disposal, the squadron does not seem to have made much use of it.

When 4th August, 1914, one of the most fateful days in the history of Mankind, dawned, bringing with it the end of an era and the start of the most appalling and tragic holocaust that the World had known, the few products of the British designers and constructors which could be classed as scouts or gun-carriers, and which were the immediate predecessors of the fighters soon to follow, were in concept and execution without doubt head and shoulders above those in the same category in any other country. The great pity was the lack of an indigenous engine to match the superb design of the airframes, a paucity which forced our designers to rely on a foreign product for what was, after all, the heart of the entire aeroplane.

In short, when Great Britain joined in World War One, she possessed a small but capable airframe industry supported by excellent designers and test pilots but the equally important engine producing facilities were missing at a time of the greatest possible gravity.

The years which led up to the 1914–18 War saw the slow but sure realization of the need for a fast armed aeroplane, capable of offensive action and of defending itself in a conflict. The men to whom this was so clear were fettered by bigoted and obdurate superiors, on whose approval they had to rely for funds to enable them to produce the new weapon, which was soon to be absolutely indispensable in a country's fight for its very survival.

Their frustration vanished overnight with the thunderous and blazing approach of war, a hellish fire in the furious midst of which was to be forged the British fighter, a class of aircraft in which the genius of our designers, engineers and test pilots was to ensure that, despite the vacillations and incompetence of politicians in whose hands the fate of the Nation depends, Great Britain should reign supreme.

The Pemberton Billing P.B.9, built in a week. (Supermarine Photo.)

CHAPTER TWO

THE FIGHTER IS FLEDGED

As the last lingering days of peace in 1914 slipped dusk by dusk to their silent transformation into the future haunting shadows of a lost past, few indeed were those among men who could have conjured into the vaults of the mind a vision even remotely resembling the scenes of reality so swiftly to be thrust upon Europe. The life-giving heat of the Sun, which had shone down that glorious Summer upon the peacefully industrious landscape of France and Belgium, was to be absorbed in the man-made furnace blazing on the ground under heaving, rolling clouds of battle-smoke, in the agonizing midst of which men fought and died as the carnage spread, destroying the very roots which had sustained their lives upon Earth. The opposing commanders lost but little time in putting to good use the aircraft at their disposal, and the armies thrusting at each other in the mortal struggle on the ground soon became used to the frail, purring machines carrying the enemy's eyes overhead on translucent wings which darted so swiftly between the sun-flecked clouds.

Before war was finally declared, the Royal Flying Corps and the Royal Naval Air Service had been steadily making themselves ready and, when the emergency came, were prepared for action. Nos. 2, 3, 4 and 5 Squadrons and the Aircraft Park crossed to France and at once engaged in reconnaissance with their Avros, B.E.s, Blériots and Farmans. The intelligence contained in the reports brought back by their crews was of immediate and utmost value to British and French planning in the field and was directly responsible for the retreat from Mons which ensured the survival of the British Army. Moving from one hastily-improvised aerodrome to another, the R.F.C.

machines and their pilots and observers maintained constant surveillance of the grey German columns as they pushed their way to the West through the noisome destruction far below. Primitive air-to-air encounters flared up quickly, with two German aircraft being forced down on 25th August, in spite of the lack of proper armament on the British machines, the crews of which were going aloft accompanied by their revolvers and rifles and, occasionally, shotguns.

Although, at first, the Allied commanders were somewhat sceptical of the ultimate value of sending aeroplanes across the lines on reconnaissance, the sterling work carried out by the few R.F.C. squadrons in action soon swept away any misgivings which might have dwelt in their minds. The pilots' and observers' reports of their findings kept the corps commanders supplied steadily with up-to-date information gleaned by peering over the sides of their fuselages, their helmeted heads lashed by the vortex of the propeller's slip-stream. Apart from their immediate tactical value, the flyers' observations provided information which enabled the commanders to assess the where-abouts of the main German forces and to forecast their intentions. The reports of the movements of von Kluck's First Army, made by the R.F.C. during the last few days of August, were of supreme importance in enabling General Joffre to plan the counter-offensive of 6th September which developed into the Battle of the Marne, an action successful in forcing the enemy back during the ensuing few days and in holding him at bay.

For three weeks the small force of four squadrons of the R.F.C. had been in the thick of the battle without a break, flying back and forth over the mêlée, and winning its spurs in its first action against the enemy. The magnificent service rendered by these few men was fully borne out by the French Commander-in-Chief, General Joffre, when he said "Please express most particularly to Marshal French my thanks for the services rendered to us every day by the English Flying Corps. The precision, exactitude, and regularity of the news brought in by them are evidence of the perfect training of pilots and observers." and by Sir John French in his initial despatch of 7th September, 1914, which contained the passage "I wish particularly to bring to your Lordship's notice the admirable work done by the Royal Flying Corps under Sir David Henderson. Their skill, energy and perseverance have been beyond all praise. They have furnished me with the most complete and accurate information which has been of incalculable value in the conduct of the operations. Fired at constantly by friend and foe, and not hesitating to fly in every kind of weather, they have remained undaunted throughout."

While Nos. 2, 3, 4 and 5 Squadrons of the R.F.C. were thus undergoing their baptism of fire in the war zone, the aircraft manufacturing industry at home was busy gearing itself to accelerated production of existing designs and to the development of new projects in the light of the latest needs. So far there had still not been any insistent demand from the R.F.C. or the R.N.A.S. for an out-and-out fighter. In the minds of those responsible for policy the scout was still envisaged in its reconnaissance rôle of acting as the forward-seeing eyes for the intelligence of the Army and the Navy. The fact that the pilots and observers were taking small arms up with them to defend themselves and to fend off any enemy aircraft which attempted to interfere with them was accepted as a matter of course and as a right that the crews were entitled to exercise in war.

The sense of urgency which rose above all other considerations manifested itself in many ways on the home front. One of those who were immediately affected was the remarkable Noel Pemberton Billing who, after several years of experimenting with various landplane designs, had veered towards the development of marine aircraft. Always a thinker on extremely original, but at the same time practical, lines of approach he had, in June, 1914, finally formed a limited company under his name at Woolston, Southampton, to manufacture his designs. As soon as war became inevitable, Pemberton Billing drew up at top speed his concept of a single-seat scout and built the machine at once. To enable it to be produced quickly in the necessary quantities envisaged, the P.B.9 was designed on lines of the utmost simplicity around the 50 h.p. Gnome engine. The sole prototype was rushed through the works at the beginning of August to completion in eight days, out of which the actual construction took a week, after which phenomenal performance it was known naturally as the Seven-Day Bus.

The P.B.9's appearance could not have been less like that of its immediate predecessor, the P.B.7 single-seat flying-boat, the sleek lines of which made the machine one of the most advanced in design practice at the 1914 Olympia Aero Show. The box-like fuselage of the Seven-Day Bus exhibited stark utility in its form in sharp contrast with the exquisite contours of the P.B.7's hull. The 26 ft. span wing panels of the P.B.9 bore out the theme of unrestrained simplicity, being square-cut, of constant chord and each in one piece. The lower set were taken straight across underneath the fuselage to be bolted direct to it. On the power of a 50 h.p. Gnome Victor Mahl flew the P.B.9 at Hendon, where it was successful enough to spend its life as a trainer for R.N.A.S. pilots. Even though the R.F.C. and R.N.A.S. were so critically short of scouts when they were plunged into war, Pemberton Billing's remarkably inspired effort at filling the gap so adroitly was wasted as the machine was not ordered into production. Although this was the case, the little P.B.9 scout deserves a corner to itself in the annals of fighter development as one of the very earliest examples of the inexpensive, quickly-built, utility type which came to be known in later years as the light fighter.

Time and time again in the future the concept of the utility fighter was to be revived in prototype form in ill-fated attempts to press home its admirable virtues. Some forty years were to pass by before a British light fighter, the Folland Gnat, was fortunate enough to achieve production status.

Since 1908 Martin and Handasyde had been numbered among the British pioneers whose courage in braving the uncertainties and perils of the early days had been rewarded in the end with success. The firm had made its mark with a series of workmanlike and exceedingly elegant monoplane designs which achieved fame in the skilled hands of Graham Gilmour, Gordon Bell and Richard Barnwell.

43

Although Martin and Handasyde had concentrated particularly on turning the monoplane layout into a sturdy, reliable type and made their name with it, the disapproval of monoplanes by the War Office, exemplified in the notorious 1912 ban, made itself felt even in such a camp of its champions.

The biplane formula was sweeping strongly into favour and by 1914 had demonstrated its qualities undeniably in the Bristol Scout, Sopwith Tabloid and the Royal Aircraft Factory's S.E.s. Biplane construction was stronger and lighter than that of the monoplane, and brought with it a brisk performance on the available power. However devoted to the monoplane its disciples might be, the only hope of obtaining production orders for a design lay in submitting to the requirements of the R.F.C., and developing acceptable biplane prototypes, whatever views a designer might hold concerning relative merits.

Martinsyde S.1. (Imperial War Museum Photo.)

The Summer of 1914, therefore, found Martinsyde abandoning the monoplane and busily engaged at Brooklands on a new design, the S.1, to the officially-approved biplane formula for a single-seat scout. When the machine made its appearance in the Autumn it was seen to present a completely conventional aspect and certainly possessed no features which could be classed as radical. Its 80 h.p. Gnome was fully and neatly cowled, the cooling air being admitted through a horizontal slot. Standard wooden construction was used throughout, with the usual fabric covering for the airframe.

At first glance, with its single-bay wings and overall compact appearance, the S.1 appeared to be remarkably similar to the Tabloid but closer inspection revealed detail differences. At their forward extremities, the undercarriage skids incorporated small auxiliary wheels and the fuselage exhibited a higher fineness ratio compared with that of the Tabloid. The S.1's wingtips possessed considerable outward rake and the complete tail unit outline set the pattern which was adhered to for all of the subsequent Martinsyde scouts. Martinsyde had also finally relinquished wing warping in favour of ailerons, of which

44

four were fitted to the S.1. The original style of landing gear was subsequently replaced by a simpler form of normal V type. Despite its trim appearance the S.1's performance was inferior to that of the Tabloid. The top speed of 87 m.p.h. was 5 m.p.h. lower than that of the Sopwith, a consequence of the slightly larger overall dimensions of the Martinsyde, and the S.1 was considered to be unstable longitudinally and to be bedevilled with poor response from its ailerons.

The Martinsydes began to come off the production lines in late 1914 and, by the end of the year, eleven had been delivered. The S.1. had not found sufficient favour to be ordered to equip any complete squadron and the four which found their way to the Western Front served with Nos. 1, 4, 5 and 6 Squadrons, R.F.C., early in 1915. On 10th May, 1915, the S.1 which had been given a home by No. 6 Squadron provided high drama for its pilot, Capt. L. A. Strange. The machine had been fitted with a Lewis gun on the upper surface of the top centre-section to give uninterrupted fire over the propeller. The ammunition drum jammed after being emptied in attacking a German machine and, while Strange stood up to free it, the Martinsyde turned over into an inverted spin. Its pilot fell out, clinging for dear life onto the ammunition drum which, luckily for him, remained lodged in place. After losing several thousand feet of height, Strange managed to swing himself back into the cockpit, regained control and lived to tell the tale.

The total estimated production run of the rather colourless Martinsyde S.1 was about sixty machines, such a small number that, had the type possessed any particular fighting virtues, it would hardly have been able to demonstrate them to any positive extent.

The S.1's more successful counterpart from the Sopwith stable, the nimble little Tabloid, had meanwhile been energetically developed into a useful scout at Kingston, following its dramatic victory in the Schneider contest at Monaco. The landplane Tabloid, fitted with the 80 h.p. Gnome, was in production for the R.F.C. and R.N.A.S. as a single-seater. A triangular fin was added at the tail and the front struts of the undercarriage were raked forward more sharply than on the original machine. Some of the production Tabloids were given an extra pair of struts in the undercarriage for additional strength.

On the outbreak of war, four R.F.C. Tabloids were taken to France and were used, unarmed, for scouting by Lts. Gordon Bell and Norman Spratt during the early operations on the Western Front. To render his Tabloid more warlike Spratt carried a supply of fléchettes, a form of sharp steel dart, which could be thrown out of the cockpit onto a target.

When the R.N.A.S. entered the conflict, one Tabloid was on strength but four finally went to Cdr. C. R. Samson's R.N.A.S. Squadron. Two of them, Nos. 167 and 168, earned immortal fame for the epic raid which was carried out by their pilots—Sqn.Cdr. Spenser D. A. Grey, who bombed Cologne railway station, and Flt.Lt. R. L. G. Marix, who destroyed the Zeppelin Z.IX in its shed at Düsseldorf.

The Tabloid went into action devoid of any armament but Samson's machines were fitted in February, 1915, with a Lewis gun mounting on the upper centre-section, an installation which was the brainchild of Wt.Off. J. G. Brownridge and Lt. T. Warner. Another Tabloid belonging to the R.N.A.S. w⸳ equipped with a Lewis gun installed on the starboard side of the fuselage, beneath the centre-section struts and enabled to fire through the propeller arc by the very rudimentary arrangement of steel deflector wedges, which were strapped around the specially shaped blades in the line of fire. Any bullet which might otherwise have hit the propeller during the uninterrupted firing of the gun was, therefore, made to ricochet off.

In addition to the few Tabloids built prior to 4th August, 1914, another thirty-six were constructed from 1st October until 30th June, 1915, with ailerons taking the place of wing warping on later examples. This comparatively small production run meant that the type was unable to make much of a name for itself, but the Tabloid stands at the head of the subsequent lengthy line of scouts and fighters which were to emanate from Kingston.

The value of a single-seat scout seaplane with good all-round performance was appreciated by the Admiralty, particularly in view of the widespread commitments of the R.N.A.S. along the coasts of the British Isles, and the Tabloid seaplane was ordered into production in November, 1914, being given in recognition of its sparkling achievement earlier in the year the well-merited appellation Sopwith Schneider. The 100 h.p. Monosoupape Gnome was standardized as its power plant and the Schneider was little altered from

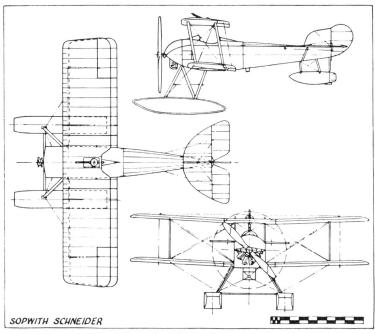

SOPWITH SCHNEIDER

Sopwith Schneider

Howard Pixton's contest mount apart from the appearance of an extra pair of struts in the undercarriage. The bull-nose cowling over the upper portion of the rotary afforded protection from oil and gases whipped back in the face of the pilot and, at the same time, gave a fair view over the blunt nose.

Original production Schneiders utilized the triangular fin shape but of slightly greater area than used on the Tabloids, together with wing warping; the fin was subsequently increased in area and given a curved leading edge and, conforming with advancing aerodynamic practice, ailerons on all four wings supplanted the strain-inducing warping. This final rejection of the warping system of lateral control was long overdue and was made not a moment too soon. The twisting of the wings' structure imposed totally unnecessary strains, particularly where biplane cellules were involved, which were eliminated when the simple and effective aileron became accepted fully.

While the Sopwith company were developing the Tabloid for war, at Bristol a pair of new prototype scouts were being completed under Frank Barnwell's direction, designated Scout B. Both were improved versions of the original Scout A which had been lost in the English Channel on 11th July, 1914. The new machines used the 80 h.p. Gnome engine and had double flying wires installed. Other differences included an undercarriage of broader track, a rudder of increased area, large skids added under the wings, and a full engine cowling with external ribs around its periphery, which had a similar appearance to the cowling fitted to Lord Carbery's le Rhône engine in the Scout A.

The two Scouts B were sent to Farnborough on 21st and 23rd August respectively for their official tests, following which both were posted to France for use with the R.F.C. during the first week of September. On arrival one was added to the strength of No. 3 Squadron, where it was armed with a rifle mounted on each side of the fuselage at an angle of 45° to fire forward outside the propeller disc; the other Scout B went to No. 5 Squadron. Two months after the pair of Bristols made their appearance on the Western Front, a further twelve were ordered for the R.F.C. on 5th November, 1914.

Just over a month later, on 7th December, the Admiralty followed with an order for twenty-four to equip R.N.A.S. units. These production machines received the designation Scout C but were basically indistinguishable from the Scout B, apart from the new version's revised engine cowling with its smooth outer surface and rather small frontal opening. The machines ordered for the R.F.C. were delivered in the following March, to be added singly or in pairs to reconnaissance units where their duty was to protect the two-seaters as they went about their dangerous observation duties over the opposing armies enmeshed in the struggle along the front line. The Bristol Scout C came on the scene before the idea had taken root of forming complete squadrons of scouts alone and so, for this reason, the type found itself spread in this way over the reconnaissance squadrons. Such a successful and reliable flying machine could well have been employed as the equipment of fighter squadrons if the concept of such formations had been realized earlier and had the machine been able, so early in the conflict, to take advantage of an interrupter or synchronous gun-firing gear.

The solitary S.E.2a, which had belonged to No. 5 Squadron of the R.F.C., found itself part of No. 3 Squadron at Moyenneville in France in October, 1914, where it flew armed with the pilot's ·45 cal. revolver and also with a rifle fitted at an angle on each side of the fuselage to fire outside the propeller. Its high speed gave it clear superiority over any of the enemy's aircraft but the S.E.2a remained at the Front for some six months only, returning to England during March, 1915, a lonely machine of brilliantly advanced design at the time of its conception and which deserved a far better fate than it received.

Yet another tractor scout had appeared within a month of the outbreak of war. This was the F.K.1, built by Sir W. G. Armstrong Whitworth and Co., and designed for them by a Dutch designer, Frederick Koolhoven, whose name was to be perpetuated by a prolific series of aircraft to appear under his signature for many years ahead. Before drafting the F.K.1, his first design for Armstrong Whitworth, Koolhoven had accumulated considerable experience through the successful Deperdussin monoplanes.

In the new scout the monoplane formula was disregarded, despite its inherent quality of speed, and the F.K.1 made its début in September, 1914. A relatively simple biplane in every way, it showed evidence of French practice in the horizontal knife-edge termination of the rear fuselage and in the omission of a fixed tailplane. The upper wings were taken over the fuselage at a considerable gap on inverted-V centre-section struts and this feature, combined with undercarriage legs spread wide apart fore and aft, gave the whole machine a rather gawky appearance. The 80 h.p. Gnome, around which the F.K.1 had been designed, was not obtainable so it flew instead with a 50 h.p. Gnome.

The machine was modified after early tests and was given a normal fixed tailplane and larger, inversely-tapered ailerons. The F.K.1's top speed of 75 m.p.h. on its low power reduced any chances that it might have had of competing with its counterparts from Bristol, Martin-Handasyde and Sopwith for orders and the design was abandoned.

Although the single-seat tractor scout was gradually beginning to come into its own at the time of the commencement of the War, the pusher layout—with its undoubted facilities for the installation and use of machine-guns—was being strongly pursued in the two-seat form.

In August, 1914, the Sopwith company were busy completing for the Greek Naval Air Service six landplane versions of their 1913 Greek Seaplane. The additional order had been placed in March, 1914, following the Greek Government's approval of the first example on floats. The new machines were to be armed with a single Lewis machine-gun in the front of the nacelle and the revised type became known as the Gunbus. The Greeks never received their expected Gunbuses as the six aircraft found themselves taken over by the Admiralty. The original Greek Seaplane had used a 100 h.p. Anzani engine but this was supplanted in the production batch of Gunbuses

Sopwith Gunbus of 1915. (Hawker Photo.)

by the 100 h.p. Monosoupape Gnome and, in order to bestow as good a field of fire as possible, the nacelle's fore part was revised in shape.

After the batch of six were delivered, the Gunbus was revised again and received increased power by the installation of the 150 h.p. Sunbeam. The

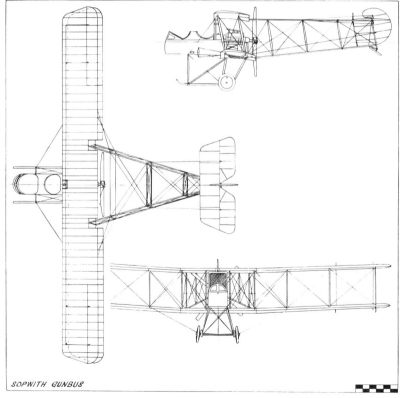

SOPWITH GUNBUS

Sopwith Gunbus

nacelle and undercarriage had to be strengthened to absorb the extra power and improved protection for the crew resulted from increasing the depth of the decking of the nacelle. In the original Gnome-powered design, the lower wings were mounted direct onto the sides of the nacelle but in the Sunbeam version they passed below it, to be attached by short struts. At the same time, a new horn-balanced rudder of increased area made its appearance and straight-edged horizontal tail surfaces were incorporated. Besides being built by Sop-with, the Gunbus was sub-contracted by Robey and Co. at Lincoln but, even though such a useful gun-carrier was available when the emergency arose, the production run of twenty-three complete machines was very small and no particularly noteworthy successes attended whatever operational use was made of the machines. The Gunbus, with its span of 50 ft., was of fair size and managed to reach 80 m.p.h. with the Sunbeam as power. Its severely restricted employment as an operational type was offset by the R.N.A.S. putting it to good use as a trainer at Hendon.

While the opening scenes of the conflict were being enacted on the Conti-nent, at Farnborough the Royal Aircraft Factory's designers were deeply involved in new projects in the midst of the greatly accelerated programme thrust on their resources in the strident urgency of war. Several Fighting Experimentals were numbered among their proposals and incorporated some widely diverse ideas in layout.

The two-seat F.E.6, built in 1914, carried on the unusual theme demon-strated in the F.E.3 of the tail unit being borne on a single metal tubular boom which passed through the pusher propeller's boss. The F.E.6 had the more powerful 120 h.p. Austro-Daimler for power and the layout again provided the gun with uninterrupted forward fire. As was the case with the majority of what might be classed as freak designs in search of the ideal, the F.E.6 was too radical to be successful as an operational machine and failed to be ordered for production.

During the opening months of the War, the outlook for the embryo British aircraft manufacturing industry changed entirely. The firms which had, some five years previously, endeavoured to set themselves up in the new field of flying to design and construct aeroplanes for sporting or service use now found that they were on a far sounder footing, with prospects of steady production runs for those of their designs which made the grade.

The main companies in being at the time were A. V. Roe, Blackburn, British and Colonial, Grahame-White, Handley Page, Martin-Handasyde, Short, Sopwith and Vickers, together with the Royal Aircraft Factory itself. As wood was the main material employed in airframe construction it was logical that sub-contract work should be handled by various cabinet-making firms, who thus had their first experience of aeroplane manufacture to which they applied their customary high standard of workmanship.

The stigma attached to the monoplane by the R.F.C. was still strongly in evidence and British design effort was concentrated wholly upon the develop-ment of the biplane to the virtual exclusion of other types. This was not so, however, in France or Germany where the monoplane was fully in favour.

Particularly was this the case in France where Blériot, Deperdussin, Morane-Saulnier and Nieuport had made their mark with an eminently successful series of monoplanes over several years.

By their devoted work in assisting the Army during the opening weeks of the hostilities, the four R.F.C. squadrons had rapidly made themselves indispensable to the field commanders and through the ensuing battles of the Marne, the Aisne and Ypres were fully engaged in reconnaissance. They were particularly useful in keeping an eye constantly on the German forces in the front line, in observing the size and disposition of reinforcements arriving at the rear areas of the battlefields and in enabling the various Allied armies to keep in close touch with each other.

Those who lightheartedly prophesied, when the storm broke in the heat of the Summer of 1914, that the War would be short-lived and would "be over by Christmas" had been proved tragically wrong. Just how wide of the mark their prognostications were was to be bitterly demonstrated for the ensuing four long, weary and terrible years. The brightly-hued poppies of Flanders, later to be adopted and worn as the symbol to recall the memory of those who gave their lives amid the carnage, faded and dropped and their place was taken by the rustic tints of Nature's demise in Autumn on the shattered trees and hedges, mutely matching the death that had come undesired to a fertile and abundant land.

Nature, in her irrepressible power, was more fortunate than Man; at least she, after her Winter's rest, could blossom again in her full beauty. The men on the fields of Flanders, once death had struck, could never rise to regain the fullness and joy of life which had been theirs. As battle succeeded battle, Winter inevitably followed Autumn and the first Christmas of the War passed, a time of afflicted homes with empty places, poignant memories of familiar faces and voices and, already, the greatest sorrow and grief.

Above the heads of the Army the airmen kept watch, within a few weeks gratefully accepted allies of the ground forces. Sir John French, in his despatch of 20th November, 1914, accorded the fullest recognition of the men of the R.F.C. in saying "The work performed by the Royal Flying Corps has continued to prove of the utmost value to the success of the operations.

"I do not consider it advisable in this despatch to go into any detail as regards the duties assigned to the Corps and the nature of their work, but almost every day new methods for employing them, both strategically and tactically, are discovered and put into practice.

"The development of their use and employment has indeed been quite extraordinary, and I feel sure that no effort should be spared to increase their numbers and perfect their equipment and efficiency."

Such unstinted and unqualified praise and appreciation bore eloquent testimony indeed to the devotion to duty of the flying and ground crews, who were in full agreement with the sentiments expressed in the last sentence of the communiqué.

As the fateful year of 1914 drew to its close, so the weather worsened. On the battlefields the once-firm soil had been transformed into a mass of mud, interspersed with water-filled shell-holes and littered as far as the eye could see with the bloody ferment of war. The deterioration in the weather made flying conditions increasingly difficult and hazardous for the pilots and observers in their machines which, in the best circumstances, had little or no power in reserve. The crews struggled on to complete their reconnaissance and artillery observation as well as they could but, in strong winds, they found that their engines had insufficient power to make much headway and, at times, they remained suspended motionless in the air so that missions had, perforce, to be abandoned.

But new equipment was on the way. Some sixteen months earlier, in August, 1913, the Royal Aircraft Factory had drawn up a two-seat pusher biplane as an original fighter design from the outset. Designated F.E.2a it remained an unbuilt project until the war started. The War Office then decided that the R.F.C. needed a potent fighter immediately and ordered twelve from the Factory. Some five months elapsed before the prototype F.E.2a was ready in January, 1915, and when it appeared it could be seen that the new machine had lost the fairly shapely lines which had graced the last version of the F.E.2. The F.E.2a, with its three-bay 47 ft. 9 in. span wings, enlarged nacelle and sturdy oleo undercarriage, was a pugnacious, hefty-looking machine powered with a 100 h.p. Green engine driving a two-blade propeller. The Green was shrouded by a metal cowling and the pilot was raised well up in his cockpit so that he could see comfortably over the observer in front of him. Between the tail booms the trailing edge of the upper wings was hinged so that, aft of the rear spar, it could be turned down to function as a landing flap. The pair of skids on the undercarriage converged at the front to carry a small third wheel as a nose-over preventative. Although the Green power plant had been exceedingly useful a few years previously in getting many different early machines into the air, its comparatively low power/weight ratio told against it in a type which, for its rôle, demanded the best possible performance.

Within two months, in March, 1915, a revised version using the more powerful 120 h.p. Beardmore appeared and was redesignated F.E.2b. The new engine was mounted without a cowling and another alteration was the deletion in the F.E.2b of its predecessor's airbrake. Although the need was so great, production was extremely slow in getting under way and it was not until another eight months had passed that the initial order for twelve was completed. The first arrived in France on 20th May, 1915, for use by No. 6 Squadron but it took a further four months to enable the unit to muster but four F.E.2bs. As a design, therefore, the F.E.2b was more or less obsolescent by the time that it started flying over the lines but, none the less, proved itself a very useful type.

Two months before the start of the War, the Royal Aircraft Factory parted with one of its most experienced and talented designers when Geoffrey de Havilland left in June, 1914, to work in the civilian industry by joining the design staff of the Aircraft Manufacturing Company at Hendon. Since being founded in 1912, Airco had been making aircraft which were not of its own design but its head, George Holt Thomas, was keen on setting up a design

The F.E.2b, doughty opponent of German scouts.

office so that the firm could establish itself as a company manufacturing its own designs.

De Havilland's first type for his new employers was to be a reconnaissance and fighting machine, perforce a biplane, and his success with the tractor B.E. series and the B.S.1 at Farnborough encouraged him to adhere to the same layout. The general form was evolving on the drawing board when it was realized by the War Office that there was still no practical means of firing a gun ahead through the propeller. Proposals for solving this problem had been submitted to the War Office by the Edwards brothers but had come to naught. The request was made that the tractor project should be abandoned and that a pusher layout be substituted.

The revised machine was to be designed around the air-cooled 70 h.p. Renault V–8 engine and was to carry a front gunner in addition to the pilot. Although the new machine was by no means de Havilland's first essay in design, it was designated D.H.1 and this and his succeeding types for the same company continued to be known by their designer's initials, the name Airco being rarely applied as well.

The D.H.1 exhibited a marked overall resemblance to the F.E.2 but was slightly smaller and heavier. One or two features of note were incorporated in an otherwise conventional two-bay pusher layout. These included a landing-gear embodying coil springs and oleo tubes for shock-absorbing, and a pair of aerofoil surfaces—some 3 ft. in span each—mounted on each side of the nacelle between the centre-section struts to act as airbrakes.

On completion in January, 1915, de Havilland carried out the tests of the D.H.1 at Hendon. Its performance was reasonably good, although the Renault's 70 h.p. was considerably lower than the 120 h.p. of the Beardmore which Airco had hoped would become available for it. Negligible effect was produced by turning the airbrakes through their 90° angle across the

Prototype D.H.1. (Imperial War Museum Photo.)

slipstream and drag was lessened when they were subsequently removed. The D.H.1 was forced to wait some time for its Beardmore engine as the few available went to the Royal Aircraft Factory. A number were built powered by the Renault and were fitted with cut-down sides to the gunner's cockpit and undercarriages which reverted to rubber-cord springing. The production version built at King's Lynn by Savages was designated D.H.1A, and benefited from the power of the Beardmore, the radiator of which was installed prominently immediately behind the pilot's head. The gunner's armament was a single Lewis gun on a pillar mounting in the nose, from which he had an excellent field of fire, and on some examples a Lewis gun was fitted for the pilot to fire over the gunner. In spite of its useful attributes, the D.H.1 never really got into its stride as a weapon of war as the F.E.2 was already well developed and the seventy-three D.H.1s and D.H.1As constructed were distributed mainly among Home Defence and training units, six of them finding their way out to the Middle East in 1916.

During 1915 designers were still faced with the two main alternatives of either the pusher or tractor layout for the armed scout. Steady evolution of the tractor type in general had endowed it with every advantage but one over the untidy pusher. The exception was still the installation and effective aiming of a forward-firing gun. In time a solution is found for every problem but, pending one for this particular obstacle, the Royal Aircraft Factory went ahead in 1915 with the design of another single-seat tractor scout.

Although little connected with the S.E.4—general overall layout and duty being about all that they had in common—the new machine was designated S.E.4a. H. P. Folland's talents as a designer were responsible for the creation of the elegant and trim little newcomer, which exhibited simpler construction than that of its predecessor. The streamlined form of the S.E.4a's fuselage was achieved by the addition of formers and stringers to the main rectangular-section, wire-braced framework of longerons and spacers. The 80 h.p. Gnome's propeller was faired into the cowling ring with a large shallow spinner, inside which a fan cooled the engine with air drawn through the

54

front orifice. Metal panels covered the nose as far back as the cockpit, the remainder of the airframe receiving the usual doped fabric covering. The staggered, equal-span wings were of single-bay cellule; the lower planes were joined to a centre-section, while the upper pair met at the centre-line to be joined to the fuselage by a pair of inverted V struts. The S.E.4a incorporated the idea, carried out on the S.E.4, of full-span ailerons which acted also as flaps. The machine's fin and rudder profile was notable as that which stamped it and many succeeding fighters as Folland designs. The S.E.4a was an excellent example of the axiom that an aeroplane which looks right should fly well, a truth which was amply demonstrated by Frank Goodden with aerobatic displays at Farnborough.

Overheating of the engine, even though the fan had been incorporated, brought about the discarding of the large spinner and the modification of the cowling to remedy the defective cooling. In all, four S.E.4as were produced by the Factory during 1915 and the 80 h.p. le Rhône was fitted as an alternative to the Gnome. To overcome the difficulty of firing straight ahead, a mounting for a Lewis gun was fitted above the upper wings at the apices of the centre-section struts so that the line of fire passed over the propeller, alternative armament being a rifle mounted at an angle on the fuselage side. Although it was a successful design and eminently suited to production, the S.E.4a constitutes yet another promising type which was unlucky enough to be passed over as a service machine. The only known military use made of it was that one was available at Joyce Green for Home Defence in the closing days of 1915.

Before the start of the War, it was realized that the Zeppelins being developed and built in Germany could prove an exceedingly dangerous menace to the United Kingdom. Their range, lifting power and silent approach to the shores of Britain posed many serious problems for the defence, the responsibility for which was assumed by the Admiralty on 3rd December, 1914. The eyes of the British public had turned skywards time and time again

The trim S.E.4a of 1915. (Imperial War Museum Photo.)

55

since the declaration of war, in anticipation of the sight of Zeppelins bent on destruction. Week after week had passed without any sign of a raider but the peace overhead was broken finally in the course of the night of 19th–20th January, 1915, when the German Naval Zeppelins L.3 and L.4 came in over Norfolk and attacked King's Lynn and Yarmouth. The long-dreaded Zeppelin raids had started and steps had to be taken quickly to combat them.

Among the aeroplanes pressed into service for anti-Zeppelin patrols were Sopwith Two-Seater Scouts, of which twenty-four had been produced and absorbed by the R.N.A.S. An unexpected tendency to slip into a spin was responsible for the nickname Spinning Jenny being earned by the type, which proved virtually useless as an interceptor of Zeppelins. Tugged aloft by its 80 h.p. Gnome the ungainly Sopwith was hard put to gain a meagre 3,000 ft. in height and wallowed far below the quarry which it was sent up to destroy from Coastal Air Stations.

The two-seat Sopwith Scout, the Spinning Jenny.

The Spinning Jenny was basically a landplane version of the Sopwith Type 807 seaplane of 1914. Two-bay wings of equal span were fitted to a fuselage which was more or less identical with that of the Type 807, the tail unit also following the same pattern. A rather mixed range of armament was fitted to the anti-Zeppelin Scouts and consisted of combinations of the German Mauser rifle loaded with incendiary ammunition in the hope of setting fire to the marauders, the normal service rifle with Hales grenades, a shot-gun containing chain-shot, and the Very pistol.

The Spinning Jenny was obviously not going to be of any use in destroying Zeppelins and another Sopwith type, the single-seat Schneider, was turned to in the hope of succeeding where its two-seat compatriot had failed. As the Schneiders came off the accelerated production lines during the first months of 1915, they were directed by the R.N.A.S. to its coastal seaplane stations and also passed to some ships as part of their equipment. The Schneider's brisk performance, allied to its incendiary bullet-firing Lewis gun which was mounted at an angle through an aperture in the upper centre-section, was

N1123, a Blackburn-built Sopwith Baby. (Blackburn Photo.)

expected to provide a satisfactory means of bringing the raiders down. Actual attempts to use the Schneiders from cruisers and seaplane-carriers in the North Sea when Zeppelins were sighted overhead in May, June and July of 1915 were failures from various causes, one of which was an unfortunate propensity for breaking their float structures on being swung into the water

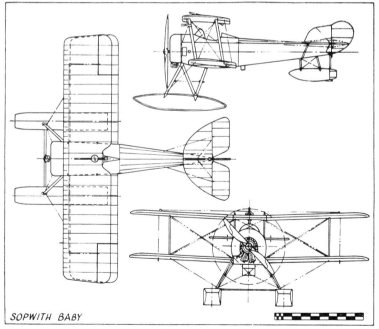

SOPWITH BABY

Sopwith Baby

57

for taking-off. To overcome this obstacle and get the intercepting Schneiders cleanly into the air with as little loss of time as possible, the idea came from Admiral Sir John Jellicoe, in a letter to the Admiralty at the end of July, 1915, that the machines should be released from the 120 ft. flying-off deck of the aircraft-carrier *Campania*. By placing a jettisonable two-wheeled dolly beneath the floats, the seaplanes could then get smoothly and quickly away. 6th August, 1915, saw the first successful take-off by this method from *Campania* when Flt.Lt. W. L. Welsh was launched in a Schneider after a run of 113 ft. while the ship steamed at 17 kt. into wind. The little Sopwith had deservedly made a niche for itself in the R.N.A.S. and increasing demands meant that extra equipment was finding its way aboard to the gradual detriment of the machine's performance. An increase in power was obviously essential and the 110 h.p. Clerget was selected as the answer. The change of engine brought with it an alteration in the cowling, which lost its old bull-nose character and assumed instead a horse-shoe aspect, open-fronted and terminating at the apices of the front landing-gear struts. With the new version's appearance in September, 1915, there came the change of name to Sopwith Baby.

While aerial activity over the Western Front steadily increased during the first half of 1915, in the Airco design office Geoffrey de Havilland was committing to the drawing-boards his concept of a single-seat armed scout of pusher layout, destined to be basically a smaller version of the D.H.1. Designated D.H.2 the machine was one of the cleanest and among the best-looking of pusher designs. The two-bay wing formula was adhered to, with the pilot seated well forward in the nacelle to command an excellent view in every direction. The 100 h.p. Monosoupape Gnome was chosen to power the D.H.2 which made its first flight in July, 1915.

The sole object of designing the new pusher was to produce an effective fighting scout, the armament of which was a single Lewis gun pivoting on a

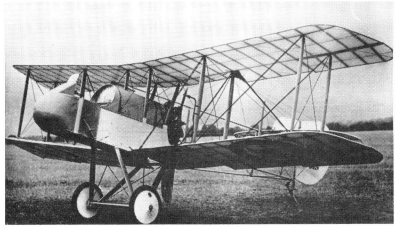

The single-seat pusher D.H.2. (de Havilland Photo.)

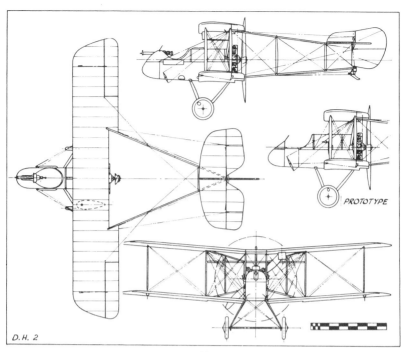

D.H.2

mounting at the side of the cockpit. The intention was that the pilot should aim the gun by hand as needed, but production D.H.2s had the gun fixed in a central trough in the upper coaming of the nacelle, a location which assisted the clearance of possible stoppages. Construction was of wood throughout with the exception of the steel-tubing booms carrying the tail unit.

In keeping with the machine's intended rôle as a fighter, the performance was brisk and the generous control surfaces gave the D.H.2 great sensitivity, a quality which was extremely useful but which required careful handling and constant attention by the pilot. Among the hazards to be guarded against were unexpected spins and the catastrophic possibility of the rotary's cylinders parting company with the crankcase and cutting through the tailbooms.

The D.H.2's great distinction is that it formed the equipment of the R.F.C.'s first single-seat fighter squadron, No. 24, a unit which arrived in France on 7th February, 1916, to be followed shortly by Nos. 29 and 32. The new fighter proved to be exceedingly useful and successful, doing great work in action for the two years following its introduction. Of four hundred D.H.2s produced, most used the standard engine but the 110 h.p. le Rhône also was employed as an alternative power plant.

At the same time as the D.H.2 was being evolved at Hendon, to the South at Farnborough J. Kenworthy was at work in the precincts of the Royal Aircraft Factory on a contemporary single-seat pusher fighter—the F.E.8.

Bristol Type 5 Scout D. (Bristol Photo.)

The time taken from conception to realization of the D.H.2 was remarkably short as the dedicated Airco staff, under the energetic George Holt Thomas, applied their resources to producing the prototype as quickly as possible. The F.E.8 was not quite as lucky as, although design work had been initiated in

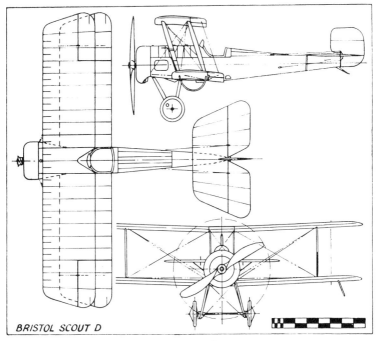

BRISTOL SCOUT D

Bristol Scout D

May, 1915, the prototype first saw the light of day during the following October and ensuing troubles delayed its introduction into service. The F.E.8's span was slightly greater than that of the D.H.2, while its weight using the same engine—the 100 h.p. Monosoupape Gnome—was a little less than that of the de Havilland machine; the speed at sea level was approximately the same for both, the F.E.8 reaching 94 m.p.h. compared with the D.H.2's 93 m.p.h. The F.E.8, as a two-bay pusher biplane, possessed little of the pleasingly-proportioned appearance which the well-rounded, balanced lines of the D.H.2 presented to the eye. Instead, the Factory product was by comparison square-cut, angular and spindly. The prototype F.E.8's four-blade propeller was embellished with a pointed spinner of generous size which could have had but a negligible effect upon performance and which

F.E.8 prototype. (Imperial War Museum Photo.)

was subsequently deleted on production examples. The F.E.8's all-important armament was a single Lewis gun which, on the prototype, was installed at a low level in the nose of the nacelle. Except for the short exposed nose portion of the barrel, the gun was completely contained within the nacelle and was intended to be remotely controlled by the pilot seated above and behind it. Accessibility was poor, particularly so in flight and the gun was consequently elevated to a normal location on top of the coaming. Only a month after its appearance the first F.E.8 was wrecked in a crash in November, 1915, Service Trials in France being delegated to the next example which was completed in time to cross the Channel in December. Pilots who flew it liked the machine and their recommendations resulted in its immediate adoption for the R.F.C. Production, however, was unpleasantly slow in getting under way, six months passing before the first arrived to do battle over the Front. Alternative trial engine installations were the le Rhône and Clerget, both of 110 h.p., but any advantage in performance which they may have offered was of little benefit to a type which was out-dated by the time that it reached operational status.

Production version of the Vickers F.B.5, 1915. (Vickers Photo.)

In company with their fellow British aircraft constructors, the Vickers company continued their efforts to produce an effective fighting machine. Their F.B.5, after being used in small numbers by one or two squadrons flying with mixed types, finally reached the Front as the sole equipment of one unit when No. 11 Squadron, R.F.C., arrived on 25th July, 1915, soon after finding its feet with its sturdy pushers. Experimental versions of the F.B.5 Gunbus which appeared in mid-1915 included an armoured example, fitted with the first of the 110 h.p. Clergets to arrive in Britain, and two for the Admiralty—Nos. 1534 and 1535—both fitted with the more powerful 150 h.p. Smith Static radial engine. All three remained as prototypes and the Vickers design staff turned their attention to something more advanced.

Under Harold Barnwell's direction a new tractor scout, the E.S.1, was

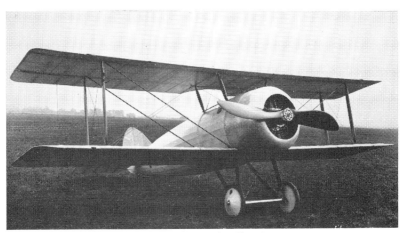

Vickers E.S.1. (Vickers Photo.)

designed and built. Powered by the 100 h.p. Monosoupape Gnome rotary, the machine was completed in August, 1915, and was a single-bay, equal-span, non-staggered biplane of very neat and refined aspect. The lines of the broad-chord cowling flowed back into the fuselage along formers and stringers applied over the main wooden fuselage rectangular structure. Taper was introduced aft of the cockpit but the practice of carrying to some distance to the rear of the engine the full circular section of the engine cowling resulted in a comparatively inferior view from the cockpit along the bulky nose-portion. Nevertheless, the E.S.1's streamlining endowed it with a creditable top speed of 114 m.p.h. at 5,000 ft., and earned it the soubriquet of the Barnwell Bullet. As No. 7509, the E.S.1 went to France for Service Trials with the R.F.C. but was ultimately written off in a crash.

The machine's excellent performance was obviously worth exploiting and a modified version, the E.S.2, was ready in September, 1915. In this, the squared-off wingtips of the E.S.1 had been replaced with those of rounded

Vickers E.S.2 7759. (Vickers Photo.)

outline and the pilot's view which, in the earlier machine had been commented on adversely, was improved in an upward direction by the provision of a generous opening in the upper centre-section. Altered also were the lower portion of the fuselage which, in the E.S.2, was flat instead of rounded and resulted in decreased depth, and the 110 h.p. Clerget's cowling which was of reduced chord.

A positive attempt was made in the E.S.2 to produce a tractor scout equipped with a fixed forwards-firing gun. This was accomplished by mounting a Vickers gun in a trough to port in the upper decking and synchronizing it to fire between the propeller blades by incorporating the interrupter gear which had been produced by Vickers in collaboration with G. H. Challenger.

Even though the E.S.2 possessed a good performance and a long-awaited answer to the old gun-aiming problem, the two built—7759 and 7760—remained as prototypes only. Despite its several attributes, the type was dogged by the relatively poor view from the cockpit, owing to the plumpness of the generous cross-section of the fuselage. Nevertheless, the E.S.2 was a

Vickers F.B.7. (Vickers Photo.)

commendable step in the right direction and provided Vickers with valuable experience which was put to good use later. As an alternative to the 110 h.p. Clerget, the le Rhône of the same power was tested also in the airframe.

While Harold Barnwell was busy designing the E.S.1 and E.S.2 for Vickers, another of the prominent British pioneer designers, R. L. Howard Flanders, was working for the same firm on a commission for a twin-engine machine capable of mounting a Vickers 1-pounder quick-firing gun. The designation F.B.7 showed that the new aeroplane was the next in line as a Fighting Biplane after the experimental F.B.6. The F.B.7 was the first design from Howard Flanders since his B.2 biplane of mid-1912 and was commenced just after the start of the War, following his enforced break with aeronautics after a serious motor-cycle crash and his subsequent recuperation far away in Australia.

The F.B.7, the first twin-engine aeroplane built by Vickers and among the earliest of multi-engine, two-seat gun-carriers, in general appearance displayed a very obvious connection with its designer's earlier B.2. It inherited the same low-slung fuselage style, together with the deep fore-fuselage and triangular-section rear portion. The undercarriage, with its very wide track and prominent central skid also owed its inspiration to the B.2. Other features common to both were the outline of the comma-shaped rudder, lack of a fixed fin, and the braced overhang of the upper wings—a feature which was even more accentuated in the F.B.7.

A pair of 100 h.p. Monosoupape Gnomes, mounted starkly in the gap between the wings, powered the 59 ft. 6 in. span biplane. The pilot was seated in a roomy cockpit to the rear of the wings, a position from which his forward view was comparatively poor and which deteriorated still further when voluminous cowlings were installed later to shroud the engines. The bluff nose of the broad fuselage provided ample room for the large gun and enabled the gunner, whose seat was attached direct to the weapon's mounting, to turn horizontally through a complete circle.

Following the F.B.7's initial flight during August, 1915, it proceeded to the C.F.S. at Upavon for evaluation, which was followed quickly on the 20th of the same month for an order for twelve production examples.

Before work commenced on the batch, several significant alterations took place in the design. The most important of these was the location of the pilot's cockpit in a greatly improved position forward of the wings and in a fuselage

64

of greatly changed structure. Gone was the old triangular section at the rear and its place was taken by a conventional rectangular structure. A less happy change was the substitution of two 80 h.p. Renault engines as a result of a shortage of Monosoupape Gnomes. Designated F.B.7A and numbered 5717, the unwieldy machine was hard put to it to achieve any worthwhile performance on even lower power than that of its original engines, which themselves had been of far lower output than required to give the reasonable speed and agility to be expected in such a type. Vickers were left with little choice but to stop work on an altogether unsatisfactory combination and the War Office agreed to the annulment of the contract.

While their S.1 was being produced in small numbers for the R.F.C., the Martinsyde design staff pressed ahead with a project by A. A. Fletcher for a long-range, single-seat fighter of good all-round performance. The new machine, designated G.100 and serialled 4735, was completed during the Summer of 1915, being designed around the reasonably powerful 120 h.p. Beardmore engine, driving a three-blade propeller. In common with its ancestor, the S.1, the G.100 found itself known as the Martinsyde Scout.

Well-proportioned and purposeful in appearance it utilized the normal fabric-covered wooden structure of the era but several modifications were embodied in the production machines which appeared during the last days of 1915. The metal cowling over the engine was considerably neater, a two-blade propeller replaced the three blader and double flying-wires were installed.

To enable the G.100's forward-firing Lewis gun to be used effectively, it was mounted on the upper centre-section at a height from which the line of fire would pass over the propeller. The only really unconventional feature about the G.100 was the second Lewis gun carried on a bracket on the port side of the fuselage just to the rear of the cockpit. This very odd arrangement was for the protection of the pilot who was expected to be able to perform the remarkable combined feats of flying the machine and firing blindly behind him with the second gun.

To fulfil its mission as a long-range fighter, the G.100 had been designed purposely as a relatively large biplane with generous wing area to carry aloft sufficient fuel for a worthwhile endurance of 5·5 hours. Consequently in combat it was at a disadvantage compared with smaller, more agile contemporaries.

On reaching the Western Front at the beginning of 1916, the G.100 was allocated to escort two-seaters of various squadrons, No. 27 Squadron, R.F.C., being the sole unit to be equipped completely with the Martinsyde G.100 and arriving at the battle front on 1st March, 1916. The fact that it was a useful weight-lifter was quickly recognised and the G.100s found themselves soon adapted as bombers.

Among the assortment of pusher scouts hopefully produced by various concerns, there appeared in 1915 a single-seater from the drawing-board of Noel Pemberton Billing. A single-bay biplane, powered by the 80 h.p. le Rhône, the P.B.23E was a sprightly-looking machine, with the pilot seated in a finely-formed, metal-covered nacelle suspended between the wings at mid-gap and containing the single Lewis gun in its nose.

Pemberton Billing P.B.23E.

The P.B.23E, soon known from its appearance as the Sparklet or Push-Proj, made its first flight at Hendon early in September, 1915, following which the Admiralty placed an order for twenty of a modified version as the Pemberton Billing Scout.

The revised model, designated P.B.25 by the designer, used wings of swept-back form in place of the straight-edged original style, and the former metal-covered nacelle was replaced by a new one enclosed in fabric. Increased power was provided by the installation of the 100 h.p. Monosoupape Gnome engine and the Lewis gun was raised to a far more accessible position in the

Pemberton Billing P.B.25. (Rolls-Royce Photo.)

66

top of the fore-decking of the nacelle. The first of the P.B.25s, 9001, received a slight increase in power over the remainder of the batch by having a 110 h.p. Clerget fitted.

Despite its competent performance, which included a top speed of 89 m.p.h. with the Monosoupape Gnome, and its advanced conception, the P.B.25 is not known to have been engaged in any operational rôle.

One of Noel Pemberton Billing's particular concerns was the lack of effective defence against the stealthy, cloud-wrapped menace of the Zeppelins. His logical and inventive mind formulated several requirements as an antidote which were transformed during 1915 into the P.B.29E, a remarkable pusher quadruplane. As an aid to good climb performance, the wings were of particularly high aspect ratio and were expected also to bestow a minimum speed of 35 m.p.h., a feature designed to contribute to endurance while on patrol, to assist materially in operating the machine in the very primitive conditions under which night flying was then taking place, and also to provide a steady gun platform. The gunner, standing in a streamlined enclosure between the two uppermost pairs of wings, had an outstandingly good all-round 360° field

Vickers F.B.8. (Vickers Photo.)

of fire. The two-bay wings each bore a pair of ailerons and the two 90 h.p. Austro-Daimler engines, driving four-blade propellers, were mounted on the underside of the lowest-but-one pair of wings which joined the fuselage level with the top longerons. Two pilots were carried in tandem cockpits; to the rear of the aft cockpit the fuselage section became triangular and terminated in a tail assembly with biplane horizontal surfaces and triple fins and rudders. A sense of urgency in the Woolston works drove the P.B.29E through to completion in some seven weeks from the start of the design but the machine's life was short as, after being flown at Chingford, it was wrecked in a crash at the same place.

Following the unfortunate failure of their F.B.7 and F.B.7A, Vickers produced in November, 1915, another twin-engine tractor biplane gun-carrier. Once again, Monosoupape Gnomes of 100 h.p. each were fitted but, this time, the airframe which they powered was of far cleaner, more advanced and more compact design. The span was only 38 ft. 4 in. on the F.B.8's upper planes of the two-bay wings, the lower surfaces of which were attached to the bottom longerons of the fuselage. The tandem cockpit arrangement, with a considerable gap between the position of the Lewis gunner in the nose and that of the pilot behind the wings, reverted to the form used in the F.B.7. The spinning rotary engines were liable to fling oil in all directions and the pair on the F.B.8 were surrounded by metal rings designed to mitigate the nuisance. The general lack of agility compared with that normally found in a single-engine fighter once again told against the F.B.8, as also did the gap between the crew's positions, and so the design fell by the wayside.

In December, 1915, a month after the début of the twin-engine F.B.8, another two-seat Vickers fighter appeared. This time it was the single-engine F.B.9—a revised F.B.5. Significant alterations in the design, bestowing an altogether more rounded appearance, were the replacement of the square tips of all horizontal flying surfaces by those of curved outline, and the shapelier nose to the nacelle. The comparatively complex form of twin-skid under-carriage was supplanted by a much neater V type. At the rear of the nacelle was fitted the 100 h.p. Monosoupape Gnome while, at the front, the gunner was given a new form of rotating circular gun-ring with a corresponding increase in the effectiveness of the weapon it supported. Although the top speed, compared with that of the F.B.5, had increased by 10 m.p.h., the F.B.9 appears to have been used mainly as a training type.

Among the firms engaged in sub-contract work which were tempted to strike out and build original designs of their own was that of Robey of Lincoln. Previously busy producing the Sopwith Gunbus for the Admiralty, in 1915 J. A. Peters evolved two contrasting single-seat biplane scouts in the company's drawing-offices; one was a pusher, powered by either the 80 h.p. Gnome or the 90 h.p. Salmson M.7, and the other was a tractor for which the engine scheduled is thought to have been the 80 h.p. Clerget. The Robey pusher was of single-bay, unequal-span wing form and the pilot was seated high up in a nacelle upon which rested the upper wings. The general appearance was com-mendably clean and, with the Salmson engine, estimated top speed was 93 m.p.h.

Vickers F.B.9. (Vickers Photo.)

Sopwith 1½-Strutter. (Hawker Photo.)

The Robey tractor, which followed the general trend of small single-seat tractor scouts of its time, possessed a very simple airframe.

The two Robey single-seaters are among the least-known of the early British scouts and little has survived concerning either machine. The pusher is reported to have come to grief during its initial flight and it is not known if the tractor flew at all.

In the course of 1915, the Sopwith Aviation Company's design office had prepared drawings for a two-seat biplane which was destined for a very successful career and for particular distinction as the first British tractor aircraft produced with a properly synchronized gun for the pilot to fire forward between the spinning propeller blades. With the construction of the prototype during the last few weeks of 1915, the Sopwith firm placed at the disposal of the Services a machine which was a great step forward in equipment.

Apart from its advanced armament installation there was nothing radical about the new Sopwith, which officially to the R.N.A.S. was the Sopwith Type 9700 and to the R.F.C. the Sopwith Two-Seater. However, neither of these designations was that under which the machine passed into its distinguished niche in the annals of British military aircraft. Universally, it became the 1½-Strutter, an appellation which is generally conceded to have evolved through the unusual arrangement of short and long pairs of centre-section struts. Powered by the 110 h.p. Clerget, the 1½-Strutter represented a logical development, embodying the valuable experience in the techniques of design and construction amassed by the Company during the past few years.

The pilot's single Vickers gun was installed centrally on the front decking and, in the case of those used by the R.F.C., was synchronized with Vickers-designed gear, while those ordered for the R.N.A.S. used the Scarff-Dibovsky gear. As well as providing for the first time a fully effective weapon for the use of the pilot, the 1½-Strutter carried a Lewis gun in its rear cockpit. The simple and rather restrictive Scarff-designed socket-and-pillar fitting for the rear gun, employed for the first 1½-Strutters, was replaced on later versions for a while by the Nieuport ring type of mounting which bestowed greater mobility on the gun. The Nieuport mounting was not ideal, owing to its awkward arrangement and size, and Wt.Off. Scarff was not long in devising a great improvement with his No. 2 ring mounting. The Sopwith-Kauper and Ross gears were also installed for the front gun in later examples of the 1½-Strutter.

In addition to its armament innovations, the type incorporated a tailplane with variable incidence, which was altered during flight by a wheel control in the pilot's cockpit, and hinged flap airbrakes in the lower wing roots.

The Admiralty was earliest to show interest in the 1½-Strutter as equipment for the R.N.A.S. and started the ball rolling with an initial order for one hundred and fifty, the first of which became available early in 1916. The R.N.A.S. commenced to use their machines with success as bombers and intended to develop such attacks on the Germans. However, the R.F.C. was so short of suitable aeroplanes prior to the opening of the Battle of the Somme, that, following a request from the War Office, the Admiralty agreed to transfer a considerable number of its 1½-Strutters. The R.F.C. had also, on its own

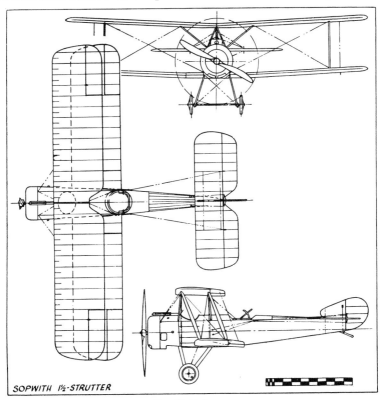

SOPWITH 1½-STRUTTER

Sopwith 1½-Strutter

The pair of A.D. Sparrow Scouts, 1536 and 1537, built by Blackburn seen under construction at Olympia Works, Leeds. (Blackburn Photo.)

account, ordered 1½-Strutters for its re-equipment, the initial machines of the procurement going to No. 70 Squadron. The type soon proved its worth over the battle front and was a welcome and reliable addition to Allied air strength.

In retrospect, the Sopwith 1½-Strutter is seen as the pioneer of the classic two-seat, tractor fighter layout, a concept which was to be exploited and developed to a very high degree for the ensuing two decades.

Throughout the 1914–18 War Harold D. Boultbee, who had previously been Chief Draughtsman to the British and Colonial Aeroplane Company, was Works Manager at Ruston Proctor of Lincoln but found time during 1915 to design a small fighter amongst other machines for the Gloucester-shire Aircraft Company at Cheltenham.

Among the single-seat fighters designed during 1915, as weapons to deal with the marauding Zeppelins, was the A.D. Scout, known also as the Sparrow, Harris Booth of the Air Department of the Admiralty being the man respon-sible for the design. The machine was intended to bear aloft the Davis recoil-less gun and this was to be housed in the lower part of the pusher biplane's nacelle.

A comparatively large gap separated the two pairs of wings, and the nacelle was attached to the underside of the upper pairs of planes. Parallel struts were incorporated in the undercarriage, their length resulting in the cockpit being at an inordinate height above ground level. Extremely large tailplane and elevator surfaces, short-coupled, were carried by the four tail-booms, in be-tween which revolved the pusher propeller and its 80 h.p. Gnome engine. The very narrow track of the wheels combined with the high centre of gravity of the machine, could have resulted only in gross unwieldiness and instability while taxiing and during take-off and landing. Strut-connected ailerons were incorporated on all four of the single-bay wings and twin fins and rudders filled the gap at the rear of the tail booms.

The whole concept was an unfortunate and unsatisfactory one, about the only point in its favour being the fine view enjoyed by the otherwise hapless pilot. Test flights soon proved the fallacy of the design, to which two airframes were constructed by Blackburn. An order for a further pair of A.D. Scouts was placed with Hewlett and Blondeau but confirmation of their actual building is lacking.

Contemporary with the A.D. Scout was the Blackburn Triplane, N502, which was designed late in 1915 and which exhibited several features in common with the A.D. machine. In particular, the Triplane possessed the same exaggerated gap between the tail booms which carried also the similar style of broad-span horizontal tail surfaces. The nacelle was mounted ahead of the centre wings of the single-bay cellules, and an undercarriage of normal

Blackburn Triplane fitted with 100 h.p. Monosoupape Gnome. (Blackburn Photo.)

height and track was provided. Additional ground stability was ensured by tip skids under the interplane struts.

The single forwards-firing gun was installed in the lower half of the nose of the nacelle, at the rear of which was fitted the 100 h.p. Monosoupape Gnome; the 110 h.p. Clerget was an alternative engine tested in the Triplane. Compared with the size of the fins, the rudders were large, and a fair measure of lateral control area was provided by fitting strut-connected ailerons on each of the six wingtips.

So passed 1915, a year of fairly significant progress in the development of the armed scout and fighter. As a distinctive class of combat aeroplane, the fighter had settled firmly into the pattern of R.F.C. and R.N.A.S. equipment and was assured of constant attention by designers and constructors to satisfy the demands for better performance continually thrust upon them by the strategists responsible for employing the machines in the field.

The opposition facing the R.F.C. and R.N.A.S. pilots was becoming steadily stronger, both in quality and quantity and also in the form of deployment. The mid-summer of 1915 had brought with it an unpleasant shock when the Fokker E.I monoplane, carrying a Fokker-synchronized Parabellum machine-gun capable of spurting a stream of bullets ahead of it, suddenly sped into action over the Western Front. Until then, only primitive and semi-organized attempts had been made to interfere with the opposing side's reconnaissance aircraft. Air fighting was now inexorably coming into its own as a deadly serious business and there was no choice but to press ahead with unrestricted speed and energy to enable the Allies to master the menacing new technique.

The German pilots were quick to capitalize on the gift of the revolutionary weapon now in their hands. New forms of attack were evolved immediately to exploit the advantage to the fullest extent and the pilots, notably Boelcke and Immelmann, adopted methods of tactical surprise to suit. The German fighters took to patrolling at a height which enabled them to pounce in a dive on any opponents, aiming and firing during the plunge. Attacks of this sort increased steadily throughout the Winter of 1915 and the Allied reconnaissance aircraft were accompanied by protective fighter escorts as an antidote. As the depredations of the Fokker grew, mid-January of 1916 brought instructions to the R.F.C. that a reconnaissance aircraft was to have an escort of a minimum of three fighters during its mission. Flying in close formation was also ordered in an attempt to reduce the alarmingly rising losses.

Fortunately, the arrival of the D.H.2 and F.E.2B units at the Front early in 1916 soon had a marked effect so that, by May, the position had improved greatly. Reorganization by Trenchard in the early part of the year had resulted in the withdrawal of fighter units from the brigades and in the concentration of the machines in wings which were then attached to each army. The fighters were thus available in compact groups for their primary purpose as offensive weapons, enabling the best use to be extracted from the numbers available.

Among the projected designs under way at the Royal Aircraft Factory when the War started was an ambitious layout by H. P. Folland and S. J. Waters for a large, twin-engine biplane armed with the Coventry Ordnance Works 1·5-pounder gun. Some time passed before the new machine, designated F.E.4 and intended for ground attack duties, was ready. The first of the two built was finished in 1916 and was powered by two 150 h.p. R.A.F.5 pusher engines which were employed to propel a machine with a span of 75 ft. 2 in.

An odd aspect of the disposition of the crew members in the front cockpit was that the forward gunner was expected to operate the C.O.W. gun from his seat behind the pilot. The third man in the crew, another gunner, was sited in the fuselage aft of the wings. The machine's large span brought about folding of the upper wingtips' overhang which was hinged to drop downwards when necessary. Some alterations were apparent in the second F.E.4, on occasion known as the F.E.4a, which made its initial flight on 16th March, 1916. The engines had been changed to a pair of 250 h.p. Rolls-Royce Eagles and the rear cockpit deleted. An experimental gunner's position was tried out in the centre-section of the upper wings, and an installation was made of a pair of Lewis guns which fired forward from each side of the fuselage gunner's position behind the pilot.

Sopwith Pup. (Hawker Photo.)

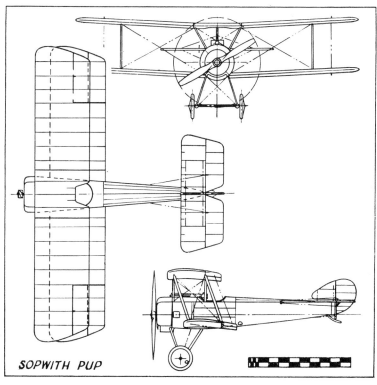

SOPWITH PUP

Sopwith Pup

74

The F.E.4 represented another attempt to carry heavy armament into action by means of a large, weighty airframe, a concept which was not a happy one as two great essential ingredients in the formula for a fighter, those of manœuvrability and speed, were lacking.

Notwithstanding, two more designs, the F.E.5 and F.E.7 biplanes, were investigated as projects, both of them being developments of the F.E.4. The F.E.5 was to have been even larger, with a span of 103 ft. and would have had twin fuselages and three R.A.F.5 engines; the F.E.7 would have exploited a theme which was a favourite one with designers now and then, namely that of a central engine bay in the fuselage driving out-rigged propellers. In the F.E.7's case, the power plant was scheduled to be a pair of 250 h.p. Rolls-Royce Eagles with shafts and gears connection to the propellers. The F.E.7 was proposed as a two-seater, with a gunner operating a battery installation of multiple machine-guns.

Both projects came to naught but a bright star was rising in the rapidly-developing single-seat firmament with the appearance early in 1916 of the Sopwith Pup. Compact and well-balanced in design, the machine did not betray by its performance and handling qualities the confidence which its appearance inspired. Pilots were unanimous in their unqualified praise for the new product from Kingston. The construction of the Pup, known originally to the R.F.C. as the Sopwith Scout and to the R.N.A.S. as the Sopwith Type 9901, was of standard wood and fabric style and carried on the successful type of split axle undercarriage pioneered by the Sopwith Company. The 80 h.p. le Rhône was chosen to power the Pup, which carried a single Vickers gun fixed on the decking in front of the pilot and synchronized with the Sopwith-Kauper gear. The first six prototype Pups went to the R.N.A.S. and production examples followed in the Autumn of 1916. Ship-board versions featured an alteration in armament in which a Lewis gun was carried on a steel-tubing mounting so that it fired upwards at an angle through the centre section cut-out.

The Pup was a success from its first appearance in service and continued to display its superiority over adversaries throughout 1917, contributing valuable assistance in the day-to-day operations in the air war.

During the early part of 1916 Sqn.Cdr. J.W. Seddon, one of the early pioneers of British aviation, was stationed at Port Victoria on the Isle of Grain and was responsible for the investigations which resulted in the construction of the Port Victoria P.V.1. This was an attempt at improving the performance of the Sopwith Baby seaplane, particularly as far as its weight-lifting qualities were concerned. As with any service aeroplane, the tendency was to continue adding more equipment to the steady deterioration of performance.

The standard Baby's wings were of the popular low thickness/chord type with comparatively little camber. This form of aerofoil gave low drag but possessed accompanying low lift properties. National Physical Laboratory experiments on aerofoil sections with greater camber had shown them to be superior for general weight lifting but a loss of speed was the penalty. Sqn.Cdr. Seddon decided to put the Laboratory investigations to practical test and had a Sopwith Baby modified by fitting a standard fuselage with new wings of identical area but with increased aspect ratio and of heavily-cambered profile. Forward stagger was also increased and new larger floats were installed. The finished conversion weighed some 300 lb. more than the normal Baby but was quite successful in proving that the revised wings enabled the P.V.1 to lift greater loads. With the 100 h.p. Monosoupape Gnome the top speed was 77 m.p.h. and the height reached was in excess of 8,000 ft. The P.V.1 later contributed to early experiments related to possibilities of launching by catapult in the course of which it took off from a railway truck on the Isle of Grain.

The R.N.A.S. Experimental Construction Depôt at Port Victoria was now getting into its stride and followed up the P.V.1 conversion with a completely original design, the P.V.2, for a Zeppelin-intercepting seaplane, single-seat gun-carrier. The armament selected was the Davis 2-pounder with ten rounds and further stipulations were that the top speed was to be 80 kt., operational cruising height 10,000 ft. and endurance 3 hours.

The P.V.2 was drawn up around the 100 h.p. Monosoupape Gnome, enveloped by a broad-chord cowling, from the periphery of which the fuselage section tapered smoothly to the tail end. The upper wings were mounted direct onto the top longerons, to avoid obstruction of the pilot's view by struts, while the narrow-chord lower planes passed in one piece well below the underside of the fuselage. Rectangular-section pontoon-type floats were fitted but were changed later for the more refined style of Linton Hope float.

The P.V.2 N.1 presented an altogether extremely attractive appearance for its time, and during its first flight tests in June, 1916, flew successfully with the exception of the aileron control. This fault was rectified by shortening the original broad-span ailerons to half their span and with strengthening them. The P.V.2 was not destined to adhere to the original project of operating with the Davis gun as development of the weapon was terminated.

Rather than abandon the P.V.2 altogether, the machine was rebuilt as the P.V.2bis with the upper wings elevated by 1 ft. on struts, together with the addition of a 2 ft. centre-section, so that they passed over the fuselage and thereby improved the forward view for landing. As a seaplane fighter the P.V.2bis was scheduled to carry a pair of Lewis guns above the upper centre-section but apparently only one was fitted eventually.

Admiralty interest in fighters continued to increase with the result that, during the first months of 1916, the Port Victoria designers received a request from the Experimental Armament Section for a two-seat fighter layout required to be an effective gun-carrier.

Plans were commenced for a pusher project on a land undercarriage and powered with the 110 h.p. le Rhône. It would seem that this machine would have been the P.V.3 but the project did not reach fruition and was dropped in favour of a revised development on floats. This was designated P.V.4 and given the serial N8. An American-designed engine, the 10-cylinder Smith Static radial which delivered 150 h.p., was scheduled to power the P.V.4.

Based on the output of this engine, the specification included a top speed of 80 kt., an initial climb rate of 5,000 ft. in 15 min., an endurance of 8 hours, wireless equipment and a Lewis gun for the gunner. The crew of two were housed in a trim, streamlined nacelle, to the top longerons of which were fitted the upper wings. The lower wings were considerably smaller than the upper set and the tail unit was carried on four slim booms. Stepped Linton Hope main floats formed the landing-gear, together with a single tail float, and a Scarff ring in the nose was used to enable the gunner to make the best use of an outstanding field of fire for his gun. The Smith Static, being produced in Britain by Heenan and Froude, was extremely slow in reaching production status, so that by the time that the P.V.4 was ready for its power unit in the Autumn of 1916 the Static was still not available. After continuing delay, a final effort was made in mid-1917 to get the P.V.4 airborne by installing a 110 h.p. Clerget. The Clerget's greater length upset the balance of the machine completely and only considerable revision of the design could have rectified the faults. By this time the cleaner tractor with its synchronized forwards-firing gun was in the ascendant and development of the P.V.4, commendable design though it was, was dropped.

Until 1916 comparatively little attention had been paid to the value of camouflage on the aircraft flown by the R.F.C. and R.N.A.S. Both the Army and the Navy had exploited the art in disguising their other equipment but their aeroplanes, for the first two years of the War, had gone about their duties in their natural finished fabric, varnished wood and polished metal.

National identification insignia had proved to be essential very shortly after the R.F.C. and the R.N.A.S. had arrived in France and the first contacts had been made with their German opponents. The troops on the ground were but poorly schooled in recognizing friendly and enemy aircraft and were apt to fire at any machines overhead.

As a means of identification, the Union Jack was adopted as a symbol to be displayed on both R.F.C. and R.N.A.S. aircraft. At first, from the end of August, 1914, the emblem was in the shape of a shield but on the publication of a Field Headquarters Memorandum in October, 1914, directing that the insignia were to be as large as possible on the machines, a straightforward rectangular form of the flag was adopted. The Union Jack did not last long, however, as a practical means of identification as it tended to become confused with the German cross insignia. After some two months in use, a G.H.Q. Order issued on 11th December, 1914, decreed that a roundel—consisting of a central red disc surrounded by a white ring and finally an outer blue ring—was henceforth to be used. For some months miniature Union Jacks were painted alongside the roundels but in May, 1915, they disappeared with the final adoption of blue, white and red vertical stripes on the rudder as an adjunct to the roundels on the wings and fuselage. As the R.F.C. adopted the roundel in place of the Union Jack, so did the R.N.A.S. but, at first, in the modified form of a red outer ring to a white centre disc.

Late in 1916 a general scheme of camouflage was brought into play, which consisted of painting the upper flying surfaces, the fin and the fuselage sides and top khaki-green. The underside of a machine remained in the clear doped natural shade.

The unqualified success of the Avro 504 prompted the parent company to construct during early 1916 a two-seat fighter variant under the type number 521. The wing structure was cleaned up by conversion to single-bay cellules and the same streamlining process applied to the undercarriage resulted in a simple V-strut structure. The rear cockpit was set some distance behind that of the pilot, above whom was a generous cut-out in the trailing edge of the centre-section.

The 110 h.p. Clerget powered the Avro 521, which was test-flown by F. P. Raynham and found to have disagreeable flying characteristics. Nevertheless, despite the crash of the prototype in the hands of an R.F.C. pilot, twenty-five production 521s were built but did not apparently reach operational service in their intended rôle.

1916 saw the completion of another of Noel Pemberton Billing's unusual designs—the Supermarine Night Hawk. The project had started the year before, following the appearance of the P.B.29 quadruplane and the Admiralty's decision to investigate the inventor's claims for his concept for anti-Zeppelin warfare. Pemberton Billing was enabled to set about designing the machine in 1915 by the agreement of the Admiralty to his release on indefinite leave for the purpose from the R.N.A.S. in which he was serving as a Flight Lieutenant.

The Night Hawk, when it saw the light of day, was a truly extraordinary creation. Once again, the quadruplane layout was followed but with sweptback wing panels in the three-bay structure. The pilot was seated in a generously-glazed enclosed pylon structure, which reached above to the upper wings and also carried the top front gunner with his 1·5-pounder Davis. To his rear was a position for a Lewis gun on a Scarff ring and the nose of the fuselage terminated in another cockpit containing a Scarff-mounted Lewis gun. Both of the machine-gun locations were provided primarily for the machine's own defence. Forward of the front Lewis gun position was a searchlight which received its power from a generator driven by a 5 h.p. A.B.C. engine, the complete unit being installed in the nose.

The Night Hawk embodied many other ingenious and advanced features but was provided with comparatively low power from a pair of 100 h.p. Anzani engines which were given the onerous task of coping with a wing span of 60 ft. and a loaded weight of over 6,000 lb. C. B. Prodger carried out the initial flights of the sole Night Hawk 1388 at R.N.A.S. Eastchurch and established the machine's top speed to be 75 m.p.h. and its landing speed the aimed-for 35 m.p.h. Substantial endurance of 9 hrs. normal and 18 hrs. maximum was part of the machine's patrol capabilities.

During the gestation period of the Night Hawk, Pemberton Billing relinquished his part in the control of the company which bore his name and the machine finally emerged from the newly-formed Supermarine Aviation Works, Ltd., under Hubert Scott-Paine.

Despite its many advanced features, the Night Hawk remained a single

A successful British triplane, the Sopwith Triplane. (Rolls-Royce Photo.)

prototype but, during the same period, the Sopwith Company was engaged on a comparably unusual design which was destined for fame and success. Supermarine's quadruplane was unable to make the grade but the Sopwith Triplane's attributes were such that it soon established itself favourably in service.

Although it bore itself on three sharply-staggered, narrow-chord wings, the Triplane prototype N.500 when it materialized at the end of May, 1916, was an eminently neat, practical design. Single interplane and centre-section struts braced the single-bay layout which was mated to a fuselage, tail unit and undercarriage close in appearance to those of the Pup. The power of the 110 h.p. Clerget engine, coupled with the small span of 26 ft. 6 in., endowed the Triplane with excellent manoeuvrability, climb and general all-round performance. Standard armament consisted of a single synchronized Vickers gun on the front decking but six were produced carrying a pair of Vickers in the same location.

Both the Admiralty and the War Office ordered the Triplane in substantial numbers but, as a result of inter-Service exchanges of aircraft in an endeavour to redress the position on the Western Front, the Triplane was operated only by the R.N.A.S. squadrons, in whose capable and enthusiastic hands it soon struck fear into the hearts of the German crews once deliveries started at the end of 1916.

The substitution of the 130 h.p. Clerget brought a corresponding benefit to the performance and the Triplane soared to its greatest heights of success with its exploits in the all-Canadian "B" Flight of No. 10 (Naval) Squadron under Flt.Sub-Lt. Raymond Collishaw. The Sopwith Triplane vindicated

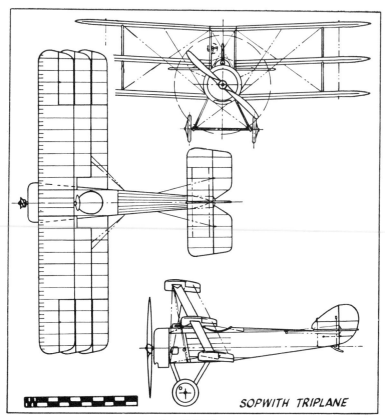

SOPWITH TRIPLANE

Sopwith Triplane

gloriously the faith which its designers had placed in the radical concept which it represented for a service aeroplane.

While the Clerget-powered triplane was establishing its reputation, two examples of a Hispano-Suiza-engined triplane single-seat fighter appeared from Sopwith—N509 with the direct-drive 150 h.p. and N510 with the geared 200 h.p. Both machines were somewhat larger than the Clerget-engined triplane but each was armed with a single Vickers gun in front of the pilot. Supplies of the engine were earmarked for the promising S.E.5 and the Hispano-Suiza triplane was not developed into a production type.

Although by 1916 the tractor layout was firmly established as the optimum for most classes of aeroplane, Vickers pressed forward during the year with another single-seat pusher fighter—the F.B.12. A well-streamlined nacelle was carried between the two-bay wings, the whole machine being designed around the 150 h.p. Hart radial engine which was expected to endow the F.B.12 with a performance superior to that of other pusher fighters extant. The F.B. 12's airframe was ready before any example of its intended engine so the 80

Prototype Vickers F.B.12. (Vickers Photo.)

h.p. le Rhône served to flight-test the machine in June, 1916. As well as flying with the le Rhône engine, the F.B.12 flew with the more powerful 100 h.p. Monosoupape Gnome and tests were made with revised wings of larger size and more angular form. Armament in each version was a single Lewis gun set well back in the upper nose of the nacelle.

Yet another version of the basic F.B.12 design, the F.B.12C, made its appearance. The scheduled engine was again the elusive 150 h.p. Hart radial but, once more, it failed to materialize and in its place the F.B.12C utilized both the 110 h.p. le Rhône and the 100 h.p. Anzani. The machine differed from the two previous F.B.12 designs in having a flat-sided nacelle in place of the circular type, and modified wings and tail. Although Service Trials were carried out at the end of the year, the pusher fighter was in eclipse and could not be expected to compete with the cleaner tractor types.

Vickers F.B.12C. (Vickers Photo.)

Even though the pusher layout had patently had its day by mid-1916, the F.E.2b continued to soldier on and was revised in two examples, designated F.E.2c, which were built as night-fighters; the main alteration was that the pilot's cockpit was the front one.

Following the pair of F.E.2cs came the F.E.2d, which set out to achieve better performance by using the excellent new 250 h.p. engine from Rolls-Royce, the first of a magnificent line of peerless aero-engines from the same firm.

Later to receive the name of Eagle, the 250 h.p. Rolls-Royce had been designed during 1914 by Henry Royce and his chief assistant A. G. Elliott. The intended rating was 200 h.p., but on test in October, 1915, under six months from the time drawings were commenced, the twelve-cylinder water-cooled engine gave 225 b.h.p. Further development produced 266 b.h.p. by March, 1916, 284 b.h.p. by the following July and 322 b.h.p. by the end of the same year.

In the F.E.2d the Eagle gave the two-seat pusher fighter an extended lease of life and the new machine arrived in France in time for the operations during the Battle of the Somme which started at the beginning of July, 1916. Unfortunately, owing to the landing of the first F.E.2d to be sent to France on 30th June in German-held territory, the potentiality of this latest arrival at the Front was revealed to the enemy before it went into action. Notwithstanding, in spite of its obsolescence as a concept and its bulk and clumsy appearance, the F.E.2d gave valiant and untiring service. The type was used to undertake varied experiments in armament and attempted also to intercept Zeppelins but its efforts to aid Home Defence were not conspicuously successful.

While the F.E.2b and F.E.2d were thus playing their part in the air war, another Royal Aircraft Factory design, the B.E.2c, was modified as a single-seat fighter in response to pressing demands from the Royal Flying Corps for such a type. Rather than set about designing a completely fresh machine, the Factory decided that the most expeditious way of meeting the case would be to modify the B.E.2c as dictated by the requirements.

Airframe 1697 was selected for conversion into the prototype B.E.12, the designation allotted to the project. A new engine, the 150 h.p. R.A.F.4a, was installed in the nose and the front cockpit was deleted. Production B.E.12s embodied several detail modifications to provide increased fuel capacity and improved performance. Normal armament applied to the B.E.12 consisted of a single Vickers gun mounted to port on the fuselage and equipped with Vickers interrupter gear. Occasionally, additional fire-power was provided by a Lewis gun installed to starboard on a Strange mounting and alternative armament fitted consisted of a pair of fuselage Lewis guns on Strange mountings.

The B.E.12 arrived in France to do battle in mid-Summer of 1916 but, in producing the conversion, the fundamental fact had been overlooked that inherent stability was a highly-developed feature of the B.E.2c but was not a quality which was in the least compatible with a fighter's primary and essential requirement of manœuvrability. The extra power and armament did nothing to meet this need and the B.E.12 was patently unable to rise to the requirements for which, in good faith, it had been designed. After but a few months' use as a fighter, the B.E.12 was relegated to duties as a single-seat bomber.

And yet, a further attempt was made to turn the B.E.12 into a successful fighter by producing a new version with single-bay wings. This was the B.E.12a which had the same 150 h.p. R.A.F.4a engine but was fitted with greatly extended tips to the upper wings. These tips terminated in ailerons given exaggerated horn balances which reached forward to the leading edge. The design proved unsatisfactory and was modified to use normal B.E.2e wings with strut-connected ailerons on each tip. At first this revised type was known as the B.E.12Ae but soon reverted in nomenclature to B.E.12a. All of this endeavour was in vain as the B.E.12a was as much a failure as the B.E.12 and served only in small numbers.

Home Defence was one of the spheres in which both types proved finally of some value and was a rôle in which a new Vickers two-seat, fighter reconnaissance tractor biplane, the F.B.14, also found itself performing. The 230 h.p. B.H.P. was the engine originally scheduled for the F.B.14 but delays in its development forced Vickers to install as an alternative the less-powerful 160 h.p. Beardmore. The combination made its first flight during August, 1916, but was unable to demonstrate a performance in keeping with that which had been expected using the intended power plant. In spite of this disappointment, an order was placed for one hundred and fifty. The F.B.14 was certainly to date the cleanest of Vickers two-seaters and in appearance looked a most promising aeroplane.

The switch to the 160 h.p. Beardmore did not, however, prove to be the panacea as difficulties with it led to the trial installation of the even lower output 120 h.p. Beardmore. With this engine the F.B.14 was quite unable to reach its required standard of performance as an operational proposition and most of the airframes constructed were passed engineless to the War Office for the search to continue for a suitable power unit.

The installation of the 150 h.p. Lorraine-Dietrich resulted in the F.B.14A, and another version with larger two-bay wings in place of the earlier single-bay type and powered by the excellent 250 h.p. Rolls-Royce Mk. IV was designated F.B.14D. The power contributed by the Eagle IV engine was responsible for the F.B.14D having the best performance of the F.B.14 series but, even so, the machine was still not able to surpass that of the redoubtable Bristol Fighter.

Vickers produced one more version of the basic design in the 150 h.p. R.A.F.4a-powered F.B.14F, which had a simplified fuselage without the curved coaming on the top surface and wings set with substantially greater stagger. Both the F.B.14D and the F.B.14F were employed on experimental work but six F.B.14s were allocated in 1917 for Home Defence operations.

Vickers F.B.14A. (Vickers Photo.)

While some progress was discernible during 1916 in the development of engines of greater power and reliability around which the aircraft designers could evolve their layouts for projected fighters, the exigencies of war dictated that large numbers of machines were required and this fact tended to militate generally against evolving new forms of structure. Although the streamlined monocoque form of fuselage had reached a high degree of perfection some three years previously, and was being used successfully in Germany—notably on the Albatros single-seaters—in Great Britain designers were adhering to the firmly-established conventional wooden box girder structures with their attendant wire bracing. In the interest of higher speeds, the addition of former and stringer fairings had become accepted practice for the minor weight penalty involved. Fabric was utilized as the main covering medium for an airframe, with plywood specified for the more highly-stressed areas, together with removable metal panels where accessibility was required. In general, airframes were becoming cleaner with a positive concentration on the tractor form, with its many advantages, once reliable synchronizer mechanisms were an established fact.

1916 was the year in which Vickers produced another single-seat fighter, the F.B.16, which was to undergo considerable development as a basic design. The F.B.16 was a neat and workmanlike single-bay biplane and was able to be fitted with the engine scheduled for it, the 150 h.p. Hart radial, which had had to be abandoned as the unit for the Vickers F.B.12. Modifications were made in the F.B.16, which included removal of the cowling over the engine, the rounding of the previously humped fin outline, the replacement of the two-blade propeller by a four-blader, and the fitting of a considerably smaller headrest for the pilot.

Vickers decided to put in hand an extensive redesign of the F.B.16 which came into the open in December, 1916, as the F.B.16A. The new fighter was of quite pugnacious aspect with sharply-staggered wings mated to a straight-sided fuselage, in the nose of which was mounted the 150 h.p. Hispano-Suiza engine. The top and bottom of the fuselage were rounded and the fin and rudder outline followed that of the modified F.B.16. The undercarriage was set well forward and the single Vickers gun, as fitted also to the F.B.16, was mounted on the front decking. In addition, the F.B.16A carried a Lewis gun on the upper centre-section on a sliding mounting.

Test flights on 20th December, 1916, carried out by Capt. Simpson, resulted in a fatal crash but Vickers constructed another F.B.16A, the trials of which R. H. Barnwell conducted. Despite the lively performance which the F.B.16A exhibited it was not to receive a production order.

Nevertheless, Vickers continued to expend time and money in developing the design still further so that, by June of 1917, F.B.16A A8963 had been transformed into the F.B.16D. As well as minor modifications to the airframe, engine power was stepped up by installing the 200 h.p. Hispano-Suiza, the armament comprising a Lewis gun firing through the propeller shaft and a second gun of the same type on the upper centre-section. The F.B.16D would have stood a good chance of being adopted for Service use as its performance was excellent for its time but engine accessibility was considered to be below the standard necessary for field maintenance.

Two other versions of the F.B.16 were to appear—the generally-larger F.B.16E with two-bay wings, 275 h.p. Lorraine-Dietrich engine and two fuselage-mounted Vickers guns, and the F.B.16H which was similar to the F.B.16E but had even greater power from a 300 h.p. Hispano-Suiza engine which brought its speed at ground level to 147 m.p.h.

August, 1916, saw the emergence of the F.B.19 Mk.I, another of Vickers Ltd.'s endeavours in single-seat fighter design. The new machine was basically the resuscitation of the E.S.1 and E.S.2 of the previous year but with a slightly smaller span and reduced overall length. The F.B.19 Mk.I's engine was the 100 h.p. Monosoupape Gnome and the armament provided was a single

Vickers F.B.16A. (Vickers Photo.)

Vickers F.B.16D. (Vickers Photo.)

Vickers F.B.16E. (Vickers Photo.)

Vickers F.B.16H. (Imperial War Museum Photo.)

86

Vickers F.B.19 Mk.II. (Vickers Photo.)

Vickers gun, mounted to port in a trough in the fuselage, and synchronized with the Vickers-Challenger gear.

A new version then appeared, designated F.B.19 Mk.II, the wings of which embodied sharp stagger, and which used either the 110 h.p. Clerget or the 110 h.p. le Rhône engine.

The Mk.I could also utilize the 110 h.p. le Rhône and both marks of F.B.19 went into limited production against orders for the R.F.C., by which service it was often called the Bullet. After being turned down for full-scale operation in France, the F.B.19 found itself flying in the Middle East and also with Home Defence units in the United Kingdom but was never fortunate enough to make a name.

An improved version of the Martinsyde G.100, the G.102, appeared during 1916, benefiting by the extra 40 h.p. available from its 160 h.p. Beardmore engine and taking to itself the name Elephant. Experimental armament installations on Elephants included one with a Lewis gun to starboard of the cockpit and firing upwards at about 45° through the centre-section and another

Martinsyde G.102 Elephant photographed at Brooklands.

The twin-engine Bristol T.T.A. (Bristol Photo.)

which was used during the Summer of 1917 in trials with the Eeman gun gear. The Martinsyde G.100 and G.102 carried out some of their most redoubtable work in the Middle East and the memory of the Elephant has been carried forward as the symbol in the badge of No. 27 Squadron, R.A.F.

In the course of September, 1915, design work had been initiated on an ambitious two-seat fighter biplane to be powered by twin engines and designated Bristol T.T.—Twin Tractor. Responsible for the project's layout were F. S. Barnwell and L. G. Frise and in its general concept, together with the gunner in the nose and the pilot located behind the wings, the T.T. resembled the Vickers F.B.7 and F.B.8. The machine was of 53 ft. 6 in. span and was scheduled to employ a pair of 150 h.p. R.A.F.4a engines. Non-availability of these units forced the installation of two 120 h.p. Beardmores, the revision resulting in a new designation T.T.A. Two Lewis guns armed the front gunner and a third Lewis was installed for the pilot to fire to the rear. The T.T.A. was ready for its initial trials in May, 1916, and these were carried out by Capt. Hooper of the R.F.C.

Bristol S.2A. (Bristol Photo.)

88

Like the two Vickers products, the Bristol T.T.A. lacked the primary requisites of a fighter and was too ponderous and low-powered to possess sufficient manœuvrability, besides denying the pilot and gunner the quick communication between them which was so essential in a fighter. There was also negligible prospect of being able to fire the guns to the rear, which left the machine defenceless from that quarter; consequently, the pair of prototypes—7750 and 7751—were abandoned.

While the T.T.A. was undergoing its trials, a completely different concept of a two-seat scout made its début—the Bristol S.2A. A single-engine biplane with pilot and gunner seated side-by-side, it was inspired by the Scout D but, as a reliable synchronizer for a forward-firing gun was still awaited, the expedient of carrying a gunner alongside the pilot was adopted in the interest of keeping down the overall size of the aeroplane. The 110 h.p. Clerget provided the power initially in 7836 and 7837, the pair of prototypes. By the time that they were ready, one during May and the other during June of 1916, fairly adequate synchronizing gears were ready and the temporary solution provided by the S.2A was not required. Its performance was commendable and one of the two S.2As was modified for further trials with the lower power of the 100 h.p. Monosoupape Gnome.

Although neither the T.T.A. nor the S.2.A passed into production, Frank Barnwell's next two-seat fighter design for the British and Colonial Aeroplane Company was destined to be an outstanding success and to have many years of excellent service ahead of it.

By the beginning of 1916, it had become quite obvious that a replacement was imperative for the primitive and obsolete two-seaters plodding their way warily across the increasingly dangerous skies over the Front. By March of that year, Barnwell was able to settle down to transferring to paper his idea of an advanced and powerful new two-seater. With a considerably enhanced fund of experience to draw upon, his versatile mind devised a layout for a biplane of eminently purposeful aspect.

At first the new project was known as the R.2A with the intended engine to be the 120 h.p. Beardmore. To obtain the desired performance it became obvious that more than 120 h.p. would be needed and thought was given to using the more powerful Hispano-Suiza as an alternative. Barnwell's mind was finally made up for him by the advent at a most propitious time in April, 1916, of a newcomer to the range of Rolls-Royce aero engines—the twelve-cylinder water-cooled V Falcon of 205 h.p. Never satisfied that significantly increased output could not be gained by intensive development, Henry Royce was able steadily to improve the rating to 228 h.p. in May, 247 h.p. in February, 1917, and 262 h.p. by April, 1917.

The Falcon was a gift to Barnwell of a fine, reliable, powerful engine around which he proceeded to completely redesign the R.2A as the Bristol F.2A Fighter. The power unit was well blended into a fuselage of rectangular section which tapered in side elevation to a knife-edge at the tail, and which was suspended by struts between the two-bay, equal-span wings. In deference to the essential requirement in a two-seat fighter that the pilot and gunner

The Bristol F.2B, among the most successful of the 1914–18 two-seat fighters. (Bristol Photo.)

should be able to communicate immediately with each other, the cockpits were adjacent and in every other way the needs of the crew for their utmost efficiency were borne in mind in the layout. The pilot's view was enhanced by adequate stagger of the wings and by cut-outs in the centre-section trailing edge and roots, while the gunner was given as broad a field of fire as could be arranged.

Two prototypes were soon ordered but incorporating different engines— one with the Falcon Mk.1 and the other with the 150 h.p. Hispano-Suiza. Work on the airframes was started during July, 1916, and 9th September saw the Falcon-powered A3303, the first machine, ready. Modification to the engine's radiators soon took place when the pair originally fitted, one on each side of the fore-fuselage, were removed to improve the view for the pilot and replaced by a neat installation around the nose ahead of the engine. A3304, the Hispano-Suiza-powered F.2A, was complete some six weeks later on 25th October. The F.2A's pilot was provided with a single Vickers gun installed in the centre of the nose and covered by the cowling so that it fired through an orifice in the radiator face. The observer's Lewis was carried on a Scarff ring.

The F.2A was an instant success and went through its trials with flying colours to achieve performance figures which exceeded those expected. An initial order for fifty was placed, to be powered with the Falcon to circumvent the shortage of Hispano-Suizas, and with revised wingtips.

The first operational squadron to use the F.2A was No. 48, which went into action with the machine on 5th April, 1917, but suffered unexpectedly high losses immediately owing to the lack of appreciation by the crews of the vastly superior capabilities of their mounts compared with previous two-seaters. Once the speed and great manoeuvrability inherent in the Fighter were recognized, the machine came into its own in combat with the pilot able to use his gun really effectively and the observer simultaneously making the most of his armament. The technique which had to be learned and exploited was one of flying and fighting with the machine in a manner hitherto reserved for a single-seater.

Even after the deletion of the side radiators, the forward view from the pilot's cockpit was still not all that it could be and was improved by incorporating downward slope in the upper longerons from the rear cockpit forward to the bearers for the engine. The modified machine went into production as the F.2B and proceeded to enhance the reputation already earned by the F.2A.

The Biff, as it soon became affectionately known, proved itself to be a brilliant design and an outstanding success among the British warplanes of 1914–18.

Although the Sopwith $1\frac{1}{2}$-Strutter had pioneered the two-seat armed tractor layout successfully, Frank Barnwell's Bristol Fighter marks the start of the classic concept and employment in battle of the single-engine, two-seat, high-performance fighter, born in the heat of war and continued into the years of peace as a type of aircraft in the development of which British designers excelled. Provided that sufficient power were available from the engine, around which the machine was designed, the two-seat fighter could prove itself to be a very welcome and useful addition to air strength. The twin-engine multi-seat concept for a fighter was a far less happy combination owing to the attendant drastic sacrifice of manœuvrability, which its size and layout involved, and which was not a pronounced feature of the single-engine formula. Some loss of performance was inevitable in the two-seat fighter, owing to increased size and the extra weight of airframe and gunner, but the Bristol Fighter was able to offset these disadvantages handsomely by virtue of its excellent, powerful Rolls-Royce engine.

Two prototypes of an all-metal, two-seat fighter, designated M.R.1 and inintended to eliminate the disadvantages attendant upon the usual wooden airframes under tropical conditions, were constructed following Barnwell's basic layout for the project during July, 1916, with the detail design work undertaken by W. T. Reid. The engine chosen was the 150 h.p. Hispano-Suiza, the airframe that it powered being a two-bay biplane which was slightly larger overall than the F.2A and F.2B. The fuselage was mounted mid-way in the gap between the wings and was a stressed-skin monocoque covered with sheet aluminium. The pilot was provided with a single Vickers gun in the cowling while the gunner had a Lewis gun on a Scarff ring. Although tested

The experimental two-seat Bristol M.R.1. (Bristol Photo.)

91

comprehensively, the M.R.1 was not selected finally for production but is of note for its use of metal for the framework and the fuselage covering.

In contrast with the situation prevailing in Britain, the monoplane had thrived on the Continent as a military machine in both France and Germany. The type had consequently received its full share of attention to development and both countries possessed a fairly useful range of monoplanes in service. By comparison, progressive experience in the design and construction of monoplanes in Great Britain had suffered severely as a direct result of the ban of 1912 and the consequent concentration, to its virtual exclusion, on biplanes, triplanes and even quadruplanes.

The advent of the Bristol M.1A single-seat monoplane fighter in September, 1916, was therefore an event of some considerable significance as Frank Barnwell had been given sanction by the British and Colonial Aeroplane Company to design it during July, 1916, despite continued official disapproval of the form for Service equipment. Such short-sighted behaviour in official circles, exhibited in various forms on many occasions, militates directly against accumulation of invaluable experience in design, construction and operation which those striving in all good faith on behalf of their country are entitled to acquire for its protection and continued well-being. Anything less than whole-hearted encouragement and assistance to those whose direct responsibility is the strength of the armed forces for the shielding of the population, is playing straight into the hands of the country's enemies and is a scandalous denial to its brave sons of the quality of equipment which they have every right to expect to be provided for them.

The monoplane ban of 1912 meant the loss of several years of steady development which Great Britain could ill afford, particularly since her traditional protection of the water surrounding her had been shown three years earlier as being no longer her complete safeguard. She could now be attacked by air from the Continent and consequently needed to exploit every conceivable means for her protection. The banning of a particular class of fast aeroplane was certainly no way of furthering this object and even the Bristol Monoplane in Barnwell's advanced style was unable to make much headway against the

C4910, a Bristol M.1C. (Bristol Photo.)

N511, an Armstrong Whitworth F.K.10 constructed by the Phoenix Dynamo Manufacturing Co.

opposition, a resistance which was to face the monoplane until the mid-1930s.

The 110 h.p. Clerget powered the M.1A and the designer aimed at achieving as streamlined an installation as possible by employing a spinner with a large diameter, leaving a cooling slot between itself and the cowling. A simple rectangular-section wooden basic fuselage was faired to circular form with the usual arrangement of formers and stringers. The wings were mounted in the shoulder position and braced by wires from a central cabane over the cockpit.

Construction of the prototype A5138 was so quick that it was ready in September, 1916, for testing by Freddy Raynham. The machine's top speed was a rewarding 132 m.p.h. and a further four examples were constructed as M.1Bs with slight modifications and armed with a single synchronized Vickers gun on the port decking.

News of the new fast and handy monoplane fighter, which soon circulated among squadron pilots, raised high hopes and anticipation of its appearance in France. Such was not to be, however, and the landing speed of 49 m.p.h. was stated to be too high in justification of the rejection for use on the Western Front. One hundred and twenty-five were, nevertheless, ordered into production as the M.1C using the 110 h.p. le Rhône and having the gun mounted centrally and synchronized by the Constantinesco gear. The M.1C did manage to see operational service in the Middle East but its denial to the pilots of the Western Front stands out as one of the worst examples of official incompetence and ineptitude extant. The issue in quantity of the M.1C to the R.F.C. in France could have wrought a great change in the Allies' favour in the fighting in the skies.

Frank Barnwell gave time to two other single-seat fighters during 1916, both projects to be powered by a single 200 h.p. Ricardo-Halford Cruciform engine. The Scout E Type 18 would have been a tractor biplane and the Type 19 a pusher biplane but neither machine materialized.

In the unending quest for fighter supremacy designers in Britain explored most layouts and, in 1916, the Armstrong Whitworth designer F. Koolhoven

The back-staggered D.H.5 prototype A5172. (de Havilland Photo.)

was responsible for a two-seat fighter reconnaissance quadruplane which, despite the complexity of its four wings, struts and pair of cockpits was, none the less, a clean and pleasing machine, especially in its final form. The proto-type used the 110 h.p. Clerget engine while the modified later version, of

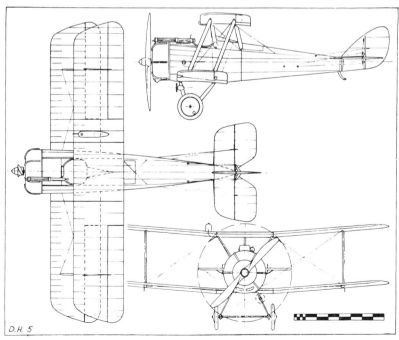

D.H.5

which a few were built, had the 130 h.p. Clerget. Tests showed that the F.K.10 was not a particularly successful machine and it remained simply one of the more unusual designs of the 1914–18 War.

An out-of-the-ordinary concept which did achieve fair success was Geoffrey de Havilland's little D.H.5 single-seat biplane of 1916, unusual in that it incorporated back-stagger in pursuit of that much-sought-after feature of a fighter—a first class view for the pilot.

Designed around the 110 h.p. le Rhône, the D.H.5 was in every other respect quite conventional in layout and construction. Unfortunately, performance at height was not a strong point with the type so, because of this fault, employment was found for it mainly in ground attack in which rôle the excellent forward view was a great asset.

In the Autumn of 1916 there appeared the first aeroplane to be both designed and constructed by the Fairey Aviation Company. Hitherto, the firm had built some Short-designed seaplanes but, with the F.2 three-seat, long-range fighter, it started the extensive line of aircraft which were to carry the

The large twin-engine Fairey F.2.

name of Fairey for the ensuing forty years. The F.2 was intended for the R.N.A.S. and was a three-bay tractor biplane with a span of 77 ft. and a pair of 190 h.p. Rolls-Royce Falcon engines. Both gunners had Lewis guns on Scarff rings, one being in the nose cockpit and the other just aft of the wings.

Although, when it flew in May, 1917, the single prototype 3704 showed the F.2 to be a competent enough design, it proved to be another of the early examples of that class of the large, multi-seat, multi-engine fighter which, owing to its inherent disadvantages, was to prove time and time again unsuitable for adoption and production.

The Fairey Company was more successful with its adaptation of the Sopwith Baby seaplane which it redesigned as the Hamble Baby to incorporate the Fairey Patent Camber Gear which consisted of wing trailing-edge flaps, used to produce increased lift and doubling as ailerons. Out of a total of one hundred and eighty Hamble Babies built, one hundred and thirty were by Parnall and Sons and, of these, seventy-four were on land undercarriages and known as Hamble Baby Converts.

During 1916, the Royal Aircraft Factory undertook the design of another

Fairey Hamble Baby, constructed by Parnall. (Fairey Photo.)

pusher fighter reconnaissance machine, the F.E.9 biplane. The 200 h.p. Hispano-Suiza provided the power and the gunner was given an excellent field of fire. By 1917, when the three F.E.9's built were completed, the comparatively untidy pusher layout was hardly expected to compete with tractor types and the F.E.9 was consequently used in various experiments.

1916 saw the appearance of another hopeful scout design from Grahame-White, the Type 20 single-seat biplane with the 80 h.p. Clerget. The machine embodied a neat, circular-section fuselage to which were fitted wings set with a pronounced gap. No progress was made with the Type 20 and the same fate befell another single-seat biplane of 1916, the Parnall Scout with the 260 h.p. Sunbeam Maori. The Scout was designed by A. Camden Pratt, who had been responsible for the Short S.81 Gun-carrier of 1913, and was a large machine of 44 ft. span intended to intercept Zeppelins. N505, the sole example built, was abandoned as it turned out to be much heavier than anticipated.

Clifford Tinson, late of Bristol and the Admiralty's Air Department, was

The Sage Type 2 with gunner's position above upper wings. (Sage Photo.)

96

engaged by Sage and Company at the beginning of 1916 as Chief Designer. His first design for the firm was a two-seat biplane fighter with a wing span of only 22 ft. 2·5 in. and arranged so that the gunner received an unrestricted field of fire by standing to fire his Lewis gun through 360° above the upper wings. The engine was the 100 h.p. Monosoupape Gnome in a neat cowling, and a glazed cabin enclosed the crew and supported the upper planes. After flying for the first time on 10th August, 1916, the Sage Type 2 crashed on the 20th of the following month at Cranwell. The design was then abandoned as the style of armament installation had been rendered unnecessary by the advent of the synchronizer gear.

While engaged in their production of scouts, the Sopwith Company built a very small single-seat biplane of 16 ft. 3 in. span and powered by a 50

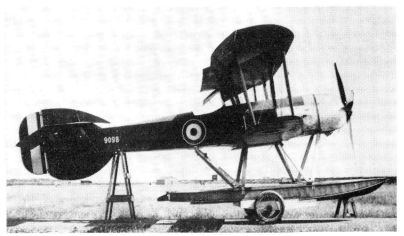

Wight Baby. (Imperial War Museum Photo.)

h.p. Gnome for the use of H. G. Hawker, their test pilot. Trials were later made with the Bee, as it was named, after a single Vickers gun had been fitted to assess its use as a lightweight fighter but the design was not adopted.

Another little-known single-seat fighter design which came to naught was the Whitehead Comet of 1916. An 80 h.p. le Rhône was fitted to the single-bay, staggered biplane which had a well-formed fuselage of circular section but an indifferent view from the cockpit.

Yet another of the unsuccessful single-seat scout prototypes of 1916 was the Wight Baby of J. Samuel White and Company of Cowes. This was a 100 h.p. Monosoupape Gnome-powered single-bay biplane which embodied the double-camber wing section evolved by Howard Wright, and folding wings.

J. Samuel White were among the few aircraft companies to attempt to exploit the quadruplane form and did so with their single-seat scout of 1916. The three upper wings were equal in span but the lowest was shorter than the others. Differing chords on each set of wings were incorporated and the 110 h.p. Clerget-engined machine was modified several times in efforts to improve it but N546 remained the only example of one more of the various unacceptable quadruplane types built.

Among the companies engaged in sub-contract aircraft work was the firm of F. C. Nestler, Ltd., and near the close of 1916 they constructed a manœuvrable 100 h.p. Monosoupape Gnome-powered single-seat biplane scout to the designs of Mons. Boudot. The Nestler Scout was quite conventional in conception but was abandoned after it crashed at Hendon on 26th March, 1917, while being flown by J. B. Fitzsimmons who lost his life in the accident.

Following the F.K.10 quadruplane design Armstrong Whitworth investigated an extraordinary development by Koolhoven to be known as the F.K.11 which was intended to be borne on a set of wings reminiscent of those tested by Horatio Phillips a decade before. The F.K.11's small-chord mainplanes would have numbered fifteen, set with pronounced stagger on the same style of fuselage as that used on the F.K.10.

The F.K.11 was not proceeded with but another design from Armstrong Whitworth, the three-seat F.K.5, also exhibited some equally remarkable features. It was built as the result of a War Office requirement for a multi-seat, long-range escort and anti-Zeppelin fighter, a specification to which Vickers and Sopwith also constructed prototypes.

The Bristol F.3A, a development of the T.T.A., using its aft fuselage, biplane wings and tailplane and the 250 h.p. Rolls-Royce Mk.1 for power, was proposed to the same requirement but was abandoned. To give the F.3A's gunners unrestricted field of fire, they were going to be installed in a pair of cockpits incorporated in the upper wings.

Armstrong Whitworth proceeded to build the F.K.5 as a large triplane with its central planes of much greater span than those above and below. The 250 h.p. Rolls-Royce engine turned its propeller immediately in front of the leading edge and between the pair of gunners' nacelles fitted to the centre wings. A revised version as the F.K.6 was built with a different fuselage, undercarriage and nacelles but, as with so many extremely unconventional designs, the machine was not a success.

The Sopwith tender to the specification was a three-seat triplane also, designated L.R.T.Tr. but less frighteningly unusual than the F.K.6. The most significant feature of the Sopwith design was the gunner's nacelle—of excellent aerodynamic form—mounted on the centre-section of the top wings. From this commanding position the field of fire was first-class and a second Lewis-gunner occupied the rear cockpit to guard the machine from attack in that quarter. The 250 h.p. Rolls-Royce Mk.I was installed in the L.R.T.Tr. and the wings, besides incorporating ailerons on each tip, embodied airbrakes in the lowest set of planes.

The Vickers member of the trio of prototype escort fighter designs was the F.B.11, which appeared also in 1916. The Vickers product showed a far more restrained approach to the problem than its competitors, being basically a

The experimental Sopwith L.R.T.Tr. three-seat triplane escort fighter. (Hawker Photo.)

straightforward tractor biplane but following the same arrangement for the disposition of the crew of three as that adopted in the Sopwith L.R.T.Tr. The upper gunner was accommodated in his lofty perch above the upper wings in a less shapely nacelle than that of the Sopwith but the Rolls-Royce Mk.1 engine of 250 h.p. was endowed with a neat cowling and radiator installation. None of the proposed escort fighters went into production as the development of synchronizing gears nullified the requirement.

At Brooklands Martinsyde had been busy building a new single-seat biplane fighter, the R.G., which was of single-bay layout and smaller than the Elephant but on generally similar lines. Powered by the 190 h.p. Rolls-Royce Falcon and armed with two Vickers guns on the front coaming, the R.G. exhibited the hallmark of a first-rate and competent fighter design. Tests at Farnborough during February, 1917, revealed a fine performance but, as both the Camel and S.E.5 had by then been adopted as replacement fighters and the Falcon was needed for Bristol Fighters, the Martinsyde R.G. unfortunately came to naught.

December, 1916, was an auspicious month for it saw the completion of two of the most successful designs in the annals of British single-seat fighters—

Vickers F.B.11 with gunner's nacelle in upper centre-section. (Imperial War Museum Photo.)

99

The prototype S.E.5 A4561, forerunner of one of the finest types of fighter of the 1914–18 War. (Imperial War Museum Photo.)

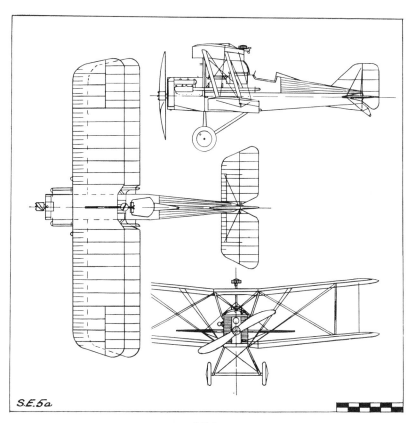

S.E.5a

S.E.5a

100

the Royal Aircraft Factory's S.E.5 and the Sopwith Camel. Both machines were destined to play outstanding parts in the turbulent air fighting over the Western Front and their names were to form a glowing part of the legend of the first great War in the Air.

The Farnborough S.E.5 was next in the line of Scouting Experimentals after the S.E.4a and its fin and rudder outline immediately indicated the hand of H. P. Folland again as the designer. Frank Goodden and J. Kenworthy contributed to the overall design and involved also were F. M. Green as design engineer, S. W. Hiscocks as his assistant, H. Grinsted as stressman, with W. S. Farren responsible for the aerodynamic and stability calculations. The S.E.5's trim, well-balanced outline stamped it undeniably as a thoroughbred and the machine lived up fully to the promise it inspired.

The machine's wooden airframe was a normal structure with fabric covering and was centred around the 150 h.p. Hispano-Suiza engine with a flat frontal radiator. The single-bay wings were set with pronounced stagger and carried four ailerons, and the tailplane embodied the refinement of variable incidence controllable during flight.

The prototype A4561 took off for the first time during December, 1916, and was soon modified with revised exhausts and increased windscreen area to the rear. The prototype's life, however, was short as the wings failed late in January, 1917, during testing by Frank Goodden who was killed in the resulting crash. Modifications were made and the S.E.5 went on to make its great name in the hands of squadron pilots, the first unit to receive the type being No. 56 Squadron, R.F.C., during March, 1917. The armament of the S.E.5 comprised a Vickers gun mounted to port on the front decking and a Lewis gun on a Foster mounting which carried it on top of the upper centresection. The first production S.E.5s were delivered complete with a large windscreen over the front and sides of the cockpit but this was quickly replaced by a small screen of simple, flat form in the interest of visibility from the cockpit.

The other fighter which was to earn undying fame for itself, the paradoxically-named Sopwith F.1 Camel, also emerged during December, 1916. The Camel paralleled the S.E.5 as a single-bay biplane of purposeful aspect but utilized the rotary air-cooled 110 h.p. Clerget engine in the prototype. Production F.1s were built with the 110 h.p. le Rhône and the 130 h.p. Clerget engines as alternative power plants.

Conventional in construction, the Camel was nevertheless an inspired design with outstanding manœuvrability as a primary feature ensured by concentrating the engine, guns and pilot in the short forepart of the fuselage around the C.G. The twin Vickers guns were under the immediate control of the pilot in the coaming in front of the cockpit. The swift response of the Camel and its pronounced sensitivity made it an ideal fighter but pilots new to it had to be very wary indeed of the considerable torque effect exercised by the engine. Once its habits and qualities were understood and mastered, the Camel was without peer in its time and ran up a score of 1,294 enemy aircraft destroyed, to better that of any rival machine during the conflict.

By mid-1916 the arrival in action of the fast single-seat scout, with its useful fire-power and its deployment in homogeneous squadrons, brought a complete and swift revision of the nature of the fighting in the air over the Western Front. A new element made itself increasingly felt, that of man-to-man duels to the death at several thousand feet in the air. In order to survive these exhausting combats, fighter pilots took to extracting every mite of performance from their mounts by making individual modifications, overhauling their guns and tuning their engines. New manœuvres and tactics were worked out among the pilots and practised to their own advantage in the struggle for mastery. The fighter squadrons set out to exploit the qualities of their small, fast machines in offence as often as possible. Attacks were launched against ground as well as air targets, with enemy observation balloons a particularly exciting form of prey, and le Prieur rockets had joined the arsenal to supplement machine-guns.

Many deeds of valour were being performed by squadron pilots and their scores of enemy aircraft shot down began to mount. The military awards made for this prowess brought the names of individual pilots to the notice of the public who were to laud Warneford, Ball, Mannock and McCudden among many others who gave their lives.

The year 1917 brought with it a marked settling down and rationalization in the development of scouts and fighters for the R.F.C. and the R.N.A.S. The extremely successful pair of single-seaters, the Camel and the S.E.5, had demonstrated undeniably that the compact, fast, manœuvrable, well-armed machine was the answer to the immediate problem of fighter supremacy. The formula was obviously the correct one to develop for great performance and was that into which available resources in design and construction should be directed. Consequently, while production of Camels and S.E.5s was increased rapidly to supply the needs of the squadrons, 1917 showed a distinct halt to comparatively freak projects and a marked concentration on improvement of existing successful designs and on the development of new designs to the now fully recognised single-seat layout.

While other firms were engaged in producing the smaller type of fighting scout, Short Brothers constructed a relatively large two-seat, three-bay biplane seaplane, powered by the 310 h.p. Sunbeam Cossack, and known as the 310 Seaplane Type B, or North Sea Scout. The machine was designed mainly to carry the 5-pounder Davis recoilless gun and was equipped also with a Lewis gun, both weapons being installed in the rear cockpit, but the cancellation of the Davis gun's development brought about the discontinuation of the Short North Sea Scout.

March, 1917, saw the appearance of another Short scout seaplane, the S.364 two-seat biplane powered with the 200 h.p. Sunbeam Afridi. Two-bay wings of equal span were used and, compared with the ungainly angularity of other Short products of the period, the S.364 presented a far tidier picture. A single Lewis gun was provided for the rear cockpit's Scarff ring but the S.364 was not developed beyond the prototype stage.

Classic dog-fighter of the 1914–18 War, the Sopwith F.1. Camel.

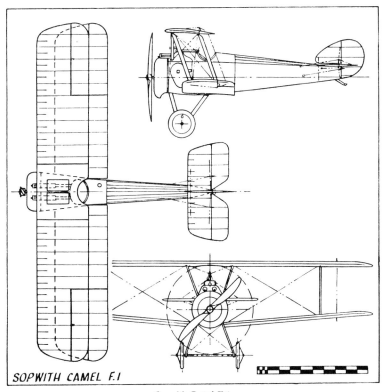

SOPWITH CAMEL F.1

Sopwith Camel F.1

Short Type B North Sea Scout. (Short Photo.)

Despite its lack of success in obtaining orders for its previous scout designs, the Grahame-White Company tried once again with the Type 21 which was completed in April, 1917. The machine was a single-seat biplane, powered by an 80 h.p. le Rhône, in which every effort had been made to streamline the airframe and cut down drag. Single I-type interplane and centre-section struts braced the wings, to which ailerons were fitted to all four tips. Despite its attributes, which included a top speed of 107 m.p.h., the Grahame-White Type 21 was not adopted.

The Sopwith designers did not rest on their laurels after turning out the Camel and followed it in May, 1917, with their 5F.1 Dolphin. The new fighter bore little, if any, resemblance to its illustrious predecessor and was notable in incorporating back-stagger in its two-bay, equal-span wings. The biplane's gap was comparatively small, so that the pilot's head projected through the upper centre-section.

Sopwith Dolphin in its early form. (Hawker Photo.)

A deep nose radiator at first served the 200 h.p. Hispano-Suiza engine in the prototype Dolphin but was afterwards replaced by side radiators mounted one on each side of the cockpit. The prototype's original fin and rudder, which followed the outline of the Camel's, were changed for new surfaces complete with horn balance incorporated in the rudder. Further alterations to the vertical tail surfaces and to the fuselage around the cockpit area to improve the view took place before the Dolphin was considered ready to be issued to the squadrons. The Dolphin's firepower was increased by the addition of a pair of Lewis guns, mounted in the centre-section on each side of the pilot, to fire forwards and upwards at around 45°. These extra Lewis guns did not prove particularly popular in use as they tended to swing during flight and to hit the pilot. Consequently, they were often discarded by the units

Vickers F.B.24C. (Vickers Photo.)

using the machine but No. 87 Squadron, R.F.C., took to mounting the Lewis guns on the lower wings to fire outside the propeller disc. In each case, however, the main armament of two Vickers guns in the decking ahead of the pilot was retained. The Dolphin proved to be a sturdy and popular machine in service, one of the few adverse criticisms of it being the risk of injury to the pilot in a nose-over on landing. To guard against this the night-flying version was equipped with metal hoops above the inner pairs of interplane struts. The normal production Dolphin used the geared version of the 200 h.p. Hispano-Suiza but, as an alternative, the direct-drive 200 h.p. Hispano-Suiza was employed in the Dolphin Mk. III and the Dolphin Mk. II had the advantage of 300 h.p. delivered by the more powerful version of the Hispano-Suiza engine.

In their endeavours to produce a successful two-seat tractor fighter, Vickers evolved several variants of their basic F.B.24 design. The machine was first discussed at the end of 1916 as a fighter reconnaissance biplane to be designed around the 150 h.p. Hart radial engine but finally appeared in 1917 with the

Vickers F.B.24E. (Imperial War Museum Photo.)

200 h.p. Hispano-Suiza installed and designated F.B.24B. Its appearance was that of a normal unequal-span two-bay biplane with rather angular and inharmonious lines.

A new version, the F.B.24C, made its bow with the 285 h.p. Lorraine-Dietrich 8Bd engine and embodied a modified fin of smaller size, besides being tried out with a pair of side radiators as an alternative to the frontal type.

The field of view from the pilot's cockpit under the upper centre-section was considered to be far too restricted for a fighting aircraft and an attempt was made in the F.B.24E to rectify the fault by raising the fuselage to the level of the upper wings and filling the resulting gap below the fuselage to the lower planes with the Hispano-Suiza's radiator. The pilot's upward view was vastly improved but at the expense of his downward vision.

The general layout of the F.B.24E was carried forward into the F.B.24G which was given larger wings of equal span and the 375 h.p. Lorraine-Dietrich 13 as its power unit with two side-mounted radiators. None of the F.B.24 variants was eventually accepted for service.

Vickers suffered equally bad luck with their F.B.25 which reverted to the pusher biplane layout for a two-seat, anti-Zeppelin fighter. The broad nacelle housed two separate side-by-side cockpits, that to starboard being set in advance of the other. The rear of the nacelle contained a 150 h.p. Hispano-Suiza engine, in lieu of the intended 200 h.p. version of the same engine which was unobtainable for the machine. A single Vickers Crayford rocket gun was intended to be the F.B.25's armament and, as an aid to night operations, a searchlight was fitted in the prow of the nacelle.

The F.B.25 made no headway as it crashed at Martlesham Heath during trials which had already disclosed that its response to its controls was very poor, causing its demise.

Contemporary with the ill-fated F.B.25 and similar in layout and purpose was the N.E.1, six of which were built by the Royal Aircraft Factory. Intended for night interception, the N.E.1 carried a searchlight in the nose of its crudely-shaped box-like nacelle, which was suspended between three-bay wings of fairly high aspect ratio. The 200 h.p. Hispano-Suiza provided the power to enable the machine to take aloft its main offensive armament of a Coventry Ordnance Works quick-firer or a Vickers rocket gun. In addition, a forwards-firing Lewis gun was mounted on the starboard side of the nacelle. Reports on the N.E.1's handling and performance were not favourable towards its use as a night fighter so that it remained but an experimental design.

Other Fighting Experimental projects investigated by the Royal Aircraft Factory were the F.E.10, a single-seat fighter intended to use the 200 h.p. Hispano-Suiza engine with the pilot in a cockpit ahead of the propeller, the obscure F.E.11, and the F.E.12 designed as a two-seat pusher biplane of 50 ft. span for use as a night fighter. The 200 h.p. Hispano-Suiza was scheduled as the F.E.12's engine and its primary offensive armament was to have been a rocket gun assisted in target detection by a pair of searchlights which accompanied the gun. Confirmation of actual construction of the F.E.12 is, however, lacking.

May, 1917, was the month of the appearance of yet another ill-fated Vickers single-seat pusher fighter—the F.B.26 Vampire. Although very similar in general appearance to the same firm's F.B.12 of the previous year, the Vampire had twice as much power in its 200 h.p. Hispano-Suiza engine and was rather larger and heavier. The two-bay style of wing cellule was retained with the nacelle fitted direct to the underside of the upper planes. A pair of Lewis guns in the nose of the nacelle armed the first F.B.26 but, after alterations to the wings, the cooling system and the vertical tail surfaces, the Vampire's offensive power was increased by a third Lewis gun, the trio being on an Eeman mounting. The triple installation was tested both high up and low down in the nacelle, trials also being made with night-flying equipment installed.

Although, the following year, one of the Vampires—B1485—appeared as the F.B.26A Vampire Mk.II, powered by the 230 h.p. Bentley B.R.2 rotary, with an armoured nacelle and twin Lewis guns for use as a trench-fighter, development was cancelled in favour of the rival Sopwith firm's Salamander.

Vickers F.B.26 prototype. (Imperial War Museum Photo.)

Mid-1917 saw the début of a two-seat fighter, the F.1, from Martinsyde at Brooklands. The machine was odd in carrying its observer in the front cockpit where he could do little that would be effective in combat. A 250 h.p. Rolls-Royce Mk.III powered the F.1, giving it a top speed at 6,500 ft. of 109·5 m.p.h. A two-bay biplane of normal appearance and construction, the F.1 had little to recommend it in its original form but Martinsyde made another effort at producing a two-seat fighter reconnaissance machine when they completed their F.2 biplane in May, 1917. A 200 h.p. Hispano-Suiza engine gave it a top speed at ground level of 120 m.p.h., the F.2 being armed with a single Vickers gun for the pilot and a Scarff-mounted Lewis for the gunner. Although a competent enough design in most respects, the indifferent view for the pilot told against the F.2 and it stood little chance of filling the place occupied by the competitive Bristol F.2B.

Another auspicious two-seat design which was unable to make the grade once the Bristol machine had gained a firm foothold was Avro's 530, completed in July, 1917. Careful attention had been paid to producing an airframe

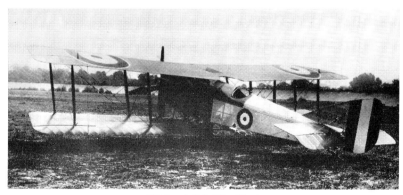

Martinsyde F.1 at Brooklands.

108

for the two-bay biplane which was designed to use the 300 h.p. Hispano-Suiza engine. The current shortage of this engine dictated the installation of the 200 h.p. version of the same make and the 530 was tested also with the 200 h.p. Sunbeam. Unusual features of the design were the deep fuselage filling the entire wing gap, the fairings applied to fill the openings between the undercarriage V struts, and the flaps which formed the trailing edges of the wings. Two guns were carried—a Vickers for the pilot and a Scarff-mounted Lewis in the rear cockpit.

Often alternative combinations of armament were experimented with on the squadrons but only comparatively rarely did a pilot fighting at the Front have a direct say in the design of a fighter aircraft itself. One such case was in the Austin-Ball A.F.B.1 single-seat biplane which was finished in

A two-seat fighter by Avro, the Type 530. (Avro Photo.)

July, 1917. Until the time of his death in action on 7th May, 1917, Ball had kept in direct touch with the evolution of the A.F.B.1. Although an ugly machine, its saving grace was a maximum speed of 138 m.p.h. at ground level on the 200 h.p. of its Hispano-Suiza engine and a good performance in rate of climb and ceiling. The installation of the A.F.B.1's pair of Lewis guns was of note; that in the fuselage fired through the centre of the propeller shaft, while the other occupied a Foster mounting on the upper centre-section. Despite its abilities the machine was not selected finally for production.

Two other single-seat fighters which were constructed during 1917 and remained prototypes only were the H.1 and H.2 designed for Mann Egerton and Co. by J. W. Carr to fall within the Admiralty's N.1A requirement. Both were square-set, two-bay biplanes, fitted with the 200 h.p. Hispano-Suiza engine and armed with a single Vickers gun on the front decking and a Lewis gun on the upper centre-section. Intended for shipboard operations, the wings were made to fold, and N44—the H.1—carried external flotation equipment

Mann Egerton H.1 Shipboard Scout. (Mann Egerton Photo.)

in the form of wing-tip floats as well as an under-fuselage float. The H.2— N45—utilized inflatable bags to provide its buoyancy. Although both machines were reasonably successful in their tests, neither version found official favour.

Following the lack of success with their F.1 and F.2, Martinsyde abandoned the two-seat formula for a fighter and turned with hope to the single-seater again as a proposition likelier to yield more positive results.

The F.3 was ready for testing by November, 1917, and lived up to its parent firm's expectations. An eminently compact, clean single-bay biplane, it was powered at first by an experimental Rolls-Royce Falcon which delivered 285 h.p., resulting in a useful maximum speed at ground level of 142 m.p.h. and

Mann Egerton H.2 Shipboard Scout. (Mann Egerton Photo.)

a service ceiling of 24,000 ft. Two Vickers guns fired forwards from beneath the cowling. Martinsyde had the satisfaction of knowing that, according to official reports, in the F.3 a machine had been designed which was considered to be superior to any other contemporary single-seat fighter. The following year production got under way as the F.4, incorporating minor alterations.

A rather curious event took place during 1917 at Mudros in the Aegean which, although it contributed nothing to fighter development, deserves to be recorded as an example of initiative and ingenuity. During his service on the station with No. 2 Wing, R.N.A.S., Flt.Lt. J. W. Alcock, well known in flying circles before the 1914–18 War and to become famous after the Armistice for his trans-Atlantic flight with Lt. A. W. Brown, designed a single-seat fighter biplane which was put together from Sopwith Triplane and Pup parts. Two engines were tried in the Alcock A.1 Scout, or Sopwith Mouse as Alcock called it; the first was a 100 h.p. Monosoupape Gnome, followed by a 110 h.p.

Port Victoria P.V.5 N53. (Imperial War Museum Photo.)

Clerget. Unluckily, Alcock was taken prisoner before his brainchild was ready but the machine was test-flown at Mudros and Stavros after completion by his colleagues. The A.1's armament consisted of a pair of Vickers guns.

During 1917 the Admiralty's Air Department continued to request designs from the R.N.A.S. Experimental Construction Depôt at Port Victoria on the Isle of Grain, the P.V.4 being followed by a single-seat fighter seaplane which was to encompass also the rôle of light bomber. Two versions were built— the P.V.5 N53 sesquiplane and the P.V.5a with wings of equal span. Floats of Linton Hope style were intended to be used and the engine scheduled was the elusive 150 h.p. Smith Static which was late in arriving for the pair of prototypes.

Finally, the 150 h.p. Hispano-Suiza was installed in the P.V.5 and the machine was mounted on floats of refined pontoon style. Its companion P.V.5a was fitted with the more powerful 200 h.p. Hispano-Suiza and received the intended Linton Hope floats. Each machine was armed with a single Vickers gun in front of the cockpit. Both machines were quite successful in their trials but neither was considered to be required for production.

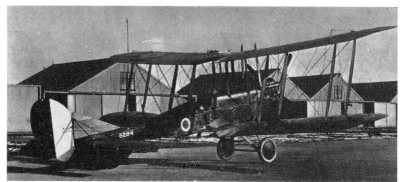

8294, a single-seat night fighter version of the B.E.2c, built by Grahame-White. (Rolls-Royce Photo.)

The next designation in the Port Victoria design series, P.V.6, was allotted to an uncompleted project for a fast scout landplane. Attention was next turned to meeting a call for a very small, low-powered scout capable of being flown from minor warships. The engine specified was the two-cylinder, geared 45 h.p. A.B.C. Gnat. Besides the Port Victoria Depôt, the Experimental Flight at Eastchurch was asked also to submit a design.

Each machine was a diminutive biplane, that designed at Port Victoria being designated the P.V.7, while the Eastchurch-conceived machine, through transference to Port Victoria for completion, became the P.V.8. Respectively, the aircraft were called the Grain Kitten and the Eastchurch Kitten.

Both types constituted early examples of the often-attempted light fighter, each being a well-conceived and competent approach to an interesting challenge.

Grain's P.V.7 was the smaller of the two, following the normal layout for a single-seat, single-bay biplane of unequal span and showed traces in its outline of its predecessors from the same design source.

The Eastchurch Kitten was rather more angular and of cleaner cut than the

The tiny Port Victoria P.V.8 Eastchurch Kitten. (Imperial War Museum Photo.)

Grain machine and received equal-span wings, set with accentuated stagger on single I-type interplane and centre-section struts.

Both the P.V.7 and P.V.8 were forced to use the lower output of the direct-drive 35 h.p. A.B.C. Gnat as the 45 h.p. version of the engine was not available. Each was armed with a single Lewis gun on the upper centre-section and each machine was modified in several respects after completion in mid-1917 and, of the pair, the P.V.8 showed itself to be the superior aeroplane.

Last of the Port Victoria series of original fighter designs was the P.V.9, a single-seat 150 h.p. Bentley B.R.1-powered sesquiplane seaplane which was completed in the last month of 1917. Two machine-guns were carried, a fuse-lage-mounted Vickers and a Lewis on the upper centre-section. The sole pro-totype, N55, proved to possess fine all-round qualities and was considered to out-perform any previous design in the same category. Despite these attri-butes, an ultimate lack of demand resulted in the abandonment of the P.V.9.

Among the firms who, during 1917, constructed prototypes specifically to carry the Admiralty-sponsored Davis recoilless gun, was that of Robey and

Production B.A.T. Bantam Mk.I.

Co. whose designer, J. A. Peters, evolved a large three-seat, three-bay tractor biplane to carry two of the large shell-firing weapons on the power of a 250 h.p. Rolls-Royce engine. Disposition of all three members of the crew was somewhat remarkable; the two gunners were located each in a nacelle faired into the upper wings on each side of the fuselage, while the pilot was situated no less comfortably in a cockpit towards the rear of the fuselage just ahead of the fin. As with the other prototypes designed to accommodate the Davis gun, the Robey-Peters Three-seater came to naught, in its own case being aban-doned after crashing during its initial flight.

While the Camel, S.E.5 and other production types continued to bear the brunt of the fighting in the air, prototypes of new fighters continued to appear in Britain. Among the companies which made bids to establish themselves as fighter constructors was the paradoxically-named British Aerial Transport Co., the chief designer of which was F. Koolhoven, late of Armstrong Whit-worth. Koolhoven's initial design for his new firm was the F.K.22 Bat, a

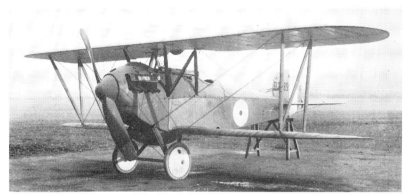

B3989, the Bristol Scout F. (Bristol Photo.)

single-seat fighter biplane drawn up around the 120 h.p. A.B.C. Mosquito radial engine, the airframe consisting of two-bay, equal-span wings fitted to a shapely monocoque fuselage. A particularly unusual feature of the F.K.22 was the location of the cockpit immediately underneath the upper wings so that the pilot's head projected above the centre-section. Failure of the proposed engine brought about redesign to make use of a later A.B.C. radial unit, the 170 h.p. Wasp, with which the Bat was renamed Bantam. Cancellation of development of the Wasp resulted in flights being made early in 1918 with rotaries—the 100 h.p. Monosoupape Gnome and the 110 h.p. le Rhône.

To distinguish it the Gnome version was referred to as the Bantam Mk.II, while the F.K.23, a smaller version, became the Bantam Mk.I. The Mk.I was bedevilled by dangerous spinning characteristics but the design's speed and manœuvrability resulted in an initial batch being ordered, with several alterations which went most of the way to eliminating the early faults. After nine Bantams had been constructed production was stopped when the A.B.C. Wasp was withdrawn as a production unit owing to persistent trouble with it. Armament of the Bantam was scheduled to be a pair of fuselage-mounted Vickers guns.

During the Summer of 1917 Bristol's designer Frank Barnwell set to work on the design of a new single-seat fighter, the Scout F, to use the water-cooled 200 h.p. Sunbeam Arab II engine. The Scout F materialized as a single-bay biplane with N-type interplane struts and a very clean engine installation which was assisted materially by the location of the radiator between the undercarriage legs. Tests revealed excellent overall performance and flying characteristics but the Arab power plant persisted in giving trouble.

Of the three Scout Fs constructed the third, B3991, was fitted with one of the new radial engines then beginning to appear. This was the 347 h.p. Cosmos Mercury with which B3991, redesignated Scout F.1, made its initial flight during April, 1918. The engine was installed to blend neatly into the F.1's nose and, with it, the machine turned in a first-class performance, carrying armament of two Vickers guns on the front decking but development of the Scout F.1 was eventually halted.

Among the various types of aircraft produced by William Beardmore and Co. was a version of the Sopwith Pup redesigned for Beardmore by G. Tilghman Richards specifically for shipboard use. Saving of space has, from the beginning, always been a primary consideration for naval aircraft and, in the W.B.III, the wings were made to fold by eliminating the stagger and fitting a revised system of struts. To reduce height the main landing-gear folded up into the belly of the fuselage, the length of which had been increased. The S.B.3D designation was applied to the version with jettisonable undercarriage; S.B.3F denoted folding landing-gear. Production W.B.IIIs served with the Fleet and were armed with one Lewis gun on the upper centre-section.

Two other single-seat fighter designs, intended for the R.N.A.S., appeared from Beardmore in the course of 1917. The W.B.IV was a two-bay biplane designed around the 200 h.p. Hispano-Suiza, the engine being installed in the fuselage above the lower wings and driving its propeller by an extension shaft, which was straddled by the pilot in his high-set cockpit in the nose ahead of the leading edge of the wings. N38, the sole W.B.IV built, was notable also

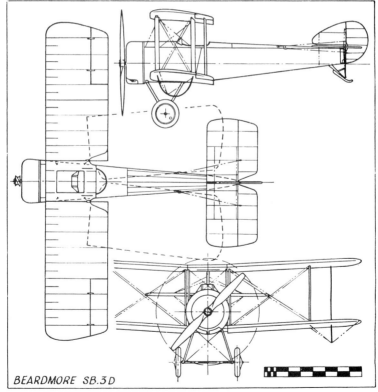

BEARDMORE SB.3D

Beardmore SB.3D

Beardmore W.B.V shipboard fighter N42. (Beardmore Photo.)

in having a streamlined flotation tank faired into the fore-fuselage and at first had floats under each wingtip. The machine carried two guns—a forwards-firing Vickers installed to port in the nose and a Lewis fitted at an upward angle in front of the pilot.

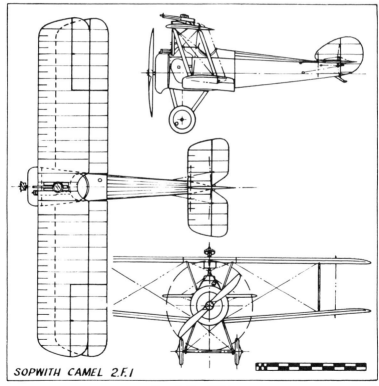

SOPWITH CAMEL 2.F.1

Sopwith Camel 2F.1

The Beardmore W.B.V single-seat fighter biplane also used the 200 h.p. Hispano-Suiza but was built specifically to make use of the 37 mm. Puteaux shell-gun which fired its rounds through the centre of the propeller shaft. In other respects the machine was of normal two-bay tractor layout but mis-apprehension concerning the safety of the pilot with the Puteaux in action led to the heavy gun's replacement by one forwards-firing Vickers and up-wards-firing Lewis gun. Interest in the W.B.V finally petered out and develop-ment stopped.

The success of the Camel and the S.E.5 led naturally to further develop-ment of both types during 1917. Various alternative engines were installed in the Camel and a special naval version went into production as the 2F.1. Successful take-offs were made from lighters towed by destroyers, trials were carried out in launching from H.M. Airship R.23 and a number of different armament installations were tested on Camels. Night-fighting Camels were produced by moving the cockpit rearwards to facilitate access to the pair of Lewis guns on their Foster mounting above the upper centre-section and a prototype trench fighter, the T.F.1, was built with a pair of downwards-firing Lewis guns in the fuselage and a third Lewis fitted above the upper centre-section.

2F.1 Camels operated from warships' platforms rendered useful service, following in the footsteps of the Pups which had pioneered such operations with the Fleet, including carrier landings.

By mid-1917 a revised version of the S.E.5, the S.E.5a, had started to reach the squadrons, No. 56 being the first to receive it. The new machine was powered by the geared 200 h.p. Hispano-Suiza and embodied minor altera-tions in the fore-fuselage. The higher-powered engine suffered from lack of reliability but the S.E.5a soon vindicated itself and established a first-class reputation amongst its pilots. The machine went into service with alternative engines which included the Hispano-Suiza of 220 h.p. and 240 h.p., the 200 h.p. Wolseley Viper W.4A and the 200 h.p. Wolseley Adder W.4B.

An addition to the Home Defence fighter force during 1917 was a more powerful version of the B.E.12 with the 200 h.p. Hispano-Suiza engine and designated B.E.12b. A pair of Lewis guns on the upper centre-section armed the machine, thirty-six of which operated with Home Defence units.

The whole of the year 1917 had been spent in expanding the R.F.C. and R.N.A.S. and in organizing their rapidly increasing resources in men and machines for the more effective prosecution of the offensive against the enemy on all fronts. Since early 1916 public concern about the air defences of the United Kingdom and the general administration of both air services had made itself heard time and again with the result that, after some eighteen months had passed, the important decision was finally taken to amalgamate the R.F.C. and the R.N.A.S. to form a third service, the Royal Air Force, which was to come into being on 1st April, 1918. The Air Ministry was formed to take over the work of the Air Board in assessing requirements in aircraft, the approval of new designs and the direction of experimental work.

Development of new, improved fighter designs continued at even greater speed and 1918 brought forth a number of machines of advanced design and increased performance. Of the aircraft actually built or merely considered as projects during this period there was not one which could be classed as an impractical freak. Indeed, all of them demonstrated plainly a sensible, rational approach to the design of single- and two-seat fighters, exemplified by an overwhelming predominance of the single-engine tractor biplane of refined form. Designers had obviously appreciated that therein lay the formula for success in the art of fighter design for the present and the immediate future. Although the final year of the 1914–18 War was notable for such an inspiring selection of prototype fighters only one, the Sopwith Snipe, was to be adopted for service in the R.A.F. in quantity. Even so, relatively few Snipes had been delivered to operational units in France by the end of the War and the main burden of aerial fighting continued to be borne until the Armistice by other fighters already in service.

B9966, fifth prototype of the Sopwith 7F.1 Snipe. (Hawker Photo.)

The Sopwith 7F.1 Snipe grew out of a requirement for a new single-seat fighter to take the fullest advantage of the 230 h.p. developed by the Bentley B.R.2 rotary engine. The prototype flew first on the power of the 150 h.p. Bentley B.R.1 engine until a B.R.2 was delivered for it, the machine's airframe using single-bay wings fitted to a flat-sided fuselage. A second prototype was constructed with curved fairings added to the sides of the fuselage, redesigned fin and rudder and other modifications. Conclusions formed following its tests in December, 1917, resulted in the appearance in January, 1918, of a third prototype, this time with two-bay wings of extended span. The Snipe's excellent climb and general manoeuvrability and its lack of the trickiness which had characterized the Camel brought general approval of its selection as the R.A.F.'s new single-seat fighter. Further minor alterations were made in the airframe to improve the machine's all-round qualities and its

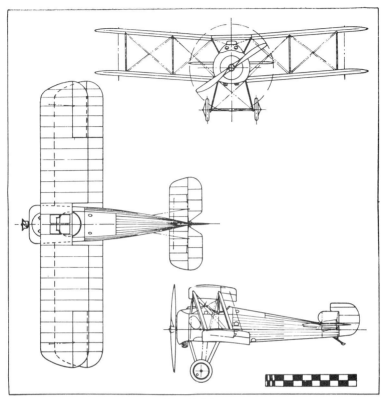

Sopwith Snipe

armament was standardized as two Vickers guns in the front decking. A long-range variant of the Snipe was designated 7F.1a and one was used to flight-test the 320 h.p. A.B.C. Dragonfly radial engine, with which it reached a speed of 156 m.p.h. The Sopwith Snipe is notable as being considered the best all-round single-seat fighter in operation by the Allies at the time of the Armistice and was to remain in R.A.F. service for some eight years.

Although by 1918 the pusher formula with the propeller revolving between tailhooms had been more or less abandoned as a proposition for projected fighters, the Royal Aircraft Factory proceeded to construct three examples of the A.E.3 Farnborough Ram, a pusher biplane carrying two and intended for use as a trench-strafer. The A.E.3's antecedent was the N.E.1 of the previous year but, as protection for its crew, armour plating $\frac{1}{4}$ in. thick clad the angular nacelle which housed a pair of Lewis guns, pivoted for firing vertically into enemy troops, and carried also another Lewis gun for firing to the rear. The two versions of the A.E.3 were the 200 h.p. Sunbeam Arab Ram Mk.I and the 230 h.p. Bentley B.R.2 Ram Mk.II. A Mk.III version of the Ram was considered as a project and would have used the lower-powered 150 h.p. Bentley B.R.1.

The experimental Austin A.F.T.3 Osprey triplane. (Austin Photo.)

As the War progressed through its final year two further Scouting Experimental designs were indulged in by the Royal Aircraft Factory designers. One, the S.E.5b, was built as a modification of an S.E.5—A8947—for comparative tests with the standard S.E.5a. The 200 h.p. Hispano-Suiza was streamlined into the nose, assisted by a large spinner, and a semi-retractable radiator of reduced area was installed underneath the engine to effect a considerable saving in drag. New unequal-span wings were fitted and the machine was tested also with normal S.E.5a wings, in which guise the designation S.E.5c was at times applied to it. The S.E.5b was given the standard S.E.5 armament of one Vickers gun and one Lewis gun.

The other S.E. design, the S.E.6, remained an incomplete project but would have been a single-seat biplane to the same requirement as the Martinsyde F.3 with the useful power of the 275 h.p. Rolls-Royce Falcon III.

After barely six years, the busy period of aeroplane design activity at the Royal Aircraft Factory came to an end but the organization could look back with satisfaction on time spent in developing a useful range of machines. Particularly noteworthy were its Scouting Experimentals, each of which had been in the forefront of advanced design and construction techniques, culminating in the outstandingly successful S.E.5 and S.E.5a.

During 1917 Farnborough's brilliant fighter designer H. P. Folland had vacated his position at the Factory and joined the Nieuport and General Aircraft Co. Ltd., at Cricklewood, where he was soon responsible for the firm's first original design, the B.N.1, which was started early in 1918. As was to be expected from the Folland drawing-board, the resulting single-seat fighter was a workmanlike design with clean and appealing lines. Although stagger was employed widely to improve view, it was not embodied in the B.N.1's two-bay cellules and another unusual feature, which Folland had used on his earlier S.E.4, was the fitting of single I-type interplane struts. The normal fuselage-mounted twin Vickers guns were augmented by a single Lewis gun on the upper centre-section. The B.N.1, wrecked in a crash on 10th March, 1918, was designed to use the 230 h.p. Bentley B.R.2 and displayed a vertical tail outline which revived the shape employed on the S.E.2a and S.E.4.

During 1917 the Austin Motor Co. decided to design a single-seat fighter to Specification A.1A but, rather surprisingly in view of the generally-conceded superiority by then of the well-developed biplane, their tender appeared at the beginning of 1918 as a triplane—the A.F.T.3 Osprey. The machine was fairly small and, as was to be expected with the power of the 230 h.p. Bentley B.R.2, the overall performance was quite creditable. The standard armament scheduled for the Osprey was a pair of fuselage-mounted Vickers but X15, the sole prototype, carried temporarily a Lewis gun in addition. However, against the new biplanes then appearing the Osprey stood relatively little chance of adoption and went the way of so many hopefully-created prototypes.

The same fate befell another aeroplane built by Austin before the War's end. This was a proposed replacement for the Bristol F.2B, named the Greyhound, and was a two-seat, two-bay biplane armed with two Vickers guns for the pilot and a single Lewis for the gunner. The machine was a promising design, constituting a serious effort to embody in every way recommendations resulting from active operation of previous types. To enable the Greyhound to fulfil its purpose of fighter reconnaissance to the best advantage, very comprehensive equipment was installed. One less happy aspect of the design was in the choice of engine, the 320 h.p. A.B.C. Dragonfly 1, a unit which was to prove unreliable and the undoing, regrettably, of a number of prototypes designed around it in the hope of making good use of its expected high output of power.

The two-seat Austin Greyhound.

121

Although as an operational type the Avro 504K was by 1918 an obsolete design, early in the year it was issued to Home Defence units in the North as a single-seat fighter armed with a Lewis gun fitted over the upper centre-section.

The prolific Sopwith design office's output was increased by yet another machine which appeared in 1918—the 2FR.2 Bulldog two-seat biplane. Intended for fighter reconnaissance, low-set on its landing-gear and heavy-jowled, the weightily-armed Bulldog was aptly named. The first prototype had single-bay wings and the 200 h.p. Clerget 11 E.B. rotary for power. Twin Vickers guns were provided in front of the pilot, while the aft cockpit was fitted with two Lewis guns, one firing forwards and the other to the rear.

A second prototype was built with two-bay wings of larger size and initially had horn-balanced ailerons which were later replaced by revised wings with plain ailerons.

The first prototype Sopwith 2FR.2 Bulldog Mk.I with single-bay wings. (Hawker Photo.)

Following the Bulldog Mk.I with its Clerget engine came another version, the Mk.II with the ill-starred 360 h.p. A.B.C. Dragonfly 1a radial for its power plant, but neither type of Bulldog was developed further.

A. V. Roe followed up their 530 two-seat fighter with another fighter design—the single-seat 531 Spider. The new prototype was completed by April, 1918, and turned out to be a 110 h.p. le Rhône-engined biplane of striking appearance. In the interest of quick production particular attention was paid to using readily-available 504K parts in the airframe but, despite this admirable object, the Spider was a distinctive machine. The main feature which caught the eye immediately was the system of three pairs of V struts on each side which braced the unequal-span wings without the assistance of bracing wires, the upper wings being set close to the top of the fuselage so that the pilot's head projected through the open centre-section. A peculiar point about the Spider's armament was the fitting of only one Vickers gun at a time when two machine-guns had become more or less standard. Tests proved the machine to be excellent for its purpose with admirable manœuvrability, its top speed at ground level with the 130 h.p. Clerget fitted being 120 m.p.h.

Avro 531 Spider. (Avro Photo.)

Another version of the Spider was planned as the 531A, based on the 130 h.p. Clerget with different biplane wing cellules and orthodox struts and wire bracing.

By June, 1918, the revised production version of the Martinsyde F.3, designated F.4 and named the Buzzard, was ready for its trials, powered by the 300 h.p. Hispano-Suiza engine. In the Buzzard an improvement in the view for the pilot was effected by moving the cockpit a short distance to the rear. In trials during August, 1918, following the fitting of improved pistons to the engine, the Buzzard Mk.I recorded a maximum speed at ground level of 144·5 m.p.h., earning itself the distinction of being the fastest type of British aircraft in production when the War ended. The machine's all-round excellence resulted in good orders for it to re-equip fighter squadrons and included a long-range version—the Mk.Ia. However, production was unable

D4263, a Martinsyde F.4 Buzzard. (Rolls-Royce Photo.)

C8655, the Boulton and Paul P.3 Bobolink. (Boulton Paul Photo.)

to get under way sufficiently during the few remaining months of the War for the Buzzard to enter service and the machine, in view of its fine qualities and advanced conception, was unfortunate in not being selected to continue the single-seat fighter tradition in the peacetime Royal Air Force.

Yet another unsuccessful contender against the Snipe was the Boulton and Paul P.3 Bobolink, a single-seat biplane fighter which was completed in 1918. Designed by J. D. North, responsible for the design of several well-known pre-War Grahame-White machines, the Bobolink—originally named the Hawk by Boulton and Paul—was a competent product, based on the 230 h.p. Bentley B.R.2 engine and fitted with staggered two-bay wings employing the increasingly popular N-type interplane struts. The Bobolink was armed with the usual pair of fuselage-mounted Vickers guns and reached a top speed at 10,000 ft. of 125 m.p.h.

The 230 h.p. Bentley B.R.2 rotary was also selected by F. Murphy as the engine for the F.M.4 single-seat biplane fighter which he evolved for

The first prototype Sopwith 3F.2 Hippo. (Hawker Photo.)

Armstrong Whitworth when, in 1917, he succeeded F. Koolhoven as designer. Named Armadillo, the machine was far from elegant in appearance and embodied a boxlike fuselage which filled the relatively narrow gap between the two-bay wings. The two Vickers guns were housed in a peculiar fairing which curved from the front face of the engine cowling to the top of the upper wings. Being tested in September, 1918, the Armadillo prototype X19 was a latecomer among the War's fighters and, with its comparatively poor view from the cockpit, stood little chance of a production order.

The feature of a deep fuselage filling the gap between the wings was adopted in a two-seat Sopwith fighter of 1918—the 3F.2 Hippo—which incorporated back-stagger in its two-bay wing layout.

Remarkable in the Hippo was that the cardinal rule in multi-seat fighter

The trench-fighting Sopwith T.F.2 Salamander. (Hawker Photo.)

design—that of close proximity of the crew members to each other in the interest of maximum co-operation for operational duty and survival—was disregarded by locating the pilot in front of the wings and the observer's cockpit in a cut-out at the trailing edge. Notwithstanding this disadvantage, both enjoyed good positions for operating their guns—the pilot with his pair of Vickers and the observer with his single or double Lewis guns. The 200 h.p. Clerget 11B rotary powered both the first Hippo and the second modified version, X11, in their trials early in the year but the type progressed no further than the pair of prototypes.

The busy Sopwith factory proceeded to produce in the Spring of 1918 another single-seat two-bay biplane fighter—the T.F.2 Salamander—with the emphasis on trench strafing. In appearance closely resembling the Snipe, the whole fore-section of the fuselage was protected by armour plating. The Salamander's engine was the 230 h.p. Bentley B.R.2, standard armament being a pair of nose-mounted Vickers guns. Experimental installations were tested consisting of batteries of multiple machine-guns, even to the extent of equipping one Salamander with eight guns concentrated to fire downwards through the bottom of the fuselage. The Salamander went into production but was too late to become operational before the Armistice and its very nature nullified use in the R.A.F. after the War.

In the course of 1918, three single-seat fighters were planned by separate companies, each machine being within the Admiralty's N.1B requirement. One of them, the Supermarine N.1B Baby, N59, is notable as being the first of an extremely select class of British warplane—the single-seat, flying-boat fighter. As was to be expected from Supermarine, the Baby was of very pleasing appearance with an elegant mahogany Linton Hope hull. The 200 h.p. Hispano-Suiza engine was installed between the folding biplane wings to drive a pusher propeller. Maximum speed at sea level when tested in February, 1918, was 117 m.p.h., combined with excellent handling and manœuvrability. Six months later, in August, the Baby was tested also with the 200 h.p. Sunbeam Arab engine but no production of the machine was undertaken.

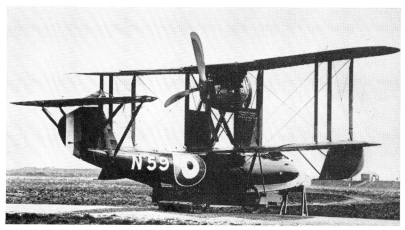

Supermarine N.1B Baby. (Imperial War Museum Photo.)

In the North, the Blackburn Company started in 1917 to construct their N.1B single-seat, flying-boat fighter—also a pusher using the 200 h.p. Hispano-Suiza and of refined aerodynamic form. Progress was slow so that, when the end of the War came, only the hull was ready. Intended armament was a single Lewis gun in front of the pilot.

The approach of the third firm, Westland, to the N.1B conditions took the form of a single-seat, tractor biplane on floats. R. A. Bruce and A. Davenport designed the machine which was intended to be operated from ships. Two prototypes, N16 and N17, were constructed, the engines chosen in each case being the 150 h.p. Bentley B.R.1. N16 used Sopwith floats, including the usual one at the tail. N17 differed in being equipped at first with a pair of long Westland-built floats which made a tail float unnecessary but the machine flew later with main and tail Sopwith floats. Tests were carried out in

Blackburn N.1B. (Blackburn Photo.)

October, 1917, and the Westland N.1Bs were armed with one Vickers gun on the front decking and one Lewis on the upper centre-section. Although performance and handling were good, the landplane Pups and Camels were considered better for the purpose of sea operations and Westland's N.1Bs were abandoned.

The Westland designers Bruce and Davenport were responsible for a two-seat fighter reconnaissance biplane which the West Country firm completed towards the end of 1918. Called the Weasel, the machine was of typical two-bay layout but was one of the unlucky types to have the unreliable A.B.C. Dragonfly 1 engine of 320 h.p. Two Vickers guns were provided for the pilot and the observer used a single Lewis on a Scarff ring. The Weasel was quite

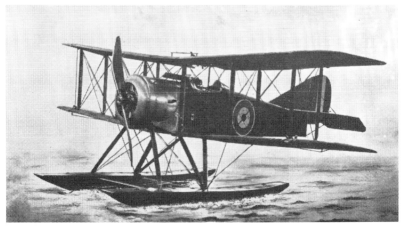

N17, the second Westland N.1B, equipped with long Westland floats. (Westland Photo.)

Two-seat Westland Weasel. (Westland Photo.)

successful in flight trials but the four built spent their lives in experimental work only.

In October, 1918, there emerged at Kingston an unusual venture for Sopwith—a single-seat, parasol monoplane fighter named the Swallow or Sopwith Monoplane No. 2. The machine was derived from the Scooter or Monoplane No. 1, which had appeared earlier in the middle of the year. The Swallow, B9276, used a Camel fuselage, a 110 h.p. le Rhône engine and carried a pair of fixed Vickers guns on the fore-decking. The machine was a very neat and attractive design but received no development beyond the single prototype.

During the final months of the 1914–18 War a number of new single-seat fighters were completed or were in the final stages to meet the requirements of the R.A.F. Type 1 Specification issued in 1918. Several prominent firms tendered to it and, among them, Sopwith produced three interesting prototypes.

May, 1918, saw the appearance of the Sopwith 8F.1 Snail Mk.I, of particular note for its finely-conceived wooden monocoque fuselage. The Mk.I was completed after its sister Snail with a conventional fuselage structure covered

Sopwith Swallow B9276. (Hawker Photo.)

A monocoque fuselage and forward stagger were features of the Sopwith 8F.1 Snail Mk.I. (Hawker Photo.)

The Mk.II version of the Sopwith Snail with stringer and fabric fuselage and negative stagger. (Hawker Photo.)

with fabric, which had been rolled out during the previous month. Both machines used the temperamental 170 h.p. A.B.C. Wasp 1 as power but the Snail Mk.II differed from the Mk.I in having its wings set with a small amount of negative stagger as opposed to the other machine's positive stagger.

A surprise Sopwith design was a new triplane, the single-seat Snark, with a monocoque fuselage mounting the 360 h.p. A.B.C. Dragonfly 1a engine following earlier installation of the 320 h.p. Dragonfly 1. Although its fuselage lines were clean, as usual with a monocoque structure, the appearance of the rest of the airframe fell far short of that of the earlier Sopwith Triplane. The Snark was designed as a high-altitude fighter and was given very heavy armament in the form of two fuselage-mounted Vickers guns and four Lewis guns fitted beneath the lowest wings. Three prototypes were built and displayed excellent performance and handling characteristics but, apart from the troubles of the Dragonfly, the day of the triplane fighter was past.

Frederick Koolhoven designed a further fighter for the B.A.T. Company to meet the R.A.F. Type 1 Specification, the F.K.25 Basilisk completed during 1918. The machine was another of those developed to use the power of the 320 h.p. A.B.C. Dragonfly radial engine and was on the general lines of the earlier Bantam but with the pilot given more conventional accommodation in a cockpit set further aft in the monocoque fuselage. Two-bay wings were again used and the undercarriage followed Koolhoven's favourite style of separate units with a broad track. The Basilisk's armament consisted of a pair of fuselage-mounted Vickers guns. The second prototype embodied minor modifications but the Basilisk failed to make any headway towards production.

F4068, the first prototype Sopwith Snark triplane. (Hawker Photo.)

F2907 B.A.T. Basilisk fitted with plain ailerons. (Flight International Photo.)

Westland Wagtail C4293. (Westland Photo.)

Westland's contribution to the series of R.A.F. Type 1 prototype fighters was provided by their design team of Bruce and Davenport and appeared in 1918 as the Wagtail. An appealing and shapely little biplane of 23 ft. 2 in. span, it mounted the 170 h.p. A.B.C. Wasp 1 engine, a unit which was one of the troublesome radials of the last part of the 1914–18 War. Construction of the Wagtail followed the usual form for a wood and fabric biplane but in its finely-conceived and balanced proportions the machine possessed an attractiveness matched by few others. Two Vickers guns on the front decking provided the Wagtail's firepower and its maximum speed at 10,000 ft. was 125 m.p.h. Five were constructed but as prototypes only.

While the remaining weeks of the 1914–18 War were passing, various British firms pressed on with the construction of the final prototype fighters conceived in the urgent stress of the costly conflict.

The Sopwith Company, which had played such a prominent and successful part in the development of British fighters, finished early in 1919 their Dragon, a well-proportioned two-bay biplane single-seater developed from the experimental prototype Snipe B9967 which had been fitted with the 320 h.p. A.B.C. Dragonfly 1 engine. The Dragon received the benefit of the extra 40 h.p. delivered by the 360 h.p. Dragonfly 1A and was in reality Snipe E7990, altered accordingly. Two Vickers guns constituted the armament and the Dragon recorded the excellent top speed of 150 m.p.h. The first flight took place during January, 1919, and production proceeded into the middle of the year but not for adoption by the R.A.F.

One more single-seat fighter, the Snapper, remained to emerge under the name of Sopwith from the Kingston factory. It was completed during the Spring of 1919 under the R.A.F. Type 1 requirement with a normal wooden

Production Sopwith Dragon with horn-balanced ailerons. (Hawker Photo.)

box-girder fuselage; the original intention was to provide it with one of mono-coque type. In common with several latecomers on the British fighter scene at the end of the War, the Snapper used the 360 h.p. Dragonfly 1A radial engine from which so much had been expected and which endowed the single-bay biplane with a top speed of 140 m.p.h. The machine's armament was the typical one of two Vickers guns and the Snapper terminated the line of Sopwith scouts and fighters which had been sparked off some five years previously with the Tabloid.

The first prototype Sopwith Snapper. (Hawker Photo.)

Two further single-seat fighters were planned under the R.A.F. Type 1 conditions. These were the Armstrong Whitworth Ara and the Nieuport Nighthawk but neither machine was ready before the beginning of 1919.

Designed by F. Murphy, the Ara shared the same unhappy type of engine as the Nighthawk—the 320 h.p. A.B.C. Dragonfly 1—and retained the same two-bay wing layout as Murphy's earlier Armadillo. The fuselage was unusually deep-sided towards the rear where it would normally have been expected to have tapered steadily in elevation. In F4971, the first prototype, the fuselage rested on the lower wings but F4972 introduced greater gap between the mainplanes, resulting in the lower wings passing beneath the fuselage. The fore-part of the fuselage housed two Vickers guns and the Ara turned in the useful top speed at ground level of 150 m.p.h. The Ara was typical of the trend of the final generation of fighters which made their début at the end of the War and this styling was shared by the Nieuport Company's Nighthawk.

In the design, H. P. Folland succeeded in raising the standard of his art as a single-seat fighter designer to a new level in laying out a two-bay biplane which displayed excellent proportions and looked every inch a fighter. In flight, the Nighthawk's behaviour was in every way compatible with the promise inherent in its appearance. Handling characteristics and performance figures were admirable, including a top speed of 151 m.p.h. at ground level and a service ceiling of 24,500 ft. The Nighthawk was given what had become the standard armament of twin fixed Vickers guns. Large-scale production of the machine was ordered even though it was powered by the Dragonfly radial but the unfortunate vicissitudes which attended the engine curtailed any chance of widespread service for it.

As the War's last days drew nearer Bristol's F. S. Barnwell proceeded with his design for a two-seat fighter to take over from the F.2B. His first approach to a successor was started in November, 1917, as the F.2C with three alternative engines—the 230 h.p. Bentley B.R.2 rotary, the 260 h.p. Salmson radial and, finally, the 320 h.p. A.B.C. Dragonfly 1—considered as the power unit. The Dragonfly was selected for the Badger Mk.I, as the F.2C was eventually named, and the prototype, F3495, was taken into the air for the first time on 4th February, 1919, by Capt. C. F. Uwins but crashed when the engine stopped suddenly owing to the failure of the petrol supply. The second Badger constructed, designated Mk.II, used the 450 h.p. Cosmos Jupiter radial with its greater power and reliability. The Badger was characterized by its single-bay, staggered, sweptback wings with their N-style interplane struts, and was armed with twin Vickers guns for the pilot and a Lewis for the observer. Three prototypes were built but no production ensued.

When the long-awaited eleventh hour of the eleventh day of the eleventh month of 1918 had struck across the shattered, stricken corner of North-West Europe to bring a barely-remembered silence to the tired, cold air of Winter, the stilling of the engines and guns of the fighters contributed to the long-sought but uncanny quiet. At the coming of war in the Summer of 1914, the aeroplane had already in a few short years established itself as a practical

J6492, the third Bristol Badger. (Bristol Photo.)

vehicle and was being developed and exploited to stretch its wings ever further afield across both land and water. Its potentialities as a weapon of war were recognized at an early stage, to come to fruition swiftly as the operations of the conflict extended in scope. The fighter's speed and handiness had soon ensured its rapid development so that, when the Armistice came, its performance was in most respects in advance of other types. The fighter was, however, purely a machine of war and its high speed was offset by strictly limited payload and range.

The urgent demands of war compelled constant research to provide ever-better performance but, over the period of the War, maximum speed showed relatively little increase from the 135 m.p.h. recorded by the S.E.4 to the 151 m.p.h. attained by the Nighthawk. In the interim, the unarmed scout had been transformed into a deadly fighter carrying as its standard armament a pair of synchronized machine-guns and endowed with superb powers of manœuvre. Relatively little change had been made in construction, the strong and quickly-built wooden box structure covered with fabric occupying a firmly-held first place. The War had allowed the fighter designer to pursue and develop his particular aspect of aeroplane design into an exacting and exciting art of its own in a field which was, in the future, to show itself to be unbounded.

Early in the War designers were feeling their way still and some explored extremely unorthodox layouts. None of the more grotesque creations succeeded in making the grade as a practical fighter and, by the middle of the conflict, the more outlandish design features had been entirely dropped so that the whole aspect of fighter design had become rationalized by 1919.

The pulsating heart of an aeroplane, its engine, had gained immeasurably through constant attention to improved reliability, reduced fuel consumption and increased power. Great Britain entered the War relying mainly on French-designed rotary engines but was quick to take advantage of her automobile engine companies' skills to evolve a wide range of aircraft engines which included also those designed by the Royal Aircraft Factory engineers. Great use was made of the rotary type of engine for the entire duration of hostilities and for some time afterwards, with much being expected of the fixed radial type of unit. Despite the amount of research and development invested in the air-cooled radial, first results were unexpectedly disappointing as far as reliability was concerned, but persistence with it finally overcame its shortcomings in the years immediately after the Armistice. The air-cooled radial possessed a number of advantages over its liquid-cooled rival, particularly as it was lighter in weight and dispensed also with the vulnerable bulk inherent in a cooling system. From the fighter designer's point of view, however, the radial's frontal area was a distinct disadvantage when he was striving to attain a clean nose entry for the fuselage. Moreover, the liquid-cooled engine's radiator could be made to retract as far as cooling requirements would allow and the radiator surface could be disposed and shaped to create minimum drag.

The need for increased performance, greater payload and improved manœuvrability under the repeated urgent calls of war had dictated decisively the general and particular lines which development of the fighter—now recognised in its full worth as an essential part of an air force—must follow.

Fighter design was destined to become a province of aircraft development in which Great Britain came to excel and for which she was in later years to be profoundly thankful to the designers of her fighter aircraft for the brilliance of their engineering achievements.

Siddeley S.R.2 Siskin. (Whitworth Gloster Photo.)

CHAPTER THREE

PROGRESS IN PEACE

The advent of the Armistice brought with it, inevitably, sweeping changes to the aircraft manufacturing industry—not least to the firms responsible for Britain's fighters. The Royal Air Force had been in existence for just seven months when the end of the War decreed that the requirements in fighters for the Service would be drastically reduced. Rapid demobilization was the order of the day in an air force which, at the cessation of hostilities, stood as the most powerful in the World with a total strength of 22,647 aeroplanes and seaplanes on charge at 30th November, 1918. 1919 was a year which was spent in reducing the numbers of aircraft and personnel at a rapid rate as squadrons were disbanded and the R.A.F. swiftly became a shamefully faint shadow of its recent robust self.

The immediate and natural reaction among the aircraft manufacturers as contracts were cancelled and orders slashed was an expectation of a bright future for private and commercial aviation to take advantage of the vastly improved techniques in airframe and engine design and construction accelerated by the War. Dreams of a speedy growth of interest and expansion in civil flying were, however, slower in realization than anticipated and nearly a decade was to pass before commercial aviation could be claimed to be truly established and reasonably thriving. Meanwhile, there was little call for new aircraft to equip a greatly depleted Royal Air Force.

The Royal Aircraft Factory had become the Royal Aircraft Establishment in June, 1918, and continued its work of research in conjunction with the National Physical Laboratory at Teddington.

During the immediate year or two after the War general Government apathy towards the aircraft industry, which had contributed by its endeavours such a great deal towards the successful conclusion of the conflict, finally brought about the exit of several firms from business, among them the greatest of the fighter suppliers—the Sopwith Aviation Company—which immediately came into being again towards the end of 1920 as the H. G. Hawker Engineering Company. For a while, the firm's main aircraft work consisted of overhauling and reconditioning the airframes and engines of the Snipes forming the country's small and pitifully inadequate force of fighters but, although automobile and motor-cycle manufacture had been taken on to keep the workshops occupied during the bad period, the main interest of the directors lay in aircraft design and construction, backed by a determination which was soon to manifest itself in a concrete form.

During this time, one of the most important of the new British single-seat fighters of the early post-War era was being developed at its prototype stage. Prior to Maj. F. M. Green's departure in 1917 from the Royal Aircraft Factory to design for the aviation section of the Siddeley-Deasy Motor Car Co. at Coventry, he prepared the preliminary layout for another fighter in the Factory's Scouting Experimental series, based on the installation of a two-row fourteen-cylinder radial engine—the 300 h.p. R.A.F.8. Once Maj. Green, J. Lloyd and S. D. Heron had settled down to work at the Siddeley-Deasy offices, the design was developed in earnest to emerge as a sprightly-looking biplane, the Siddeley S.R.2 Siskin, in mid-1919. At the same time, at Maj. Green's instigation the Company had gone ahead with the development of the R.A.F.8 engine and completed it as the Jaguar.

The Siskin flew first in July, 1919, with the unfortunate choice of the 320 h.p. A.B.C. Dragonfly 1 as its power plant, but this was eventually replaced by the Jaguar which had been turned into a reliable and successful unit by the Summer of 1922. The prototype Siskin followed the usual all-wood construction and fabric covering of the war period and carried the standard pair of Vickers guns on its nose-decking as armament. The Siskin was not ordered at the time but much was to be heard of it later in its revised and developed version.

A decision was made during 1920 which was to have in the future a momentous effect, unforeseen at the time, on the subsequent development of the British single-seat fighter. This was the agreement among the directors of the Gloucestershire Aircraft Co. of Cheltenham to continue in business as aircraft manufacturers despite the lack of potential orders. The Company's experience of aeroplane manufacture originated during the War when H. H. Martyn of Sunningend undertook at first sub-contract component work, finally progressing to producing complete aeroplanes of de Havilland and Bristol design. The firm was noted particularly for the outstanding workmanship put into its aircraft and set about continuing its aspirations by acquiring the designs of the Nieuport and General Aircraft Company when that firm closed down at Cricklewood in 1920. Of substantial advantage to Gloucestershire in the project was that the British Nieuport chief designer, H. P. Folland,

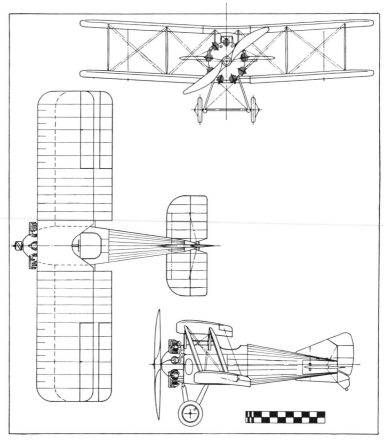

Nieuport Nighthawk

agreed to join the firm. Under this set of circumstances there was set in motion the production of a long line of excellent fighters from Cheltenham and Gloucester originating in the gifted brain of Folland.

The Dragonfly-engined Nighthawk was shown at the initial R.A.F. Pageant at Hendon on 5th July, 1920, but, for the time being, no sign was forthcoming from the Air Ministry of interest in promoting and encouraging new designs in fighters for the Royal Air Force. Foreign governments, however, were keen on building up air arms for themselves, having witnessed what strength could be wielded by the air forces of the belligerent powers in the late war. Consequently, a batch of fifty modified 230 h.p. Bentley B.R.2-powered Nighthawks, under the original name of Mars Mk.II, Mk.III and Mk.IV but redesignated Sparrowhawk Mk.I, Mk.II and Mk.III respectively, were sold to the Imperial Japanese Navy, thus providing the firm in 1921 with its first fighter contract.

J6926 Gloster Mars VI, developed from the Nighthawk. (Gloster Photo.)

By 1922 the reliable 385 h.p. Bristol Jupiter II radial was available and the obsolete rotary type of engine could be finally discarded and the troublesome Dragonfly forgotten. The Nighthawk was re-engined as a high-altitude fighter with the excellent Jupiter II to be followed, under Specification 35/22, by two more with the 385 h.p. Jupiter III and another two with the 325 h.p. A.S. Jaguar II. These re-engined Nighthawks, designated Mars Mk.VI by the G.A.C., went out to the Middle East during 1923 for Service Trials with No. 1 Squadron, then flying Snipes. Another foreign order was received during 1922 for twenty-five Mars Mk.VIs for Greece, a further help in spreading the name of the Company as producers of first-class fighters.

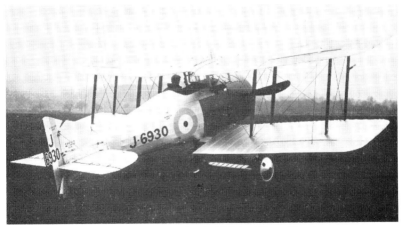

Gloster Mars X, produced as the Nightjar. (Gloster Photo.)

A projected version, the Mars Mk.VII, was dropped but Folland proceeded to develop the Sparrowhawk design still further into the Mars Mk.X as a naval fighter of which twenty-two, designated Nightjar, were ordered. They retained the 230 h.p. Bentley B.R.2, and had a wide-track, long-stroke undercarriage and arrester hooks to catch the fore-and-aft wires then in use.

While these contracts were helping to promote the fortunes of the Gloucestershire Aircraft Co., Folland was busy in the midst of extensive research to improve the overall efficiency of the biplane as a fighter. The investigations were directed particularly towards evolving high-speed wing sections and resulted in an extremely clever arrangement, the H.L.B. combination of differing aerofoil sections, the upper wings utilizing a high-lift H.L.B.1 profile, while the lower wings were of medium-lift H.L.B.2 type. The overall effect was an approach to monoplane efficiency as the lower wings, although providing useful lift at take-off, at high speeds created little lift or drag. The small span thus made possible, combined with reduced centre of pressure travel and shorter fuselage, contributed to the manœuvrability of any machine embodying the H.L.B. combination, the arrangement being incorporated for the first time in the single-seat B.R.2-engined Grouse of 1923 which was a Mars Mk.III modified.

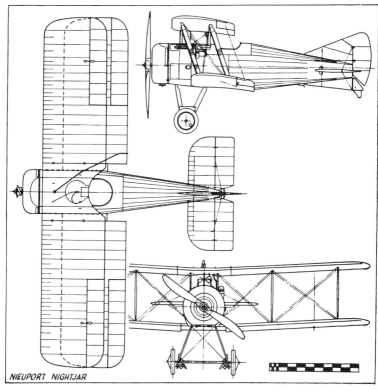

NIEUPORT NIGHTJAR

Nieuport Nightjar

G–EAYN Gloster Grouse Mk.I. (Gloster Photo.)

During 1920 there was a brief revival of interest in the single-seat flying-boat type of fighter when Supermarine built the Seaking Mk.I amphibian with a pusher 160 h.p. Beardmore engine. The machine's armament was a single Lewis gun and it attained a top speed of 110 m.p.h. A later version, the Seaking Mk.II, appeared in 1922 with a 300 h.p. Hispano-Suiza. Excellent powers of manœuvre were claimed for the design which could be looped, rolled and spun.

In April, 1921, another waterborne machine, the Fairey Pintail Mk.I fighter reconnaissance seaplane was tested by Lt.-Col. Vincent Nicholl. Designed in 1920 by F. Duncanson to the R.A.F.'s Type 21 requirement for a two-seat amphibian which could operate from land, water and carrier, N133 —the first prototype—was fitted with the 450 h.p. Napier Lion I and carried a Vickers gun for the pilot and a Lewis gun on a Scarff ring for the observer. The field of fire to the rear was excellent as all vertical tail surfaces were mounted below the tailplane. The Mk.I had retractable wheels between the

Fairey Pintail Mk.IV with wheels inset in the floats as supplied during 1924 to the Imperial Japanese Navy. (Fairey Photo.)

141

Fairey Flycatcher Mk.I, one of the most popular of early Fleet Air Arm fighters. (Fairey Photo.)

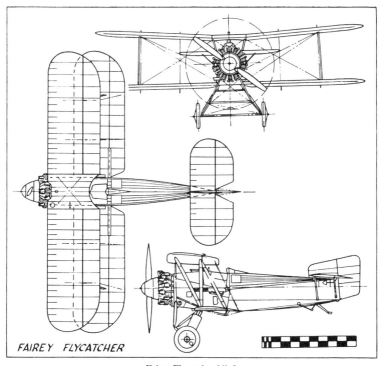

FAIREY FLYCATCHER

Fairey Flycatcher Mk.I

142

floats, the Mk.II N134—tested at Hamble in 1921 by Capt. Norman Mac-millan—had a longer fuselage and retracting wheels outside the floats, the Mk.III N135 was like the Mk.II but incorporated fixed wheels inset in the floats, while the Mk.IV was the version of the Mk.III supplied in a small batch to the Imperial Japanese Navy in 1924.

The Bristol Aeroplane Company projected their Type 35 two-seat seaplane with a Jupiter engine to the R.A.F. Type 21 conditions and another Bristol project, for the U.S.A. A.H.2 requirements, was the Type 38 two-seat fighter on floats with the 180 h.p. Wolseley Viper for power. The Bristol Type 39 would have been a single-seat version of the Type 38 and the pro-jected Type 40 was scheduled to be a two-seat biplane fighter with the 240 h.p. Siddeley Puma engine.

The Bristol Type 76 two-seat fighter, however, was built. A revised version of the F.2B, with the 425 h.p. Jupiter IV as its power plant, the single proto-type G–EBGF appeared in 1923. Unwanted by the R.A.F. a variant, the Type 76B, was sold to the Swedish Army.

By 1922 it became obvious to even the acutely economy-conscious Air Ministry that a replacement for the Nightjar could no longer be delayed. Specification 6/22 for a new deck-landing single-seat fighter, powered by either the Jupiter or the Jaguar engine, was therefore issued.

Two firms, Fairey and Parnall, constructed prototypes to the requirement, both machines in their landplane versions sharing the common span of 29 ft., length of 23 ft. and height of 12 ft. In plan view they were much alike but the Plover from Parnall possessed slightly the greater wing area of the two.

The stocky little Fairey machine was designed by F. Duncanson and named the Flycatcher, the prototype N163 being flown initially during 1922 by Lt.-Col. Nicholl with the 400 h.p. A.S. Jaguar III engine. In 1924 it was re-engined with the 425 h.p. Bristol Jupiter IV but the Flycatcher went into production in 1923 with the 400 h.p. Jaguar IV, to reach a final total by 1930 of one hundred and ninety-two machines. The Flycatcher had an appealingly compact and aggressive appearance that was all its own, with dihedral on its upper wings only, and an impression conferred by its heavily-staggered wings of thrusting forward. The machine was specially arranged to dismantle into sections not exceeding 13 ft. 6 in. long and was fitted with full-span Fairey camber-changing trailing-edge flaps on both sets of wings which, together with hydraulic brakes for the wheels, helped it to land in a stretch of 50 yards. The brakes were used in conjunction with the early type of fore-and-aft arrester gear on the Fairey oleo-pneumatic undercarriage. Capt. Norman Macmillan flew a Flycatcher through the first diving tests officially called for by the Air Ministry for an aircraft, and the machine soon became known to the annual Hendon Air Display audiences through the noise created by the fluttering of the tips of its propeller blades as it pulled out of a dive. The Flycatcher was operated also on floats and as an amphibian with its pair of wheels set into the floats' undersides. Two Vickers guns, one ·5 and one ·303, were synchro-nized to fire past the propeller.

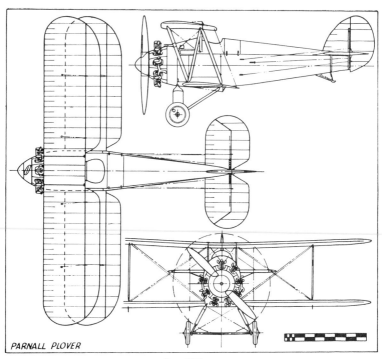

PARNALL PLOVER

Parnall Plover

The Flycatcher was immensely strong but this admirable characteristic was not shared to the same extent by its competitor from Parnall to the 6/22 specification—the Plover. Harold Bolas drew up a machine which matched to an uncanny degree the Fairey product in many respects but which was of all-wood construction as opposed to the Flycatcher's use of metal in the fore-part of the fuselage. The first pair of Plovers—N160 and N161—mounted the 436 h.p. Jupiter IV, while the third prototype—N162—used the 385 h.p. Jaguar. Six Jupiter-engined Plovers were delivered to the Service during 1923 but the Flycatcher soon asserted itself as the better machine under operating conditions and was therefore ordered in quantity to become the standard single-seat fleet fighter for the ensuing nine years.

The Fleet Air Arm was formed in April, 1924, and while its requirement for a fighter was thus being met, attention was turned similarly towards catering for the needs of the R.A.F., still making do with its outmoded Snipes. Under J. Lloyd's direction at Armstrong Whitworth the Siskin had undergone a transformation and emerged from its metamorphosis as the Siskin Mk.III, with a fuselage and wing spars of high-tensile steel tubing and strip, a material which was a great improvement in strength and for maintenance. With a 325 h.p. Jaguar III engine and a pair of synchronized Vickers guns, the Siskin Mk.III was ordered in 1923 and entered service with No. 41 Squadron during May, 1924. Camouflage was now a thing of the past, except

Handley Page H.P.21. (Handley Page Photo.)

for heavy bombers, and the new fighters' fabric covering was resplendent in silver dope. Fighter units also revived the practice of painting on the upper wings and the fuselage sides of their machines distinctive squadron markings. During the War these had consisted of small bars or geometrical figures on the aft portion of the fuselage but the new markings of the 'twenties evolved as far brighter and bolder gaily-coloured bands of checks, bars, stripes or other devices. The Siskin presented a somewhat untidy appearance for a fighter and was characterized by the far greater size of the upper wings compared with the lower set.

In the course of 1923 Short Bros. constructed two examples—J6974 and J6975—of a purposeful-looking two-seat fighter, the S.3 Springbok Mk.I, to Air Ministry Specification 19/21 based on the experience of stressed-skin construction gained with their Silver Streak of 1920. The Springbok, with its all-metal framework and stressed-skin covering, had an exceedingly well-formed and shapely fuselage which mounted a 400 h.p. Jupiter IV engine in its nose. The fuselage was suspended between the equal-span, two-bay biplane wings, the entire centre-section of which was left uncovered in the upper planes. The top wings' front and rear tubular spars rested at a tangent on the upper curve of the fuselage, with the front cockpit set between them so that the pilot's head was on a level with the exposed spars. The rear cockpit, complete with Scarff gun-ring, was immediately adjacent to the rear spar. A Vickers gun mounted on the port side of the fuselage was provided for the pilot while the observer had a Lewis.

Normally accustomed to building large aircraft, Handley Page not only went suddenly to the other end of the scale during 1923 and produced a single-seat shipboard fighter but also, in an era of biplanes, designed the machine daringly as a cantilever low-wing monoplane. Designated H.P.21, three proto-types were ordered by the United States Navy in its class VF27 and known

J7297, the silver dope and white enamel last Short Springbok Mk.II. (Short Photo.)

as the H.P.S–1 or S.B.24 and were required principally to evaluate the high-lift, slow-speed devices incorporated in the machine's wings.

The sole H.P.21 finally constructed was completed in September, 1923, and fitted with a Gwynne-built 230 h.p. Bentley B.R.2, constituting rather an extraordinary anomaly in installing an obsolete rotary engine of low power in an airframe of such advanced and modern concept. Throughout, the all-wood H.P.21 was an ingenious design with a ply-covered fuselage, the rear section of which was connected by six bolts to the fore-portion built integrally with the wings.

Leading-edge slots were mounted full span and were connected to the ailerons which operated also as flaps, the combination producing the remarkably low landing speed of 44 m.p.h. Plywood covering was used on the wings and all control rods carefully faired or enclosed so that the H.P.21 reached a top speed of 145 m.p.h. at sea level, had a climb of 1,800 ft./min., a service ceiling of 21,000 ft. and an endurance of 3 hours. Provision was made for a pair of synchronized ·300 Marlin machine-guns but these were not fitted before the eventual scrapping of the aircraft after trials by the U.S. Navy. An alternative float undercarriage was embodied in the design and, while under evaluation, a plain rounded rudder replaced the horn-balanced style at first fitted.

In 1924 the Air Ministry ordered a further three Springboks, J7295, J7296 and J7297, with the same system of metal fuselage structure and stressed-skin covering, but with lighter, fabric-covered wings. The redesigned S.3a Mk.IIs were altered so that the lower wings were mounted direct onto the fuselage. Instead of the equal span and chord of the Mk.I, the lower planes of the Mk.II were of smaller span and chord with a consequent splay in the mounting of the interplane struts. The tailcone was deleted to make way for a rudder of full depth, the fin was shortened and horn balances were added

146

to the rudder and elevators. Although not adopted, the Springbok is of particular importance historically as the first aeroplane designed for the R.A.F. to possess originally both an all-metal structure and covering.

By 1922 the Air Ministry had decided that the time was ripe to remedy the deficiency in the R.A.F.'s fighter force by issuing Specification 25/22 for a single-seat interceptor night fighter. Capt. Thomson, the Hawker chief designer, produced a two-bay biplane—the Woodcock Mk.I—to meet the requirement. The machine has the honour of being the first of the magnificent line of Hawker fighters to be designed to the present day, but the prototype J6987 was not at first an unqualified success. Freddy Raynham, successor to the late Harry Hawker as the firm's test pilot, put the machine through its trials on completion in 1923 and found wing flutter and poor rudder control present.

Nevertheless, the Woodcock was considered worth developing and on Capt. Thomson's departure from Hawker in 1923, the new chief designer, W. G. Carter, took over and redesigned the machine. The Mk.II prototype, J6988, when flown in 1924 featured single-bay wings of reduced span, increased overall length and a 380 h.p. Jupiter IV in place of the Mk.I's 358 h.p. Jaguar II. The Woodcock Mk.II was a far superior aeroplane but still underwent minor modifications before being accepted by the R.A.F. and going into service in 1925 with two units only—Nos. 3 and 17 Squadrons. All-wood construction with fabric covering was employed in the Woodcock which carried its pair of synchronized Vickers guns mounted one on each side of the fuselage. The Mk.II's top speed at sea level of 141 m.p.h. showed no advance over the maximum speed attained by fighters in small-scale production at the end of the War a few years earlier. Even so, the Woodcock played a useful and important part in filling the gap in Britain's nocturnal defences at a period when her combined fighter resources were dangerously low.

Official concern over economy during the immediate post-War period was sharply highlighted in the Type 52 Bullfinch single-seat fighter from Bristol

Early version of Hawker Woodcock Mk.II. (Hawker Photo.)

147

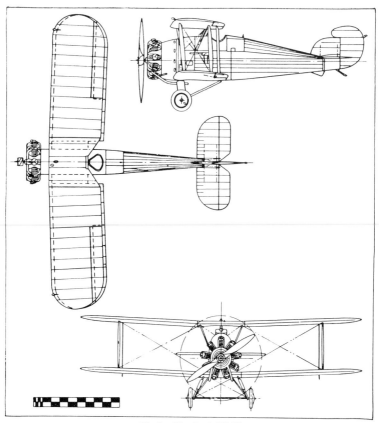

Hawker Woodcock Mk.II

designed by Frank Barnwell in 1921. The Type 52 M.F.A. parasol monoplane was drawn up so that it was easily convertible on the production line into a two-seat biplane with the extra lifting power of an additional wing mounted well-staggered below the fuselage. Each version used the 450 h.p. Jupiter III installed in a steel-tubing fuselage which formed part of what was, for Bristol, a comparatively inelegant airframe. An upper fin was omitted but a pair of underfins were faired into twin tailskids which incorporated a pair of small rudders as well. In the two monoplanes which flew in 1923, the 240 sq.ft. wings were swept back and of parallel chord but tapered very sharply in section from the strut attachment points to the centre and to the tips. Twin synchronized Vickers guns formed the pilot's armament and C. F. Uwins took the third monoplane J6903 on its initial flight on 15th February, 1924.

Following this the machine was converted to be flown by Uwins in the middle of the following month as the biplane Type 53 M.F.B. An extra bay inserted in the fuselage immediately behind the pilot carried the second cockpit with its Scarff-mounted single Lewis gun, the lower wings being

148

Bristol Type 52 Bullfinch as a monoplane. (Bristol Photo.)

Bristol Type 53 Bullfinch in biplane form. (Bristol Photo.)

suspended just beneath but without interplane struts. The Bullfinch achieved its object of being a reasonably fast single-seat monoplane which was readily adaptable in production to emerge also as a two-seat biplane if necessary but, despite successful results in its official trials, the idea was dropped.

Following a display at Hendon of the powers of the Gloucestershire Grouse with its H.L.B. wings, enough enthusiasm for Folland's innovation was aroused in the Air Ministry for an order to be placed with the Company for three prototypes of a new design incorporating H.L.B. which had demonstrated convincingly that, with it, structural weight could be lower, wing area reduced, wing loading increased and stalling speed brought down, all being accomplished with an increase in stability and manœuvrability.

The customary Folland touch resulted in the dainty little Grebe single-seater to meet the Air Ministry request, and was the machine which really set its parent firm in large-scale business as fighter constructors. The two-row 14-cylinder 325 h.p. Jaguar III nestled compactly into the short nose and the fin and rudder proclaimed descent from Folland's earlier S.E.5. Modified and improved production Grebe Mk.Is of 1924 were given the extra power of the 400 h.p. Jaguar IV, resulting in a top speed of 153 m.p.h. at sea level. Although the service version carried the usual pair of Vickers guns, Grebes

Gloster Grebe of No. 25 Squadron. (Gloster Photo.)

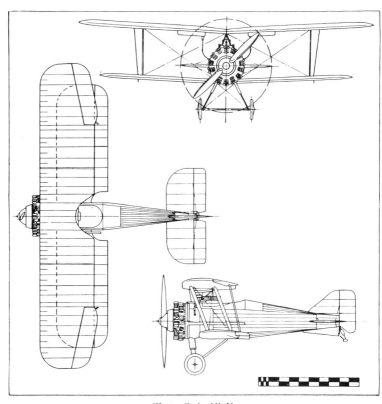

Gloster Grebe Mk.II

were used in tests of ·5 Brownings and Vickers guns, other experiments including the first official terminal velocity dive in which it reached and survived a speed of 240 m.p.h., trials with three different sets of wings in an endeavour to improve the pilot's view, and the successful launching from the airship R.33 on 21st October, 1925, of one Grebe over Pulham and another above Cardington. The Grebe Mk.II was a revised version with thinner centre-section and improved ailerons and a projected variant would have had the powerful 700 h.p. Rolls-Royce Condor IV engine. The R.A.F.'s Grebes used fixed-pitch wooden propellers but the demonstrator G–EBHA was employed to test the Gloster-Hele-Shaw-Beacham variable-pitch type.

At Kingston, in the course of 1924, Sydney Camm designed a new single-seat biplane fighter, the Heron, to incorporate the ingenious system of metal construction which he and Fred Sigrist had devised. This consisted basically of steel or duralumin tubing which was bolted together to form the primary structure, thus eliminating welding and making repair work far easier. The Heron's wings used another Hawker innovation, the dumb-bell section metal spar. Only one Heron, J6989, was built as a Private Venture, being test-flown by P. W. S. Bulman—newly-joined chief test pilot—at the beginning of 1925. The 455 h.p. Jupiter VI engine was fitted, giving a top speed of 156 m.p.h. at 9,800 ft. During trials in 1926 at Martlesham Heath, a Fairey Reed metal propeller was fitted and the Heron spent its days in experimental flying. Official tests of the machine brought unqualified praise in every way for the first all-metal Hawker aircraft but no order for it.

To cope with the greater stresses imposed by higher speeds and generally increased performance inherent in progressive fighter development, the Bristol

Hawker Heron. (Hawker Photo.)

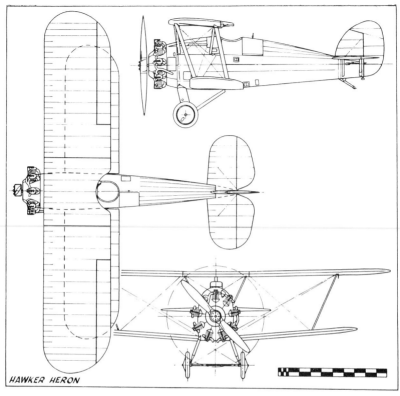

HAWKER HERON

Hawker Heron

Company also became aware to a greater degree of the many advantages of metal construction and produced the Type 84 Bloodhound two-seat fighter biplane which was flown for the first time on 8th June, 1925, by Cyril Uwins. The machine, developed from the earlier Fighter Type 78 of 1923, utilized composite construction as it had a fuselage of steel tubing and wooden wings, the mainplanes being swept back fairly sharply. Metal wings were later fitted and the scheduled armament comprised a pair of Vickers guns for the pilot and a Lewis gun on the Scarff ring in the rear cockpit. The Bloodhound was employed mainly for extended testing of its 436 h.p. Jupiter V engine and propeller trials. A project at Bristol for a two-seat monoplane Fighter D Type 80 with Jupiter engine was investigated but not built.

By the mid-1920s there was considerable activity in the drawing-offices and factories of those British constructors evincing an interest in the technique of fighter production. The aged rotary-engined wartime Snipes were rapidly nearing the end of their safe and useful life and, with a slowly-gathering momentum, specifications detailing the requirements of the Royal Air Force and the Fleet Air Arm, emanated from the offices and conference-rooms of the Air Ministry. In these specifications the manufacturer was, on the whole, allowed in the particular design a high degree of latitude in the form that the actual machine could take as a prototype. The requirements issued by the Air Ministry stated the primary purpose for which the proposed machine was required, together with any additional capabilities or features. The number of crew members would be specified, as would also the engine if the aeroplane were to be designed to make use of a definite type or make of power plant. An important feature of the specification was the armament which the machine would be required to carry and the general upper and lower limits of performance called for would be laid out. At the same time the designer was informed of any special items of interior equipment which were to be incorporated to enable the resulting aircraft to achieve the desired performance or to carry out the specified duties.

With no known potential enemy at the time or in the foreseeable future, the country was resting contentedly and complacently in its security, bent on enjoying the fruits of victory after the bloodiest and costliest of all wars. Little wonder then that the Treasury was far from keen to sanction expenditure in building up forces, in particular the R.A.F. which, with its comparatively brief span of life, was hardly able to bring to bear the same influence in its call for funds as the far more deeply-rooted Army and Navy. Automatically the practice had evolved of making one type of aircraft perform as many jobs as possible—army co-operation, light bombing, reconnaissance, transport, torpedo dropping and other functions—out of which had appeared the ubiquitous general-purpose machine which gave such valiant service over two decades, especially abroad under very trying climatic conditions in the British Empire when the Nation was still fortunate enough to possess sufficient spirit, courage, initiative and strength to stand up for itself and command immediate respect in any part of the World.

The fighter was one class of aeroplane in which the demands for the highest overall performance could not be compromised by inclusion as part of a general-purpose specification.

Bristol Type 84 Bloodhound. (Bristol Photo.)

During the mid-1920s the biplane was still firmly regarded generally as the form for a fighter but, occasionally, a designer allowed his mind the luxury of a digression towards the monoplane. One such instance occurred in February, 1925, at Kingston when Sydney Camm drew up the basic design for a Hawker single-seat, low-wing cantilever monoplane fighter, to be powered by a Bristol Jupiter and armed with a pair of Vickers guns. Some ten years, however, were to elapse before Camm's dream of a Hawker monoplane fighter came to pass in a form which was a little later to achieve undreamed-of glory and honour.

Meanwhile, like those of the Gloucestershire Aircraft Co., the excellence of Hawker products was attracting business from abroad and 1925 found Camm redesigning the Woodcock in minor respects as the Danecock for production of twelve in Denmark under the designation L.B.II Dankok, following the export of three prototypes across the North Sea.

1924 saw the Gloucestershire firm commencing to transfer its production from Sunningend at Cheltenham to a new factory at Brockworth Aerodrome near Gloucester. The Company was determined to maintain its hard-won position and reputation in the front rank of fighter constructors, despite the somewhat precarious financial nature of the business, and felt that judicious investment in manufacturing and flying facilities would be bound to pay handsome dividends eventually. The move was spread over five years but February, 1925, witnessed the Service Trials at Martlesham of a new Gloucestershire single-seat biplane from Henry Folland—the nimble little Gamecock—destined to become one of the best-known of R.A.F. fighters in the late 1920s. The prototype J7497, with the 425 h.p. Jupiter IV, was designed to Specification 37/23 as a development of the Grebe, with but seven months elapsing from the start of detailed design in mid-1924 to delivery of the prototype to Martlesham. Wood and fabric construction was adhered to still, with the single-row, nine-cylinder engine conferring a dumpier appearance to the fuselage lines blended to it. The machine's outstanding agility and general performance in its trials brought a production order without delay to Specification

153, one of three Hawker-built Danecocks. (Hawker Photo.)

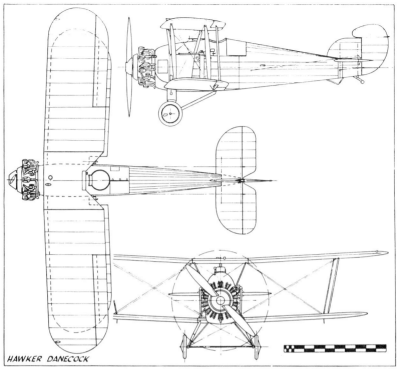

HAWKER DANECOCK

Hawker Danecock

18/25 as the Gamecock Mk.I for the R.A.F. Silver finish overall was now the order of the day for fighters and this, combined with national insignia and individual squadron markings and crests, made the Gamecock one of the most colourful of fighters to be employed at any time by the R.A.F.

The first prototype Gamecock used the Grebe's style of fin and rudder, changed in May, 1925, to incorporate a horn-balanced rudder. The first two prototypes—J7497 and J7756—had the Jupiter IV but the third prototype—J7757—was fitted with the Jupiter VI, the engine installed in the ninety production machines. Last wooden fighter to be ordered for the R.A.F., the Gamecock carried on the H.L.B. concept and successfully went through severe tests in experimental flying, including reaching a speed of 275 m.p.h. in a dive and pulling out of a spin after making twenty-two turns. Investigations were made into wing and tail flutter with J7910 with narrow-chord ailerons in 1927, resulting in additional struts being fitted later to R.A.F. Gamecocks to brace the tips of the upper wings. In the Gamecock the pair of Vickers guns were moved from the traditional location on the top decking to troughs inset in the fuselage sides.

During 1928 J8047 was completed for spinning tests with wings moved to the rear, a longer fuselage, narrow-chord ailerons, modified rudder and a wide-track undercarriage. The same machine carried out trials of the 450 h.p.

Jupiter VII engine and the Gloster-Hele-Shaw-Beacham variable-pitch propeller in 1929. In 1927 a pair of export Gamecocks, designated Mk.II and fitted with narrow-chord ailerons, modified wings and windscreens, greater fuel capacity and the 400 h.p. Jupiter IV, went to Finland where production was undertaken with the Gnome et Rhône engine and where the type flew also on skis. Mk.IIs tested in the United Kingdom included J8804 in 1928 with the 425 h.p. Jupiter VI, narrow-chord ailerons and new fin, rudder and centre-section, and J8075 used at the R.A.E. to evaluate the 480 h.p. Bristol Mercury IIA.

Another Bristol engine, the exhaust-turbo-supercharged Orion of 495 h.p., was scheduled to be tested as a Private Venture in Gamecock G–EBOE but the unreliability experienced with the power plant caused the cancellation of the project.

The appellation Gloucestershire Aircraft Company had always been something of a mouthful, particularly to the firm's foreign customers, so that on

Prototype Bristol Type 76 Jupiter Fighter. (Bristol Photo.)

Fairey Flycatcher floatplane.

Gloster Gamecock Mk.II. (Gloster Photo.)

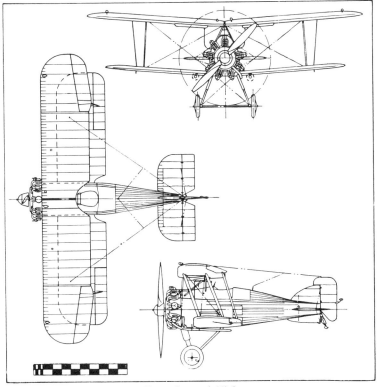

Gloster Gamecock Mk.I

157

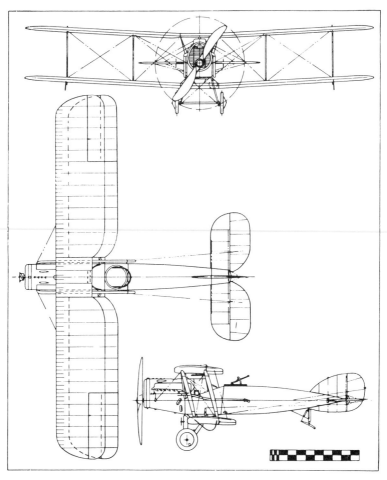

Bristol Fighter Mk.III

11th November, 1926, the name was changed to the Gloster Aircraft Company —to the satisfaction of all concerned.

While the company at Gloucester had been steadily and carefully consolidating its position in the Industry, development of fighter designs was proceeding concurrently within other firms connected with their production. Efforts to improve engine performance at greater heights by resorting to supercharging were bearing fruit and Armstrong Whitworth's designer J. Lloyd redesigned the Siskin Mk.III to take advantage of the 450 h.p. supercharged Jaguar IVS, the prototype Siskin Mk.IIIA making its first flight on 20th October, 1925. Orders were placed for the R.A.F. in 1926, so that the new fighter went into service in the middle of 1927. The Mk.IIIA's top speed at sea level was 156 m.p.h., not a particularly significant increase but its

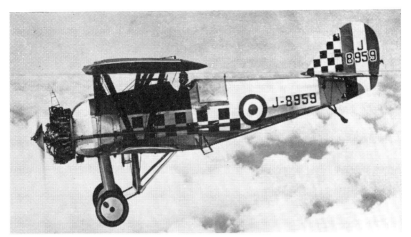

Sqn.Ldr. C. N. Lowe, C.O. of No. 43 Squadron, flying his colourful Armstrong Whitworth Siskin Mk.IIIA. (Armstrong Whitworth Photo.)

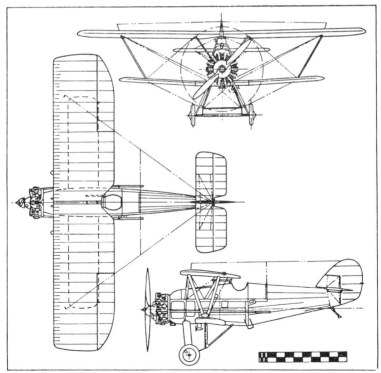

A. W. Siskin Mk.IIIA

Beardmore W.B.26. (Beardmore Photo.)

service ceiling rose to 27,000 ft. The Mk.IIIA retained the general layout of the previous mark but the after portion of the fuselage was raised appreciably towards the rear, thus carrying the tailplane in a higher position. At the same time the small underfin was deleted and the dihedral of the upper wings reduced. The Mk.IIIA carried its pair of Vickers guns on the decking in front of the cockpit.

Following its successful entry into the aircraft industry just prior to the 1914–18 War, the firm of Beardmore continued its aviation interests and in 1925 produced the W.B.26, a stocky-looking two-seat biplane fighter designed by W. S. Shackleton. The 360 h.p. Rolls-Royce Eagle IX engine blended

Avro 566 Avenger in original form with 525 h.p. direct-drive Lion VIII. (Avro Photo.)

cleanly into a slab-sided fuselage which bore deckings above and below. The parallel-chord, single-bay wings were square-cut, in common with the tail surfaces, and carried the fuselage suspended mid-way between them, the lower wings being faired into the underside of the fuselage by the Lamblin radiator block. The W.B.26's structure was of fabric-covered wood, armament comprising two Constantinesco-synchronized Beardmore-Farquhar machine-guns for the pilot and a single similar gun on a Scarff ring in the rear cockpit. The 37 ft. span W.B.26's clean design gave a top speed of 145 m.p.h. and the machine, which was produced for Latvia, made its maiden flight in 1925 piloted by Capt. A. N. Kingwill.

Avro made a bid for the single-seat fighter market during 1925 when the Type 566 Avenger, designed by Roy Chadwick, was constructed at Hamble with the particular purpose of testing a system of wooden monocoque fuse-

J7502 Gloster Gorcock with direct-drive Lion VIII. (Gloster Photo.)

lage construction. The prototype G–EBND was the sole example built and received a neatly-cowled direct-drive 525 h.p. Napier Lion VIII engine with which the Avenger had a top speed of 180 m.p.h., making it one of the fastest fighters flying at the time. The Lion's twin radiators were of the Lamblin type set in flat panels, one under each of the upper wings. Two Vickers guns, mounted one on each side of the fuselage, formed the armament.

The Avenger was rebuilt as the Type 567, to participate in the 1928 King's Cup Race, fitted with the geared 553 h.p. Lion IX which gave it a longer nose. At the same time the original N-type interplane struts were replaced by single I struts and strut-connected ailerons were added to the lower wings. Demonstrations of the sleek Avenger were made by H. J. L. Hinkler but the design was not developed further.

By 1924 the Gloucestershire design staff, impelled by the active and searching mind of Folland, had realized that the limit of usefulness of wooden construction for fighters—and other military types—was being approached and they consequently turned to the development of metal structures. The Air Ministry assisted the Company by placing a contract in mid-1924 for three experimental single-seat fighters—two to have steel fuselages and wooden wings, the third to be all-steel.

The Company's experience of their Lion-engined Bamel and Gloster racers was a great asset in the design of the three Gorcock biplanes built to the contract, two of which—the Mk.Is—appeared in 1925, J7501 powered by the geared 450 h.p. Lion IV and J7502 with the direct-drive 525 h.p. Lion VIII. The all-metal Mk.II J7503, using the geared 450 h.p. Lion IV, was ready in 1926. J7503 was the fastest of the trio, reaching a top speed of 174 m.p.h. at 5,000 ft.

Divided opinions about the relative merits of geared and ungeared engines resulted in the Gloster experimental department taking the Gorcocks over for research. Finally, the direct-drive Lion was fitted to J7501 and J7503 also but preoccupation with production of the Gamecock, which had meanwhile been ordered for the R.A.F., meant that little flying was done by the Gorcocks until 1926. The Company's extended trials with the machines delayed delivery of the Mk.Is to the Air Ministry until 1927 and that of the Mk.II until 1928. Wing flutter manifested itself in both versions but the Gorcocks repaid the investment by their good service in research. During 1929 three types of duralumin propellers were tested on the direct-drive Lion VIII Gorcock and each machine bore its pair of Vickers guns in channels on either side of the fuselage.

Among the many interesting prototype fighters to emanate from Kingston during the 1920s was the single-seat Hawker Hornbill, Camm's initial completely original military aircraft to be designed since he joined the firm. A single-bay biplane, it was of fabric-covered wooden construction, with the exception of the steel-tubing fore-part of the fuselage enclosed with metal panels. J7782, the single prototype, made its first flight in May, 1925, at Brooklands, powered by the 698 h.p. Rolls-Royce Condor IV engine which gave it a top speed of 187 m.p.h. The Hornbill was rather singular in being armed with only one Vickers machine-gun which was installed on the port side of the fuselage. Handling trials at Martlesham disclosed trouble with directional stability and engine cooling, with the result that a revised rudder had to be fitted and twin under-wing radiators replaced the former single one. The Hornbill's life was spent in extensive experimental flying after being transferred for the purpose to the R.A.E. towards the end of 1926.

As in other countries, fighter design in Great Britain was to benefit enormously through research into airframes, engines, control, stability, performance and innumerable related aspects of development instigated by the construction of new aircraft specifically designed for racing or by the modification of existing types for the purpose. National events, such as the King's Cup Race, the Aerial Derby and lesser contests, all acted as a strong spur but none with the same vital strength or sense of urgency as the international Schneider Trophy in which British prestige was at stake before the eyes of the World. Following Britain's initial Schneider victory in 1914 by Pixton's

Hawker Hornbill in its early form. (Hawker Photo.)

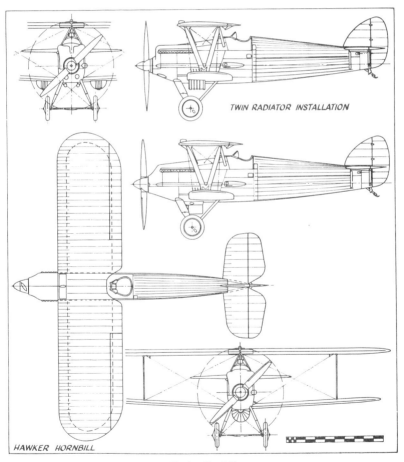

TWIN RADIATOR INSTALLATION

HAWKER HORNBILL

Hawker Hornbill

Sopwith Tabloid, other companies took on the challenge after the contest was revived in 1919. As constructors of waterborne aircraft, Supermarine were immediately eager to compete and entered their Sea Lion Mk.I in 1919 and won the Trophy in 1922 with the Sea Lion Mk.II, piloted by Henri Biard at 145·62 m.p.h. In 1923 the Sea Lion Mk.III was outclassed by the fast American seaplanes, one of which won.

1924 saw the Gloucestershire Aircraft Co. joining in and Folland prepared the Gloster Mk.II seaplane for participation but it was wrecked at Felixstowe before the contest, putting Great Britain out of the running for that year. In the event, as there was no challenger against America in 1924, the contest was abandoned and postponed until 1925.

Appreciation of the great value to the Nation of the experience and knowledge to be gained of high-speed flight from taking part in the Schneider Trophy duels finally brought Air Ministry support and assistance to Supermarine and Gloucestershire in their praiseworthy endeavours. For the 1925 event, Folland proceeded to redesign the Gloster Mk.II as the Gloster Mk.III, a pair of the biplanes being built—N194 and N195—each with a 670 h.p. Napier Lion VII.

While Folland had retained the single-bay biplane formula for the Gloster Mk.IIIs, the Supermarine designer, R. J. Mitchell—whose name was destined to be immortalized in British aviation by the Spitfire—chose the mid-wing monoplane as his solution in the S.4. Powered by a 700 h.p. Napier Lion, the machine was a twin-float seaplane with cantilever surfaces, and its superb beauty of line gave a broad hint of what Mitchell was to achieve later in the outstanding elegance of his magnificent Spitfire.

On 13th September, 1925, the S.4 set up a new World's Air Speed Record of 226·9 m.p.h. but crashed just after take-off in the tests being flown the day before the Schneider contest was held at Baltimore, U.S.A. One of the pair of Gloster Mk.IIIs was wrecked also but Hubert Broad finished second in the competition flying the remaining Gloster Mk.III.

By the middle of the 1920s the various influences at work—the enthusiasm and ability of the designers of the interested manufacturers, the steady issue of Air Ministry specifications, official support and financial assistance for projects, the call for new equipment for R.A.F. and F.A.A. units, and the indirect but invaluable stimulus of the annual Schneider contest's challenge—were all factors which showed that the wind was set fair for progressive and steady development in the art of British fighter design.

Avro 584 Avocet. (Avro Photo.)

CHAPTER FOUR

THE BIPLANE SUPREME

By the time that the middle of the 1920s had been reached the Royal Air Force's needs in fighters were being met by Armstrong Whitworth, Gloster and Hawker, with Fairey—already firmly ensconced in the field of marine aircraft—catering for the Fleet Air Arm.

As the Industry settled down after the War a fairly well-defined pattern became evident, with certain manufacturers concentrating their design and production resources on a preferred type of aeroplane for which the company eventually became noted through its expertise in one or more particular classes. This is not to say that any firm devoted itself to a single class of machine to the exclusion of all others; in most cases, each was able to undertake a relatively broad range of work. As the issue of Air Ministry specifications increased in frequency, so it became the custom for Hawker and Gloster to tender a design for most of the fighter requirements with, in many cases, several of the other companies accepting the challenge and producing prototypes. A practice which, at the same time, steadily gained favour, was that of constructing a Private Venture prototype, either in non-conformity with an official requirement or to meet the conditions of an Air Ministry specification but without a definite contract for a prototype. In many cases these Private Venture fighters were developed for export in small batches to foreign air forces or for production under licence in the countries concerned. Another cogent reason for the design and construction of Private Venture machines was the need for testing in actual practice of new design features or methods of construction which had been developed in research by the company involved. The soundest way to evaluate such principles was, and always will be, to embody them in the aircraft itself and to test it in its element.

Avro Avocet N210 equipped with floats. (Avro Photo.)

After constructing their Private Venture Type 566 Avenger during 1925 to assess the merits of a wooden monocoque fuselage, A. V. Roe and Co. in 1926 built another fighter, this time to appraise a metal stressed-skin structure. Its use on the Type 584 Avocet's fuselage was the first made by Avro, the machine being a single-seat, all-metal, fleet fighter biplane, designed by Roy Chadwick to Specification 17/25. The Avocet's fuselage, of small-diameter circular section and exemplary streamline form from spinner to tailcone, was suspended mid-way between the staggered, unequal-span wings. A curious aspect of the design was that, after so much trouble had been taken with low-drag fuselage design to ensure as high a performance as possible on the comparatively low power of the supercharged 230 h.p. Armstrong Siddeley Lynx IV installed, the benefits of such streamlining should be compromised by the square-cut tips to the wings and tail surfaces—both in plan and section—without the incorporation of taper in section except on the lower wings. In place of flying wires, the fabric-covered wings were braced by heavy diagonal struts from the lower roots outwards. A feature was made in the design of horizontal tail surfaces which folded vertically upwards, and of wings which were easily removed completely to facilitate shipboard stowage. A pair of Vickers guns were housed in troughs in the fuselage sides.

Two Avocets were built during 1926—N209 and N210. Both flew on land undercarriages and N210, fitted with twin floats, was used for a while to assist in training Schneider Trophy pilots. Some two years of trials were carried out with the Avocets, among the modifications made being the fitting of a new horn-balanced taller rudder to N210. On wheels a top speed of 133 m.p.h. at 10,000 ft. and a service ceiling of 23,000 ft. were attained.

Among Bristol projects investigated during this period but not built was one for a single-seat pusher biplane fighter, designated Type 94, to be powered by a Jupiter engine.

Fairey licence-production of the 430 h.p. Curtiss D.12 engine as the Felix was put to good use in the elegant Firefly Mk.I single-seat fleet fighter built by the firm in 1926. The machine was designed by Marcel Lobelle as a Private Venture to Specification 24/23 and its uncluttered appearance was in marked contrast with that of Duncanson's Flycatcher. The Firefly Mk.I's general effect was that of a scaled-down Fox with the closely-cowled engine blended equally cleanly into the fuselage lines. An airframe of composite construction was covered with fabric and twin Vickers guns fired from troughs on each side of the fuselage; a retractable radiator was fitted below the fuselage together with another of fixed type in the wings. The prototype Firefly Mk.I was the sole machine built and achieved a top speed of 188 m.p.h.

During 1926 Vickers showed that they had not lost their interest in fighters when they produced their Type 121 version of the Wibault Scout 7.C1, a parasol monoplane design by Mons. Michel Wibault, which was powered by a 455 h.p. Jupiter VI engine. The machine was built to investigate the Wibault system of all-metal airframe structure which featured also a covering of dural overall. The Wibault Scout's wings were of parallel chord and were notable for their deep section.

Although, by the mid-1920 period, Vickers had concentrated their attention to a great extent on the large, heavy class of aircraft, the firm's interests were such that they continued intermittently to construct prototype single-seat fighters. Another appeared during 1926, the Type 123 biplane using a 400 h.p. Hispano-Suiza 52 engine with its semi-circular radiator set under the lower wings' centre-section. The wings themselves were equal in span and well staggered, carrying the fuselage mid-way in the gap. Metal was used in the airframe of the fabric-covered prototype G–EBNQ which made its first flight on 11th September, 1926, development flying proceeding until, in 1928,

Fairey Firefly Mk.I with Felix engine. (Fairey Photo.)

Vickers Type 121. (Vickers Photo.)

the Type 123 prototype was converted into the Vickers Type 141 with a consequent increase in performance.

Gloster's Folland was still convinced that greater heights would have to be attained by interceptor fighters so, in spite of the abandonment of the project for a Gamecock with the turbo-supercharger Bristol Orion, a development of the Gorcock was planned, still designed around exhaust-driven supercharging.

Named Guan, three prototypes were ordered under contract by the Air Ministry to evaluate three different Napier engines. Design was started in 1925 and the first machine, J7722 with the geared 450 h.p. Lion IV, was completed in August, 1926. Its top speed was 155 m.p.h. at 16,000 ft., but this was bettered by the second Guan, J7723 fitted with the direct-drive 525 h.p. Lion VI, which reached 175 m.p.h. The pair of Lion-powered Guans were delivered to the R.A.E., at which establishment all of their trials were made.

Vickers Type 123, later rebuilt as Vickers Type 141. (Vickers Photo.)

168

Constant breaking down of the exhaust-turbo-superchargers led finally to their relinquishment and was responsible for the cancellation of the third Guan which was to have had the inverted, geared Lioness engine, supercharged also by an exhaust-driven blower and which, by virtue of its inversion, would have resulted in an improved view for the pilot. The unhappy experiences with attempts made to obtain satisfactory supercharging by exhaust-driven turbine systems led the R.A.E. to decide that supercharging by gearing was a superior and more reliable method. During their tests the Guans showed that they could climb to 31,000 ft. but the exhaust-driven supercharging units led to an untidy nose, with a prominent array of exposed piping as part of the installation.

Prototype Gloster Guan J7723 powered by direct-drive Lion VI. (Imperial War Museum Photo.)

During an era in which the single-engine biplane was almost uncontested among single-seat fighters, J. D. North took a drastic step when he designed the Boulton and Paul P.31 Bittern, a twin-engine monoplane which was a decade before its time in general design and in its special features. Appearing in 1927, the machine was one of the earliest of single-seat fighters with two engines and was intended for use against formations of raiding enemy bombers.

Two prototypes were built, J7936 and J7937, both of them unusual in being fitted with a pair of Lynx engines which developed only 230 h.p. each. Alternative power plants of double this output were available which would have conferred a far superior performance on the Bittern in every respect in its allotted task of speedy interception. The wings were mounted at the shoulder position, the pilot's open cockpit being located at the leading edge with an excellent view over the finely-shaped nose. Aft of the leading edge the fuselage sides were flat and the wingtips of J7936 were square-cut in plan and

The twin-engine, single-seat Boulton and Paul P.31 Bittern. (Boulton Paul Photo.)

Bristol Type 101, shown in its original form. (Bristol Photo.)

section. The same machine's engines were set centrally with the thrust line passing through the wings' profile. Two Lewis guns were carried and the top speed of J7936 was 145 m.p.h.

The second Bittern, J7937, differed in several prominent ways from the first example. Instead of being mounted with close cowlings in their nacelles, the two Lynx engines were underslung with open fronts and in Townend rings. The parallel-chord wings retained the same thickness until they tapered in section at their tips, in place of the constant taper in section used on J7936. J7937's wings were braced below by V struts to the undercarriage, the whole arrangement of bracing struts displaying greater complexity than on the first Bittern. Instead of being fixed to fire forwards, J7937's pair of Lewis guns were mounted in barbettes on each side of the nose to incline from 0° to 45° in elevation, with the complete ring-and-bead gunsight hinged on a frame and connected to the guns so that it was elevated in concert with the guns. The entire armament system could therefore be raised as a single unit to fire upwards at hostile bombers.

The Bittern was extremely advanced and purposeful in conception for its time but possessed a layout and innovations which were not to make their mark and find official favour for a number of years.

Bristol's interest in the two-seat fighter was still alive during 1926 so that, towards the end of the year, Frank Barnwell started a new design which made its initial flight on 5th August, 1927, piloted by Cyril Uwins. Designated Type 101 and powered with the 450 h.p. Jupiter VI in place of the Mercury engine scheduled originally, the machine was an eminently clean biplane of equal span and with well-staggered, single-bay wings. The wooden fuselage, hexagonal in section, was mounted at mid-gap and faired into the lower centre-section on a pylon mounting. Plywood was used as a fuselage covering, the metal-framed wings utilizing fabric. The pilot was provided with twin Vickers guns in fuselage side-troughs while the rear cockpit, set close behind that of the pilot, carried a single Lewis gun on a Scarff ring. The field of fire for the gunner was particularly good by virtue of the low setting of the upper wings and the relatively high location of the gun mounting. The Type 101 reached a top speed of 150 m.p.h. and was employed extensively for engine testing. It was registered G–EBOW, being converted later to a single-seater and used for air racing.

Bristol thoughts in the single-seat fighter field were centred for a while in 1927 on a project for an adaptation of the Type 99 Badminton racer, to be powered by a Jupiter engine and designated Type 102A; the scheme, however, was not pursued.

1926 had found Gloster, in company with several other manufacturers, in the midst of the transition to metal construction, resulting in a decision to adapt the Gamecock to the new form and, concurrently, to test one or two other recent innovations. The single prototype G.30 Goldfinch, J7940, was ready by 1927 and incorporated two new types of high-tensile steel wing spar. The deep-section upper wings made use of the Gloster-developed Lattice Girder spar, while the thin lower wings were formed around the box-section spar devised by the Steel Wing Company. The Goldfinch used a supercharged 450 h.p. Jupiter VII engine and carried the standard fuselage-mounted armament of two Vickers guns. J7940's fin extended forwards along the upper decking and the all-metal airframe was covered with fabric.

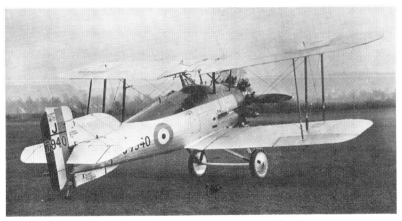

Gloster Goldfinch with extended fin. (Gloster Photo.)

Vickers Vireo. (Vickers Photo.)

The Goldfinch's all-round performance was excellent with a top speed of 157 m.p.h. at 20,000 ft., a service ceiling of just on 27,000 ft., and rate of climb of 1,500 ft./min. Air Ministry trials were satisfactory so that, when the call came for a replacement all-metal, day-and-night fighter for the R.A.F., the Goldfinch should have stood a good chance of winning. Ultimately, when the official specification was issued, the Gloster design fell short of the requirements in payload and fuel capacity and Bristol reaped the reward with their Bulldog to Specification F.9/26.

The experience which Vickers had gained with construction of the Wibault Scout in 1926 was incorporated in the Vireo experimental single-seat naval fighter of 1927. The machine was, for its time, very advanced in conception as a cantilever low-wing monoplane with commendably clean lines, the flying surfaces being tapered and angular at their extremities. N211, the single Vireo built, carried on the Wibault system of a metal airframe throughout, covered overall with metal sheeting. The Vireo was yet another of the fighters of the period to be fitted with the relatively low-power 230 h.p. Lynx engine. Although no production was undertaken, the machine is notable as a praiseworthy predecessor of the all-metal low-wing monoplanes which were to become the accepted basic layout some ten years later.

Concurrently, Gloster were continuing and cultivating their successful and remunerative association with the Imperial Japanese Navy and started the design in July, 1927, of a new single-seat, shipboard fighter as a potential successor to the Sparrowhawk. Named the Gambet, Folland's new venture resembled the Gamecock and was completed by December, 1927. A 420 h.p. Jupiter VI was installed in the nose of the wooden fuselage and the wings carried on the Gloster H.L.B. concept. Two Vickers guns, with 600 rounds each, fired from channels in the fuselage sides and four 20 lb. bombs could be carried in the rack. Comprehensive equipment included flotation bags in the rear fuselage and oxygen for the pilot. In its trials the Gambet was as pleasant to handle as the Gamecock, recording a top speed of 148 m.p.h. and a service ceiling of 22,950 ft. The Gambet was shipped to Japan where it was entered as J–AAMB by the Mitsui Company in the 1928 Ship Fighter Competition. In the face of stiff opposition, the Gambet won the contest and a production order for Mitsui who subsequently constructed a sizeable number for the Imperial Japanese Navy.

Gloster were encouraged by their success to suggest to the Air Ministry that a Gambet should be submitted for trials at Martlesham Heath as, with a top speed some 15 m.p.h. faster than contemporary service shipboard fighters and a superior overall performance, the machine could well have proved a useful successor to the Fleet Air Arm's current equipment. The Air Ministry were, however, "...... regretfully, not interested".

As fighter development proceeded, the never-ending demand for increased all-round performance meant more powerful engines which needed stronger and heavier airframes to absorb their greater power. New internal equipment of a more comprehensive nature sent the weight up to an even higher level. The Air Ministry perceived that heavier firepower would have to be incorporated in future designs and, accordingly, issued in 1924 Specification 4/24 calling for a multi-seat, twin-engine fighter capable of bearing aloft two automatic shell-firing guns to meet and defeat enemy aircraft which might appear armed with heavy calibre cannon. Two firms, Bristol and Westland, felt the requirement to be worthy of their attention, each producing prototypes of widely-differing concept.

For Westland Arthur Davenport started in 1925 the design of the Westbury relying on the quite conservative layout of a large three-bay, non-staggered,

Gloster Gambet prototype J–AAMB. (Gloster Photo.)

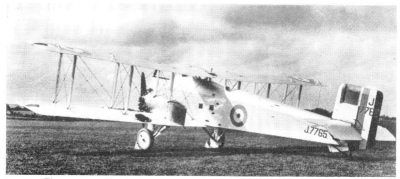

First prototype Westland Westbury, fitted with wooden wings. (Westland Photo.)

J7767, the Bristol Type 95 Bagshot. (Bristol Photo.)

Westland Wizard Mk.II with revised ailerons and thin centre-section. (Westland Photo.)

174

biplane with its pair of 450 h.p. Jupiter VI engines faired into nacelles on the upper surface of the lower wings. Two versions were built—J7765 with composite fuselage construction and wooden wings, and J7766 with wings using dural spars. The Westbury's main feature was its armament which comprised two 37 mm. C.O.W. guns, that in the nose being fitted on a rotatable ring platform, while the second was installed to fire forwards and upwards from a cockpit just aft of the trailing edge. In addition, the rear gunner was expected to deal with any attacks from below by firing a Lewis gun through an opening in the floor of the fuselage. An alternative to the rear C.O.W. gun installation was provided by making the portion of the rear decking around it replaceable with another section complete with a Scarff-mounted Lewis gun. Equipment included oxygen for the crew of three and radio. After completion in 1927 J7765 made its first flights in the hands of Capt. Frank Courtney; Maj. L. P. Openshaw, who undertook the rest of the flying programme of the Westburys, flew J7766 in its initial trials.

Bristol's prototype, the Type 95 Bagshot, was vastly different from the Westbury in its approach to Specification 4/24. Barnwell adopted the radical and advanced layout of a shoulder-wing, cantilever monoplane which was christened originally the Bludgeon. Aft of the nose turret which housed one of the pair of 37 mm. C.O.W. guns the fuselage was triangular in section and wide-chord fairings, amounting almost to stub wings, were attached to the undercarriage axles. The second C.O.W. gun was carried amidships behind the wings and the same cockpit mounted also a single Lewis gun to the rear. Two 515 h.p. Jupiter VIs provided the power for the Bagshot and Capt. Uwins made the maiden flight on 15th July, 1927, at Filton. Despite the deep section used in the wings, flexing of the planes was encountered, resulting in aileron reversal. The Bagshot, with its wingspread of 70 ft., was 2 ft. greater in span than the Westbury, and was of metal throughout covered with fabric.

Although official interest in the specification's requirements eventually lapsed, both the Westbury and the Bagshot provided useful experience for their respective constructors in solving structural and armament problems. When the cannon was finally adopted in later years its form of installation was quite different from that envisaged by the designers of the late 1920s, trying to evolve with the means at their disposal the best method for the use of the heavy guns in a fighter.

While work had been proceeding on the big multi-seat Westbury, Westland turned also to a new single-seat fighter, the Wizard, as a Private Venture design of parasol monoplane type, based upon experience with their successful Widgeon lightplane. Davenport favoured an all-wood structure for the machine, with a fuselage of oval section, in the nose of which was mounted an exposed 490 h.p. Rolls-Royce Falcon III installed with surprisingly little attempt to blend it cleanly into the otherwise well-streamlined fuselage. Outboard of the ailerons, the trailing edge tapered very slightly on wings of constantly thick section from tip to tip.

The Wizard made its first flights with Maj. L. P. Openshaw as pilot, who was faced with a forced landing when an air lock occurred in the fuel pipes.

The machine was badly damaged on turning over during the ensuing alighting in a field near Yeovil and there were doubts about the advisibility of reconstructing it.

Finally, however, it was decided that repair was worth while, but a new fuselage was designed using a system of metal-tubing structure devised by Westland. J9252, designated Wizard Mk.I, was a great improvement in appearance over the original version. The engine, a 490 h.p. Rolls-Royce F.XI, was cowled in a finely-shaped nose, complete with spinner, which did justice to the rest of the fuselage. A new rudder of refined outline replaced the earlier crude, angular type and a retractable radiator was housed in the belly. In addition to the pair of Vickers guns in side troughs, the Wizard could carry four 20 lb. bombs in an under-fuselage rack.

The Air Ministry had shown enough interest to award Westland a development contract to assist in a small way financially and, early in 1928, testing was resumed by Flt.Lt. L. G. Paget. The Wizard Mk.I showed its paces in public at the R.A.F. Display at Hendon in July, 1928, with particular emphasis on its excellent climb rate of 2,000 ft./min. at 10,000 ft. At the request of the Air Ministry the wings were then revised to embody a thinner centre-section in an attempt to improve the view. At the same time the engine was changed to a 480 h.p. Kestrel IIS. Hopes were entertained that the Wizard in its new Mk.II form might be ordered to equip the R.A.F. but, following the modifications, the performance deteriorated and official policy still continued to favour the biplane as a standard fighter formula.

The R.A.F.'s Gamecocks and Siskins were giving good service with thirteen squadrons in the United Kingdom but, with the speed of bombers increasing sharply in the constant battle of wits to elude fighter defences, the time had come to prepare for re-equipping the fighter units.

The first step was taken with the issue in April, 1926, of Specification F.9/26 to cover a replacement single-seat, day-and-night fighter with an air-cooled radial engine and armament of two Vickers guns. F.9/26 was an extremely interesting challenge to Britain's fighter designers and was the first specification to produce a sizeable new crop of prototypes, nine of which were ordered.

At Hawker Sydney Camm was quickly off the mark and despite the rapidly-increasing complexities in design brought about by steady, unceasing development, his Hawfinch—which made its first flight in March, 1927—was the first of the F.9/26 contenders to take to the air. The Bristol Jupiter, reliable and well-developed, found itself as the engine selected for the majority of the machines built to the requirement and was chosen initially in its 455 h.p. Mk.VI version for the Hawfinch. The aircraft, J8776, possessed excellent, well-balanced proportions in an unequal-span, two-bay biplane with accentuated stagger, and which used the Hawker all-metal structure in its airframe. The Hawfinch went to Martlesham Heath for its official tests in July, 1927, but with a 450 h.p. Jupiter VII as its power. In company with the Bristol Bulldog, it led the field in the F.9/26 competition but was finally narrowly beaten by the Bristol product.

Hawker Hawfinch with double-bay wings and Watts wooden propeller. (Hawker Photo.)

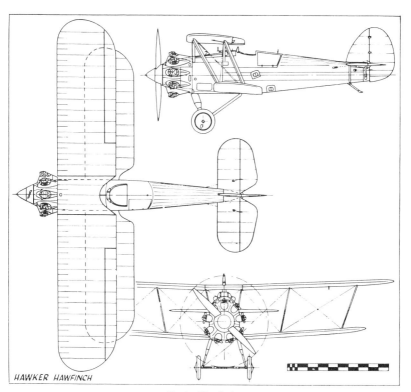

HAWKER HAWFINCH

Hawker Hawfinch

On return to its parent firm in mid-1928, the Hawfinch was converted by September to single-bay wings for a while and went to Felixstowe for trials as a seaplane. During 1929 and for the ensuing two years, flying also with the 400 h.p. Jaguar V, it was employed on experimental work which yielded useful information to Hawker as a valuable guide in future designs.

The winner from Bristol of the F.9/26 production contract, the Type 105 Bulldog, was a compact single-bay biplane of all-metal construction, conceived by Frank Barnwell with detail design by L. G. Frise, which Cyril Uwins took on its maiden flight on 17th May, 1927. A particular feature of the design was the special attention paid to providing the pilot with a good field of view. The rebuilt prototype Bulldog Mk.I reappeared late in 1927 but was markedly different from the original in having wings of greatly increased area while retaining single-bay layout. The whole appearance was disproportionate in the attempt to attain an improved ceiling and rate of climb.

Following testing second thoughts were evident in the Bulldog Mk.II prototype of 1928 which was somewhat different from the first Mk.I. The fuselage was longer and the vertical tail surfaces were far shapelier than before. The general result of the alterations was to give a far more balanced effect to the entire design, and in this form with minor changes—among them the deletion of the headrest—the Bulldog went into production for the R.A.F. to become one of its best-known fighters. Making its first flight on 21st January, 1928, J9480—the first production Mk.II—had a 450 h.p. Jupiter VII engine as had the initial production examples but later models used the 490 h.p. Jupiter VIIF.

Development of the Bulldog continued and by 1931 the Mk.IIA had made its appearance. Modifications incorporated over a period included an improved oil system, a stronger airframe, an undercarriage of broader track and with larger tyres, a new fin of greater area, and a tailwheel in place of the skid. With the Jupiter VIIF engine, the Mk.IIA returned a top speed of 174 m.p.h. at 10,000 ft., production taking place to Specification 11/31.

The Bulldog was such an outstanding success that a number of foreign air arms soon became interested in acquiring it. Even the United States Navy, normally entirely dependent on the products of American companies, thought it worth investigation and a Bulldog Mk.II was sent to Anacostia in 1929. Testing revealed aileron flutter and failure of wing ribs during T.V. dives, resulting in another Bulldog, U.S.N. serial A8607, being sent out in 1930 with mass-balanced ailerons and strengthened ribs.

Another entry in the list for F.9/26 honours was provided by Boulton and Paul of Norwich with their P.33 biplane, which was named Partridge in July, 1926. Out of the specified F.9/26 choice of engines of Armstrong Siddeley Jaguar V, Bristol Mercury, Bristol Orion with turbo-supercharger, or steam-cooled Rolls-Royce Falcon X, J. D. North selected finally the Mercury after a preliminary design had been laid down using the Jupiter in advance of the ultimate settling of details of the specification. As with a number of other

The first prototype Bristol Bulldog Mk.I. (Bristol Photo.)

The prototype Bristol Bulldog Mk.II developed from the second Mk.I prototype. (Bristol Photo.)

K1080, a production Bristol Bulldog Mk.II. (Bristol Photo.)

179

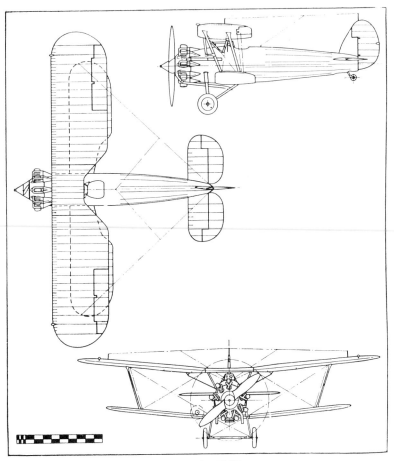

Bristol Bulldog Mk.IIA

aircraft of the period scheduled to use the Mercury, a substitute had to be found eventually owing to the teething troubles experienced during the Mercury's development. J8459, the prototype Partridge of 1928, ultimately received the 440 h.p. Jupiter VII for its flight trials with the later-unrealized intention of installing a Mercury II engine in the unbuilt Partridge Mk.III. The Partridge itself was an entirely conventional single-bay biplane with fairly square-cut flying surfaces and attained a top speed of 167 m.p.h.

During this period a serious and successful attempt was made by Dr. H. C. H. Townend to evolve a means of cowling the radial engine which, with its large diameter, gave rise to considerable drag. The problem was to avoid impairing the cooling of the cylinders and this was effectively accomplished by Dr. Townend and the Department of Scientific and Industrial Research, in conjunction with Boulton and Paul, whose manufacturing facilities were

Bristol Bulldog Mk.IIIA. (Bristol Photo.)

employed to develop the Townend ring-cowling. The invention was instrumental in increasing the speeds of aircraft fitted with it and was a popular
device with designers for many years to improve the efficiency of their aircraft.

The S.S.18, Gloster design to the F.9/26 formula, made its first flight in
January, 1929. Fitted with a 480 h.p. Mercury IIA engine, the new machine
carried on Folland's long-established reputation of designing a product of
original but exemplary appearance. J9125, the prototype S.S.18, reverted to
two-bay layout in its staggered equal-span wings and was unusual in having
inner interplane struts of broader chord than the outer pairs. The all-metal
airframe was covered with fabric and the pair of Vickers guns fired from side
troughs in the fuselage.

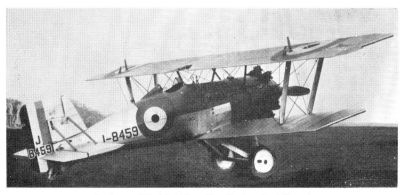

Boulton and Paul P.33 Partridge. (Boulton Paul Photo.)

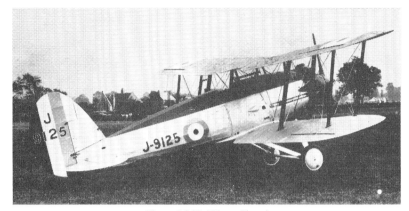

Gloster S.S.18. (Gloster Photo.)

Originally designed to use the Jaguar III as an alternative power plant, J9125 was re-engined in 1929 with the 450 h.p. Jupiter VIIF, bringing a corresponding slight increase in weight and redesignation to S.S.18A. Under S.S.18B, a proposal was made—again during 1929—to fit the higher-powered 550 h.p. Armstrong Siddeley Panther III but nothing came of the idea. Nevertheless, a great deal more was to be seen of airframe J9125 in the immediate future years.

While various fighter-inclined firms had busied themselves with F.9/26 and other requirements, Blackburn made an attempt during the late 1920s to revise the light-fighter concept and succeeded in producing in the Type 14 Lincock, designed by Maj. F. A. Bumpus with G. E. Petty as assistant chief

Blackburn Lincock Mk.II. (Blackburn Photo.)

182

engineer, a compact single-seat biplane with attractive lines—a machine which was considered by many pilots to outshine most other types for aerobatics.

Appearing in the early Summer of 1928, the all-wood Lincock Mk.I carried its finely-shaped plywood-monocoque fuselage suspended mid-way between the staggered single-bay wings. Mounted in the nose and faired well into its lines was the 235 h.p. direct-drive Lynx IV engine. The Lincock Mk.I was registered G–EBVO and armed with a pair of synchronized Vickers guns. Flown by Sqn.Ldr. J. Noakes, it took part in the 1928 King's Cup Race at an average speed of 115·32 m.p.h., later being bought by the Air Ministry.

At the Olympia Aero Show of 1929, Blackburn displayed the Lincock Mk. II, a revised version of all-metal construction with the fuselage faired into the lower wings and with a redesigned undercarriage incorporating a split axle. A geared version of the Lynx, with Fairey metal propeller, supplanted the direct-drive type and was carried by the nose mounting, which formed one of the three detachable portions of the fuselage—the two other parts being the centre unit and the rear fuselage. It was intended to show the Lincock Mk.II at the 1930 Hendon Air Display in the New Types Park but, owing to damage to the machine, its place was taken at the show by the original Mk.I version. The Lincock Mk.II was quite diminutive, with the same span of 22 ft. 6 in. as the Mk.I and an increased length of 19 ft. 6 in., compared with the Mk.I's 18 ft. 1 in. Top speed was 150 m.p.h. against 168 m.p.h. for the Mk.I.

The Lincock Mk.II was developed still further into the Mk.III, which incorporated a transverse axle in its landing gear and could be powered with the Lynx IVC as an alternative to the Lynx Major. Of the four Mk.IIIs built two were shipped to China and two to Japan, this version reaching 164 m.p.h. at 3,000 ft.

Although the three marks of Lincock possessed excellent handling qualities, the low power used—as part of the general design basis of the light fighter—limited the top speed, compared with the conventional types of fighter, to such an extent that there was no place to be found for it in an air force.

This fault was to have been rectified in the all-metal Blackcock with the 510 h.p. of the Rolls-Royce Falcon X, increased overall size and weight, and an expected top speed of 197 m.p.h. but the design, by Maj. F. A. Bumpus and B. A. Duncan, remained a project only to Specification F.20/27.

Blackburn interest in fighters persisted, however, to the extent of constructing a single Turcock during 1928 to the order of the Turkish Government. The machine was a revision of the Blackcock, fitted with the 490 h.p. Jaguar VI engine which gave it a top speed of 181 m.p.h. Completed at the beginning of 1928 and registered G–EBVP, the Turcock crashed on 13th February of the same year, ending for the time being Blackburn aspirations in the realm of single-seat fighters.

Changes in operating techniques of fleet fighters, resulting in a demand for ever-increasing performance, brought forth Specification N.21/26 for a new single-seat, deck-landing fighter for the Fleet Air Arm. Amendment of the original requirements took place in 1927 and Fairey quickly submitted a new design by Marcel Lobelle—the Flycatcher Mk.II. One prototype only, N216, was constructed and, although it shared the same name as its illustrious predecessor, the machine was a completely fresh product with no resemblance to the Flycatcher Mk.I. With Fairey airframe F873, the Mk.II was of metal throughout, covered with fabric, and mounted the 480 h.p. Mercury IIA engine with two-speed supercharger. The Flycatcher Mk.II was characterized by being a compact, single-bay biplane with strut-connected ailerons, Fairey oleo-pneumatic undercarriage and a clean nose entry around the engine. Two Vickers Mk.II ·303 machine-guns were housed in the top decking. With the Mercury engine installed N216 reached a top speed of 164 m.p.h. at 10,000 ft. but during the year of its appearance—1927—the machine was re-engined

Fairey Flycatcher Mk.II. (Fairey Photo.)

with the more powerful 540 h.p. Jaguar VIII. The Flycatcher Mk.II incorporated flotation gear and could carry four 20 lb. bombs.

The Vickers contribution to N.21/26 turned out in 1928 to be the Type 123 biplane G–EBNQ, converted into the Type 141 with the supercharged 510 h.p. Rolls-Royce F.XI in place of the Hispano-Suiza of the Type 123. The new engine conferred a much blunter appearance to the nose and its place was taken later on by the Rolls-Royce F.XII.

N.21/26 attracted, as was to be expected, a Folland-designed entry from Gloster. Designated G.28 Gnatsnapper Mk.I, the machine was an unequal-span, single-bay staggered biplane with dihedral on the upper wings only. Generous horn balances were incorporated in the tail control surfaces and the engine selected was the 480 h.p. Mercury IIA. The contract for N215 was received in June, 1928, and variable-camber wings, with Gloster lattice spars, were embodied in the aircraft.

N215 was unfortunately destroyed and a second prototype, N227, was prepared with the 485 h.p. Mercury IIIA engine to replace it. The Mercury,

Vickers Type 141 shipboard fighter to N.21/26. (Vickers Photo.)

still in its experimental stage, was in the middle of its teething troubles and was finally discarded. The 440 h.p. Jupiter VII was installed but the delivery of N227 to Martlesham in May, 1929, was too late for the Ship Fighter competition.

As a result of the difficulties encountered with the Mercury power plant, the Air Ministry decided to postpone the selection trials until 1930.

Gloster received notification in January, 1929, to redesign the Gnatsnapper

N227, second prototype Gloster Gnatsnapper, in its original form. (Gloster Photo.)

The Gloster S.S.37 Gnatsnapper Mk.III. (Rolls-Royce Photo.)

to take the supercharged 540 h.p. Jaguar VIII, N227 being delivered to Martlesham during 1930 as the Gnatsnapper Mk.II. In the course of the reconstruction the vertical tail outline was revised completely. N227 was giving a good account of itself in the contest when fate stepped in near the end and the machine turned over while landing in a high wind. After the crash it was rebuilt and used for armament trials until it went back to the Gloster factory to emerge again in June, 1930, as the S.S.35 Gnatsnapper Mk.III with two-bay wings and the 600 h.p. Rolls-Royce Kestrel V engine. Wing condensers were installed for tests of the evaporative cooling system. N227 then passed to Rolls-Royce for testing of the 600 h.p. Rolls-Royce Goshawk III which also utilized evaporative cooling.

The Hawker contribution to the field for N.21/26 took the form of the Hoopoe N237, designed by Camm during 1927 as a Private Venture which was near to the requirement but did not conform fully to it. In fact, of the designs

Hawker Hoopoe N237 with single-bay wings. (Hawker Photo.)

submitted to N.21/26, not one completely met the specification but the Hoopoe was sufficiently well favoured in the official reports of its trials at Martlesham in 1928 for continued development to appear worth while. In its original form the machine was a two-bay biplane powered by a 450 h.p. Mercury II but this was changed to the 520 h.p. Mercury VI when N237 was tested as a seaplane at Felixstowe during 1929. Later in the year, on reverting to a landplane, a drastic revision was made to the Hoopoe when shorter-span single-bay wings were fitted and the engine replaced by a 400 h.p. Jaguar V complete with Townend ring. Following further Service Trials an inner ring was fitted to the engine in the early part of 1930, but later in the year the entire

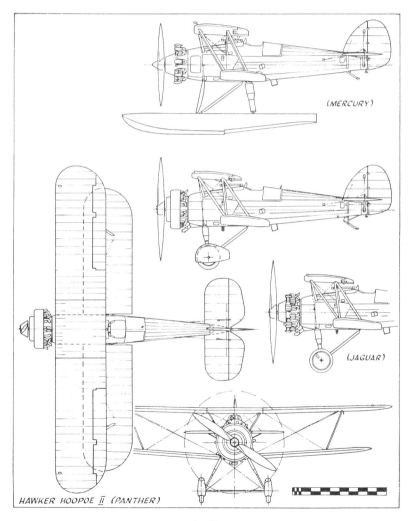

(MERCURY)

(JAGUAR)

HAWKER HOOPOE II (PANTHER)

Hawker Hoopoe

S1591, the Armstrong Whitworth A.W.16 to N.21/26, shown in its original form with horn-balanced rudder, small fin and inner ring to engine cowling. (Armstrong Whitworth Photo.)

J8027, the A.W.14 Starling Mk.I. (Flight International Photo.)

J8028, the A.W.14 Starling Mk.II. (Armstrong Whitworth Photo.)

engine installation was changed to the 560 h.p. Panther III, together with concentric Townend rings, spats and other alterations. With the Panther the Hoopoe reached a very creditable top speed of 196·5 m.p.h.

Although the naval authorities evinced a strong preference for the air-cooled radial type of engine, Hawker were convinced of the ultimate superiority of the rapidly-developing in-line, liquid-cooled power plant and were actively engaged in demonstrating its virtues, so that development of the Hoopoe came to a halt.

The A.W.16, Armstrong Whitworth contender to the N.21/26 formula, appeared in 1930 and was a well-proportioned biplane conceived by J. Lloyd. The A.W.16 was designed also as a Private Venture to conform to Specification F.9/26, being intended to embrace separately the rôles of fleet fighter, day-and-night fighter and interceptor. In the first two cases it carried W/T equipment.

The naval version, to N.21/26, was S1591 with its 540 h.p. Panther engine surrounded by a Townend ring, the exhausts being of the stub type. Extensive tests were carried out on the machine at the A.&A.E.E. for some two years and resulted in modifications being made to S1591 which included deletion of the horn balance on the rudder, the provision of a new fin which extended forwards and was of increased area, and the removal of the inner ring of the Townend cowling from the front of the engine.

Another Armstrong Whitworth single-seat fighter of the 1928 period was the A.W.14 Starling Mk.I interceptor J8027, a rather portly unequal-span, single-bay biplane fitted with an uncowled 385 h.p. Jaguar VII and twin Vickers guns. Wings and tailplane were square-cut and the Starling Mk.I was exhibited at the 1929 Olympia Aero Show in the form of J8027 in civilian markings G–AAHC, with the supercharged 450 h.p. Jaguar IV in a Townend ring.

The second Starling, the Mk.II J8028, differed in several respects from the Mk.I J8027, while bearing the same name. A taller undercarriage permitted the use of a larger-diameter propeller and simplified pairs of interplane struts replaced the N type of J8027. A Panther II engine was fitted and J8028 was used to test modifications for the A.W.19 two-seat general-purpose biplane. The Mk.II's lower wings were of considerably shorter span than those of J8027.

A third A.W.14, also under the name Starling, appeared during 1935 but, although the two later Starlings differed considerably from the Mk.I J8027, it was not felt necessary to redesignate them as production was not contemplated, construction being confined to the three examples only.

1929 brought forth another single-seat biplane fighter from Vickers, the Type 143, developed from the Type 141 of the previous year and fitted with the 450 h.p. Jupiter VIA. Apart from the change to a radial engine, the Type 143 used a split-axle undercarriage and was of note in being equipped with tip skids under the lower wings. The fuselage, as in the Type 141, was suspended mid-way between the wings and bore a pair of Vickers guns in side channels. The 34 ft. span of the Type 143 was the same as that of the Type 141, but

Vickers Type 143 produced for Bolivia. (Vickers Photo.)

wing area was lower by virtue of a reduction in chord. The fabric-covered all-metal Type 143, tested also with the 440 h.p. Jupiter VII, was produced for the Bolivian Air Force specifically to be able to cope successfully with flying from an aerodrome situated at a height of 14,000 ft. All-round performance of the Type 143 was slightly better than that of the Type 141.

Specification F.10/27 for a multi-gun, high-altitude single-seat, interceptor fighter resulted in 1928 in the A.10 from Saunders-Roe and the S.S.19A from Gloster.

Henry Knowler's design for Saro was a single-bay unequal-span biplane drawn up around the in-line 490 h.p. Rolls-Royce F.XIS engine which had a tunnel radiator fitted with a shutter of the roller-blind type. The centre-section of the large upper wings was thinned considerably to improve the pilot's view and the A.10 carried four fuselage-mounted machine-guns—one each side and a pair on the top decking. The first flight of the A.10 took place on 10th January, 1929, but no production ensued.

Saro A.10 with tambour radiator shutter open. (Saro Photo.)

The Gloster entry for F.10/27 consisted of the versatile J9125 airframe which, since it had been the S.S.18A, had become the S.S.19 in 1932 with the 450 h.p. Jupiter VIIF in a Townend ring and had reached, in this form, a top speed of 193·5 m.p.h.

To conform to Specification F.10/27 J9125 was redesignated S.S.19A and retained the Jupiter VIIF but had its armament increased to, for the period, the phenomenal number of six machine-guns installed as two in the fuselage sides, two in the upper centre-section and two in the lower wings. The S.S.19A was the most heavily-armed single-seat fighter of its time and represented a positive step forward in Folland's design philosophy. The S.S.19A's two-bay wings conferred the necessary rigidity for aerobatics and fast dives, its narrow-chord Frise ailerons endowed it with excellent handling characteristics in the air, and Palmer pneumatic brakes assisted its qualities on the ground. Although not adopted in its S.S.19A form, the design was progressing steadily nearer to acceptance.

Blackburn Nautilus. (Blackburn Photo.)

Among the naval specifications issued during 1926 was O.22/26, calling for a new two-seat, fleet spotter reconnaissance aircraft with high performance and able, if necessary, to act as an interceptor fighter to a limited extent. It was not until 1929 that the requirement began to bear fruit as several firms hope-fully produced their interpretations as prototypes. Handley Page tentatively prepared their H.P.37 design but it progressed no further than the project stage.

The Blackburn contribution to O.22/26, designed by Maj. F. A. Bumpus, appeared in 1929 as the Nautilus N234, a handsome, staggered, unequal-span, two-bay biplane fitted with the 520 h.p. Rolls-Royce Kestrel F.XIIMS. The engine was faired superbly into the fuselage by its cowling and the radiator filled the gap very neatly between the fuselage and the lower wings. The pilot's Vickers gun fired from a trough on the port side of the fuselage, while the observer used a single Lewis gun.

Fairey were naturally in the running and Marcel Lobelle designed the Fleetwing N235, Fairey airframe F.1132, for completion in 1929. The machine was a very clean single-bay biplane with a finely-cowled 480 h.p.

Fairey Fleetwing with wide-chord interplane struts, wire aileron link and rudder without horn balance. (Fairey Photo.)

Kestrel IIS which replaced the Kestrel I with which the Fleetwing first flew. N235 was modified with slimmer interplane struts, a larger fin, a horn-balanced rudder and a strut connecting the ailerons in place of the cable link. The rear Lewis gun utilized the Fairey high-speed mounting and the pilot was provided with a single Vickers gun in the usual fuselage channel to port.

From Short Bros. came the Gurnard biplane to O.22/26, two of which were built—the landplane N228 with the 540 h.p. Jupiter X, and the 525 h.p. Kestrel F.XIIMS-powered N229 which was tested with normal land under-carriage, with twin floats and also as an amphibian using forwards-retracting wheels on each side of a single central float in conjunction with two wingtip

Short Gurnard N229 with Kestrel F.XIIMS and amphibian undercarriage. (Short Photo.)

Short Gurnard N229 on twin floats. (Short Photo.)

stabilizing floats. The Gurnard was designed with the accent on the fighter rôle and carried the usual pilot's single Vickers gun and observer's single Lewis gun, the rear weapon being fitted on a Short ring mounting.

The O.22/26 requirement was met finally by Hawker after modifying J9052, the Hart prototype, following the machine's evaluation by the R.A.F. After acceptance by the F.A.A. the type went into production as the Osprey under Specification 19/30 and served well for many years. Several different marks of Kestrel were used in the various versions of the Osprey and a stainless-steel main structure was later adopted in place of the earlier steel-tubing and aluminium framework to avoid corrosion in naval use.

Short Gurnard N228 fitted with Jupiter X. (Short Photo.)

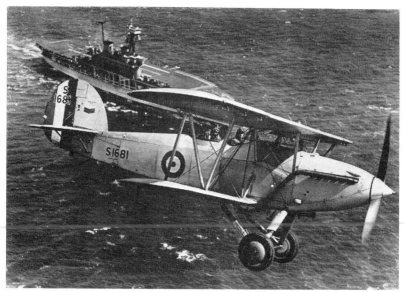

Hawker Osprey Mk.I. (Rolls-Royce Photo.)

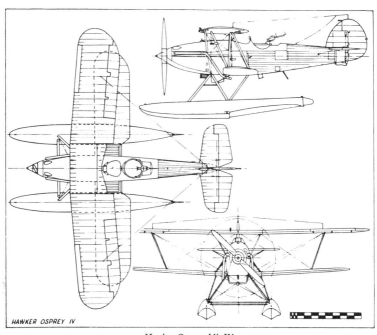

HAWKER OSPREY IV

Hawker Osprey Mk.IV

194

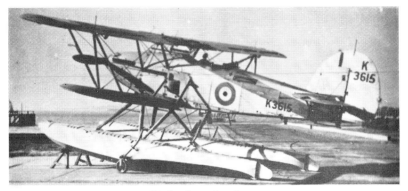

Hawker Osprey floatplane.

While fighter performance was increasing in every respect, bombers were being developed concurrently to outstrip a defence force's interceptors. To combat the ever-mounting capabilities of the hostile bomber the Air Ministry in 1927 found it necessary to issue Specification F.20/27 for a single-seat, high-altitude, interceptor fighter, armed with a pair of Vickers machine-guns and powered by an air-cooled radial engine.

The prospect of a useful order tempted a number of companies to submit an interesting selection of contrasting prototypes. Among the biplanes was the Hawker F.20/27, designed by Sydney Camm and using the 450 h.p. Jupiter VII engine. The single prototype J9123 made its first flight at Brooklands in August, 1928, flown by P. W. S. Bulman. Martlesham Heath trials late in 1928 returned a top speed of 190 m.p.h. and a change of engine in 1930 to the 520 h.p. Mercury VI increased it to 202 m.p.h. at 10,000 ft. The in-line liquid-cooled engine was rapidly asserting its particular quality of superior streamline form over the radial and Hawker did not pursue the F.20/27 design any further.

Hawker F.20/27 J9123. (Hawker Photo.)

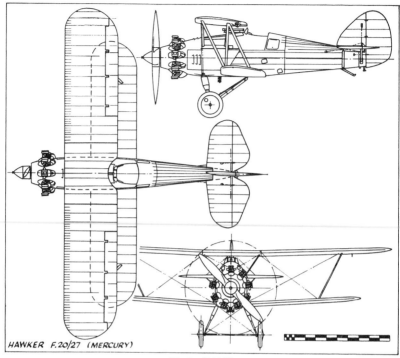

HAWKER F.20/27 (MERCURY)

Hawker F.20/27

The Bristol aspirant to F.20/27 consisted of the Type 107 Bullpup J9051, a 450 h.p. Mercury II-powered revised smaller version of the Bulldog which, although faster and considered to be pleasanter to fly than the Bulldog, did not possess its predecessor's generally well-balanced and pleasingly-proportioned appearance. Capt. Uwins made the initial flight with the Bullpup on 26th April, 1928, and J9051 subsequently flew with a short-stroke version of the Mercury and appeared at the 1934 S.B.A.C. Display equipped with the sleeve-valve Bristol Aquila III engine. Included in the Bullpup's design was provision for increased armament consisting of either two or four Lewis guns installed under the lower wings.

At Fairey Marcel Lobelle designed the Firefly Mk.II, a very competent-looking Private Venture biplane with excellent lines and the supercharged 480 h.p. Kestrel IIS for power, which first flew on 5th February, 1929. Although no production ensued in Britain, the Firefly Mk.II was built in Belgium by Avions Fairey at Gosselies for the Belgian Air Force.

The main reason behind the F.20/27 specification was the desire of the Air Ministry to encourage the development of a new class of fast-climbing inter-ceptor fighter in place of types used to carry out the old concept of maintaining standing patrols. The radial engine was far from favoured for the purpose by some constructors and de Havilland produced a low-wing monoplane, the

Bristol Type 107 Bullpup fitted with Mercury. (Bristol Photo.)

D.H.77 J9771, as a Private Venture to the requirement, a machine designed by W. G. Carter which employed the 301 h.p. Napier Rapier I and later the 295 h.p. Rapier II with their superbly-low frontal area. The D.H.77's first flight was made early in December, 1929, by Hubert Broad at Stag Lane.

For the Westland entry, Arthur Davenport designed the F.20/27 Interceptor low-wing monoplane around the 440 h.p. Mercury IIA engine. Features of the design included cut-away wing roots to improve vision, oxygen, exhaust-heated guns, a door to the cockpit, Frise-type ailerons and oleo-pneumatic undercarriage legs and brakes. The Interceptor J9124's initial take-off was made during 1929 by Flt.Lt. L. G. Paget but the Mercury was still in the

Bristol Type 107 Bullpup with Aquila engine. (Bristol Photo.)

Fairey Firefly Mk.IIM to F.20/27. (Fairey Photo.)

throes of its development difficulties. A change was made to the 420 h.p. Jupiter VII and, at the same time, other modifications were carried out which included the fitting of a fin and rudder of high aspect ratio, a shorter headrest and slightly shorter ring cowling in front of the new engine. Although not developed beyond the single prototype J9124 provided a useful fund of experience when the time came to design the Westland C.O.W. gun monoplane.

In common with de Havilland and Westland, Vickers also decided to adopt the low-wing monoplane layout for their F.20/27 entry—the Type 151 Jockey Mk.I. The machine, J9122, was a pleasing design of 1929 with square-cut, metal-covered flying surfaces, constructed on the Wibault principles. The rear portion of the fuselage was clad with fabric and the nose mounted an uncowled 450 h.p. Jupiter VIIF which was changed later to a 500 h.p. Mercury IIA. The divided-axle undercarriage incorporated hydraulically-operated Vickers brakes and the pair of Vickers guns were installed in the fore-decking to fire between the engine cylinders. The Gloster F.20/27 contender which made a late appearance in 1933, designated S.S.19B, was J9125 modified yet again, using the 530 h.p. Mercury IVS.2 and with its armament reduced from the six machine-guns of the S.S.19A to but two Vickers in the nose. In this final form S.S.19B J9125 served as the prototype of the Gauntlet.

The Air Ministry eventually recognised that the slim, powerful in-line engine was destined inevitably to be the power unit of the future for fighters and accordingly amended Specification F.20/27 during 1928 to require the Rolls-Royce F.XI Kestrel to be the engine used. The employment of the Kestrel as a bomber's power plant had so increased the performance of that type of aircraft that, while the prototypes to the original F.20/27 were being evolved, the specification's requirements fell far short of being able to produce

de Havilland D.H.77 J9771. (de Havilland Photo.)

an interceptor with sufficiently advanced capabilities to combat the new class of bombers emerging.

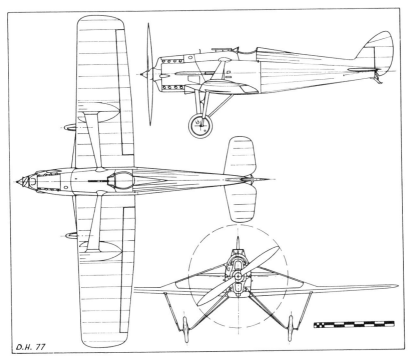

D.H.77

Vickers Type 151 Jockey Mk.I with Mercury IIA. (Vickers Photo.)

Westland F.20/27 with Jupiter VII and high aspect ratio fin and rudder. (Westland Photo.)

J9124, the Westland F.20/27, fitted with Mercury IIA and low aspect ratio fin and rudder. (Westland Photo.)

200

J9125 as the Gloster S.S.19B. (Gloster Photo.)

At Kingston, Sydney Camm swiftly produced a new design, the Hornet, to meet the amended F.20/27 formula and the machine, a compact biplane with superb lines and performance to match, aroused great interest when on display at the 1929 Olympia Aero Show. The Hornet's first engine, the Rolls-Royce F.XIA, was soon exchanged for the 480 h.p. Rolls-Royce F.XIS and the aircraft became J9682. Official trials at Martlesham Heath quickly confirmed the Hornet's potentialities, resulting in orders being placed for it during 1930 for the R.A.F. as the Fury.

1929 saw the appearance of a new design from Harold Bolas for a single-seat shipboard fighter—the Parnall Pipit N232. The promising 495 h.p. Rolls-Royce F.XI was chosen for it and was cowled to give an extremely fine nose entry. Four ailerons formed part of the staggered, equal-span, two-bay wings and the cooling system utilized a retractable radiator beneath the fuselage, in conjunction with an auxiliary skin-type radiator forming part of the upper centre-section. An alternative two-float undercarriage could be fitted and the Pipit's armament consisted of the standard pair of nose-mounted Vickers guns.

The second half of the 1920s had witnessed the rapid rise of the biplane fighter until it was approaching the zenith of its designers' art. All-metal airframe construction had supplanted wood and the liquid-cooled in-line engine was well on the way to displacing completely the air-cooled radial.

The wearing of parachutes, incredibly long overdue, had finally become compulsory during 1925, after an untold number of brave lives—those of dearly-loved sons, husbands and fathers—had been allowed to be lost needlessly over the years in the most scandalous manner, as though human life were of no value whatsoever to those in whose hands lay the responsibility for providing adequate equipment for the Nation's aircrew.

Hawker Hornet prototype J9062, predecessor of the Fury. (Hawker Photo.)

The Schneider Trophy Contests continued to act as a stimulant of the greatest value to Britain's airframe and engine development, the contending seaplanes coming chiefly from Supermarine and Gloster, powered by engines produced by Rolls-Royce and Napier. Mitchell at Supermarine and Folland at Gloster continued to contribute superb examples from their drawing-boards to form the British Schneider teams which, from 1927, were composed of R.A.F. personnel. The multitude of formidable problems met and overcome

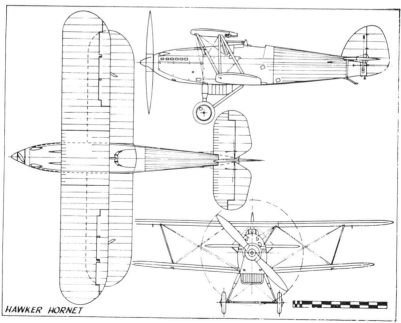

HAWKER HORNET

Hawker Hornet

Parnall Pipit. (Rolls-Royce Photo.)

in the course of designing for the exciting series of Schneider duels enabled the designers and engineers concerned to add to their store of knowledge of high-speed flight as no other means would have done. 1927 witnessed the Supermarine S.5 triumphant at Venice and the following year Vickers (Aviation) Ltd. took over the Supermarine organization. 1929 was another Schneider victory year for Supermarine with the S.6 and the 1931 success for the S.6B brought the Trophy to a permanent home in Great Britain without any realization of just how much the sporting triumphs were to contribute towards the fighters which, a few years hence, would save the British Isles in perilous times.

Vickers Type 177 Private Venture shipboard fighter. (Vickers Photo.)

CHAPTER FIVE

CHANGE—AND A CHOICE

The winds of change have shown themselves to blow more swiftly, perhaps, across the field of aircraft development than over any other area of technical achievement.

The time for the first great metamorphosis for the fighter came during the 1930s when the advanced ideas which had been simmering in the brains of designers for many years, appearing briefly now and then in prototype form, finally came to be accepted in the revolution which forcibly took place in fighter concepts.

Nothing could stem the ultimate replacement of the biplane by the developed monoplane, but some years were yet to elapse before the monoplane had finally liquidated the opposition.

Official specifications continued to issue forth from the Air Ministry, engaging the attention of interested concerns, but the occasional Private Venture fighter still made its appearance. From Vickers in 1930 there came the single-seat Type 177, a biplane of conventional and purposeful appearance, powered by the 540 h.p. Jupiter XF in a Townend ring. The Type 177's top speed was 190 m.p.h. at 13,120 ft., and the design carried on the feature favoured in the previous Vickers Types 123, 141 and 143 of a fuselage mounted at mid-gap in the wings.

The Hawker Hornet, in its final form as the Fury, epitomized the peak of development of the liquid-cooled biplane single-seat fighter as a production entity for the R.A.F. The renaming of the Hornet took place to conform to the new 1927 system of Air Ministry nomenclature in which land-based fighters were to have names beginning with the initial F and fleet fighters with the initial N.

In competitive trials of J9682 with the Fairey Firefly Mk.IIM, the Fury won its right to selection as the R.A.F.'s new interceptor and went into production to Specification 13/30 in its Mk.I version, an initial batch of twenty-one being ordered in August, 1930. Rated at 14,000 ft., the 525 h.p. Kestrel IIS drove a two-blade wooden Watts propeller and the first production Fury, K1926, was test-flown at Brooklands on 25th March, 1931, by P. E. G. Sayer. Initial proud recipients of the R.A.F.'s first fighter with a speed exceeding 200 m.p.h. were the members of No. 43 Squadron at Tangmere, who quickly became adept at showing off their dazzling new mounts to an admiring public. Although it showed a great advance in performance in one step, the Fury—as with many great and successful designs—was essentially a straightforward, practical product, simple to construct and to maintain in service.

Not to be outdone by the Royal Air Force, the Fleet Air Arm lost little time in showing interest in a fleet fighter version of the Fury and Specification 16/30 was drawn up around Hawker proposals. The outcome was the Rolls-Royce F.XIMS-powered Norn, H.N.1, first flown early in 1930, followed by the first prototype Nimrod, S1577, and the first production Nimrod Mk.I, S1578, with Kestrel IIMS. Wingspan was greater than that of the Fury and naval equipment added included flotation bags in wings and fuselage. The all-metal airframe was designed to take an alternative detachable wheel or float undercarriage.

In addition to S1578, S1577 was tested as a seaplane and M.A.E.E. Felix-stowe Report F/119 of February, 1934, issued on S1577 fitted with twin dural floats noted that the machine was excellent for maintenance but that take-off was rather dirty until it was planing on the step. In the air it tended to remain inverted after rolls, was unstable longitudinally and required careful control in steep dives. No-wind take-off was achieved in 13·5 secs., top speed was 159 kt., service ceiling 26,000 ft. and climb 1,520 ft./min. at sea level.

Star of the Hendon Air Displays of the 1930s, the Hawker Fury Mk.I. K1926, the first production example, is seen at Brooklands. (Rolls-Royce Photo.)

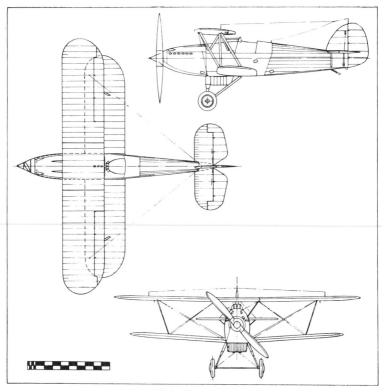

Hawker Fury Mk.I

Nimrod K2823 was altered to have sweepback on upper and lower wings and fitted with a Kestrel VFP, developing 608 h.p. at 11,000 ft., and rams-horn exhaust manifolds. Known as the Intermediate Nimrod, it served to develop the Nimrod Mk.II to Specification 11/33, earning for itself good recommendations in A.& A.E.E. Martlesham Report M/594a/2 of December, 1935. Flown to 28,600 ft., the estimated absolute ceiling was 29,800 ft., a speed of 192 m.p.h. being reached at 14,000 ft. The landplane Nimrod was some 250 lb. lighter than its counterpart on floats and K2823 with its Kestrel V, tested against K2824 using a Kestrel IIS, was 15 m.p.h. faster at 20,000 ft. and reduced the time to reach the same height by 3·5 min. The Nimrod was an extremely useful addition to the Fleet Air Arm and was supplied abroad to Denmark, with Japan and Portugal receiving one each.

By standards obtaining in 1930 the Hawker Hart had a remarkably high performance, particularly compared with that of the single-seat fighters in service, and the point was emphasized sharply in the 1930 Air Exercises when the Hart showed itself faster than the defending interceptors. The machine appeared to be worth transforming into a two-seat fighter, a class of machine neglected since the days of the Bristol F.2B, and J9933—the first production

Hawker Nimrod Mk.I. (Hawker Photo.)

Hart—was selected for the purpose to Specification 15/30. The pilot's armament was increased to two Vickers guns and the gunner's Lewis was given an improved field of fire by setting the mounting at an upward angle

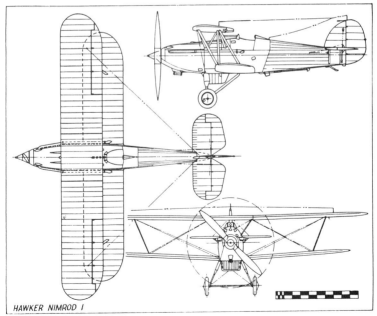

HAWKER NIMROD I

Hawker Nimrod Mk.1

The first production Hawker Demon. (Hawker Photo.)

towards the rear. As the Hart Fighter, one flight of the new machine joined
No. 23 Squadron in March, 1931, for comparative trials beside two flights
of Bulldogs.

Following experiments to improve the efficiency of the rear gun position,
the Hart Fighter went into production in 1932 to Specification 6/32 as the
Demon. No. 23 Squadron gave up its Bulldogs in April, 1933, to re-equip

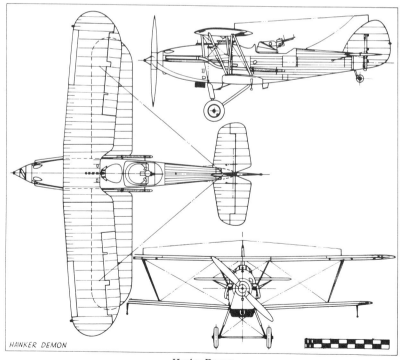

HAWKER DEMON

Hawker Demon

208

J9933, the first production Hawker Hart, as trials aircraft for Frazer-Nash turret later fitted to Demons. (Hawker Photo.)

completely with the initial batch of Demons, thus becoming the first of the new generation of two-seat fighter squadrons in the R.A.F. Development of the Demon continued, J9933 serving to prove the hydraulically-driven Frazer-Nash turret with its shield of folding segments, the object being to protect the gunner from the interference of the slipstream. The Turret-Demons were fitted with the 584 h.p. Kestrel VDR in place of the 485 h.p. Kestrel IIS of the earlier versions and appeared from the middle of 1936.

In the late 1920s, the Air Ministry was still attracted by the possibilities of the 37 mm. Coventry Ordnance Works shell-firing gun and issued Specification F.29/27 for a single-seat fighter using the C.O.W. gun as its armament.

Bristol prepared the Mercury III-powered Type 112 monoplane project but did not build it.

Westland C.O.W. gun fighter J9565 to F.29/27 as first constructed with Mercury IIIA, low aspect ratio fin and rudder and four-blade propeller. (Westland Photo.)

Westland F.29/27 with C.O.W. gun installed, two-blade propeller and taller vertical tail surfaces.
(Westland Photo.)

For Westland Arthur Davenport produced a modified version of the Interceptor low-wing monoplane of 1929. Completed in 1931 and test-flown by Flt.Lt. L. G. Paget, the C.O.W. Gun Fighter J9565 in its early form was powered by the 485 h.p. Mercury IIIA engine driving a four-blade propeller and featured a low aspect ratio fin and rudder. Following early tests a new vertical tail of substantially higher aspect ratio was fitted and a propeller with two blades replaced the four-blader. The single C.O.W. gun was then installed at an angle of 55° on the starboard side of the cockpit under the direct control of the pilot.

If Westland's C.O.W. gun prototype followed the growing and inevitable trend towards the low-wing monoplane, the extraordinary response which appeared from Vickers in 1931 to the F.29/27 requirement looked—at first glance—as though it were harking back to the long-abandoned pusher biplane formula of some fifteen years earlier in the 1914–18 War. Designated Type 161, J9566 resembled the F.B.12 and F.B.26 Vampire but in a far cleaner and more powerful form. Unequal-span, two-bay wings with single interplane struts were part of the square-cut flying surfaces and carried a short bluff-bowed nacelle, at the rear of which were mounted the 450 h.p. Jupiter VIIF engine and its four-blade propeller; the power plant originally intended was to have been the 485 h.p. Mercury IIA. Aft of the engine a tapered cylindrical tube acted as an extended spinner to fair the propeller into the boom-supported tail unit.

J9566's initial flight was made at Brooklands during 1931 by Capt. J. Summers but tests showed poor directional stability. Consequently, the Type 161 was modified with an enlarged fin and rudder and a fan-shaped fin added on each side at the rear of the tail booms. In this form the Type 161 is thought to have been redesignated Type 162. The machine's 37 mm. C.O.W. gun was housed to starboard in the nacelle and mounted to fire upwards at a high angle.

Neither of the two designs to F.29/27 was proceeded with after its trials and official interest in promoting the quick-firing C.O.W. gun lapsed.

In September, 1932, Martlesham Report M/598 was issued, following tests of the Armstrong Whitworth A.W.16 single-seat biplane fighter built as a Private Venture to Specification F.9/26. Carrying the registration A–2, the machine was the zone fighter counterpart of the naval A.W.16 S1591 constructed to N.21/26. Powered by the Panther IIIA No.A.S.8508, developing 501·8 h.p. at 12,000 ft., A–2 revealed a serious disparity in its climb performance compared with that of S1591 recorded in Report M/579 of November, 1931. As a result, A–2's climb tests were carried out at airspeeds appropriate

Vickers Type 161 in its original form. (Vickers Photo.)

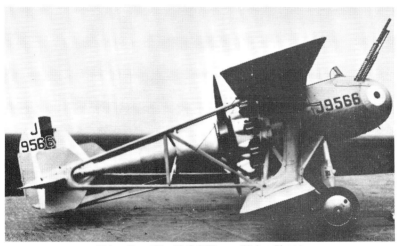

Vickers Type 161 with C.O.W. gun. (Vickers Photo.)

The Private Venture Armstrong Whitworth A.W.16 A–2 to F.9/26 in original form with small fin, horn-balanced rudder and concentric Townend cowling rings. (Armstrong Whitworth Photo.)

to those of S1591. A–2 reached a top speed of 195 m.p.h. at 14,500 ft., stalled at 55 m.p.h., climbed at 1,140 ft./min. at sea level and gave its best climb rate of 1,300 ft./min. at 10,000 ft. After preliminary trials, the fin area was increased by 3 sq. ft. from 4·55 sq.ft. to 7·55 sq.ft. by extending it forwards, and the rudder area was reduced from 11·8 sq.ft. to 10·7 sq.ft., the rudder's horn balance being deleted. At the same time, the chord of the elevators was increased, the leading edge of the ailerons was made blunt and the tail navigation light was moved from the trailing edge of the rudder to the top of its hinge line. These alterations gave the A.W.16 far better handling characteristics for ailerons and elevators but made the rudder slightly less effective at the stall. All normal aerobatics were accomplished with ease but the lightness of the ailerons was somewhat disquieting to the pilot, particularly at high speeds. The machine was steady in a T.V. dive, reaching a terminal true airspeed of 350 m.p.h. and recovering satisfactorily from the dive.

The general summing-up was that A–2 was satisfactory as a zone fighter, being very manoeuvrable in the air and on the ground, with a reasonable view for the pilot. It was pleasant and easy to fly, with normal take-off and landing, but the harmonization of the controls was spoiled somewhat by the lightness of the ailerons which proved disquieting in aerobatics.

Martlesham Report M/598/2 of August, 1933, covered tests with A–2 as an interim day-and-night fighter, fitted with the 565 h.p. Panther VII, the machine reaching 195 m.p.h. at 15,000 ft. and an initial climb rate of 1,545 ft./min. While at A.&A.E.E. two engine failures occurred and, from February until May of 1933, modifications were made to the cockpit and headrest and the structure strengthened to the level expected by Specification F.7/30.

New tyres and spats were fitted and the rudder acquired a mass balance. The view was improved but aileron control harmony was still imperfect and, although spin recovery was easy, fore-and-aft instability at over 250 m.p.h. brought forth the comment that A-2 was not a stable platform at above that speed for its pair of Vickers guns.

Three of the A.W.16s were supplied to China in 1932 but, despite its good all-round qualities, the type was not favoured for service in either the R.A.F. or the F.A.A.

Fairey preoccupation with naval designs made it natural that the firm should seek to adapt the Firefly Mk.II as a shipborne fleet fighter. Sixty of the Mk.II were built by Avions Fairey at Gosselies for successful use in the Belgian Air Force and 1932 saw the début of the Firefly Mk.III S1592—Fairey airframe F1137—as a prototype single-seat naval fighter with the 480 h.p. Kestrel IIS. Flotation bags occupied the rear of the fuselage and, in the same year, S1592 was mounted on twin floats as a High-Speed Flight trainer but development then ceased.

During 1932, while Air Ministry interest in the C.O.W. gun was still warm, Bristol prepared their Type 132 design for a two-seat, low-wing monoplane, powered by a Bristol Hydra engine and carrying one 37 mm. C.O.W. gun. Construction of a prototype was started but subsequently cancelled.

Sydney Camm's superb Fury possessed considerable development potential and 1932 witnessed several variants emerging, particularly for foreign governments who were eager to equip their air forces with the matchless British fighters. Customers at Hawker included Yugoslavia, Norway, Persia, Portugal and Spain. One Yugoslav Fury was fitted temporarily with a 500 h.p. Hispano-Suiza 12NB engine for evaluation at Brooklands in 1931 but, as the performance was poor, reverted to the Kestrel. The Norwegian Fury of 1932 with the 530 h.p. Panther IIIA tended to nose over on the ground and the Panther installation was abandoned. The Persian Fury, produced in 1933,

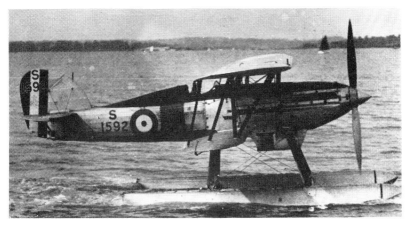

Fairey Firefly Mk.III as a floatplane. (Fairey Photo.)

The single Hawker Norwegian Fury with Panther engine. (Hawker Photo.)

Hawker Persian Fury 203 with Hornet engine. (Hawker Photo.)

Hawker Yugoslav Fury. (Hawker Photo.)

Bristol Type 105 Bulldog Mk.IIA fitted with Aquila III. (Bristol Photo.)

used the American Pratt and Whitney Hornet S2B1G for power but cooling difficulties resulted in the substitution of the 550 h.p. Mercury VI in the next batch of Persian Furies produced in 1934. During the same year, three Furies with de-rated Kestrel IIS engines were supplied to Portugal.

A repeat order from Yugoslavia proposed the installation of the 720 h.p. Lorraine Petrel H Frs engine but, as a better performance was forthcoming using a later Kestrel, it was decided to fit the 745 h.p. Kestrel XVI. The incorporation of a cantilever undercarriage, with internally-sprung wheels, a new low-drag radiator and accommodation for an extra gun under each lower wing, resulted in a handsome aircraft with a top speed of 242 m.p.h. The first example of the order for ten flew initially on 14th September, 1936. 7th April,

Bristol Bulldog Mk.4A with Mercury engine. (Bristol Photo.)

1936, saw the first flight of the Spanish Fury, a version similar in appearance to the Yugoslav machine but powered by the 700 h.p. Hispano-Suiza 12X Brs engine.

For several years Westland had been experimenting with the unique and successful tailless Pterodactyl designs by Capt. G. T. R. Hill. This work culminated in 1932 with the construction of the third of the type by Westland, the Pterodactyl Mk.V, an astonishingly original two-seat, sesquiplane, tailless fighter, powered by the steam-cooled 600 h.p. Rolls-Royce Goshawk fitted in the nose of the nacelle, whereas previous Pterodactyls had followed the pusher layout. The sweepback of the leading edge of the outer panels of the upper wings was 42·5°, that of the trailing edge from the centre line being 24°.

Westland Pterodactyl Mk.V in its early form. (Westland Photo.)

A tandem, two-wheel undercarriage helped further to reduce drag, a pair of small out-rigged wheels supported the machine on the ground. The main front wheel was steerable and the rear wheel was fitted with brakes. A pair of forwards-firing Vickers guns armed the pilot, the rear gunner using two Lewis guns from his electrically-operated turret. The Pterodactyl Mk.V could carry a normal load of bombs and was equipped with receiving and transmitting radio and oxygen. The pilot view was excellent and the gunner was able to obtain a superb, unobstructed field of fire from his commanding position immediately behind the pilot.

Registered P8, the machine was tested by H. J. Penrose and proved to be capable of full aerobatics and inverted flight. A structural failure during the initial ground runs at Yeovil caused a delay of some months before the first flight but the radical fighter afterwards proved itself to be an eminently practical flying machine. Directional stability was subsequently improved by the addition of a slender fixed fin on the underside of the wings outboard of the interplane struts.

Although in its basic layout the Pterodactyl Mk.V represented an echo from the prehistoric past of winged creatures, it also presaged the sweptback and tailless forms which fighters of some thirty years hence were destined to employ in their designers' successful endeavours to attain supersonic speeds. For its time, the Pterodactyl Mk.V was a unique and courageous example of outstanding vision and a remarkable achievement in combining in a practical, graceful and effective form so many of the often-conflicting ideals which face a designer.

A requirement which might have produced some interesting prototypes, but which came to naught, was specification F.5/33 for a two-seat fighter with turret armament. Two unbuilt projects to meet it were the Armstrong Whitworth A.W.34 and the Bristol Type 140, the last-named a pusher monoplane powered by a Bristol Perseus engine and carrying its guns in a spherical nose turret.

Further unbuilt designs were prepared by Armstrong Whitworth and Bristol to Specification F.22/33, which also required turret armament but in a three-seat aircraft. The Armstrong Whitworth project was the A.W.33 and the Bristol the Type 141. The Bristol machine was designed as a monoplane with two Bristol Aquila engines and armament in a spherical turret in the nose.

Concentration by Hawker on development of the Fury produced several interesting variants, each aimed at improving general performance at what was inevitably the close of the biplane era. Specification F.7/30 demanded a new generation of single-seat interceptor fighters of advanced design and it was felt at Hawker that a considerably revised Fury might meet the case.

Some time would have to elapse before the machine could be ready for flight so, in the meantime, work was initiated on a Private Venture version of the Fury to assist in assessing the alterations proposed for a machine to be designed to F.7/30. The result was G–ABSE, the aptly-named Intermediate Fury, which P. E. G. Sayer flew for the first time on 13th April, 1932, with a Kestrel IIS installed. For the next three years G–ABSE put in many hours of work proving points for the P.V.3 to F.7/30 and flew with the Kestrel IVS to test the Goshawk's supercharger, the Kestrel VI, the Goshawk III and an up-rated Kestrel VI Special.

To Specification F.14/32, the High-Speed Fury K3586 was built as a Private Venture, making its first flight on 3rd May, 1933. The machine underwent more drastic alterations to its airframe than the Intermediate Fury G–ABSE as, in addition to changes in engine, the wings were altered. In some 800 hours of intensive trials K3586 flew with the 525 h.p. Kestrel IIS, the 600 h.p. Kestrel S, the 525 h.p. Kestrel IIIS, the 600 h.p. Kestrel VIS, the 695 h.p. Goshawk III, the 700 h.p. Goshawk B.41 and the 790 h.p. Rolls-Royce P.V.12. The lower wings of the High-Speed Fury were tapered on the trailing edge and the upper wings were tapered on the leading edge, interplane struts being of the V type on the Mk.I. When the steam-cooled engines were being tested on the Mk.II version, however, parallel-chord upper

Hawker Intermediate Fury. (Hawker Photo.)

wings of standard type and N struts were used, the upper wings carrying flush-set condensers extending—on the upper surfaces—half-chord from the leading edge.

The evaporative cooling of the Goshawk was plagued with constant trouble during the unit's development. It seemed inevitable that the engine would never pass into service, but thought had to be given to an interim replacement for the fighter squadrons' Fury Mk.Is during the long gestation period. The answer was found in the Fury Mk.II, designed to Specification F.14/32 and equipped with the 640 h.p. Kestrel VI engine. K1935, an early Fury Mk.I, served as the prototype and reached 228 m.p.h. in A.&A.E.E. trials. The main external distinguishing feature between the two Furies was the addition of spats to the undercarriage. Production Fury Mk.IIs were to Specification 6/35, which decreed that endurance should be maintained by an extra fuel tank in the fore-fuselage, with which the top speed dropped to 223 m.p.h. Specification 19/35 covered a second production batch in 1936–37.

Hawker High Speed Fury Mk.I fitted with Kestrel VIS. (Hawker Photo.)

Although the writing was plainly on the wall for the biplane fighter, the type was still considered by a number of designers to possess sufficient attributes--one of the most important of which was manœuvrability—to warrant further development. Among the new biplanes to appear in the course of 1934 was the Armstrong Whitworth A.W.35 Scimitar, a revised version of the A.W.16 and a machine of handsome aspect fully representative of the peak of progress in its class. Extra power was provided by the installation of the Panther IXA rated at 624 h.p. at 5,000 ft. Overall dimensions were similar to those of the A.W.16 and the armament was the normal pair of Vickers guns, with accommodation for light bombs under the lower wings. The most noticeable external differences in the A.W.35 from its forebear were the new spats,

Hawker High Speed Fury Mk.II with steam-cooled Goshawk. (Hawker Photo.)

divided undercarriage axle, full cowling over the engine and the cut-down portion of the fore-decking in front of the cockpit.

The prototype made its first flight on 29th June, 1934, and comparative tests undertaken at Martlesham Heath between two A.W.35s were recorded in A.&A.E.E. Report M/681 of December, 1935. The aircraft were finished in Norwegian Air Force colours and carried the registrations 405 and 407 respectively. The report commented that the Norwegian dope scheme did not compare favourably with the standard British service finish as, with it, splits occurred in the fabric during dives. Spins were steep and fast with recovery quick and easy using the normal method of control column moved forwards and application of opposite rudder. In dives the machines behaved well and were steady with recovery easy at up to 290 m.p.h.

Hawker Fury Mk.II. (Hawker Photo.)

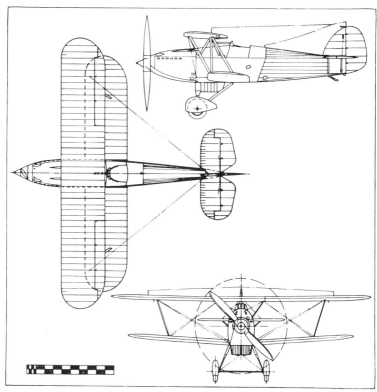

Hawker Fury Mk.II

Following early assessment of 405 and 407 at Martlesham, for comparative purposes a cleaning-up process was applied to 405 at the A.&A.E.E. In addition to surface polishing, fabric fairings were added, the gun ports were covered and the exhaust extensions removed. As received at Martlesham in its original state 405 reached a top speed of 208 m.p.h.; following the cleaning-up and an increase in r.p.m. this was improved to 216 m.p.h. at 10,000 ft. The original maximum climb rate of 2,230 ft./min. and of 1,720 ft./min. at sea level was increased to 2,510 ft./min. at 3,600 ft. In contrast 407, at empty and loaded weights of 2,989 lb. and 4,133 lb. respectively, recorded as received 206·5 m.p.h. at 6,500 ft., a climb rate of 2,610 ft./min. at sea level and best climb rate of 2,670 ft./min. at 1,500 ft. The Scimitar was not selected for production in Britain but was built under licence in Norway.

Stable-mate of the Fury in the R.A.F. fighter squadrons from the mid-1930s was the Gloster Gauntlet until the advent of the monoplane in service. Gloster and Folland were finally rewarded for their patience, industry and persistence in promoting and modifying the basic S.S.18 design since 1929 with the evergreen J9125 airframe until, in its S.S.19B form in 1933, it reached the status of prototype for the Gauntlet as a day-and-night fighter replacement for the Bulldog to production Specification 24/33.

Until the acceptance of the Gauntlet, previous Gloster fighters in the R.A.F. had been of wooden construction, and to the Gauntlet fell the distinctions of becoming the first Gloster fighter of all-metal structure to enter the Service and the last production R.A.F. fighter with an open cockpit. The Gauntlet Mk.I was equipped with the 645 h.p. Mercury VIS.2 and the first and second

The Armstrong Whitworth A.W.35 Scimitar G–ACCD. (Armstrong Whitworth Photo.)

machines of the order for twenty-four were fitted with spats, the remainder receiving Dunlop fairings between the main wheels.

J9125 was sent to A.& A.E.E. Martlesham for acceptance tests and Report M/654 of April, 1935, was notable for its comments on the excellence of the Gauntlet. Delivered under contract No. 279522/33, J9125 was flying with a Mercury VIS.2 No. M4527, rating 643 h.p. at 12,500 ft. at 2,400 r.p.m. The machine was tested at an empty weight of 2,654 lb., loaded 3,910 lb. and recorded a top speed of 230 m.p.h. at 15,800 ft., climb rates of 2,320 ft./min. at sea level and 2,555 ft./min. at 10,000 ft., and a landing run of 150 yards with brakes in a 5 m.p.h. wind. Since being tested at A.& A.E.E. Martlesham in August, 1933, J9125 had acquired a new exhaust manifold and Townend ring, a revised petrol system, Dowty oleo legs in place of Vickers type, a tail-wheel instead of the skid previously fitted, and stronger spats. When tested with Dunlop fairings on the undercarriage in place of the spats, a loss of 1 m.p.h. resulted.

General improvements in detail since August, 1933, included a larger wind-screen and modified gunsights, consisting of Aldis and ring and bead. The machine acted as a steady platform for the two Vickers Mk.V guns forming the armament and which were housed in mild steel troughs replacing the earlier light alloy type which sustained damage from blast. The guns, from which 12,000 r.p.g. were fired in trials, operated satisfactorily at 31,000 ft. in −54°C. and at night produced no dazzle and only a small flash. Initial firing resulted in damage to the tail bracing wires from empty cases or links but this was remedied by modifying the chutes. The engine mounting had been strengthened and the Dowty undercarriage legs gave improved shock absorbing but, with them, J9125 tended to bounce on rough surfaces. Equipment fitted included T.R.9 radio and G.22 camera gun. Handling characteristics were unaffected by the change in J9125 from the Mercury IV of 1933 to the Mercury VIS.2 used in 1934. During the armament trials, engine No. M4527 completed its permissible flying hours and was replaced by a Mercury VIS.2 No. 108700 which gave 10% less power than the first unit. Using a Watts propeller the greatest height reached in the A.&A.E.E. tests was 34,400 ft. but estimated absolute ceiling was 35,000 ft., with service ceiling 34,000 ft.

A.&A.E.E. Report M/654A of June, 1935, on comparative tests with K4081, the first production Gauntlet Mk.I which was used for development and fitted with a Mercury VIS No. M4549 giving 619 h.p. at 12,500 ft., at empty and loaded weights of 2,688 lb. and 3,937 lb. respectively, recorded a service ceiling of 33,200 ft.

Development flying of the Gauntlet proceeded in the charge of Flt.Lt. P. E. G. Sayer, who had transferred from Hawker to Gloster. Following the twenty-four Mk.Is came production of the improved Mk.II Gauntlet, carrying the more powerful 650 h.p. Mercury VI, two hundred and four of the new mark being produced during 1936–37 commencing with K5264. The Gauntlet Mk.I joined the R.A.F. in May, 1935, when the pilots of No. 19 Squadron at Duxford took delivery of their new mounts; eventually, Gauntlets were flying with twenty-two fighter squadrons.

Gloster S.S.19B Gauntlet Mk.I J9125.

During 1934 the Gloster Aircraft Company joined forces with Hawker Aircraft, bringing a consequent immediate strengthening of the resources available to both organizations at a most propitious and vital time. A practical result of this amalgamation was soon evident as the Gauntlet Mk.II

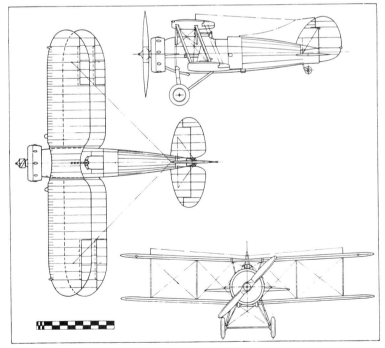

Gloster Gauntlet Mk.I

went into production with revised fuselage construction and wing spars after Gloster became identified with the Hawker-Siddeley Group. Later examples of the Mk.II featured a Fairey three-blade metal propeller in place of the original two-blade wooden Airscrew Company type and, in the Gauntlet, the R.A.F. possessed the fastest fighter that it had received.

1930 had witnessed the announcement from the Air Ministry of Specification F.7/30, one of the most important requirements formulated to date for a fighter. The swiftly-changing pattern of the international scene and the rapid advances under way technically in the field of aeronautical design called for extremely imaginative thinking and accurate foresight to ensure the re-equipment in reasonable time of Britain's fighter squadrons with aircraft able to cope adequately with any type of hostile aircraft with which they might be confronted. Many factors, among them an increase in maximum and cruising speeds, rate of climb, range and endurance, had to be borne in mind.

Of utmost importance also was the fact that rising operational speeds meant a direct reduction in the time for which a fighter's guns could be brought to bear. One obvious answer to this pressing problem was an immediate increase in the weight of fire, a measure long overdue and which could be accomplished reasonably easily by doubling the number of machine-guns. The heavy and awkward 37 mm. C.O.W. gun had lost its transient fascination for the Air Ministry and the only alternative readily available—short of developing an entirely new machine-gun—was to use the existing well-established and proven types which were a known quantity. These amounted to the drum-fed Lewis—normally aimed by a gunner from a ring mounting, the belt-fed Vickers—usually fixed to fire forwards—and, possibly, the American Colt-fabricated belt-fed Browning.

Issued at the end of 1930, Specification F.7/30 numbered among its requirements for a single-seat, day interceptor and night fighter an armament of four Vickers guns, a maximum speed of over 250 m.p.h., and an improvement in ceiling, rate of climb and manoeuvrability. Implicit in the night-fighter aspects of the requirement were a low wing loading, ease of landing, good field of view from the cockpit and elimination of exhaust glare.

Encouragement was given to designers to draw up their projects around the Rolls-Royce Goshawk, an evaporatively-cooled development of the reliable Kestrel.

Trials of the F.7/30 contenders were scheduled to be undertaken at A.& A.E.E. Martlesham Heath during 1932. However, development of the Goshawk was not proving to be as straightforward as expected and the most suitable and powerful air-cooled radial available, the Mercury—favoured by some designers in spite of the subtle official guidance towards use of the Goshawk—was also struggling to meet its specified performance and degree of reliability. These difficulties, allied to the additional problems inherent in indulging in an advanced specification, were responsible for the postponement of the evaluation of F.7/30 prototypes until 1933 and once again until 1934, with trials eventually being carried out during 1935.

Meanwhile, the obvious prospects of a healthy production order for the winner of the contest had generated intensive activity in more aircraft companies than any fighter requirement so far issued. F.7/30 presented the design teams with a tremendous challenge. The prize to be won appeared, when the specification was presented, to be great but, to earn it, judgment had, perforce, to be unerring at a time of complex change in the development life of the aeroplane.

Perhaps the most pressing of the conflicting factors was the basic choice between biplane and monoplane. To achieve the augmented speed expected, the monoplane was receiving increased attention steadily and was making inroads relentlessly into the domain so far dominated by the biplane. Had the time arrived at last to stake all on an immediate and abrupt switchover to the monoplane? Would it be sounder policy to attempt to carry the biplane

Vickers Jockey Mk.I J9122 rebuilt and fitted with Jupiter VIIF. (Vickers Photo.)

one stage further? If the choice were to be that of the biplane, would it be better to attempt to improve a design which had already proved itself, or was it worthwhile to prepare a completely new biplane layout—at the same time introducing radically new features into it? Had the time arrived yet to complicate the pilot's job by, in one step, making him responsible for a machine of entirely different layout and, therefore, different flying and handling characteristics? Was it correct policy to burden him further, at the same time, with a retractable undercarriage, take-off and landing flaps, a variable-pitch propeller, adjustable cooling gills, a new type of gunsight, together with appurtenances such as a cockpit canopy, and other refinements then under active development? These and numerous other questions had to be investigated and assessed before the step could be taken. Eventually, the fruits of the protracted deliberations emerged over a period of three years until several F.7/30 prototypes of remarkable variety had made their début.

Vickers were swift to present their rebuilt Type 151 Jockey J9122, a 450 h.p. Jupiter VIIF-powered development of the Type 151 low-wing monoplane of 1929. The machine was completed in 1931 and, apart from the change in engine, differed externally from the earlier Type 151 in having a ring cowling around the Jupiter and spats on the undercarriage. The wing section was R.A.F. 34. The revised Jockey displayed nothing that was radical and achieved a moderate top speed of 218 m.p.h. at 9,840 ft., a rate of climb of 1,850 ft./min. and an absolute ceiling of 31,500 ft. There was little opportunity for extensive trials or modifications as J9122 was lost during 1932 through getting into an uncontrollable flat spin during spinning trials.

After R. J. Mitchell's outstanding success with his low-wing monoplane designs in the Schneider Trophy, it was natural that he should carry on the formula in his proposal for an F.7/30 prototype from Supermarine. Both Vickers and Supermarine, with their F.7/30 tenders, broke away from the biplane in spite of the diehard official preference for it.

In the case of Vickers, the redesigned Jockey represented a refinement of an earlier monoplane fighter, but for Supermarine Mitchell set to work on a completely original layout for a monoplane fighter. The design became the Type 224 in March, 1932, and was centred on the officially-preferred 660 h.p. Goshawk III engine. The Type 224 K2890, unofficially known as the Spitfire, lacked the fine grace of line and the elegance which Mitchell had achieved with his Schneider S.4, S.5 and S.6 monoplanes. This was possibly to be expected in a workaday fighter and yet was not essential as part of the functional design, as Mitchell showed immediately afterwards with his supremely comely Type 300 Spitfire. K2890 featured inverted-gull wings with the surprisingly large span of 45 ft. 10 in., the condensers for the steam cooling of the Goshawk being incorporated in the wings' surfaces. The cranked wing roots carried two of the four Vickers guns, while the other pair were housed on each side of the engine. Fairly voluminous trouser fairings enclosed the undercarriage members and a streamlined headrest completed the open cockpit.

The Type 224 was finished late in 1933 and returned a maximum speed of 230 m.p.h. instead of the 235 m.p.h. expected by its designer. While the machine was under construction, Mitchell had second thoughts about the whole design and started to commit to paper an advanced development of the Type 224. The use of smaller wings was envisaged, complete with split flaps, the undercarriage was to be retractable outwards and the pilot was to be enclosed, with a cockpit fairing behind him atop the slender rear fuselage. The four guns and the Goshawk engine, as required by F.7/30, were still to be incorporated in the layout.

This first development of the Type 224 led to yet another which was accepted as a proposal by the Air Ministry at the beginning of 1934. The new design carried on the straight-taper wings but with broader root chord and increased-span ailerons. These wings were to carry the four guns set well outboard. The depth of the rear fuselage was increased so that the cockpit hood was faired in a direct line to the tail, and the outwards-retracting main undercarriage members became single-leg units. The top speed of this revised design

Supermarine Type 224 to F.7/30. (Rolls-Royce Photo.)

was expected to be 265 m.p.h. As the original Type 224 K2890 had to be completed for the Martlesham evaluation, and as a new engine of great promise—the PV-12—was in the offing from Rolls-Royce, neither of these two developments was proceeded with but the second of them formed the basis of Mitchell's next design proposal.

Among the F.7/30 projects that of Westland was the most unorthodox. Designed by Arthur Davenport as the P.V.4, the machine was a biplane embodying that very attractive proposition to designers—the installation of the power plant inside the fuselage about the centre of gravity. Basic advantages attending this set-up were improved balance and increased manœuvrability, a vastly cleaner nose entry with the possibility of concentrated grouping of offensive armament in the fore-fuselage, and a far better view for the pilot approaching the ultimate with the deletion of a long bulky nose normally enveloping the engine. Advantages are usually attended by disadvantages and in the buried engine's case, the main point of detraction is in providing the transmission to the propeller location. Extension shafts and straight or bevel gearing are automatically involved and therein lies the primary weakness in the concept.

Westland P.V.4 to F.7/30 as it appeared at first with low aspect ratio fin and rudder, open cockpit and separate exhausts. (Westland Photo.)

227

The Westland F.7/30 P.V.4 K2891 was completed in 1934 to Contract No. 189221/32 and powered by the Goshawk IIS which developed 600 h.p. at 12,000 ft. at 2,600 r.p.m. with a Watts two-blade wooden propeller. The engine was installed at the C.G. in the gap between the wings, the entire depth of which was filled by the fuselage. An extension shaft and gearing carried the output to the propeller mounted in the short nose, the upper decking of which sloped downwards very sharply from the pilot's open cockpit set at the leading edge of the wings to give an unrivalled field of view. Immediately below in the nose were grouped the battery of four Vickers guns with converging lines of fire, the lower pair staggered to the rear of the upper pair.

K2891's wings were single-bay and of unequal-span, the upper planes incorporating sharp dihedral at the roots and automatic slots. The Goshawk's deep radiator block was mounted between the undercarriage legs and equipment installed in the P.V.4's fabric-covered, all-metal airframe included two-way radio, oxygen and night-flying equipment.

Although recent previous Westland fighter concepts had progressed steadily to the monoplane, and the monoplane had been favoured as the preliminary Westland F.7/30 design, the P.V.4 had finally been settled as a biplane to meet best the specification's dictates for low landing speed and manoeuvrability.

Following early tests, K2891's cockpit was enclosed, the fin and rudder were increased in height and single exhaust manifolds replaced the original separate stubs. Despite the modifications made to the design, the Westland F.7/30 contender was not a success and Report M 676 issued by A&A.E.E. Martlesham Heath during 1935 averred that early in the trials the performance of the aircraft was found to be considerably below that of other aircraft built to the specification and that, in compliance with instructions received from the Directorate of Technical Development, the trials were abandoned. Performance figures recorded at A.&A.E.E. at 3,687 lb. empty and 5,207 lb. loaded in climb tests to 20,300 ft. included a rate of climb of 1,455 ft./min. at sea level at 85 m.p.h. and 2,260 r.p.m., the machine taking 8 min. to reach 10,000 ft. Uncorrected approximate top speed was 147·5 m.p.h. at 13,000 ft. and 142 m.p.h. at 10,000 ft. K2891 subsequently spent its time in experimental flying and, at one period, bore a revised vertical tail in which the rudder hinge line was raked sharply forwards.

Following trial F.7/30 installations in the Intermediate G–ABSE and High-Speed K3586 Furies, Hawker went ahead with the P.V.3 biplane in full conformity with the F.7/30 requirements after exploring the way ahead with the experimental versions of the Fury.

A complete breakaway into untried radical concepts possessed little appeal to the Hawker assessment of the specification. The employment of a steam-cooled engine posed a formidable enough installation problem for a service fighter without complicating the issue still further. Accordingly, Camm evolved in the P.V.3 a highly developed but practical version of the Fury. For some three months before the P.V.3 made its initial flight on 15th June, 1934,

The P.V.3, epitome of Hawker biplane fighter development. (Hawker Photo.)

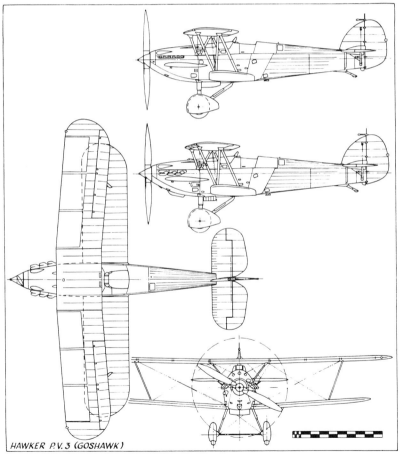

HAWKER P.V.3 (GOSHAWK)

Hawker P.V.3

the 695 h.p. Goshawk III engine, cooling system and propeller which powered it were extensively tested in K3586. There was sufficient room in the elegant nose to house two Vickers guns above the engine and the remaining pair one on each side of it. Spats enclosed the main wheels and the entire structure was strengthened to absorb the increased power of the Goshawk compared with that of the Kestrel. To improve operating capabilities at night, flame-damping exhaust manifolds were fitted later but they exhibited an alarming tendency to explode when hot.

As Hawker had taken the trouble well in advance to make extensive F.7/30 preparations and to indulge in trial installations, the P.V.3 was ready in 1934 in ample time for Martlesham. Other F.7/30 prototypes were still being completed and Hawker had time, therefore, to install in the P.V.3 later improved versions of the Goshawk. First flight with the 700 h.p. Goshawk B.41, with liquid cooling and a fixed radiator under the fuselage, was made on 26th June, 1935. This was changed shortly to the 700 h.p. Goshawk B.43 which reverted to steam cooling and which made its initial take-off in the P.V.3 on 9th July, 1935. It was with the B.43 that the machine, registered I–PV3, was delivered finally to A.&A.E.E. Martlesham and reached a top speed of 224 m.p.h. at 14,000 ft.

Bristol entered the F.7/30 contest with vigour, preparing several projects, two of which were built. The firm explored fully both the biplane and the monoplane concepts for the purpose, preparing three proposals which were discarded. These consisted of the Type 127 monoplane to be powered by the Goshawk, the almost identical Type 128 Mercury-engined monoplane and the Type 129 Mercury-powered pusher monoplane with the tail unit borne by twin booms.

Finally, in 1934, a pair of F.7/30 aspirants made their appearance from Bristol. One, the Type 123 biplane—destined to be the last biplane from Bristol—was envisaged originally in a tender of January, 1932, as a machine with wing cellules devoid of bracing wires and with V interplane struts. Extensive revision was then initiated and the Type 123 in its final form emerged as an attractively-contoured, sharply-staggered biplane of advanced type, engineered around the 600 h.p. Goshawk III with evaporative cooling. The upper wings were swept back and all four planes incorporated strut-connected, narrow-chord, broad-span ailerons. Interplane bracing wires were absent. Full-span slots were mounted on the leading edge of the upper wings and flaps were another refinement in the design. The undercarriage, faired with trousers and spats, was constructed around a reaction-type shock-absorber system. The wing and horizontal tail surfaces were of parallel chord and the vertical tail was unusual in having the generous horn balance of the rudder set deeply forwards into the fin. The ailerons, serving also as flaps for landing and take-off, were coupled to the Handley Page slots.

Flight trials of the Type 123 began on 12th June, 1934, in the hands of Capt. Uwins but, as was the case with most aircraft which attempted to use the Goshawk, continual trouble manifested itself in the cooling system. In addition, testing in the air disclosed lateral instability which was not eased

Bristol Type 123. (Bristol Photo.)

Bristol Type 133 R-10. (Bristol Photo.)

Blackburn F.7/30 fitted with tailwheel and with spats removed. (Blackburn Photo.)

231

by an increase in fin and rudder areas. Despite the care taken in the development of the design and the resources behind it, no simple and direct method could be found to remove the cause of the buffeting encountered and the decision had regretfully to be taken to discontinue work on the Type 123.

All along, Bristol had not been too happy with the prospect of using an engine of design and manufacture other than their own and, for this reason, had prepared the Types 128 and 129 proposals. Although its Type 123 design had been accepted for prototype construction, the firm had commenced in 1933 a Private Venture project to F.7/30 for a low-wing monoplane based on their own 605 h.p. Mercury VIS.4 air-cooled radial. Designated Type 133 and registered R–10, the machine was constructed concurrently with the Type 123 and made its first flight on 8th July, 1934, with Capt. Uwins in control, shortly after that of the biplane. With a free hand for a Private Venture project Bristol made a fine job of the Type 133, which was of particular note as the first of the new generation of monoplane fighter prototypes to be built for potential R.A.F. equipment. All-metal structure and covering, apart from fabric for the control surfaces, were employed and the wing panels were joined to the fuselage by an anhedralled centre-section. The hydraulically-operated main undercarriage units retracted rearwards and the armament of four guns was disposed with two Vickers in the upper front decking and one Lewis on each side in the wings just outboard of the landing-gear fairings. First tests were made with an open cockpit, ailerons-cum-flaps along the entire trailing edge of the outer wing panels and a tailskid.

Significant alterations then followed and included provision of an enclosed cockpit with sliding hood and headrest, a larger fin and rudder and installation of a tailwheel. The original aileron and flap system was discarded and replaced by normal split flaps under the centre-section and outer wing panels and by shorter-span ailerons.

Test flights made prior to expected delivery to Martlesham were satisfactorily carried out by Uwins and T. W. Campbell, the machine attaining a top speed of 260 m.p.h. at 15,000 ft. and a rate of climb of 2,200 ft./min. High hopes were entertained for the success of the Type 133 in the forthcoming F.7/30 evaluation but they were dashed completely when, on 8th March, 1935, the machine crashed at Longwell Green after Campbell had been forced to bail out when an uncontrollable flat spin developed during final tests at Bristol. The Bristol Aeroplane Company was therefore left without any entrant for the F.7/30 trials despite having constructed in the Type 133 the most advanced design among those submitted.

Next to the Westland P.V.4, the Blackburn F.7/30 entrant K2892, designed by George E. Petty, was the most unorthodox of the prototypes constructed. Petty decided to retain the biplane layout and adhered also to the specification's preference for the Goshawk, K2892 being fitted with the steam-cooled 660 h.p. Mk.III. The engine was located in the normal nose position but the machine's main claim to unorthodoxy lay in the siting of the pilot high in the middle of the upper wing's centre-section. The fuselage was set so high in the wing cellules that the upper planes were located at the mid-wing position while the lower planes were suspended well below, with the Goshawk's radiator filling the deep gap under the belly. The sleek fuselage was completely metal-skinned but fabric was used to cover the flying surfaces. The Blackburn F.7/30's armament of four Vickers guns was disposed in the nose, two being above the engine and two below it. The undercarriage installation was commendably clean, both a tailskid and tailwheel being tried.

The radical layout of K2892 furnished the pilot with a remarkably fine view but miserably poor protection in the event of nosing-over. When ground tests were commenced the usual cooling difficulties with the Goshawk made themselves manifest, together with instability of the undercarriage. In spite of the amount of work involved in creating the Blackburn F.7/30, it was never flown and finally found its way to Halton for use as a ground instruction airframe.

Although the requirements contained in Specification F.7/30 when it was issued held out such high hopes of bringing forth a first-rate new single-seat fighter for the R.A.F., and although so many firms attempted to achieve the ideals set out in it, bad luck attended the whole venture. The Kestrel engine had been a great success but the derivative Goshawk had failed owing to the final impracticability of its heavy and complex evaporative cooling system. This unforeseen setback rebounded to a great or a small degree on most of the F.7/30 contenders designed around the Goshawk, resulting in an inordinate loss of time in getting the competitive trials under way. Furthermore, the specification's needs were revised at intervals and so much valuable time was lost that, as each year was succeeded by the next, the whole concept of the specification became outdated when seen in the light of the rapidly advancing techniques in aircraft and engine design.

The protagonists of the monoplane were still having an uphill struggle against the deeply-rooted prejudice of twenty years against the type but it was now only a matter of time before the death of such a warped and short-sighted dogmatism.

Sydney Camm and Reginald Mitchell had finally eschewed the biplane as a formula worthy of any further attention and were actively engaged in promoting the monoplane to take over the mantle of the fighter in the Royal Air Force. Both Camm and Mitchell, pre-eminent men in their professional field with unrivalled experience behind them, knew without further doubt that the moment of the monoplane's entry had arrived. Nevertheless, the diehard champions of the biplane at the Air Ministry were to have one final fling before having to concede undisputed victory to the monoplane.

The delay and vacillation which had attended the whole conduct of the F.7/30 requirement came to an end in July, 1935, when an order for the Gloster S.S.37 was placed on behalf of the R.A.F. Preoccupation by Gloster with getting the Gauntlet accepted and into production precluded immediate attention to Specification F.7/30 by the company but, by September, 1934, the S.S.37, a refined successor to the Gauntlet, was ready for flight.

K5200, the Gloster Gladiator prototype. (Gloster Photo.)

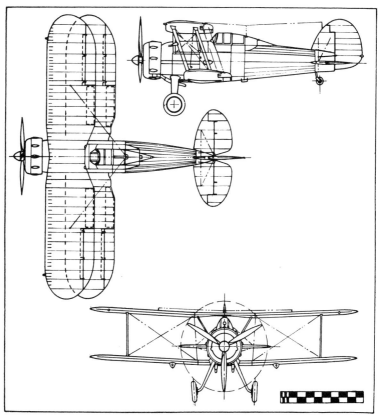

Gloster Gladiator Mk.I

234

The machine was designed by Folland as a Private Venture to F.7/30 and was entered at a late date for evaluation. After adopting two-bay wing cellules for the Gauntlet, Folland reverted to single-bay layout for the S.S.37, which utilized a fuselage and tail unit basically the same as embodied in the Gauntlet. The prototype's engine was the 645 h.p. Mercury VIS.2 and its armament consisted of a pair of fuselage-mounted Vickers guns, together with a single Lewis gun under each lower wing. A particularly distinctive feature was the low-drag cantilever main undercarriage unit with the added refinement of Dowty internally-sprung wheels. Compact and workmanlike, the machine was well-suited to fill the place as representative of the last of the R.A.F.'s biplane fighters to be chosen for service. The prototype S.S.37 became K5200, passing to the Air Ministry from 3rd April, 1935, and being given the name Gladiator Mk.I when ordered into production to Specification F.14/35.

Gloster Gladiator Mk.II of No. 72 Squadron. (R. T. Riding Photo.)

Revisions made in the Mk.I for service use included the fitting of the more powerful 840 h.p. Mercury IX, a sliding cockpit canopy and hydraulically-operated flaps on each wing panel. As soon as sufficient quantities of Browning machine-guns became available, the Gladiator's armament was changed to consist of four of the type.

As part of the Gladiator's development, extensive trials were carried out. Report M/666B/Int.2 of 10th September, 1937, from A.&A.E.E. Martlesham detailed comparative tests made in July, 1937, with K7964 fitted with a 10 ft. 6 in. diameter Fairey-Reed three-blade metal propeller driven by a Mercury IX giving 840 h.p. at 14,000 ft. with a special ·572:1 reduction gear against K5200 flying with a standard Mercury IX using its normal ·5:1 reduction gear. K5200 was tested with both the two-blade Watts wooden propeller and the metal three-blade Fairey type. The trials were conducted with the primary objective of achieving smoother running of the engine. With the Fairey propeller K5200 reached a top speed of 253 m.p.h. and climbed to 32,000 ft. without any tendency for the engine to cut. With the Watts propeller, the same machine achieved a maximum speed of 248 m.p.h. By comparison

235

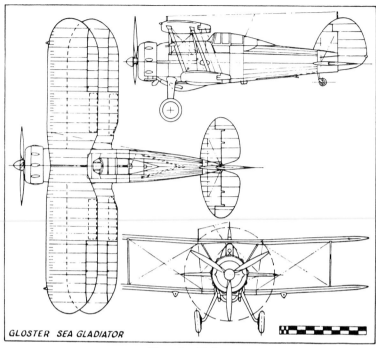

GLOSTER SEA GLADIATOR

Gloster Sea Gladiator

K7964, tested at an empty weight of 3,276 lb. and a loaded weight of 4,646 lb., reached 245·5 m.p.h. at 14,200 ft., climbed at 2,390 ft./min. at 5,000 ft., and attained a service ceiling of 32,000 ft., with an estimated absolute ceiling of 34,000 ft. Conclusions reached were that take-off run with the increased gear ratio was cut but that top level speed was reduced also. It was decided later to adopt the three-blade metal propeller and ·572:1 gear ratio to Specification F.36/37 as the Gladiator Mk.II.

The success of the Gladiator attracted the attention of the Admiralty so that a version of the Mk.II was produced in 1938 for the Fleet Air Arm as the Sea Gladiator Mk.II. The usual naval equipment—comprising arrester hook, catapulting points, and a collapsible dinghy housed in a fairing between the undercarriage legs—was added for the Gladiator to succeed the Nimrod in the Navy.

As the last British fighter biplane passed into production, its place in the minds of its creators at Gloster had been taken swiftly by thoughts of the exciting and satisfying prospect ahead of freedom at long last to concentrate on development of the monoplane, a process which was already engaging the resources of the rest of the industry.

Although the train of events which attended more or less every aspect of the F.7/30 specification over several years had resulted in little more than downright frustration and disappointment to all actively engaged in trying to meet its originally well-conceived and far-sighted requirements, the evolution of the Gladiator was, at least, some vindication and compensation. By the time that Gloster received the production contract for the Gladiator, the events and state of affairs, which to a great degree dictated the terms of a requirement, had sped at ever-gathering momentum past Specification F.7/30 so that the Gladiator—although it brought with it in one step a ridiculously delayed increase of double the fire power in an R.A.F. single-seat fighter—constituted merely a stop-gap before the triumphant advent of the monoplane, an event which, perhaps, had been worth waiting for, as it brought not one but two brilliant examples destined for unprecedented fame and undying glory.

The peak of biplane elegance, the Fairey Fantôme G–ADIF. (Flight International Photo.)

CHAPTER SIX

REARMAMENT — AND THE MONOPLANE

In retrospect, the decade leading up to the unleashing of the hounds of war in 1939 is one of rapid advance in all aspects of aeronautical design in the early 1930s with, from 1934 onwards, a sense of urgency introduced once the utter futility of the dangerous and misguided policy of disarmament was realized and appreciated.

In 1923 it had been agreed that the strength of the Royal Air Force should be increased over a period to eighty-one squadrons. After ten years the planned programme had not been implemented as, by the end of 1933, the total had reached only seventy-four squadrons. The schedule had lagged owing to financial stringency brought about by the Depression of the late 1920s and early 1930s and also as a result of the indiscretion of the Government in placing the safety of the Nation in jeopardy by contributing to the folly of limitation of the armed services, which the British people have the right to expect to be provided for them out of the hard-earned money extracted by way of taxation. The failure in 1933 of the International Disarmament Conference held in Geneva, and the subsequent growth in the size of the air forces of other nations, finally provided the impetus needed to give the Royal Air Force and the Fleet Air Arm the chance to expand.

The first step envisaged was the speedy completion of the programme planned in 1923 and six new squadrons were authorized in the March, 1934, Air Estimates. A bare three months later, in July, a fresh scheme—designated A—was announced for far greater expansion of the R.A.F., including the stepping-up of the Home Defence Air Forces from fifty-two to seventy-five squadrons, with the formation of eighteen extra units designed to give a total R.A.F. strength in all areas of one hundred and twenty-eight squadrons at the end of a five-year period. After a further three months, the decision was taken in November, 1934, to expedite the whole programme to provide, during 1935–36, twenty-two of the Home Defence squadrons plus three for the Fleet Air Arm.

The primary reason for the sense of urgency which at last seeped its way into the inert minds of the inept individuals responsible for the well-being of the millions of inhabitants of the United Kingdom was the alarm occasioned by the disclosure on 27th March, 1935, that Germany possessed a resuscitated air force. Once again, in spite of the plainest evidence visible for all to see, allied to the events of past history, the infamous German military machine had been permitted to rise through the weak-kneed behaviour of incompetent politicians.

The immediate outcome was the announcement on 22nd May, 1935, of Scheme C to hasten the expansion of the home-based R.A.F. to reach, by March, 1937, a total of one thousand, five hundred first-line aircraft, the number considered necessary to reach by that date parity with France and Germany. As the international situation continued to worsen and the chances of maintaining peace grew slenderer, so another programme—Scheme F— was brought into being in February, 1936, which provided for a greater proportion of fighters than had Scheme C.

The turn of events had finally forced the Government, who in the contingency of an air war, would suffer equally as much as the population whose interests they had been elected to protect, to abandon completely their wanderings in the wilderness of disarmament and to effect an unqualified aboutface into feverish rearmament.

Fairey Fox Mk.VII. (Fairey Photo.)

In the midst of this expansion—unprecedented in peacetime—Britain's fighter designers strained to provide the squadrons with the aircraft for which they were calling. By now, however, the fighter had changed completely from the relatively simple aeroplane of a few years before into a highly-complex and increasingly-expensive machine. Correspondingly, its gestation period had lengthened considerably—so there was no time to lose if the squadrons were to be brought up to a decent level of strength.

Specification F.35/35 for a single-seat, high-speed fighter failed to produce anything but unrealized projects. Bristol proposed the Type 151 monoplane and Hawker also submitted a tender on 21st February, 1936. The project from General Aircraft consisted of a Bristol Hercules-powered monoplane with variable-area wings.

The most unorthodox design to F.35/35 came as the A.S.31 from Airspeed and was one of the most extraordinary—and, at the same time, elegant —fighters ever to be drawn up. The A.S.31's wings, with straight trailing edge and tapered leading edge, carried its tractor Rolls-Royce Merlin engine embedded in the centre-section. The tail unit was carried at the rear by slender twin booms, the outstanding feature of the A.S.31 being the fantastic proposal to house the pilot in a cupola forming the front portion of the fin set in the centre of the tailplane. The machine was planned to carry eight guns and to have an estimated top speed of 450 m.p.h. As the A.S.31 was not built it was never ascertained whether the prediction that the large moments which the pilot would experience in his tail cabin would make him airsick might prove to be true.

Although serious development of the biplane fighter had virtually ceased in Britain by the mid-1930s, two Private Venture examples were designed by Marcel Lobelle of Fairey. The Fox Mk.VII was a single-seat fighter development of the two-seat Fox bomber and was evolved for the Belgian Air Force, by whom it was known as the Kangourou. An 860 h.p. Hispano-Suiza 12Y gave the Fox Mk.VII a top speed of 232 m.p.h. as a single-seater and the machine could be converted into a two-seater in one hour. Armament was heavy and comprised a cannon firing through the airscrew hub and four machine-guns, disposed one on each side of the fuselage and one in each upper wing. Alternatively, six machine-guns could be fitted.

Lobelle's other biplane fighter was the outstandingly beautiful Fantôme, designed in 1934 and entered in the 1935 Belgian International Fighter Competition. The Fantôme, powered by the 925 h.p. Hispano-Suiza 12 Ycrs was armed with a 20 mm. Oerlikon cannon firing through the propeller shaft, two nose-mounted Browning machine-guns and a Browning in each lower wing. Registered F–6, the Fantôme made its first flight in June, 1935, and later flew as G–ADIF. With a top speed of 270 m.p.h., it was one of the cleanest and most elegant biplane fighters to be conceived but G–ADIF was unlucky enough to crash at Evère during the Competition on 17th July, 1935, killing its pilot S. H. G. Trower. Despite this setback, three more examples— known as the Féroce—were assembled in Belgium from British parts during

Vickers Type 279 Venom. (Bristol Siddeley Photo.)

1936, two being sold subsequently to Russia but delivered to Spain; the third Belgian-assembled machine underwent armament trials at A.&A.E.E. Martlesham as L7045.

Following Specification F.7/30, the next fighter requirement of importance to result in several prototypes was F.5/34, calling for a single-seater equipped with six or eight Browning machine-guns with 300 r.p.g. to fire for 15 sec., a reflector sight, a retractable undercarriage incorporating wheel-brakes, enclosed cockpit, oxygen for the pilot, and capable of 275 m.p.h. at 15,000 ft., 265 m.p.h. at 20,000 ft., a service ceiling of 33,000 ft., a landing run of 250 yards and an endurance of 90 min.

There was no further sign of a biplane being envisaged to meet F.5/34. Instead, each contender's designer had turned without hesitation to the low-wing monoplane as the best all-round layout for the purpose.

From Vickers there appeared in 1936 their interpretation in the form of the lowest-powered and smallest of the F.5/34 machines, the dainty-looking, square-cut little Private Venture Type 279 Venom. Basically a closed-cockpit adaptation of the Jockey Mk.II, the Venom was designed around the 625 h.p. Bristol Aquila AE–3s engine housed in an N.A.C.A. cowling, complete with cooling gills. The polygon-section, monocoque, dural after-fuselage was metal-skinned, the same covering being used for the R.A.F.34-section wings, which incorporated split flaps and housed the eight Browning machine-guns. The Venom's Vickers oleo-pneumatic undercarriage retracted inwards and the engine turned a three-blade de Havilland-Hamilton variable-pitch propeller. Registered PVO–10, the machine had a top speed of 312 m.p.h., an initial climb rate of 3,000 ft./min. and a 32,000 ft. service ceiling.

Early in 1935 H. P. Folland, in collaboration with H. E. Preston, began the layout of the G.38 to F.5/34, destined to be the last of his fine designs for Gloster. As well as being his final Gloster fighter, the G.38 was Folland's most elegant product for the Company and, indeed, one of the best-looking single-seat fighters of its era. Completed in December, 1937, the machine was a low-wing monoplane powered by the 840 h.p. Mercury IX enclosed in a long-chord cowling with controllable gills and driving a de Havilland three-blade, controllable-pitch propeller. In one stage the specification had encouraged

Flt.Lt. P. E. G. Sayer flying the elegant Gloster F.5/34. (Gloster Photo.)

designers to take the plunge and embody in the new prototypes all of the advanced features being promoted in the interests of higher performance and fighting efficiency. The G.38's fuselage was an oval-section, light-alloy monocoque structure with stressed-skin sheathing the wings and tail unit and with fabric covering the control surfaces. The Dowty-designed main undercarriage retracted simply by swinging rearwards and upwards, leaving a portion of the wheels exposed under the wings. The armament of eight guns was housed in the wings, the method followed generally on the adoption of the

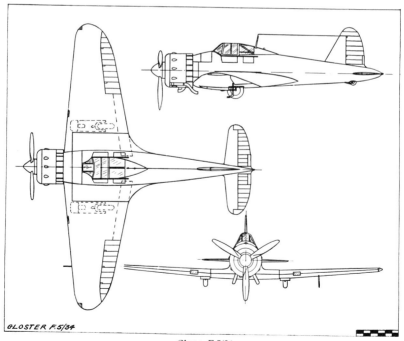

GLOSTER F.5/34

Gloster F.5/34

Browning. The elimination of synchronizing gear allowed an unimpeded rate of fire, an advantage which could be grasped fully with the reliability of the Browning under remote control.

Pre-occupation with development and production of the Gauntlet and Gladiator was behind the comparatively slow progress made with the Gloster F.5/34. Following the first flight in December, 1937, of K5604, a second prototype—K8089—flew in March, 1938. By then, the Hurricane and Spitfire were in production as the start of the new generation of R.A.F. single-seat fighters and the Gloster G.38, in spite of its excellent performance, failed to obtain a production order. Nevertheless, it embodied virtually all of the newly-accepted features of fighter design, including hydraulically-operated split flaps, cantilever flying surfaces, and a faired cockpit canopy bestowing an

The shapely Bristol Type 146 to F.5/34. (Bristol Photo.)

excellent view from the pilot's position. The top speed of the trim G.38 was 315 m.p.h. at 16,000 ft., with an initial climb rate of 2,080 ft./min. and a service ceiling of 32,500 ft. Both machines continued to be occupied on experimental flying until the middle of 1941.

Representative also of the new style of all-metal, stressed-skin, low-wing monoplane was the Bristol prototype to F.5/34—the Type 146. Drafted around the 835 h.p. Bristol Perseus PRE–IS nine-cylinder sleeve-valve radial engine, the machine differed considerably from its precursor—the Type 133. The Type 146 was far more elegant and less bulky in appearance, combining a slim fuselage with tapered wings and tailplane and elevators. Of particular note in the Type 146 was the finely-shaped sliding bubble cockpit canopy—a feature adopted universally for fighters some years afterwards. All three components of the undercarriage retracted completely, the main wheels turning inwards to be housed in the centre-section. The original wing-mounted armament of four guns was later increased to eight.

The machine, registered K5119, was completed during 1937 but it was not until 11th February, 1938, that it made its first flight with Cyril Uwins in the cockpit. Instead of the Perseus engine, the power plant installed was the 840 h.p. Mercury VIII. Flight trials were cut short, however, after three months by an accident at Filton on Empire Air Day during May, 1938, when the Type 146 collided with a set-piece while taxiing. The fact that, by that date, Specification F.5/34 had been superseded and that the Company's resources were being devoted to production of the Blenheim, led to the decision to forgo further development of the Type 146. With a three-blade, controllable-pitch propeller fitted a speed of 287 m.p.h. at 15,000 ft and a useful service ceiling of 38,100 ft. were attained.

During the 1914–18 War, quite a number of small aircraft firms had designed and constructed examples of their own prototype single-seat fighters. The ensuing years of peace had witnessed virtually no activity of this nature until, in 1937, the Martin-Baker Aircraft Company of Denham, led by their energetic and brilliant founder and designer James Martin, built the M.B.2 as a Private Venture conforming to F.5/34.

The design started what was to be an unusual and peculiar episode in the history of British fighter development—the story of the Martin-Baker fighters covering a span of some eight years. The Company was small and, compared with other illustrious names in the Industry, relatively obscure. Martin's inventiveness had originated a number of original constructional ideas, notably a system of simple, strong, tubular metal structure which could be assembled easily with unskilled labour. The M.B.2 was the third aircraft designed by Martin. Of the two previous machines—both civil monoplanes— the first was abandoned when partly completed and the second, the M.B.1, flew successfully in 1935 but was destroyed later by fire in the factory. Nonetheless, the M.B.1 proved the feasibility of the simply-built and easily-maintained structure which had low cost also in its favour.

In 1937 James Martin demonstrated his outstanding versatility by switching straight to the design of the fighter. The M.B.2, however, was not an ordinary fighter and exhibited no sign of being a slavish copy of any other machine. Its creator possessed very definite ideas of his own and took the opportunity to incorporate as many of them as possible in the airframe. Prior to the renaissance which took place in British fighter design in the 1930s and which produced the modern monoplane, the production of the wooden or metal biplanes was a relatively simple matter. The fast monoplane of the new and vastly more powerful and complex breed of fighters now appearing, by its very nature made far greater demands on the resources of its parent company. To produce such a prototype would have engaged a considerable proportion of the skill and capacity of any of the large organizations, and Martin-Baker showed remarkable courage and determination in tackling the project. From beginning to end the whole design was governed by the principles of simple, easy production and repair, allied to as high a performance as possible.

The engine chosen by Martin for the M.B.2 was the air-cooled Napier Dagger III, nominally rated at 805 h.p. but specially boosted to provide over 1,000 h.p. at take-off. The small cross-section of the twenty-four-cylinder H-type power plant was carried on into the slim fuselage, the lines of which were kept exceedingly clean; the only major excrescence on the fuselage was the framed tear-drop, full-vision cockpit canopy situated mid-way along its length. The deep rear to the fuselage was intended to provide sufficient keel area to dispense with a fixed fin and the rudder was a simple surface set into the back of the fuselage. The structure was built up on Martin's steel-tube system, metal panels covering the fuselage to the rear of the cockpit. Aft of this point to the leading edge of the tailplane, fabric was used. Although provision was made in the design for a retractable undercarriage, the prototype M.B.2 was equipped with fixed landing-gear of 9 ft. 8 in. track in prominent trousers, the port fairing incorporating the oil cooler in a further effort to reduce drag. The eight ·303 Browning machine-guns were mounted in the fabric-covered wings outboard of the undercarriage units, particular attention being paid in the installation to swift rearming which could be completed in five minutes.

Marked M–B–1—and allocated civil registration G–AEZD—the M.B.2 made its first flight on 3rd August, 1938, at Harwell piloted by Capt. V. H. Baker, who demonstrated the machine in public at Heston in May, 1939. An unusual feature of the M.B.2's aerodynamic layout was that the length of 34 ft. 2 in. exceeded the span of 34 ft., a practice which was to become increasingly evident and accepted in the future. Although stability was promoted by using the long fuselage, the disposition of the fin area was faulty and a fixed vertical surface made its appearance above the tail.

As P9594, the M.B.2 underwent trials at Martlesham Heath during 1938, many of its features earning enthusiastic praise in A.&A.E.E. Report M/730/Q.1 of 1st December, 1938. The Dagger III No. 77101 was rated at 798 h.p. at 5,500 ft. and the engine's installation was reported as excellent, the time taken to remove and replace being the fastest encountered in recent years for a power plant of similar size. The type of spinner and its means of attachment were thought very good. The report commented that many features of the M.B.2 were excellent and seemed hardly capable of improvement. Among those which drew particular praise were the first-class accessibility of the guns through panels released by half a turn of a key, the sorbo-covered platform for kneeling armourers—recommended as well worth standardization on fighters, the quickly-removable unit-built seat and control-box system, and the retractable crash-pylon which automatically extended behind the pilot's head in the event of a nose-over—another feature recommended to be made standard. The ailerons were mass-balanced inside the wings and the specially-developed Martin-Baker jacking pads facilitated removal of parts. The machine was found to be directionally unstable while taxiing on its undercarriage units of pneumatic and oleo shock absorbers and Dunlop low-pressure tyres and brakes. Entry to the cockpit was assessed as rather difficult but, once inside, it was noted as roomy and comfortable, warm and free from draught and with a good view in all directions both in flight and while taxiing.

In every way, the arrangement of the cockpit elicited unstinted praise but the test pilots were not so happy with the M.B.2's overall flying characteristics in its earlier form after the fixed fin had been added. A general lack of

Martin-Baker M.B.2 P9594 with final conventional vertical tail surfaces. (Martin-Baker Photo.)

flying stability was noted, the machine being considered as just stable with engine on but unstable with engine off. Great concentration was necessary in level flight and in turns, the elevator being found too sensitive when gliding and was recommended to have lower gearing. With flaps up the stall occurred at 73 m.p.h. I.A.S. and at 58 m.p.h. I.A.S. with flaps down. In banks it was found to be unpleasant as, owing to the lack of lateral stability, the M.B.2 would not take up a natural banking angle and threw the pilot from side to side of the cockpit. Accurate slow rolls were difficult and gun-firing trials showed that it was hard to hold steady aim owing to the abnormal feel of the

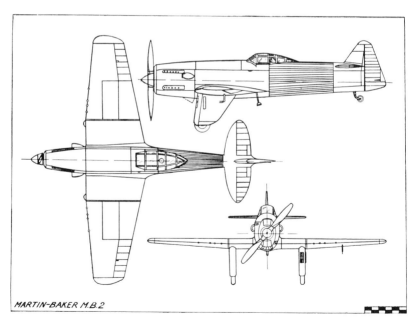

Martin-Baker M.B.2

controls. Martlesham's general assessment of the Martin-Baker fighter was that, owing to the peculiarities of rudder and ailerons, it was not pleasant to fly and that longitudinal, lateral and directional stability were not good and should be improved. To render the M.B.2 acceptable, the report called for alterations to make the ailerons lighter and more effective, increased aft keel area and a larger and more positive rudder, greater tailplane area to bestow glide stability, and the provision of dihedral to improve lateral stability.

By the time that the Heston demonstration took place in May, 1939, the new fin and rudder—of normal triangular form—had been installed. The A.&A.E.E. tests of the M.B.2 were carried out at a loaded weight of 5,537 lb. and a wing loading of 26 lb./sq.ft. The machine's particularly clean design enabled it to attain a top speed of 350 m.p.h., between that of the contemporary slower Hurricane and faster Spitfire. In spite of the M.B.2's many fine attributes, the fact that its system of structure would have enabled simple and swift quantity production and that the prototype could have been developed into a very useful addition to the R.A.F. at a period when it was absolutely essential for the country to possess adequate reserves of fighters, the brilliantly-conceived M.B.2 was not ordered and P9594 was eventually dismantled at Denham.

Although numerous laudable attempts to provide an up-to-date single-seat, multi-gun fighter for the R.A.F. were made by way of Specifications F.7/30 and F.5/34, the impasse was destined to be resolved in another way, mainly by the determination, sagacity and foresight of the two men to whom Great Britain is so deeply indebted—Sydney Camm and Reginald Mitchell. By the early 1930s, Camm was preparing to concentrate his talents on the monoplane and, to further the object, in August, 1933, discussed the topic with Maj. J. S. Buchanan of the Directorate of Technical Development at the Air Ministry. Camm's proposal was eventually presented some four months afterwards in December as a low-wing monoplane Private Venture adaptation of the Fury, designed around the 660 h.p. steam-cooled Goshawk and armed with two machine-guns in the nose and two in the wing roots. It retained in general the outline of the fuselage and tail surfaces of the Fury, to which were mated the 38 ft. span wings, embodying straight taper from the roots to the rounded tips. A fixed, spatted undercarriage was proposed and the pilot was given the protection of a cockpit canopy faired into a tapered headrest on the rear decking. Clean and typically Hawker, the Fury Monoplane was designed to a loaded weight of 3,802 lb. and expected to reach 280 m.p.h. at 14,000 ft.

The Fury Monoplane was not built as, matching the strong stirrings in the field of aeroplane design, were the steps being taken by engine manufacturers to increase the power available for the new generation of aircraft. The in-line unit undoubtedly possessed the great merit of low frontal area and reduced drag, its main disadvantage compared with the bulky, air-cooled radial being the necessity of providing the extra complexity and weight of a liquid cooling system. The radiator imposed also a certain drag penalty but this was mitigated to a large extent by careful design of its shape, area and housing to keep the loss to the absolute minimum. Hawker were naturally aware of Rolls-Royce intentions and progress in development. The unhappy diversionary episode of the steam-cooled Goshawk was coming to a close and attention was concentrated fully on a normal liquid cooling system applied to the P.V.12, the Rolls-Royce successor to the Kestrel, for which the drawings had been started in January, 1933. Development proceeded apace with steady increments in output in successive models. The P.V.12 benefited immeasurably from the invaluable experience gained by Rolls-Royce when they designed and produced the superlative "R" series of twenty racing engines for the Schneider Trophy seaplanes. The Merlin, as the P.V.12 was eventually christened, turned out to be one of the most successful aero-engines ever produced and, over the years, earned for itself a name as illustrious as the numerous aircraft which it powered in so many different marks.

Backed by the superb engineering skill of Rolls-Royce, the Merlin was a magnificent engine for Camm to use as the basis around which to begin to draw up in May, 1934, the detailed design of his successor to the Fury line. Specification F.5/34 served as a broad outline for the new monoplane at first but, as the design conformed to it only partly, in August, 1934, a completely fresh requirement—F.36/34—was formulated to envelop the machine as envisaged by Camm. The tender for the Interceptor Monoplane, as it had by then become known, was submitted on 4th September, 1934, and approval was received on 21st February, 1935, for Hawker to proceed with the construction of a prototype F.36/34 single-seat, high-speed, monoplane fighter. As originally conceived, F.36/34 expected a top speed of approximately 320 m.p.h. at about 15,000 ft., the machine to carry four machine-guns able to fire for a minimum time of twenty seconds. While awaiting the decision of the Air Ministry to order a prototype, Hawker proceeded in December, 1934, to construct a mock-up of the F.36/34 monoplane.

One extremely important point was still far from Camm's liking. Specification F.5/34 had made provision for six or eight guns and there seemed to be little sense in preparing a design for a considerably more advanced aeroplane to carry but four guns. Negotiations were in progress in 1934 to obtain the licence to adapt the American Colt-manufactured ·300 Browning gun to ·303 calibre and to produce it in England. Ultimately, the Birmingham Small Arms Company undertook the production of this very reliable machine-gun with its high rate of fire and its adoption on this side of the Atlantic immediately opened up the way for its incorporation in the Hawker Monoplane so that, upon the conclusion in July, 1935, of the agreement between Colt and B.S.A., F.36/34 was amended to cover the use of a set of wings housing eight ·303 Browning machine-guns.

The Hawker system of metal tubular construction with fabric covering had proved itself over many years. Its cardinal virtues of simple and speedy construction and repair—in particular the ease with which battle damage could be rectified—made the Company loth to relinquish it and it was decided that the system still should prove adequate for the performance expected from the F.5/34 monoplane. Nevertheless, the Hawker design staff proceeded to evolve metal stressed-skin wings in anticipation of their subsequent adoption for the machine. Construction went ahead smoothly so that the prototype F.36/34—K5083—was ready to be taken on 23rd October, 1935, from Kingston for assembly at Brooklands.

In one step, Sydney Camm had effected what was destined to be an extremely successful changeover from biplane to monoplane with a design which bore the typical Hawker stamp of a first-class, purposeful and thoroughbred design. Fitted with the Rolls-Royce Merlin C engine No. 11 giving 1,029 h.p. at 11,000 ft. and driving a Watts two-blade, fixed-pitch, wooden propeller, K5083 made its first flight at Brooklands on 6th November, 1935, piloted by the renowned Hawker chief test pilot P. W. S. Bulman. Bulman continued to carry out development flying with the machine for the next three months

Hawker F.36/34 Hurricane prototype K5083. (Hawker Photo.)

until, on 7th February, 1936, following incorporation of minor modifications, K5083 was ready for the A.&A.E.E. pilots at Martlesham Heath to assess the potent newcomer.

A.&A.E.E. Martlesham Report M/689 of April, 1936, recorded their impressions of K5083. As received from Hawker, the machine weighed 5,672 lb. loaded. The covered cockpit drew praise for enabling the pilot to look aft without risk of having his goggles blown off. The cockpit was considered to have a small blind spot to the rear but its comfort was excellent. Adverse criticisms of the machine were that, at over 150 m.p.h., it was impossible to slide the canopy to the rear for emergency exit and that the machine was unacceptable until the canopy would open at any speed. A modification was recommended to the flap which covered the lower half of the main wheels when folded as it struck a tuft of earth and grass on landing, resulting in the fracture of a brake pipe line. The brakes were assessed as good but care was needed to prevent the machine turning up on its nose at the end of the landing run.

A fair amount of trouble was experienced with the Type C Merlin fitted during the trials. Merlin No. 11 was exchanged for No. 15 in which the supercharger tail and roller bearings failed in the course of tests by Bulman. This was replaced by No. 17 which later had piston failure and was then exchanged for No. 19. Various types of engine failure had arisen in K5083 and the carburation of the Merlin C test engines was considered unsatisfactory for service use.

Flight trials established a top speed of 315 m.p.h. at 16,200 ft. and a rate of climb of 2,550 ft./min. at sea level. As speed increased, the ailerons were found to change steadily from light to heavy until, at maximum level speed and in dives, they became heavy for a fighter. Response to the ailerons was rapid and, in general, they were considered satisfactory but would be improved at high speed if made lighter without over-balancing. The same effect was noticed with the rudder as speed increased and it became extremely heavy in a dive. The suggestion was made that the rudder should be lighter at over 150 m.p.h. The elevators were satisfactory but the tail-trim cables tended to stretch, thereby giving an unpleasant effect of fore-and-aft instability. Although K5083 tended to fly left wing down in the climb and right wing down at top speed, the machine was considered generally simple and easy to fly and to have no apparent vices.

Development flying continued and, on 3rd June, 1936, Hawker received a contract covering the production of six hundred machines, the name Hurricane being agreed a little later on 27th June. The Merlin C had been abandoned and replaced by the Merlin F, to be produced as the Merlin I. After a number had been built, production of the Merlin F was stopped, its place being taken by the Merlin G which passed into quantity production as the Merlin II.

So, with initial deliveries being made on 15th December, 1937, to No. 111 Squadron at Northolt, the R.A.F. was on the way to being modernised, receiving in one step an excellent monoplane which brought with it double the armament of the Gladiator and an increase in speed of nearly 70 m.p.h.

L1547, the first production Hurricane to Specification 15/36, went to A.&A.E.E. Martlesham for tests together with L1696, evaluation proceeding from 2nd September, 1938, until 17th January, 1939. Both machines

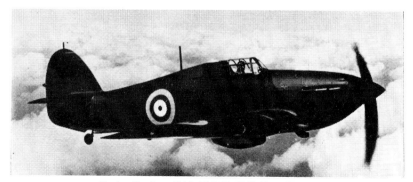

Hawker Hurricane F.Mk.I L1648. (Rolls-Royce Photo.)

Supermarine Spitfire prototype K5054. (Supermarine Photo.)

incorporated various modifications, including revised rudder and rear fuselage and the addition of an underfin for extra keel surface. L1547 was fitted with a tail parachute and A.&A.E.E. Martlesham Report M/689A of 10th February, 1939, noted that the average total height lost in three turns of a spin was 3,800 ft., 5,800 ft. being lost in an eight-turn spin but no trouble was experienced in recovering. The same report covered dive tests carried out with L1696 which disclosed that the cockpit hood was still difficult to open at around 380 m.p.h. in a dive and that, after preliminary dives to 395 m.p.h. I.A.S., the bottom fuselage panel failed. Several of the wooden formers and stringers were broken and it was thought that the damage had been caused by a large puddle of water at take-off but, when the same thing happened again at 385 m.p.h. I.A.S. to a replacement panel, the remedy was found to lie in the insertion of an extra former which was satisfactory at up to 390 m.p.h. I.A.S.

While Sydney Camm had been busy at Hawker with his Hurricane, Reginald Mitchell was actively pursuing his own ideals at Supermarine. Just as Camm was aware of the great potential of the new engine from Rolls-Royce—the P.V.12—so was Mitchell; his ultimate redesign of the Type 224—the Type 300—was based on the installation of the P.V.12 and accepted in January, 1935, for construction as a prototype. To cover the Supermarine Type 300, Specification F.37/34 was prepared and Mitchell's masterpiece—the prototype Spitfire K5054—emerged to make its first flight on 5th March, 1936, at Eastleigh, Hants., in the skilled hands of Capt. J. Summers. Mitchell's health had given rise to increasingly serious anxiety yet, despite pain and worry, he did not spare himself in producing in the Spitfire his finest design, which was in itself ultimately to provide a world-renowned memorial for him by becoming synonymous with his name.

The prototype Spitfire's Merlin C was faired into an elegantly slim, light alloy monocoque fuselage but the most striking feature of the dainty fighter lay in the beautifully conceived elliptical eight-gun wings. The neat single-strut main undercarriage legs folded outwards and the undersides of the wings carried the radiator to starboard and the oil cooler to port. In contrast with the fabric-covered prototype and early production Hurricane, the Spitfire was designed for stressed-skin overall with the exception of its control surfaces.

A.&A.E.E. Martlesham Report M/692/Int 2 of September, 1936, was liberal in its praise for the new Supermarine single-seater. Tested at a loaded weight of 5,332 lb., ground handling was assessed as exceptionally good with take-off and landing straightforward and easy. The Spitfire's cockpit was found to be well arranged, roomy and with good controls. In flight, the control surfaces were thought to be entirely satisfactory for the type of machine, were well-harmonized and appeared to constitute an excellent compromise between manœuvrability and steadiness for shooting. The suggestions were made that the elevator control might be improved by reducing the gear ratio between the control column and the surfaces and that the rather flat glide could be remedied by fitting flaps of higher drag. The Spitfire earned itself an excellent all-round report which concluded that it was simple and easy to fly, had no vices and, in general, could be flown without risk by an average, fully-trained service fighter pilot.

The stage was set to provide the Royal Air Force with a magnificent stablemate for the Hurricane, the pair of which would give the Service possession of the finest single-seat fighters extant. The first production order for Supermarine to construct three hundred and ten Spitfire Mk.Is was placed on 3rd June, 1936, to Specification F.16/36 but, before the first machine of the batch could fly, Reginald Mitchell succumbed on 11th June, 1937, at the early age of forty-two, to the illness which he had fought for so long and with such courage. And so Great Britain lost a genius indeed among her aircraft designers, a man of determination and valour deserving the highest honours in recognition of the gifts which he bestowed upon his country, to contribute so profoundly to its salvation in the dark and dangerous days ahead.

The privilege of introducing the Spitfire into the R.A.F. fell to No. 19 Squadron at Duxford when its Mk.Is arrived in June, 1938. After Mitchell's sad and untimely death, his place as chief designer at Supermarine was taken by Joseph Smith who was subsequently to be responsible for the evolution of the numerous variants of the Spitfire to follow.

While the Royal Air Force was thus acquiring its new modern equipment, the Fleet Air Arm was beginning also to think in terms of the monoplane and Specification O.27/34 was issued to bring forth a two-seat fighter dive-bomber. Several firms were drawn to devise projects to meet the requirement, including Avro, Blackburn, Boulton Paul, Hawker and Vickers.

The Blackburn tender was accepted, resulting in the Air Ministry placing an order for two prototypes in April, 1935, the first of which, K5178, appeared during 1937. Named Skua and designed by G. E. Petty, the machine was a comely low-wing monoplane armed with four Browning guns in the wings and a Lewis gun in the rear cockpit. Both K5178 and the second prototype K5179 flew with Mercury IX engines but the production Skuas, of which one hundred and ninety were ordered in July, 1936, used the 905 h.p. Bristol Perseus XII sleeve-valve engine.

Blackburn Skua. (Blackburn Photo.)

No. 800 Squadron, F.A.A., took over the first Skuas in November, 1938, and the type's main claims to distinction are that it was the Fleet Air Arm's first operational monoplane and its first specially designed dive-bomber. All-metal stressed-skin construction was used and the wings folded for carrier stowage.

At the same time as the Fleet Air Arm decided to continue employing the two-seat fighter, the Royal Air Force became conscious of the increasing shortcomings in its own Demons. A replacement was obviously needed if the two-seat fighter concept were to continue to retain its place in the squadrons. The Frazer-Nash type of turret had provided a partial answer to shielding the all-important rear gunner at higher speeds but could patently find no place in the new generation of monoplanes with their considerably enhanced performance.

Specification F.9/35 was accordingly devised to cover a new two-seat interceptor fighter replacement for the R.A.F.'s Demons, based on the installation of a power-operated multi-gun turret. To render the new machine effective it was required to possess speed and manœuvrability reasonably comparable with single-seat fighters in spite of the handicaps inherent in the bulky turret.

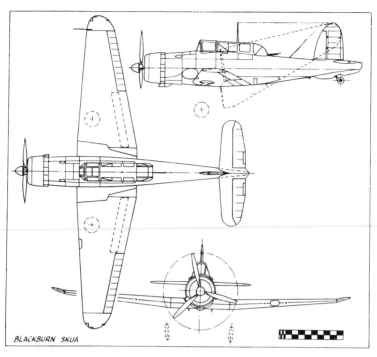

BLACKBURN SKUA

Blackburn Skua Mk.II

Several F.9/35 projects were prepared, that by Armstrong Whitworth—a 39 ft. span mid-wing monoplane—being designed around an engine installation of two Armstrong Siddeley Terriers. No progress was made with the A.W. F.9/35 proposal and it was soon abandoned.

Bristol submitted the Type 147, a single-engine low-wing monoplane which shared many parts in common with the Bristol Type 148. The rear gunner was intended to sit immediately behind the pilot and to fire his four Browning guns, which were to be mounted a little further aft in a sunken turret, by remote control. The first version of the Type 147, submitted in August, 1935, was expected to attain a top speed of 280 m.p.h. at 15,000 ft. with a Perseus engine and the alternative Type 147 proposal of the following month, using a Bristol Hercules, should have reached 318 m.p.h. at the same height. Neither of the Bristol tenders met with Air Ministry approval and both remained solely projects.

Two firms, Boulton Paul and Hawker, were successful in receiving orders during the Autumn of 1935, for prototypes of their F.9/35 designs. Designed by J. D. North, the Boulton Paul P.82 Defiant K8310 made its first flight two years later at Wolverhampton on 11th August, 1937, in the hands of Cecil Feather. At first its appearance was that of a conventional single-seat, low-wing fighter as the turret was not fitted and its position was faired over. With the 1,030 h.p. Merlin I installed the Defiant returned a maximum speed of 302 m.p.h. and, as its initial trials showed it to be a satisfactory, stable aircraft, the Boulton Paul A.Mk.IID turret with four Browning machine-guns was installed. At the same time, slight modifications were made to the airframe and retractable fairings fore and aft of the turret helped to streamline its bulk when it was not in use. Perhaps the most extraordinary and lamentable feature of the Defiant was its complete lack of any forwards-firing armament for the pilot. Production of the Defiant Mk.I was ordered during 1937 to Specification F.5/37, with the 1,030 h.p. Merlin III as the selected power

Boulton Paul Defiant F.Mk.I N1581 of No. 264 Squadron. (Dowty Photo.)

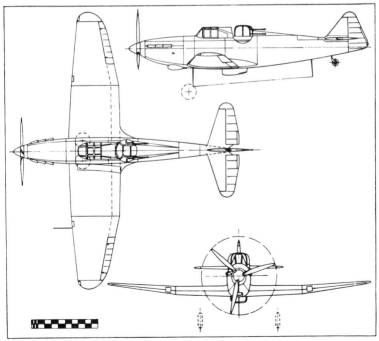

B.P. Defiant Mk.I

255

The Hawker Hotspur, K8309, with turret. (Hawker Photo.)

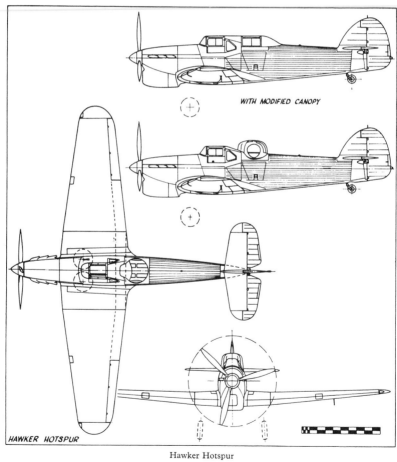

WITH MODIFIED CANOPY

HAWKER HOTSPUR

Hawker Hotspur

256

plant, the first examples going to No. 264 Squadron in December, 1939. As experience in combat was to show later, the design philosophy behind the Defiant was not a sound one and, when opposed by a single-seat fighter, the type stood little chance of survival with its top speed of 304 m.p.h. and the imposition of its heavy dorsal turret.

The Defiant's only serious rival to F.9/35 was the Hotspur, of which Hawker constructed a single prototype K8309. Similar in general layout to the Defiant, the Hotspur was in the main a major redesign of the Henley light bomber in which the rear gunner's position was replaced by a fully-exposed four-gun Boulton Paul turret. The pilot of the Hotspur was provided with a single Vickers gun housed in the port half of the nose. A 1,025 h.p. Merlin II engine powered the Hotspur which flew eventually on 14th June, 1938, when P. G. Lucas took it into the air for the initial flight. By that time the Defiant had received its production order and, although Specification 17/36 had been drawn up to cover possible production by A. V. Roe, the sole Hotspur built was used for experimental work.

As fighters grew steadily heavier, faster and more complex and their engines increased in power, so the armament which they were developed to carry was receiving attention. The tendency was to increase the weight and size of the missile and to fire it by automatic cannon. The Coventry Ordnance Works quick-firers had made little progress in Great Britain but on the Continent considerable attention had been paid to developing heavier calibre armament.

Fairly obviously, unceasing technical advance was going to bring about the adoption of the cannon as a fighter's weapon and Specification F.37/35 was issued to embrace a single-seat, day-and-night fighter equipped with four 20 mm. cannon. Unbuilt F.37/35 projects included the Supermarine 313, the Bristol Type 153 Hercules-powered adaptation of the Type 151 monoplane, and a version of the Hurricane tendered by Hawker on 23rd April, 1936, intended to carry four Oerlikon guns.

The Westland P.9 Whirlwind was eventually selected for prototype construction, L6844 making its first flight at Yeovil on 11th October, 1938, piloted by Harald Penrose. Designed in 1936 by W. E. W. Petter, the Whirlwind was a strikingly attractive and original low-wing monoplane with a pair of geared and supercharged 885 h.p. Rolls-Royce Peregrine I engines installed in line with the nose of the slim fuselage. The centre-section of the thin wings enclosed the radiators and the fuselage nose housed the battery of four 20 mm. Hispano Mk.I cannon. The tailplane was set high up on the tail fin and the entire undercarriage retracted completely. Some trouble was experienced at first with the Peregrine engine, a development of the Kestrel, but, on the successful conclusion of trials, the Whirlwind was ordered into production in January, 1939. Official reluctance to disclose its existence lasted until 17th December, 1941, when Lord Beaverbrook revealed its name despite the fact that details were known abroad for many months before, since 1939. The Whirlwind earned itself the distinction of being the first Westland fighter to serve with the R.A.F. and was also the first twin-engine single-seat

Westland Whirlwind P7110. (Rolls-Royce Photo.)

fighter to enter any service. In addition, the machine was the sole type to serve using the Peregrine. Only two R.A.F. squadrons—Nos. 137 and 263—were equipped with Whirlwinds which, despite their high top speed of 360 m.p.h. at 15,000 ft., found their choice of aerodromes restricted by the rather high landing speed. When used on operations, the Whirlwind established its *forté* as low-level escort and attack for which its speed, range and heavy firepower rendered it particularly suitable.

Little was done to develop the Whirlwind beyond its original form but L6844 was fitted experimentally with twelve Browning ·303 guns and then with four Hispano Mk.II cannon as an alternative installation. Trial armament in another example was a single 37 mm. cannon.

While Britain's aerial defences against daylight attack had been scandalously weak for many years, provision for dealing with assault under the cover of darkness was even less satisfactory. The night-fighter particularly needed long endurance to carry out its work with any effect and, in searching for a speedy and effective remedy for the deficit, it was decided to adapt the powerful and fast Bristol T.142M Blenheim. Accordingly, from 1938 onwards some two hundred Blenheim Mk.I bombers were converted into night-fighters in the Southern Railway workshops at Ashford. The normal armament of one fixed forwards-firing Browning gun for the pilot and one Vickers K gun in the dorsal turret was augmented by four Brownings with 500 r.p.g. housed in an under-fuselage pack. The two-seat night-fighter Blenheims went a long way towards filling the gap in Britain's nocturnal defences at a crucial time until specifically-developed types could be brought into action.

In an endeavour to provide the Fleet Air Arm with a competent heavily-armed, two-seat fighter, Specification 0.30/35 was issued. A project for converting the Defiant was discussed but, finally, Blackburn produced a modification of the Skua to meet the requirement under the name Roc. George Petty was responsible for the design which used the 905 h.p. Perseus XII. The three initial production examples served as prototypes, L3057 making the first flight on 23rd December, 1938. The most obvious difference in the Roc compared with the Skua was the installation of the Boulton Paul A turret with its four Brownings to the rear of the pilot.

To render the Roc even more useful, it was tested as a seaplane to Specifications 26/36 and 20/37 by fitting L3059 with twin floats but showed directional instability and crashed after taking-off on 3rd December, 1939. Experiments were continued and M.A.E.E. Helensburgh Report H/155 of 30th April, 1940, covered subsequent trials with L3057, the first prototype on floats, to see if a simple modification would effect a cure. Extra fin area was

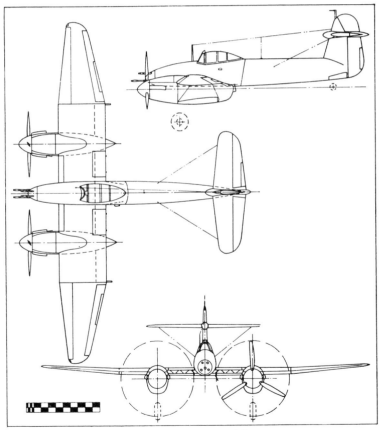

Westland Whirlwind F.Mk.I

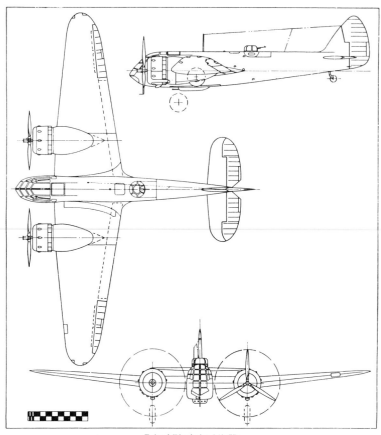

Bristol Blenheim Mk.IF

added under the tail and greatly reduced the instability but care was still needed in turns at low heights. Taxiing was good and take-off normal after a run that was long but not unduly so. Landings were made easily and the Roc was assessed as suitable for service use with the underfin fitted and once the pilot was accustomed to restrictions being imposed on turns at low altitudes owing to subsequent slipping inwards and loss of height. The maximum speed of the float-equipped Roc was reduced to 178 m.p.h. at 6,000 ft. and the idea was subsequently abandoned. The landplane Roc was not particularly successful as a concept and, produced to Specification O.15/37, served shore-based with only Nos. 801 and 806 Squadrons, F.A.A.

Specification F.34/35, in itself derived from an Aquila-powered project to F.5/33 for a two-seat, twin-engine fighter with a four-gun, power-driven turret, resulted in a project from Gloster but the proposal was dropped when the Defiant was accepted for service. However, when Specification F.9/37 was

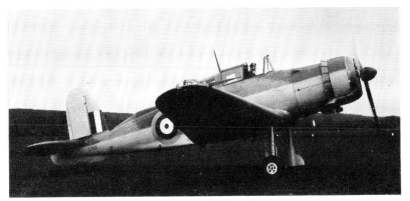

Blackburn Roc. (Blackburn Photo.)

issued Gloster revived the earlier design and modified it to meet the new requirement.

Designed by W. G. Carter, successor to H. P. Folland who had severed his long and successful connection with Gloster to found his own firm, the F.9/37 was Carter's first design for the company. Two prototypes were ordered, L7999 fitted with 1,050 h.p. Bristol Taurus TE/1 engines and L8002 using 885 h.p. Peregrines. The F.9/37 emerged as quite an attractive

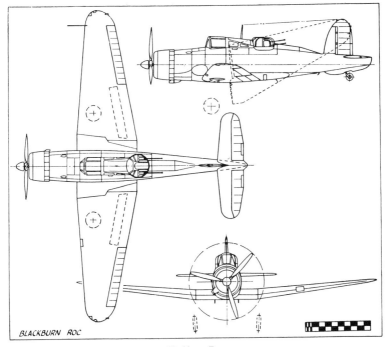

BLACKBURN ROC

Blackburn Roc

Gloster G.39 L7999 fitted with Taurus engines. (Gloster Photo.)

L8002, the Peregrine-engined Gloster G.39. (Gloster Photo.)

and powerful looking low-wing monoplane with twin fins and rudders. The original intention was to construct the F.9/37 as a two-seater but, in the early development stages, it was decided to delete the rear gunner's cockpit and complete the machine as a single-seater. L7999 was ready first and made its initial flight at Brockworth on 3rd April, 1939.

On 23rd May, 1939, the F.9/37 was flown at high speed across Northolt over the assembly of M.P.s and in July, 1939, arrived at Martlesham. The handling report issued from the Establishment in July, 1939, stated that the cockpit was easy to enter and to leave, and was comfortable and of good lay-out. The view appeared to be good in all directions except rearwards. Flown at a loaded weight of 11,653 lb., L7999 was stable about all axes and under all conditions of flight but, with the cooling gills open, stability in the climb was poor but found to be satisfactory when they were either half-open or closed. Approach speed was 90–95 m.p.h. and the undercarriage and flaps descended quickly. A.&A.E.E. Boscombe Down Report 756 of 31st July, 1940, noted that L7999 had been badly damaged on landing after a few preliminary flights at A.&A.E.E.

Returned to Gloster for reconstruction, the F.9/37 was sent back to A.& A.E.E. in April, 1940, with its original troublesome Taurus T–S(a) engines replaced by a pair of 900 h.p. Taurus T–S(a)III units in which the super-chargers had been derated to reduce boost pressure from $+5\frac{1}{4}$lb./sq.in. to $+4\frac{1}{2}$lb./sq.in. maximum. Top speed was thereby brought down from 360 m.p.h. at 15,200 ft. with the original engines to 332 m.p.h. at the same height. Unserviceability prevented completion of tests before L7999 again left A.& A.E.E. but the machine had been assessed as easy and pleasant to fly, with stability considered satisfactory and controls not heavy for a twin-engine fighter. L8002, L7999's 885 h.p. Peregrine-powered sister prototype, made its initial take-off on 22nd February, 1940, and reached a top speed of 330 m.p.h. at 15,000 ft.

Specification F.18/40 required a two-seat, Merlin-engined fighter for day-and-night interception with fixed guns and tests were carried out with ballast carried in L8002 to approximate to the requirement. A mock-up was prepared for an F.18/40 prototype but the project was abandoned. The F.9/37's fuse-lage-mounted armament comprised two 20 mm. Hispano cannon and four ·303 Browning machine-guns installed in an extremely useful long-range fighter which, but for the delaying mishap early in its trials, might well have gone into production to fill an important gap in Britain's fighter force.

By 3rd September, 1939, when—for the second time in twenty-five years—the German war machine moved into action to bring in its own murderous, bestial and incredibly inhuman way undreamed-of terror and misery to the innocent peoples of Europe, the Royal Air Force and, to a lesser degree, the Fleet Air Arm had managed to equip themselves with modern classes of fighter aircraft. In 1937, on 30th July, the Admiralty had regained control of the Fleet Air Arm and was, thenceforth, able to order its affairs to its own liking. To follow the now-camouflaged Gladiators, Hurricanes, Spitfires, Defiants and Blenheims filtering through to the operational squadrons, new fighters—equipped with more powerful engines and armament—were being developed to play the greatest part so far enacted by air power in any war.

P5224, the second prototype Hawker Tornado. (Hawker Photo.)

CHAPTER SEVEN

PISTON VERSUS JET

Once the Hurricane was accepted and production under way, it was natural that little time would be lost at Hawker in commencing a new design. Engines were becoming still more powerful and two which were of particular interest to Sydney Camm were the X-type Vulture from Rolls-Royce and the H–type Sabre produced by Napier. Both were twenty-four-cylinder liquid-cooled units around which, in 1937, Specification F.18/37 was drafted and issued on 9th March, 1938.

The requirement called for twelve ·303 Browning guns to be carried with 500 r.p.g. in a high-speed fighter to follow the Hurricane and Spitfire and able to operate in all parts of the World. Of great importance was the attainment with high density of fire of the greatest possible superiority over enemy bombers. The guns were to be heated and the machine was to be capable of ground attack work and to incorporate utmost turn-around speed. The maximum loaded weight was to be 12,000 lb. and a tricycle undercarriage could form part of the design if considered necessary to meet the demand to land within 600 yards over a 50 ft. obstacle. A two-speed supercharger was thought essential to operate at speed below 15,000 ft., at which height a minimum speed of 400 m.p.h. was required. Minimum service ceiling was to be 35,000 ft. and the original armament requirement was later altered to four 20 mm. cannon.

Two designs were prepared at Hawker to F.18/37—the N-type, using the Sabre and later to achieve fame as the Typhoon, and the R-type with the Vulture, the ill-fated Tornado. The much higher performance demanded from the new machines meant the final abandonment by Hawker of fabric as a main covering medium. The fore-part of the fuselage retained the firm's usual tubular-steel construction but, to the rear of the cockpit, a change was made to a monocoque shell structure. The Tornado prototype, P5219, was started during 1938 and made its first flight from Langley with P. G. Lucas on 6th October, 1939. Two months later P5219 flew with the 1,760 h.p. Vulture II's radiator moved under the nose from the earlier amidships location, a change brought about by unsatisfactory airflow at high speed in the original position. A second prototype Tornado, P5224, was flown over a year later on 5th December, 1940, with wings constructed to house the revised armament of four 20 mm. Hispano cannon. A few months afterwards, both P5219 and P5224 received Vulture V engines but the Napier unit had been in trouble for some time.

Production of the Tornado had been arranged with A. V. Roe and the one example, R7936, completed there spent its time as a test-bed for various

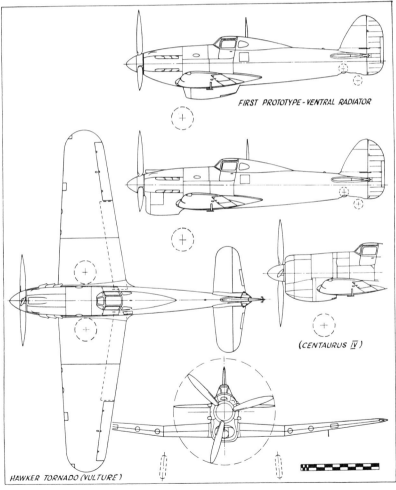

FIRST PROTOTYPE - VENTRAL RADIATOR

(CENTAURUS IV)

HAWKER TORNADO (VULTURE)

Hawker Tornado

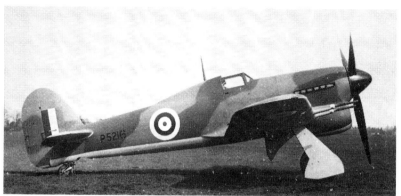
The second Hawker Typhoon prototype, P5216, equipped with four cannon as the prototype F.Mk.IB. (Hawker Photo.)

propellers. Another Tornado prototype, HG641, found itself making its first flight on 23rd October, 1941, with P. G. Lucas, under the power of the radial 2,210 h.p. Bristol Centaurus CE.4S.

Although the Centaurus installation was far more satisfactory than that of the Vulture, production of the Tornado was stopped and facilities switched

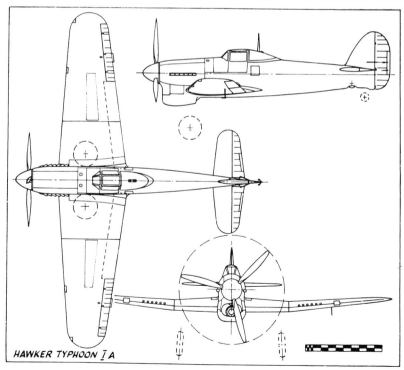
HAWKER TYPHOON I A

Hawker Typhoon F.Mk.IA

to producing the Typhoon. P5212, the 2,100 h.p. Sabre I-powered prototype Typhoon was ready for Lucas to take it on its initial flight on 24th February, 1940. In common with the Vulture, the Sabre had its share of teething troubles, and a particularly nasty experience came Lucas's way on 9th May, 1940, when the monocoque portion of the fuselage at the rear of the cockpit of P5215 failed in flight. The pilot's courage in staying with the machine and in landing it intact so that the trouble could be set right earned him the award of the George Medal.

On the outbreak of War in 1939, the Aircraft and Armament Experimental Establishment was moved from Martlesham Heath to Boscombe Down, to provide extra protection from enemy raids and improved flying facilities.

Report 761 of 29th October, 1940, issued by A.&A.E.E. Boscombe Down, dealt with tests conducted on Typhoon P5212 at the Hawker airfield at

Hawker Typhoon F.Mk.IB. (Hawker Photo.)

Langley, Bucks., by an A.&A.E.E. team of pilots between 26th September and 15th October, 1940, to clear the type for production. Powered by a Sabre I No. 95108, developing 2,055 h.p. at 2,500 ft. and driving a 14 ft. diameter de Havilland three-blade hydromatic propeller, the machine's tare weight was 8,148 lb. and its wing loading 39·5 lb./sq.ft. A failure in the radiator, which had to be removed for repair, terminated the trials. The first take-off of P5212 was made at a weight of 10,485 lb., the performance recorded being a maximum climb rate of 2,730 ft./min. at 15,500 ft., a service ceiling of about 32,300 ft., an absolute ceiling of about 33,000 ft., a take-off run of 525 yds., and a maximum level speed at 19,800 ft. of 410 m.p.h. T.A.S. The view to the rear of P5212 was criticized as not good enough and demanding improvement. The level of noise in the cockpit was found to be very low compared with that of contemporary fighters and pleasant for the pilot. The low noise level up to the limiting speed was thought a very good feature. Stalling tests revealed that P5212 stalled at 88 m.p.h. I.A.S. with flaps up and at 70 m.p.h. I.A.S. with flaps and undercarriage lowered. Dives were made by the A.&A.E.E. team to 475 m.p.h. I.A.S. but the firm's pilot had reached 505 m.p.h. I.A.S., a speed which resulted in the cockpit's door to port being unlocked through the suction on the external handhold.

The prototype Typhoon earned itself a generally good report, being found quiet, easy to fly and without vices. Although fast, P5212 was considered to get along without obvious effort, resulting in a good psychological effect on the pilot. The controls were light and well-harmonized, showing signs of careful and painstaking development towards a very effective fighting machine, the ceiling of which, however, called for an increase to meet its operational needs.

The Typhoon with the twelve Browning machine-guns was the Mk.IA and that with the more favoured armament of four 20 mm. Hispano cannon was designated Mk.IB. Among improvements investigated were the provision of six 20 mm. guns, the use of an exhaust-driven supercharger for the Sabre, increased span wings and an annular radiator around the engine. An interim measure to improve vision to the rear was the substitution of clear-view panels in the fairing behind the cockpit; this was subsequently superseded by a rearwards-sliding, completely transparent canopy which then became standard.

The comparatively poor rate of climb, the Sabre's continued teething troubles and the failure of the rear fuselage joint militated against the immediate success of the Typhoon in service. The Sabre II engine was a more reliable unit but, as high altitude performance was still disappointing, the Typhoon finally came into its own as a magnificent weapon for low-altitude attack in which it excelled with its high speed low down, combined with the terrific hitting power of its batteries of eight rockets and four cannon. R7881 was the sole Typhoon N.F.Mk.IB built to test the type's potential as a night-fighter, but the general difficulty of handling the Typhoon in darkness resulted in the dropping of the project.

During the fateful year of 1938, despite the pathetic, humiliating sight of the deception of a British minister by the infamous German dictator and the promise of "peace in our time", the Bristol staff under L. G. Frise pressed ahead with the design of the Type 156 Beaufighter, a two-seat, twin-engine machine conceived to fill the glaring gap in our long-range fighter defences. The philosophy behind the decision to formulate the machine around as many components as possible of the Type 152 Beaufort was to speed the whole project of producing a new prototype and of phasing it into production at a time when all resources were committed to sustaining the vast rearmament programme.

Although created in this way, the Beaufighter—among the most powerful and pugnacious in appearance of all fighters—turned out to be extremely successful. The first prototype, R2052, made its initial take-off with Cyril Uwins on 17th July, 1939, powered by a pair of 1,425 h.p. Hercules III engines. Originally started as a Private Venture, the Beaufighter was covered from 3rd July, 1939, by Specification F.17/39 in respect of four prototypes with

R8694, the Hawker Typhoon F.Mk.IB used in trials with a Napier experimental annular radiator. (Napier Photo.)

three hundred production Beaufighter Mk.IFs to follow. To ease the strain on the supplies of Hercules engines, an alternative Beaufighter, the Mk.II, was developed using a pair of Merlin engines. The Beaufighter's four cannon were carried in the lower nose, while the six ·303 Brownings were disposed four in the starboard wing and two in the port wing with 1,000 r.p.g. Carrying A.I. Mk.IV radar, the Beaufighter was soon asserting itself and proving its worth against enemy night raiders on its introduction into squadron service in the Autumn of 1940.

Two slim-fuselage versions of the Beaufighter, proposed but not built, were designated Type 158. These would have been the Hercules VI-engined Mk. III and the Rolls-Royce Griffon-engined Mk.IV.

Trials carried out with the 1,280 h.p. Merlin XX-engined Beaufighter Mk.II R2274, modified to carry a four-gun Boulton Paul turret immediately behind the pilot and redesignated Mk.V, were recorded in A.&A.E.E. Boscombe Down Report 758/a of 7th August, 1941. The object of the modification was to overcome the nose-down tendency experienced through the recoil of the cannon when firing. The Mk.V was fitted with one pair of cannon and had the wing machine-guns omitted. Tested at a weight of 18,695 lb., R2274 was considered to handle satisfactorily on the whole but in some ways in an inferior manner to the standard Mk.II. Installation of the turret produced no noticeable change in take-off, approach or landing and at dives up to 390 m.p.h. I.A.S. the turret operated satisfactorily. The emergency exit was criticized as extremely difficult to use and was not considered to be good enough. At 19,300 ft. the Mk.V recorded a top speed of 302 m.p.h.; R2306 was the second Mk.V built.

In its original form the Beaufighter exhibited some awkward tendencies. The directional instability encountered in the Mk.II was counteracted by setting the tailplane with 12° dihedral and the swing experienced on take-off was cured by fitting a long dorsal fin.

Bristol Beaufighter Mk.IF. (Bristol Photo.)

Bristol Beaufighter Mk.IIF with Merlin engines. (Bristol Photo.)

R2274, the Bristol Beaufighter Mk.II fitted with four-gun turret as the prototype Beaufighter Mk.V.
(Bristol Photo.)

A.&A.E.E. Boscombe Down Report 758/a dealt also with tests carried out on the Merlin XX-engined Beaufighter Mk.II T3032 from 26th January until 6th February, 1943. The extension added 13·1 sq.ft. to the fin area and had no adverse effect. The straight tailplane was fitted and, tested at a loaded weight of 20,400 lb., T3032 was found to be reluctant to sideslip.

Beaufighter Mk.I R2268 was unusual in being used to test twin fins and rudders and T3177 was tested with Griffon IIBs for power.

Among unbuilt fighter projects suggested were two single-seaters by Airspeed—the A.S.48 with a Sabre engine and six 20 mm. cannon and the A.S.56

Bristol Type 156 Beaufighter Mk.VIC. (Bristol Photo.)

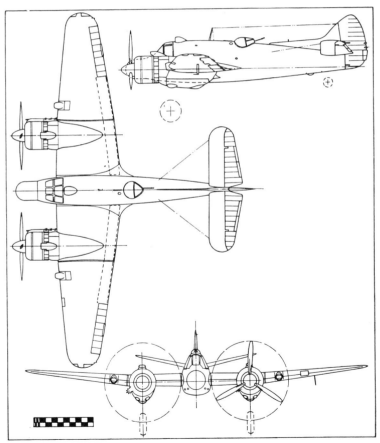

Bristol Beaufighter T.F.Mk.X

Bristol Blenheim Mk.IVF. (Bristol Photo.)

powered by the Sabre VI and carrying four 20 mm. guns, a single-seat version of the Defiant and the Supermarine Type 324.

During 1940 the Blenheim Mk.IV was developed into the Mk.IVF fighter by the addition under the nose of a pack containing four ·303 Brownings.

In 1937 two Fairey P.4/34 light bomber prototypes, designed by Marcel Lobelle, had flown. Resembling a scaled-down Battle, the P.4/34 was not adopted as a bomber by the R.A.F. but was subsequently developed into a two-seat, carrier-borne fighter for the Fleet Air Arm to Specification O.8/38 and called the Fulmar. The machine was an elegant, well-proportioned low-wing monoplane possessing the great virtue of a heavy, forwards-firing, fixed armament of eight ·303 Brownings mounted in the wings. N1854, the proto-type Fulmar Mk.I—Fairey airframe F3707—was piloted by Duncan Menzies on its first flight on 4th January, 1940, from Ringway. As the Fleet Air Arm's first eight-gun fighter, the Fulmar was a very welcome newcomer to the Navy, despite its inferior speed when compared with contemporary single-seaters.

In company with Fulmars N1855 and N1858, N1854 underwent trials at A.&A.E.E. Boscombe Down and Report 757 of 5th November, 1940, recorded the Establishment's pilots' impressions. N1854 and N1858 were fitted with the Merlin RM3M developing 1,060 h.p. at 7,500 ft., while N1855 used the Merlin VIII No. 140836 which gave 1,035 h.p. at 7,750 ft. and drove a three-blade Rotol hydraulic, variable-pitch propeller of 11 ft. 6 in. diameter and 20° pitch range. Noise level in the front cockpit was thought to be high but was found to be lower in the aft position and communication between the crew members by voice pipes was poor. Heating and ventilation also received unfavourable reaction. In flight the Fulmar was found to be very sensitive to directional trim changes, the controls being quick, light and responsive. Although the machine was generally easy and pleasant to fly, the rate of climb, ceiling and top speed were low for a fighter. The armament was thought very good but, since no rear weapon was fitted, the top speed should have been higher. In steep spins with the nose well down a good deal of height was lost. Dive tests with N1855 from 16,000 ft. at an angle of 90° took the machine to 415 m.p.h.; with throttle closed and pulling out of the dive at 4,000 ft. it reached

The third production Fairey Fulmar Mk.I N1858. (Fairey Photo.)

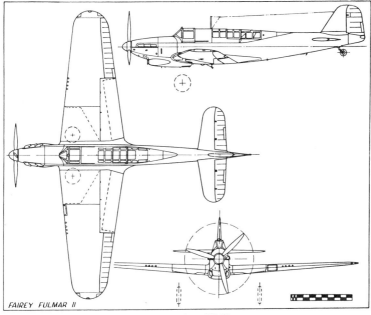

FAIREY FULMAR II

Fairey Fulmar Mk.II

4g. The aircraft was extremely steady in the dive but the covers of both starboard inner stowage and the rear ammunition box were torn off, the lower portion of the engine cowling bulged inwards and the starboard side of the cowling cracked along its lower edge. During the dive recovery the pilot's canopy closed itself although it was locked back open.

Carrier tests on H.M.S. *Illustrious* revealed a tendency to crab bodily to port on take-off but landing on deck was easy. Top speed recorded with N1854 was 255·5 m.p.h. at 2,400 ft.; N1858 reached 246·6 m.p.h. at 9,000 ft.

Rate of climb at 7,000 ft. was 1,220 ft./min. and estimated service and absolute ceilings were 22,400 ft. and 23,700 ft. respectively. Fulmar Mk.I prototypes N1856 and N1857 were scheduled to receive floats but were eventually completed as landplanes.

During 1941 the Fulmar Mk.II made its appearance, using the 1,260 h.p. Merlin XXX with which the maximum speed was raised to 272 m.p.h.

A Mk.II version of the Defiant, with the extra power of the 1,260 h.p. Merlin XX which raised its top speed to 315 m.p.h. at 16,500 ft., appeared in 1940, making its first flight as N1550 on 20th July.

Specification F.11/37 of 26th May, 1937, was issued to produce a two-seat day-and-night fighter for Home Defence or to operate with a Field Force. The requirement insisted on the embodiment in the machine of a number of exacting qualities, with primary emphasis on very high speed and heavier armament than previously used to cope with fast enemy bombers. The gunner was to be completely sheltered from the slipstream in a power-operated turret containing four 20 mm. Hispano cannon or belt-fed guns, the armament to be capable of firing straight ahead and over 360° azimuth with an elevation of at least 60° and a minimum of 15° depression. If the guns could not fire immediately ahead alternative fixed forwards-firing armament was to be provided. For effective search and attack an unimpeded view of the upper hemisphere was required with the field of view to exceed the field of fire. The gunner's seat was to possess 4 in. vertical adjustment and to be coupled with the horizontal swing of the guns. The same vertical seat adjustment was to be provided for the pilot, together with 6 in. horizontal adjustment for the rudder bar. F.11/37 called also for full night-flying equipment, a blind-flying hood, electric starters for the British engines specified, a good view for night-landing, a high degree of manœuvrability and good low-speed control, easy egress by parachute, speedy quantity production and the possibility of the engines being changed in two hours. In addition to being a steady gun-firing platform, in which the gunner could be seated in a position remote from the guns, the machine had to carry a bomb load of 250 lb. internally for use in breaking up enemy bomber formations. Minimum speed was to be 370 m.p.h. at 35,000 ft., and the fighter had to be able to maintain height at 15,000 ft. on one engine.

Several firms were drawn to scheme projects to meet the formidable challenge of F.11/37, among them Armstrong Whitworth, Short, Bristol—with a Beaufort Fighter later revised to F.17/39, Hawker, Supermarine and Boulton Paul with the P.92.

Out of the six tenders the P.92 by J. D. North was selected and a contract was placed with Boulton Paul in March, 1938, for one prototype powered with Vulture IIs, another using Sabres and a third example for development of the turret and armament. To assess the general feasibility of the concept V3142, a single-seat, fixed-undercarriage, half-scale flying version of ply-covered, all-wood structure, powered by a pair of 130 h.p. D. H. Gipsy Major 11s and designated P.92/2, was constructed in 1940 by Heston Aircraft. The most notable feature of the entire design lay in the gun turret which was of

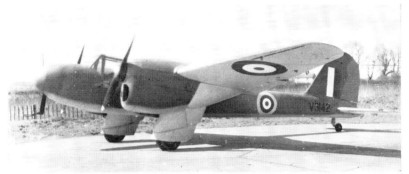

The Boulton Paul P.92/2 half-scale version of the P.92. (Boulton Paul Photo.)

large diameter and very shallow so that it lay nearly flush with the wing centre-section into which it was sunk in a well. Boulton Paul indulged in a great deal of development work on the design, but, in March, 1940, the Air Staff began to consider the advisability of concentrating on fewer types in the interest of the prosecution of the War and finally cancelled the project two months later on 26th May, when the two prototype P.92s were 5% complete.

The P.92/2 was tested at A.&A.E.E. Boscombe Down during July, 1943; Report 812, issued in the following month on 25th August, summarized the results. The P.92/2's turret was a dummy devoid of guns but the machine was equipped with a tail parachute and three-section trailing-edge flaps. Normal loaded weight was 2,716 lb. but V3142 was flown also at 2,778 lb. The cockpit was found to be long, narrow and cramped, with an uncomfortable seating position and could be entered only by steps and with the engines stopped. The cockpit hood had to be removed completely and replaced by external aid. Noise level was not unduly high but it was thought that it might have been excessive in the full-size P.92 owing to the proximity of the engines and their exhausts. The pilot's view ahead was good but bad to the rear and sides. Beyond 85° it was obstructed entirely by the engines and there was no rear view below 30° elevation, although above 30° it was considered good. Flying characteristics generally were pleasant but required improvement in the lateral plane. The gliding angle was very flat and needed steepening with additional flap area.

During the critical days of 1940, when the Germans were expected to invade the British Isles, alarm was naturally felt lest our fighter defences should prove inadequate. Several ideas were put forward with the good intention of boosting available stocks of fighters. A. A. Bage, the Percival chief designer, prepared a project for adapting the existing 205 h.p. Gipsy Six Series II-powered Mew Gulls for anti-invasion ground-attack defence. Designated P.32AA, the superb little racers were to be armed each with a pair of ·303 Vickers machine-guns at a loaded weight of 2,400 lb., with which a top speed of 210 m.p.h. was expected.

Miles M.20 Mk.I AX834. (Miles Photo.)

As their contribution to the fighter reserve in 1940, Miles converted twenty-five M.9B Master Mk.Is on the production line into the M.24 single-seater armed with four ·303 Brownings carried two in each wing. The M.24's Kestrel engine's radiator was moved forwards under the nose and the rear cockpit was covered over and faired into the fuselage.

F. G. Miles was responsible for a particularly brilliant example of improvisation during 1940 when he produced his Private Venture M.20 single-seat, medium-and-high altitude day fighter. The idea for the machine was another manifestation of the aircraft manufacturers' concern over a possible shortage of fighters for the Services. Permission to proceed with the project was given at the end of the first week of July, 1940, and such was the energy and enthusiasm of all involved that the Mk.I, U–9 AX834, to Specification F.19/40, flew at Reading only nine weeks and two days later on 14th September after completion on 12th September. In order to promote fully the concept behind the all-wood M.20, the greatest possible use was made of Miles Master components and hydraulics were eliminated by using a fixed undercarriage. The 1,240 h.p. Merlin XX engine utilized the power-egg installation from a Beaufighter Mk.II and the eight ·303 Mk.II Brownings were housed in the wings under easily-removable panels for quick rearming. A fine point about the M.20 was the excellent view from the bubble canopy. Performance of AX834 was first-class, the top speed of 345 m.p.h. at 20,400 ft. falling between the Hurricane and the Spitfire, its range of 1,200 miles was greater than that of either of them and so was its ammunition capacity.

The feared Hurricane and Spitfire shortage did not arise but Miles proceeded to construct the Naval Mk.II version of the M.20 to Specification N.1/41, completing it in April, 1941, as U–0228 DR616. As part of its naval equipment, the machine was fitted with catapult spools and had provision for an arrester hook. A noticeable external difference compared with the Mk.I was the alteration in shape of the wheel spats.

Fitted with Merlin XX No. C10229/137235 the M.20 Mk.II was sent to Boscombe Down for trials and A.&A.E.E. Report 768/Pt.1 of 23rd May, 1941, commented on inadequate fuel drainage for the wooden structure. Adverse criticism was levelled also at the hood which, although of neat design for jettisoning, was still considered most unsatisfactory if the pilot had to bale out as both hands at once were needed to move it without sufficient elbow room, a feat found almost impossible. The pilot could not insert a gloved finger in either of the operating levers and the hood was impossible to open from outside as there was no provision for doing so; also, if frosted over, it would not open. The lack of a crash pylon over the pilot's head was another point noted. Report 768/Pt.2 of 24th May, 1941, recorded that the unserviceability of the engine had delayed tests and that sitting on the floor with his legs stretched out was an uncomfortable position for the pilot, particularly as he was expected to wear a collapsible dinghy on his back. The view, especially to the rear, was exceptional, but a bullet-proof windscreen was essential for operations. Cockpit layout was good but no reserve tank was provided. The flaps were not very effective and the controls were assessed as heavy, particularly in aerobatics. Flaps-up stalling occurred at 90 m.p.h. and the flaps-down stall was at 73 m.p.h. The machine was dived to 450 m.p.h. I.A.S. with remarkable acceleration and the absence of wind noises around the hood made the high speed feel quite pleasant. The 100 m.p.h. I.A.S. approach speed was fairly high, the machine touching down at 80 m.p.h. I.A.S. The fixed undercarriage was thought to introduce a real source of danger to the pilot in a crash landing, especially in the absence of a crash pylon.

A.&A.E.E. Report 768/Pt.3 of 18th September, 1941, noted that the M.20 Mk.II was tested as a land and as a ship-catapulted fighter with all external items fitted except landing hook, camera and certain radio gear. Loaded weight was 7,560 lb. with an 11 ft. 3 in. diameter three-blade Rotol propeller No. 5, possessing variable pitch range of 35°, the wing loading being 32·5 lb./sq.ft. Maximum climb rate was 2,300 ft./min., take-off run was 270 yd., top speed 333 m.p.h. at 20,400 ft., estimated service ceiling 32,800 ft. and estimated absolute ceiling 33,700 ft.

Among unbuilt projects considered during 1940 were a single-seat night fighter to Specification F.18/40 for which the Hawker P.1008 and Miles M.22A were tendered, a Gloster night fighter design to F.29/40, the single-seat, high-altitude General Aircraft G.A.L.46 to F.4/40 with a 1,270 h.p. Merlin, the single-seat Percival P.33AB with a 1,300 h.p. Merlin and four ·303 Brownings—which was expected to have a top speed of 352 m.p.h. and would have resembled an enlarged Mew Gull fitted with a retractable undercarriage, and the Hawker P.1009 fleet-fighter version of the Typhoon to Specification N.11/40.

Under the exigencies of war numerous schemes were devised to improve the overall effectiveness of the fighter. The Hurricane was selected to assess an idea for increasing range by the addition of jettisonable upper wings. Its feasibility was tested first on a smaller scale with the Hillson Bi-mono designed by Ernest Lewis and built by F. Hills of Manchester in 1940.

L1884, the Hurricane converted into the Slip-Wing Hillson F.H.40 Mk.I. (Hawker Photo.)

Successful trials with the Hillson Bi-mono led to the construction of a set of plywood-covered wooden wings of 328 sq. ft. area, 7 ft. root chord, Clark YH section and 693 lb. weight, which were mounted on Hurricane Mk.1 L1884—ex-R.C.A.F. 321—by means of N struts and diagonal supports. Fuel tanks were embodied in the extra wings and release was by electric solenoid slip gear. Elevator area was increased by 10% to maintain effective control as a biplane. Under the designation Hillson F.H.40 Mk.I, tests were conducted at Sealand but the device never found official favour.

Hurricane Mk.I L1750, equipped with two 20 mm. Hispano cannon for armament, was the subject of A.&A.E.E. Boscombe Down Report 689/b, which noted that, compared with L1547, the maximum climb rate was down by 350 ft./min. and top speed reduced by 8 m.p.h. T.A.S. L1750 reached 302 m.p.h. at 16,800 ft. and had a best climb rate of 2,200 ft./min. at 10,200 ft. The machine handled just like a standard eight-gun Hurricane but yawed slightly with one gun firing and dropped its nose a little during long bursts.

Report 689/c on Hurricane Mk.I L2026, fitted with a Rotol constant-speed propeller, recorded a much better climb and take-off than with the previous wooden fixed-pitch propellers. Weight was increased to 6,750 lb. and level speed fell by 4 m.p.h. compared with the two-pitch propeller version. General flying and handling were hardly affected by the change to the Rotol constant-speed propeller.

Following its introduction into service, the basic Spitfire design was subjected to continual improvement. A.&A.E.E. Martlesham Heath Report M/692/a of 15th June, 1939, on K9787—the first production Mk.I—noted that the ailerons had been modified following an earlier recommendation and that the flap range had been increased to 90° with a consequent improvement in landing qualities. Initial climb and climb-away from an abortive landing were considered poor.

Boscombe Down Report 692/f of 31st October, 1940, dealt with trials carried out on Spitfire Mk.I P9565, flying with a Merlin III and D.H. two-pitch propeller, to assess the merits of a special extra 30 gallon fuel tank—7 ft. 3·5 in. long and 2 ft. 1·75 in. deep—mounted about mid-way beneath the port wing. With an approximate increase in weight of 440 lb., the top speed was 353 m.p.h. at 17,900 ft. P9565 behaved as a normal Spitfire except that a little right aileron was needed in climb and level flight. The port wing dropped in a dive; the same wing dropped in a stall, from which a spiral dive ensued. In a dive at over 350 m.p.h., the ailerons became so stiff that it was practically impossible to carry out any fighting manœuvres.

During the Norwegian campaign of 1940, a scheme was prepared for a float-equipped Hurricane to assist in the operations. Twin floats were constructed but the idea was dropped. The Hurricane did, however, go to sea in 1941 when a number of land fighters were converted as Mks. IA, IB, IC and IIC Sea Hurricane for use on carriers and catapult-equipped merchant ships.

Following the navalized Hurricane came the Seafire version of the Spitfire in 1941, beginning with the adaptation of the Mk.VB as the Seafire Mk.IB. The adaptation brought to the Fleet Air Arm a first-class single-seat fighter with a performance which was comparable with that of fighters based on land.

Although the proposed seaplane Hurricane was never completed, Spitfire Mk.VB W3760 was converted onto twin floats 25·59 ft. long by Folland late in 1941. Report H/164 of 6th June, 1943, from M.A.E.E. Helensburgh noted that water handling was very good and that, with the 1,475 h.p. Merlin 45 No. 37287/217057 driving an 11 ft. 3 in. diameter Rotol variable-pitch hydraulic propeller at 7,580 lb. loaded weight, the machine reached 324 m.p.h. at 19,500 ft. Two further Mk.VBs—EP751 and EP754—were converted but attention was then focused on adapting Spitfire Mk.IX MJ892, powered by the 1,720 h.p. Merlin 66 with which it attained 377 m.p.h. at 19,700 ft. Eventually, no official requirement existed for a floatplane fighter and the project was terminated.

One of the greatest success stories of World War Two was that of the superb two-seat de Havilland D.H.98 Mosquito, astounding with its performance achieved by using two Merlins set in an airframe of wood, a complete contradiction of contemporary all-metal design practice.

Supermarine Spitfire F.Mk.IB. (Dowty Photo.)

Hawker Sea Hurricane F.Mk.IIC NF717. (Hawker Photo.)

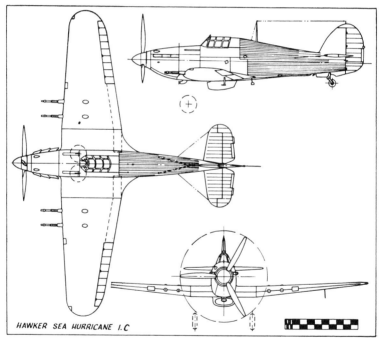

HAWKER SEA HURRICANE I.C

Hawker Sea Hurricane F.Mk.IC

The night-fighter prototype Mk.II, W4052, was constructed to Specification F.21/40 and flew for the first time on 15th May, 1941, when Geoffrey de Havilland Jr. piloted it from its birthplace at Salisbury Hall, Herts. The Mosquito confounded the sceptics completely and proved to be among the finest and most versatile aircraft conceived. The Mosquito N.F.Mk.II's armament comprised four 20 mm. Hispano cannon and four ·303 Browning

EP754, the third Spitfire F. Mk.VB converted by Folland into a floatplane. (Rolls-Royce Photo.)

machine-guns, allied to A.I. Mk.IV or Mk.V radar. W4052 was for a while fitted experimentally with a four-gun Bristol B.XI turret mounted immediately to the rear of the cockpit and then tested with a bellows-actuated, segmented airbrake which encircled the fuselage just behind the wings.

In the course of 1938 two specifications were prepared by the Admiralty for a replacement two-seat fleet fighter. N.5/38 and N.6/38 were subsequently revised as N.8/39 and N.9/39 for a turret fighter respectively, Fairey and Hawker submitting tenders for each requirement. Eventually, both specifications were amalgamated under N.5/40, which resulted in a new design by H. E. Chaplin—the Fairey Firefly, a compact, powerful and handsome low-wing monoplane fitted with the 1,735 h.p. Rolls-Royce Griffon II and heavily armed with four 20 mm. cannon. Z1826, the first of four prototypes made its initial take-off on 22nd December, 1941, with C. S. Staniland as pilot. Range at cruising speed, manœuvrability and low-speed characteristics benefited greatly by the embodiment of retractable Fairey-Youngman flaps which could be extended behind the trailing edge. Modifications were introduced on

de Havilland Mosquito N.F.Mk.II. (Rolls-Royce Photo.)

281

The prototype Fairey Firefly Mk.III Z1835, a converted Mk.I. (Fairey Photo.)

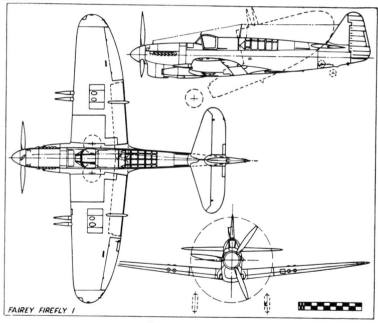

FAIREY FIREFLY I

Fairey Firefly F. Mk.I

later production F.Mk.Is and, from the four hundred and seventieth machine, the engine fitted was the 1,990 h.p. Griffon XII.

A night-fighter version of the Firefly F.Mk.I was developed as the N.F. Mk.II with an A.I. Mk.X radar-occupied radome mounted on each wing near the roots, but disturbance of the C.G. by rear cockpit installation of radar equipment forced an 18 in. extension of the nose as a counter measure.

The fitting of the 2,035 h.p. Griffon 61 resulted in the F.Mk.III, which was

Blackburn Firebrand T.F.Mk.IV. (Blackburn Photo.)

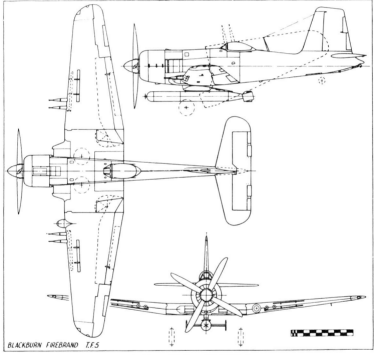

BLACKBURN FIREBRAND T.F.5

Blackburn Firebrand T.F.Mk.5

generally similar to the F.Mk.I and had a top speed of 349 m.p.h. but was not put into production.

The idea of incorporating a retractable float underside in a fuselage was one that received some practical attention in prototype form during the 1914–18 War. The concept was revived in the course of 1942 to Specification N.2/42 for a single-seat fighter. The Blackburn B.44 low-wing monoplane was designed by Maj. J. D. Rennie around a Sabre engine with a pair of three-blade

283

contra-rotating propellers. Intended to operate from small escort carriers out of range of shore bases, the B.44's planing bottom was designed to retract to lie flush with the fuselage underside and the pair of stabilizing tip floats were to retract inwards under the wings. A top speed of 360 m.p.h. at 25,000 ft. was expected but the idea was not developed beyond the design office.

A design conference held by Blackburn on 25th July, 1940, to consider Specification N.11/40, calling for a naval short-range, shipboard interceptor fighter with cannon armament, resulted in the 2,305 h.p. Sabre III-engined B.37 Firebrand prototype DD804 making its first flight on 27th February, 1942. Designed by G. E. Petty, the Firebrand was a large, low-wing monoplane built to carry four wing-mounted 20 mm. cannon.

DD804 was tested at A.&A.E.E. Boscombe Down from 23rd June until 28th July, 1942, and Report 787 noted that, following criticisms, the machine embodied new tailplane and elevators, changes in Irving balance and in the balance tab ratios of ailerons and rudder, and a modified oil cooler. The alterations had improved DD804's flying characteristics but the curved side panels of the windscreen distorted the view for deck landings. Longitudinal stability and all control surface characteristics needed improving and a 20% to 25% increase in rudder area was necessary. In addition, greater flap area was essential to reduce float on landing.

As the Firebrand F.Mk.I did not display any worthy improvement in performance over the Seafire, it was decided that it would be developed into a torpedo-strike fighter. The second prototype F.Mk.I, DD810, served for conversion into the prototype T.F.Mk.II NV636 but, after a small batch had been produced, priority of the R.A.F. over Sabre engines for Typhoons led to the fitting of the 2,520 h.p. Bristol Centaurus to Specification S.8/43.

The first T.F.Mk.III, DK372, flew with a Centaurus VII and was tested at A.&A.E.E. Boscombe Down from March until April, 1944, Report 787/a of 17th May, 1944, noting that spring tabs were fitted on all three control surfaces, aft keel area had been reduced, and that chord and area of the rudder and the span of the wings and tailplane were increased. An offset of 3° to starboard of the fin on the second prototype T.F.Mk.III, DK373, to counter swing on take-off brought with it undesirable characteristics.

1942 provided another chapter in the history of the remarkable Martin-Baker fighters. On 1st May, 1939, the Air Ministry issued Specification F.18/39 for a high-speed, single-seat replacement for the Hurricane and Spitfire, able to operate in any part of the World. The machine was to be capable of ground attack work and of very quick turn-around. Armament demanded comprised two cannon with 60 r.p.g. or eight machine-guns and a tricycle undercarriage could be incorporated if necessary. Maximum all-up weight was to be 12,000 lb., the machine was to be equipped with a two-speed supercharger operating at high speed below 15,000 ft., minimum top speed called for was 400 m.p.h. at 15,000 ft. and service ceiling required was a minimum of 35,000 ft.

Undaunted by the formidable prospect of tackling such a project, James

Martin-Baker M.B.3 R2492 in its initial version with rear fuselage decking. (Martin-Baker Photo.)

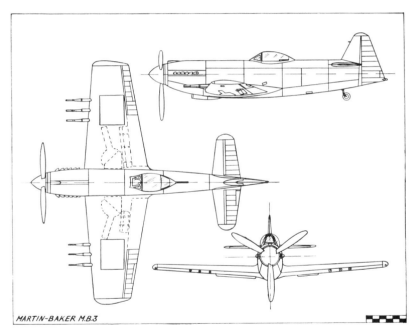

MARTIN-BAKER M.B.3

Martin-Baker M.B.3

Martin and his relatively small company set to work to design and construct the M.B.3, a machine which met and exceeded the requirements of F.18/39, as was amply demonstrated following R2492's first flight on 31st August, 1942, conducted by Capt. V. H. Baker at Wing, Bucks. The 2,020 h.p. Sabre II provided the power for the potent fighter and gave it a top speed of 415 m.p.h. at 20,000 ft. With six 20 mm. Hispano cannon and 200 r.p.g.

housed in the wings under large, easily-removable panels, the sleek and compact M.B.3 was at that time the most heavily-armed fighter extant. Martin's sensible predilection for easy, speedy maintenance was emphasized by the covering of the steel-tubing fuselage also with large, readily-detachable metal panels. An admirable endeavour to reduce head-resistance was made by installing radiators of commendably low frontal area under the wings—that of the coolant beneath the starboard plane and the smaller one for the oil under the port surface. In its original form, the M.B.3's cockpit was faired by raised decking into the rear fuselage but this was soon removed and replaced by a finely-shaped, full-view, transparent blister canopy. The M.B.3 was showing up well in its tests but fate stepped in cruelly when its Sabre failed in the air on 12th September, 1942, and Capt. Baker was killed when the machine caught fire on hitting a haystack during the subsequent attempt at landing.

Despite the shocking blow of Capt. Baker's untimely death and the total loss of R2492, another fighter project—the M.B.4—was considered by matching the M.B.3 airframe to the powerful Griffon engine. This idea was eventually discarded and James Martin started work on a completely new design which was to take some eighteen months to complete.

In an endeavour to improve the basic Typhoon design a revised version, the Typhoon Mk.II, was prepared by Camm during 1941, two prototypes being ordered by the Air Ministry on 18th November, 1941, to Specification

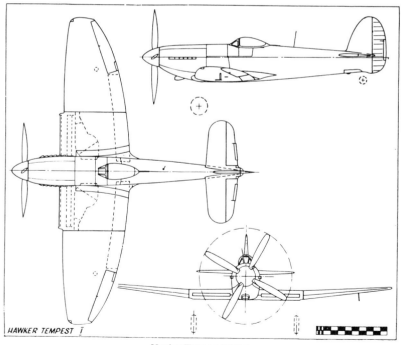

HAWKER TEMPEST I

Hawker Tempest F.Mk.I

Hawker Tempest F.Mk.V. (Hawker Photo.)

F.10/41. Main developments in the design were the incorporation of elliptical wings of low thickness/chord ratio, radiators in the leading edge of the centre-section and the Sabre IV engine. The designation Typhoon Mk.II was soon changed in favour of Tempest, six prototypes being ordered during

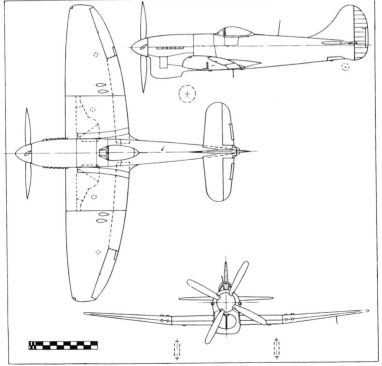

Hawker Tempest F.Mk.V

1942 with a variety of engine installations. The Tempest Mk.I HM599 was to have the Sabre IV, the Mk.IIs LA602 and LA607 the Centaurus, the Mks.III and IV the Griffon, and the Mk.V HM595 the Sabre II. Eventually, the Mk.V HM595 was the first in the air when P. G. Lucas flew it on 2nd September, 1942, the Sabre's radiator being mounted beneath the nose. Sleekest of the Tempests was the Mk.I, which made its initial flight on 24th February, 1943, and reached 466 m.p.h. at 24,500 ft. The Mk.V went into production in advance of the Mk.II and carried four 20 mm. Hispano cannon. Engines used were the Sabre IIA and IIB.

Boscombe Down Report 807 of 30th May, 1943, on the prototype Mk.V fitted with Sabre II No. S–3195/A.406805 and tested during April, 1943, at take-off weight of 11,225 lb., recorded best climbing speed as 185 m.p.h. I.A.S. to 16,000 ft., 3,760 ft./min. rate of climb at 3,600 ft., and maximum speed 420 m.p.h. at 19,000 ft. Experiments conducted included fitting a Mk.V NV768 with an annular radiator and a massive ducted spinner.

The need for a single-seat fighter with emphasis on high altitude capabilities resulted in the issue of Specification F.4/40. Tenders prepared were the General Aircraft G.A.L.46, Hawker P.1004 and the Westland Welkin, but the requirement was revised later as F.7/41 and issued on 26th April, 1942.

F.7/41 called for a single-seat fighter able to operate at great heights and in all parts of the World. Armament was to consist of six 20 mm. Hispano cannon with normal ammunition 120 r.p.g. and maximum 150 r.p.g. A pressure cabin was mandatory, the machine was to provide a steady gun platform, the view all around for the pilot was to be good—particularly to the rear, and, although designed as a single-seater, provision was to be made for an observer or for A.I. radar for the pilot's use only. Minimum top speed required was 415 m.p.h. at 33,000 ft. and service ceiling demanded was to be over 42,000 ft. with a pair of Merlin 61s for power.

Two prototypes eventually emerged to conform to F.7/41—the Vickers Type 432 and the Westland P.14 Welkin Mk.I. The Vickers machine,

Vickers Type 432. (Vickers Photo.)

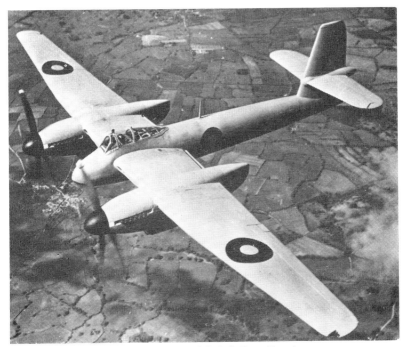

DZ217, was the final manifestation of two earlier projects—the Type 414 to F.22/39 and the Type 420 to F.16/40—both requiring a high-altitude, cannon-armed single-seat fighter. Designed by R. K. Pierson, the Type 432 was an extremely elegant and refined low-wing monoplane in which all flying surfaces were of elliptical shape. The pilot was housed under a pressurized dome in the nose of the slim, circular-section fuselage, the six 20 mm. British Hispano cannon being borne externally mid-way under the fuselage in a bath-shaped pack. Two 1,565 h.p. Merlin 61s drove Rotol four-blade, constant-speed propellers and an anti-spin parachute was concealed in the rear fuselage. The Merlins' radiators formed the wings' leading edge at the roots, while split four-section flaps were at the trailing edge. The Type 432, unofficially named Mayfly, made its first take-off in December, 1942, and continued tests until December, 1944. Top speed was about 440 m.p.h. at 28,000 ft.

W. E. W. Petter was responsible for the design of the Welkin, the Westland contender to the F.7/41 specification, which, with its span of 70 ft., was the largest single-seat fighter to be constructed. Although in general layout reminiscent of the Whirlwind, the compound taper and dihedral of the high aspect ratio wings and the general angularity of the massive Welkin denied it the compact elegance which characterized the Whirlwind. Engine combinations of 1,650 h.p. each consisted of either a Merlin 72 or 76 to starboard and a Merlin 73 or 77 to port, the port-side unit being employed to drive the cabin pressure Rotol supercharger. Four 20 mm. Hispano cannon were installed in the nose. The first flight of the prototype Welkin F.Mk.I DG558/G took place on 1st November, 1942, with H. J. Penrose and the second prototype was followed by sixty-seven production examples.

DX279, the second production Welkin F.Mk.I went to Boscombe Down for testing during October, 1943. A.&A.E.E. Report 808 of 2nd March, 1944, records that the two Merlin 73s drove D.H. four-blade, hydromatic, non-feathering propellers and that empty and loaded weights were 14,420 lb. and 19,840 lb. respectively. The instrument layout was criticized as generally poor with small dials which were difficult to read. Taxiing, take-off and climb were good and the angle of climb was steep but the ailerons were not effective enough at any speed. The rate of roll was slow and, at about 10,000 ft., a full roll took about 12–15 seconds, about 4 seconds being required to bank 60°. Besides being sluggish on the glide, the ailerons were not sufficiently effective at high altitudes. General stability was satisfactory but single-engine characteristics were unacceptable owing to very severe rudder oscillations with one engine off at below single-engine cruising speed which was at about 170 m.p.h. I.A.S.

In mock combat trials with a Mosquito Mk.IX at 35,000 ft., the Welkin found it difficult to keep the diving speed below that at which compressibility effects manifested themselves, and it was impossible for it to follow when the Mosquito dived away at quite a small angle. The ineffectiveness of the ailerons at high altitudes precluded rapid reversals of bank and all attempts to employ usual single-seat fighter techniques of a fast roll into a diving approach with quick changes of bank to obtain a sighting line were unsuccessful by a large margin. The poor downwards view from the cockpit made it difficult for the pilot to keep the target in sight, particularly when climbing above and in front of the quarry to attack. During tests, the Welkin's pilot frequently lost sight of the target when climbing to a suitable position for attack. All controls were considered sluggish at high altitudes and an improvement in the ailerons was of prime importance. To give a fair assessment DX279 was tested against another Welkin at 38,000 ft. to 40,000 ft. The summing-up felt that the Welkin should prove capable of dealing successfully with an enemy bomber or reconnaissance aircraft but would undoubtedly be outmanœuvred, especially in the rolling plane, if pitted against another single-seat fighter. The Welkin's low limiting diving speed was a considerable handicap as any adversary could escape by diving away quickly.

During 1944 PF370—later re-serialled WE997—made its appearance as the two-seat Welkin N.F.Mk.II day-and-night fighter to Specification F.9/43. A.I. radar was housed in the extended nose and other modifications were carried out. Top speed was 360 m.p.h. at 30,000 ft. compared with 387 m.p.h. at 26,000 ft. for the Mk.I. As it transpired, the expected attacks from great heights never developed and the Welkins were subsequently employed usefully in high-altitude research.

Hawker Hurricane F.Mk.IIA. (Hawker Photo.)

Hawker Hurricane F.Mk.IIB. (Hawker Photo.)

Hawker Hurricane F.Mk.IIC. (Hawker Photo.)

Naturally, in the constant endeavour to win the life-or-death struggle with the Axis Powers, unremitting research and development were directed towards producing fighters with considerably better performance than that of their predecessors. Concurrently with the design of new machines, existing types were the subject of unceasing attention. By reason of their proved success the Hurricane, Spitfire and Mosquito came in for prolonged and intensive development.

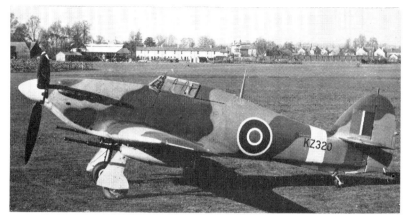

Hawker Hurricane F.Mk.IID carrying two Vickers S 40 mm. guns. (Hawker Photo.)

A.&A.E.E. Report 689/g of 10th September, 1941, on the Merlin XX-engined Hurricane Mk.IIB Z3564 with twelve ·303 Brownings and external tanks, assessed the machine's handling as acceptable on the ground but very unstable initially in the climb until 150–160 m.p.h. was reached. At this speed

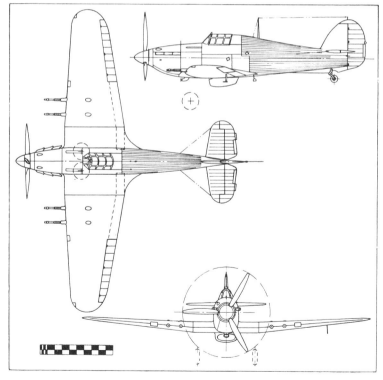

Hawker Hurricane F.Mk.IIC

it was considered fairly satisfactory but the aircraft was therefore unstable at its best climbing speed. Stalling speed had increased but behaviour was satisfactory during manœuvres. Dives were performed at speeds reaching 410 m.p.h. I.A.S.; at 380 m.p.h. high-frequency vibration began which was extremely painful as the greater part of the oscillation was transmitted to the pilot's body through the rudder bar. The cause was not ascertained and it was assumed that Z3564 was a bad aeroplane and not representative of the type.

Projected were versions of the Hurricane using the Dagger, Hercules and Griffon engines but none was taken further than the drawing-board. Main variants built consisted of the Mks.IIA Series 1 and 2, IIB, IIC, IID and IV. The IID came into its own as a very successful tank-buster in the North African campaign where its pair of 40 mm. cannon wrought havoc among the enemy's armoured corps. Rolls-Royce B.F. or Vickers Type S cannon were fitted and Z2326, equipped with a Merlin XX and a pair of 40 mm. Vickers guns, underwent trials at A.&A.E.E. at a loaded weight of 7,656 lb. as recorded in Report 689/Pt.18 of February, 1942. The Mk.IV, redesignated from the Mk.IIE, was developed to carry a variety of wing-mounted armament, including eight 60 lb. rockets.

Although the Hurricane was subjected to a fair amount of development, the Spitfire's list of variants was far longer. Following the Mk.I came the Mks.II, III, IV, V, VI, VII, VIII, IX, X, XI, XII, XIII, XIV, XVI, XVIII and XIX.

Spitfire Mk.V N5053, fitted with a Merlin R.M.5S driving a Rotol four-blade, hydraulic, variable-pitch propeller, was the subject of A.&A.E.E. Boscombe Down Report 692/1 dealing with comparative trials with a three-blade propeller on the same machine. The four-blader increased the ceiling by 1,200 ft. to 40,500 ft., the maximum rate of climb by 210 ft./min. to 3,190 ft./min. at 18,000 ft., while normal top speed remained the same at 369 m.p.h. at 23,000 ft.

A.&A.E.E. Boscombe Down Report 692/i of 16th February, 1943, covered trials with Spitfire Mk.VB AA937, fitted with a Merlin 45 and normal and clipped wings. The metal tips were replaced by wood fairings to reduce the span from 36 ft. 10 in. to 32 ft. 7 in., the area changing from 242 sq.ft. to 231 sq.ft. Normal loaded weight was 6,540 lb., clipped loaded weight 6,510 lb. Maximum speed of both types was 353 m.p.h. at 19,600 ft., but the clipped wings reduced best climb rate at 15,200 ft. from 2,840 ft./min. to 2,670 ft./min. and the service ceiling from 38,000 ft. to 36,200 ft.

The results of a request from the Photographic Reconnaissance Unit at Benson for all-out and cruising tests at altitude to be carried out on Spitfire P.R.Mk.XI MB789 with a Merlin 63 for the information of the Unit were summarized in A.&A.E.E. Report 692/r of 12th September, 1943. With radiator flaps closed at a loaded weight of 8,040 lb., maximum level speed was 417 m.p.h. at 24,200 ft., maximum cruising 397 m.p.h. at 31,000 ft. The machine used a Rotol four-blade propeller, was in operational condition, had individual ejector exhausts, was without armament and bullet-proof

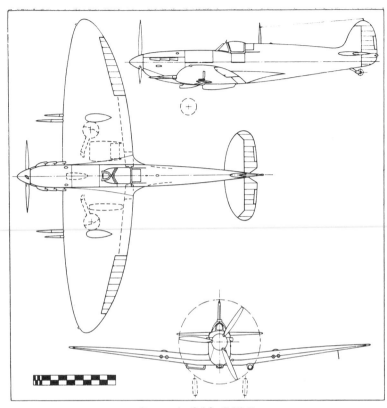

Supermarine Spitfire F.Mk.V

windscreen and aerial wires, had a rounded windscreen without formers, and a retractable tailwheel.

A.&A.E.E. Boscombe Down Report 692/q of 27th October, 1943, dealt with Spitfire F.Mk.VIII JF319 which had been converted to form the prototype Mk.XIV. The engine was a Griffon R.G.5SM driving a five-blade Rotol propeller and fitted with a larger radiator than on the Mk.VIII and individual ejector exhausts. The machine embodied universal wings, small-span ailerons, two 20 mm. cannon and four ·303 machine-guns, a highly polished exterior and a modified fin and rudder incorporating a straight edge. Maximum speed reached was 446 m.p.h. at 25,400 ft.

As the War progressed and spread to new theatres, with one country and continent after another being drawn into the holocaust, so the demands made upon the fighters increased steadily. In every point of performance and function the fighters' capabilities were pressed to the limits and speed, ceiling rate of climb, range and firepower were forced ever higher. The Hurricane had finally reached the end of its development potential and was being superseded by later Hawker products, but the Spitfire found itself with the honour

Supermarine Seafire F.Mk.III MA970. (Dowty Photo.)

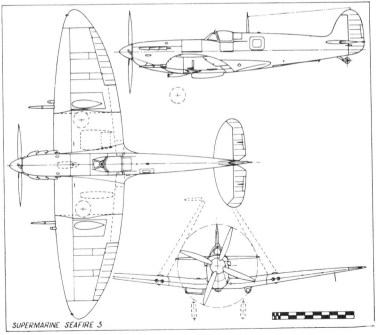

SUPERMARINE SEAFIRE 3

Supermarine Seafire F.Mk.III

de Havilland Mosquito F.B.Mk.VI. (de Havilland Photo.)

of being the only fighter in continuous production before, during and after
the war years. Its potentialities were exploited successfully for low and high
altitude fighting and for photographic and fighter reconnaissance.

Concurrently, the Seafire evolved through Mks.I, II, III and XV, with
the Griffon engine replacing the Merlin in the Mk.XV.

Once the concept of the fast, all-wood Mosquito had silenced its critics and
secured acceptance, the machine's outstanding attributes brought about development for multifarious rôles. Among those concerned with fighting which
these embraced were the night-fighter, the fighter-bomber and the anti-
shipping strike fighter.

A.&A.E.E. Report 767/g of 3rd February, 1943, covered the testing in
January, 1943, of Mosquito N.F.Mk.XV MP469. The engines were a pair of
Merlin 61s, driving four-blade metal D.H. Hydromatic propellers and with a
single Marshall supercharger in the port unit for supplying low-pressure air
by way of a heater to the pressure cabin. For high-altitude night-fighting, the
wings were extended by 8·4 ft. to 62·6 ft. span, with an increase of wing area
of 29 sq.ft. taking place to a total of 479 sq.ft., and four ·303 Brownings were
housed in an external fuselage fairing, 500 r.p.g. being normal and 750 r.p.g.
maximum. Tested at 17,465 lb. MP469 attained a service ceiling of 43,000 ft.
in 32·75 min. but, by careful use of the radiator flaps, it was thought that
another 800 ft. could be reached. Top speed was 408 m.p.h. at 27,800 ft. and
initial rate of climb 2,995 ft./min.

In A.&A.E.E. Report 767/k of 3rd October, 1943, tests of the Mosquito
F.B.Mk.XVIII were described. A modification of the F.B.Mk.VI HJ732,
the machine was converted by deleting the four 20 mm. Hispano cannon
carried in the bomb-bay and substituting a 6-pounder 57 mm. Molins
Mk.IV gun stripped of its carriage and equipped with a special Molins feed
to form what was christened the Tse-tse installation.

With the new gun installed slightly to starboard under the fore-fuselage
beneath the cabin, and with armour plating added around the nose and bomb-
bay and four ·303 Brownings mounted in the nose, the tare weight reached
14,810 lb., plus 1,580 lb. for the Tse-tse installation and twenty-four rounds

for the 6-pounder gun. At full throttle, HJ732 was dived to 470 m.p.h. I.A.S. and considered satisfactory for service use but the suggestion was made that pilots should be warned to use care when braking in landing as the weight concentrated forwards gave the machine a tendency to nose over. Caution was needed also in out-of-trim dive recovery. Twenty-seven Mk.XVIIIs were ultimately built with the heavy quick-firer and proved their worth in the hands of Coastal Command against enemy shipping in particular.

The appearance of the Gloster E.28/39 Pioneer W4041 in 1941 and its successful first flight on 15th May, 1941, when Flt.Lt. P. E. G. Sayer took it into the air at Cranwell, represented the culmination of years of intensive work by Frank Whittle and the team who brought the gas turbine to a practical stage for use as an aircraft engine. The new noise in the sky marked the beginning of the end for the faithful piston engine in the saga of fighter development and signified the opening up of a vast new vista in fighter design, the limits of which were to prove unpredictable.

The progress made with the Whittle jet engine in its tests prior to the completion of the E.28/39 gave rise to sufficient confidence in its ultimate use as a fighter power plant for the Air Ministry to feel justified in planning ahead on such lines.

During 1939, the Gloster design staff were involved in a project for a Sabre-engined, twin-boom, single-seat fighter of pusher layout and thought was given to its adoption as an airframe to house the jet engine. Eventually, the twin-boom formula was discarded and the E.28/39 emerged with the engine installed in a normal full-length fuselage but provision was made in the design for the accommodation of four ·303 Brownings. Although so successful as a test-bed for the Whittle engine, the E.28/39 held out little prospect of serving as a useful fighter.

By mid-1940, W. G. Carter was preparing plans for a single-seat fighter using two jet units to give sufficient power for the machine to prove successful in an operational rôle. Specification F.9/40 was drawn up to cover the new design and the maiden flight of DG206—the first of the Gloster F.9/40 prototypes to fly—was performed on 5th March, 1943, at Cranwell by Michael Daunt. DG206 flew with a pair of 2,300 lb.s.t. de Havilland Halford H.1 engines and other units used by the batch of eight prototypes were the Metropolitan Vickers F.2, Power Jets W.2/500, Rolls-Royce W.2B/23 and Rover W.2B.

A.&A.E.E. Boscombe Down Report 817 of 31st March, 1944, covered tests carried out on 24th and 29th February, 1944, on DG205/G, the fourth prototype, by A.&A.E.E. pilots at the Gloster Company's airfield. General conclusions were that the machine was easy to fly and quiet and pleasant in the absence of vibration and fumes. The controls were considered to be badly harmonized as the rudder was immovable at ordinary level and diving speeds after the first few degrees of movement and the elevators were too heavy and the ailerons too light. The seat required tilting back a few degrees and recommended also was the repositioning of fuel and throttle controls and some instruments. An emergency braking system was thought essential and so were continuous-reading fuel contents gauges. The rate of roll compared favourably with that of the Spitfire.

Four A.&A.E.E. pilots made five short flights at the manufacturer's field in order to gain preliminary experience with, and impressions of, such a revolutionary mode of propulsion. At 16,900 r.p.m. the pair of W.2B/23 engines gave a nominal static thrust of 1,600 lb. Most tests were made on DG205/G but some were with DG208/G. The visitors found the starting and use of the engines simple and taxiing straightforward but throttle response to be much slower than with conventional aircraft. Take-off swing was absent and the run fairly short but initial climb rate poor. An approach speed of 120 m.p.h. I.A.S. was used for gliding turns, reducing to 95–100 m.p.h. I.A.S. over the boundary, the approach and landing being found simple and easy. Removal of the 10 seconds restriction on minimum time for opening up from idling to maximum r.p.m. was recommended as it was considered to be a serious disadvantage, especially on a baulked landing at 110 m.p.h. I.A.S. with flaps and undercarriage down as the aircraft lost 100 ft. in height before commencing

Gloster Meteor F.Mk.I. (Armstrong Siddeley Photo.)

to climb away. The F.9/40 was completely free from engine noise but aerodynamic noise was found appreciable at higher speeds. There was no vibration but, ironically, its absence made the pilot more aware of atmospheric bumps.

Following the eight prototype F.9/40s, the Gloster jet fighter—originally named Thunderbolt—went into production in its G.41A Meteor F.Mk.I form with, initially, Rolls-Royce W.2B/23 Welland I engines and four nose-mounted 20 mm. Hispano cannon. To No. 616 Squadron went the honour of receiving the R.A.F.'s first jet fighters, EE219 arriving on 12th July, 1944. The Meteor was also the first British-designed single-seat fighter with a tricycle undercarriage to take its place in the R.A.F. and the sole Allied jet fighter on operations during the Second World War.

In the course of 1942, layouts were prepared for both mid- and low-wing versions of the General Aircraft G.A.L.53 single-seat, jet fighter project which would have used a single 1,600 lb.s.t. Power Jets W.2B engine and have carried four 20 mm. cannon in its nose at a cruising speed of 380 m.p.h.

While the revolutionary new jet fighters were being developed in strict secrecy—the first public announcement of their existence being made on 7th

Hawker Tempest F.Mk.II MW742. (Hawker Photo.)

January, 1944—the piston-engine fighters had still to be improved for the purpose of winning the War as quickly as possible.

On 28th June, 1943, LA602—the first Hawker Tempest Mk.II—made its maiden flight piloted by Philip Lucas. The machine, designed to Specification F.10/41, was fitted with the 2,520 h.p. Centaurus IV and carried four wing-mounted 20 mm. Hispano Mk.II cannon.

The results of tests carried out on LA602 at A.&A.E.E. Boscombe Down between 3rd and 10th May, 1944, were summarized in Report 807/a of 10th July, 1944. A Rotol four-blade propeller of 12 ft. 9 in. diameter was fitted but the engine was without a cooling fan. The cockpit was found to be quieter than that of the Mk.V as the noise level was considerably lower. The machine was considerably pleasanter and less tiring to fly. However, compared with the Mk.V, the view from the Mk.II for taxiing was not as good owing to the broader nose. At 11,590 lb. the designed limiting diving speed was 580 m.p.h. I.A.S.

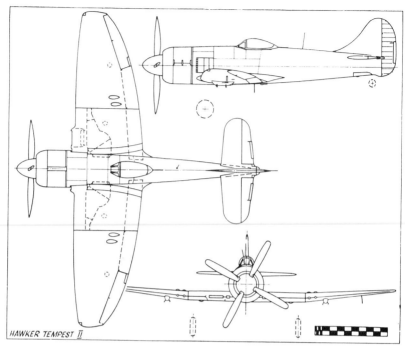

HAWKER TEMPEST II

Hawker Tempest F.Mk.II

The slow tempo of production resulted in the arrival of the Tempest Mk.II at No. 54 Squadron—the first unit—in November, 1945, too late to see any action in the War but it gave extensive service overseas.

On 9th May, 1944, W. Humble conducted the first flight of HM595, the Tempest Mk.VI prototype, converted from the Mk.V prototype. The machine was fitted with the 2,340 h.p. Sabre V engine and NX119 was tested on 11th

Production Hawker Tempest F.Mk.VI. (Hawker Photo.)

December, 1945, at Boscombe Down, Report 807/b of 23rd February, 1946, covering the trials. Intended for tropical use, the Mk.VI arrived in service after the end of World War Two to serve with a few squadrons in Germany and the Middle East.

The de Havilland Aircraft Company made an early start in jet fighter design, beginning their first—the D.H.100 Spider Crab—to Specification E.6/41 in 1942. The requirement, issued on 8th December, 1942, called for a single-seat jet fighter test-bed using a D.H. jet unit and armed with four 20 mm. Hispano cannon backed by 150 r.p.g. A minimum speed of 490 m.p.h. was demanded, together with a service ceiling of over 48,000 ft.

LZ548/G made its first flight when Geoffrey de Havilland Jr. eased it from the ground at Hatfield on 20th September, 1943. With its twin-boom layout, the Spider Crab—soon to be renamed Vampire—made the most of the engine installation in the nacelle by cutting losses in the 2,700 lb.s.t. D.H. Goblin I to a minimum. Eight months afterwards, the Vampire F.Mk.I was ordered into production, later models receiving the more powerful 3,100 lb.s.t. Goblin II. The War was over by the time that the attractive little Vampire reached its first unit—No. 247 Squadron—but the type went on to become one of the most successful and best-known of the early jet fighters.

Handling trials of the 2,500 lb.s.t. Halford HIA-engined third prototype Vampire MP838/G during April, 1944, at A.&A.E.E. Boscombe Down were

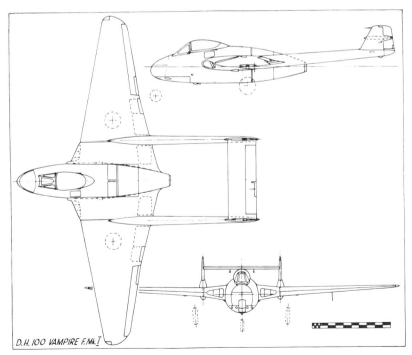

D.H. Vampire F.Mk.I

The magnificent Martin-Baker M.B.5 R2496. (Martin-Baker Photo.)

described in Report 819 of 1st June, 1944. Tests were at a loaded weight of 8,495 lb. and the machine's cockpit was considered one of the best among contemporary single-seat fighters, being comfortable, well-arranged and with easy access to all controls and instruments. The view directly forwards was very good but, in general, was thought disappointing with distortion and thick windscreen and side panels limiting visibility. Comfort in taxiing at up to 110 m.p.h. was outstanding but the rate of climb was found to be poor compared with other single-seat fighters. Good points were the Vampire's excellent aileron control, the extremely low noise level and the high speed at low levels. Criticized were slow acceleration in level flight and the directional unsteadiness which militated against its efficiency as a gun platform.

A.&A.E.E. Report 819/a of 29th May, 1946, dealt with handling trials of Vampire F.Mk.I TG274, the first production example, carried out during June, 1945. The engine installed was a de Havilland Goblin I rated at 2,700 lb.s.t. and loaded weight of the machine was 8,610 lb. The view from the English-Electric-built production machine still provoked adverse criticism and take-off run, in comparison with that of piston-engine fighters, was found to be long, the machine appearing to "leap" into the air at 110 m.p.h. I.A.S. At 9,500 r.p.m., 220 m.p.h. I.A.S. appeared to be the best climbing speed. TG274 was a very pleasant machine to fly and directional behaviour was an improvement on that encountered in the third prototype MP838/G.

Following the loss of the M.B.3 and the abandonment of the projected M.B.4, Martin-Baker pressed ahead with the M.B.5. In his last fighter design to fly, James Martin excelled himself by producing one of the finest of all piston-engine single-seat fighters. The M.B.5 R2496 retained Specification F.18/39 as its basis and used the same wing form as that of the ill-fated M.B.3. The engine used was the powerful 2,340 h.p. Griffon 83 driving two three-blade D.H. contra-rotating propellers. Four 20 mm. Hispano cannon were installed in the wings and the entire structure was in accordance with Martin's strict adherence to the principles of simplicity and ease of maintenance, the fuselage consisting of the Martin system of steel-tubing basic framework covered with large removable metal panels. The view fore and aft was exceptionally good and the ingenious engineering features such as the hinged instrument panels, the cleanly and sensibly arranged cockpit, the ease of access to the entire engine installation and the simple and reliable form of undercarriage retraction all brought a wealth of thoroughly deserved praise.

L. Bryan Greensted made the first flight of the M.B.5 on 23rd May, 1944, at Harwell and the machine's performance—with a top speed of 460 m.p.h. at 20,000 ft.—and superb handling qualities were the subject of enthusiastic reports from all pilots who sampled the magnificent machine. Nevertheless, although James Martin's brilliant M.B.5 was possibly the finest all-round single-seat piston-engine fighter ever designed, it was not lucky enough to be put into production to contribute its share in defeating a determined and brutal enemy.

As the Second World War entered its closing stages, the prototypes of the last generation of piston-engine fighters emerged. Specification F.1/43 resulted in the Spiteful from Supermarine's J. Smith. Although the fuselage carried on the fine lines of the immortal Spitfire, gone were the elegant elliptical wings, their place being taken by laminar-flow surfaces with compound-taper plan-form. NN660, consisting of a Spitfire Mk.VIII fuselage and tail, the new laminar-flow wings and a Griffon 61 engine first flew on 30th June, 1944, with J. K. Quill piloting. The second Spiteful prototype, NN664, was finished late in 1944 and had a deeper fuselage and other modifications. A small number only of the Type 371 Spiteful F.Mk.XIV with the Griffon were

The first production Supermarine Spiteful F.Mk.XIV RB515. (Rolls-Royce Photo.)

de Havilland D.H.103 Hornet F.Mk.I with W. P. Fillingham at the controls. (Rolls-Royce Photo.)

built, followed by the Mk.XV with the Griffon 89 or 90, and the Mk.XVI with the Griffon 101 which was notable in reaching a top speed of 494 m.p.h. at 28,500 ft.—the fastest recorded by a British piston-engine fighter.

The A.&A.E.E.'s engineering and maintenance assessment of the sixth production Spiteful F.Mk.XIV NN667, was contained in Boscombe Down Report 836/Pt.2 of 7th August, 1947. NN667 was evaluated from 1st February until 6th June, 1946, during which it was flown for 25 hr. 40 min. with particular attention paid to the speed with which it could be serviced. In this respect the machine was assessed as below average and the cockpit layout as bad, as too much time would be consumed in routine operations and it was thought that the Spiteful would prove difficult in servicing and maintenance. NN667 was fitted with the 2,375 h.p. Griffon 69 turning a five-blade Rotol hydraulic variable-pitch type R42/5F5/3 propeller. The report was critical of the butt-jointing of the fuselage sheet-metal covering which militated against the attainment of a superfine surface finish, but the ingenious automatically-retracting, spring-loaded plunger picketing shackle drew praise and was recommended for adoption on other aircraft types. The cockpit received particularly critical comment on the grounds of the inaccessibility of equipment seemingly situated in a series of ledges or in deep cavities, thus providing dirt traps and absorbing an excessive amount of man-hours in maintenance.

The Spiteful did not reach any squadrons but the de Havilland D.H.103 Hornet, to Specification F.12/43, of which the prototype RR915 made its first flight on 28th July, 1944, with Geoffrey de Havilland Jr., was the fastest piston-engine fighter to enter the R.A.F., proving very successful. Compared with the eminent Mosquito, wood and metal construction was employed in the slim and graceful Hornet, and this, combined with the power of a pair of 2,030 h.p. Merlins—a 130 to port and 131 to starboard—gave the sleek single-seater the excellent top speed of 485 m.p.h. in the prototype.

The Hornet was designed in the first place as a Private Venture by de Havilland and developed as a long-range fighter for Far East operations against the Japanese. Installation of four 20 mm. Hispano cannon and operational equipment in the production F.Mk.I reduced the maximum speed to 472 m.p.h. at 22,000 ft. but the War was over by the time that the first unit, No. 64 Squadron, received its Hornets at the commencement of 1946.

A.&A.E.E. Boscombe Down Report 828 was concerned with the handling tests of PX211, the second production Hornet F.Mk.I, during September and October, 1945. The machine was found to be deficient in longitudinal stability, to suffer from a tendency for the rudder to move to full travel of its own accord under conditions of sideslip and to possess dangerous engine failure characteristics. In the case of engine failure, if swift action were not taken by the pilot, the machine quickly entered a vertical dive with the rudder held immovably fully over towards the stopped engine. To cure these defects, a larger horizontal tail was introduced and the F.Mk.3 featured a dorsal fin,

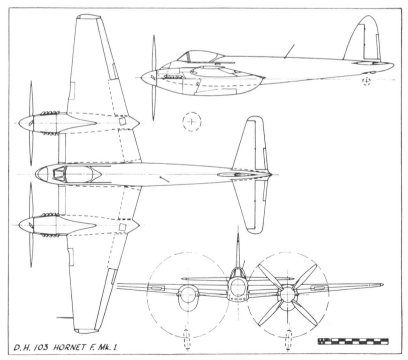

D.H. Hornet F.Mk.I

305

NX798, the Hawker Fury F.2/43 prototype. (Dowty Photo.)

which was installed retrospectively on earlier Hornets, and increased internal fuel capacity.

The Mk.3 prototype, PX312, underwent A.&A.E.E. trials from July, 1947, until May, 1948, as recorded in Report 828/b of 24th March, 1950, when the Mk.3 was considered as acceptable for service use in the form in which PX312 was tested.

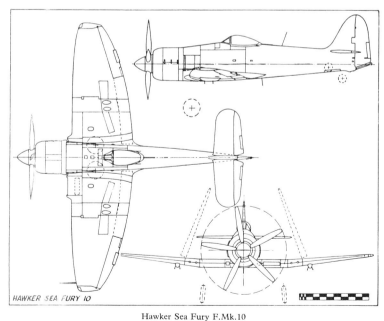

HAWKER SEA FURY 10

Hawker Sea Fury F.Mk.10

1st September, 1944, witnessed Philip Lucas making the maiden flight with the prototype Hawker Fury NX798. Specification F.2/43, to which the machine was built, had evolved by way of F.6/42 which had brought tenders from Folland, English Electric and Westland, and the Hawker proposal of a Tempest Light Fighter. The object behind the project was to try to arrest the constant increase in weight which was taking place in fighters and the Fury eventually showed a slight advantage in that direction. Prototypes were constructed powered by the Griffon 85, Centaurus XV and the Sabre VII. Concurrently, a naval variant, the Sea Fury, was developed by Boulton Paul through Specifications N.7/43, F.2/43 and finally N.22/43.

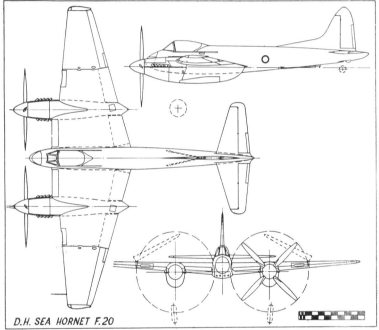

D.H. SEA HORNET F.20

D.H. Sea Hornet F.Mk.20

SR661, the Sea Fury F.Mk.X prototype, after making its first flight on 21st February, 1945, underwent A.&A.E.E. tests for deck operation assessment from 19th until 29th May, 1945. Report 830/Pt.1 of 22nd August, 1945, noted that the machine was not considered suitable for deck operation owing to insufficient rudder power to counter the tendency towards right swing on take-off, irregular and slow engine response to the throttle and disappointing acceleration on take-off. A.&A.E.E. Report 830/Pt.2 of 15th October, 1945, summarized handling tests from 2nd until 10th July, 1945, on SR661 which had been modified with a larger rudder, five-blade Rotol propeller and higher reduction gear ratio of ·444. The machine was improved sufficiently for deck trials to proceed but still required attention in several respects.

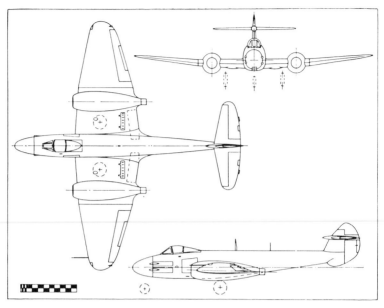

Gloster Meteor F.Mk.III

As the War drew to its close, there was no doubt that it was but a question of time—and a short time at that—before the piston-engine fighter was finally ousted by the jet. Naval adaptations of land-based jet fighters were under development and the last generation of propeller-driven fleet fighters began to enter service. A revised version of the Firefly, the F.R.Mk.4, with clipped wings and leading-edge root radiators, made its appearance, as did the N.F.Mk.4, the F.R.Mk.5, the N.F.Mk.5 and the A.S.Mk.5.

Little time was lost in producing the Sea Hornet F.Mk.20 prototype PX212 to Specification N.5/44, which first flew on 19th April, 1945, to provide the F.A.A. with a fast, long-range fighter. Power plants were a 2,030 h.p. Merlin 133 and 134, with which the maximum speed was 467 m.p.h. at 22,000 ft.

Specification N.5/45 was responsible for the Supermarine Seafang F.Mk.31 with the Griffon 61 and fixed wings, and the F.Mk.32 with the Griffon 89, contra-rotating propellers and folding wings. A naval version of the Spiteful, only eighteen production examples were produced at the tail end of the piston-engine fighter era.

The Meteor provided a good basis for exploration into the field of jet fighters and development proceeded apace. The G.41C F.Mk.III prototype EE230 took to the air in September, 1944, the first fifteen machines being fitted with Welland engines, subsequent examples receiving Derwent Is under designation G.41D, those with the lengthened engine nacelles becoming Type G.41E.

From September until November, 1944, the third production Meteor F.Mk.I, EE212/G, fitted with a pair of Rolls-Royce W.2B/23C engines, was assessed for general handling as noted in A.&A.E.E. Boscombe Down Report 817 of 23rd May, 1945. Directional oscillation was apparent and the short engine nacelles caused buffeting at comparatively low Mach numbers and were eventually replaced by longer cowlings. EE212/G was easy and pleasant to fly and possessed better longitudinal stability than any other British fighter. At normal cruising speeds it could be trimmed to fly accurately hands-off but take-off and climb performance were poor.

After nearly six terrible years of bloodshed and tragedy, spread over a greater portion of the world than in any previous conflict, the Second World War came to an end in 1945. Britain's fighters, flown with zest, skill and consummate bravery by her aircrew, had contributed their full share to the defeat of the evil and guilty nations of Germany, Italy and Japan. In the inferno of war, the fighter had undergone its most radical change yet, with the establishment of the revolutionary gas turbine engine as a practical proposition placing unprecedented power at the disposal of fighter aircraft designers.

Supermarine Seafire F.R.Mk.47. (Rolls-Royce Photo.)

CHAPTER EIGHT

THE TURBINE TAKES OVER

The end of the world-wide conflict of 1939–45 brought with it the conclusion of the concept of fighters which had been developed to such a high degree over three decades. The piston engine had served to bring about the final annihilation of the diabolic forces of Germany and Japan, but was about to be eclipsed by the vast potential inherent in the gas turbine. The new engine was the greatest single factor in precipitating the fresh generation of fighters evolved, even though peace brought rapid and enormous cuts in the size of fighter forces.

Throughout the war period, airframe and engine designers had worked wholeheartedly to produce as quickly as practicable the finest weapons that they could devise to place in the hands of Britain's fighter pilots. In basic layout the piston-engine aircraft had changed but little from the accepted retractable-undercarriage, low-wing monoplane. Performance and hitting power, however, had improved vastly through the colossal increase in engine power, the adoption of machine-guns and cannon of heavier calibre, the introduction of rockets, the ability to carry heavier bombs, the evolution of long-range drop tanks, cockpit pressurization and enhanced radio facilities.

The advent of the radical gas turbine brought a complete revolution in fighter design and performance. The tricycle undercarriage was adopted practically universally from the start and the new style of engine installation enabled the designer to make the nearest approach so far to his ideal airframe profile, tempered with R.A.F. and F.A.A. operational equipment requirements.

Before the piston-engine fighter was eschewed entirely, the last marks of Spitfire, Seafire and Mosquito rolled from the production lines.

Spitfire development tapered off into the F.Mks.21, 22 and 24. Boscombe Down Report 692/s of 29th June, 1945, expressed dissatisfaction with the handling characteristics of LA187, the prototype Spitfire F.Mk.21. Interaction was noted between longitudinal and directional changes of trim and the machine exhibited undesirable directional behaviour, these qualities resulting in its assessment as unsuitable for high-altitude operations owing to their dangerous nature at such heights.

Shortcomings reported in the handling of the Mosquito N.F.Mk.38 were responsible for trials carried out at Boscombe Down during August, 1949, and recorded in an A.&A.E.E. Report of 28th October, 1949. A Mk.36 RL114 and a Mk.38 VT658 were used, each powered by a pair of Merlin 114As, and were appraised for failure of one engine after take-off. Neither aircraft was able to maintain height on one engine at the required speed of 175 m.p.h. I.A.S. Behaviour in such a case was assessed as dangerous, especially at night, owing to poor stability and the need for constant attention to trimming. In the circumstances it was concluded that neither machine reached the standard required for a modern night fighter. The N.F.Mk.36 was a development of the N.F.Mk.30 using American A.I.Mk.X radar and the N.F.Mk.38 was basically the same but had British A.I.Mk.IX fitted and a cabin situated 5 in. further forward.

A noteworthy feature of the Spitfire F.Mks.21, 22 and 24 was the change in wing plan-form from the finely shaped ellipse—which had typified the Spitfire from K5054—to new blunt-tipped planes. The F.Mk.21s and 22s saw most of their service with the post-war auxiliary squadrons. The last Seafires to be represented in the Fleet Air Arm after the War were the F.Mk.15 and the F./F.R.Mks.17, 45, 46 and 47, naval counterparts of the Griffon-engine R.A.F. Spitfires.

July, 1945, witnessed the first take-off of EE360, the prototype G.41F Meteor F.Mk.4 fitted with 3,500 lb.s.t. Rolls-Royce Derwent 5s. The F.Mk.4, used widely, was a very successful version and, on 7th November, 1945, EE454 *Britannia* was flown by Gp.Capt. H. J. Wilson to set a new

Supermarine Spitfire F.Mk.21 employed by Rotol for test with contra-rotating propeller.

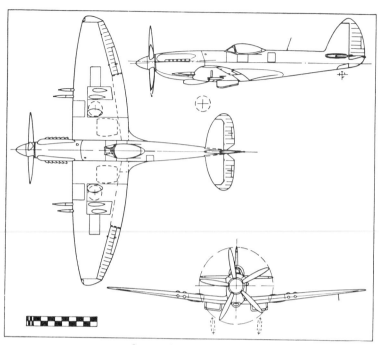

Supermarine Spitfire F.Mk.24

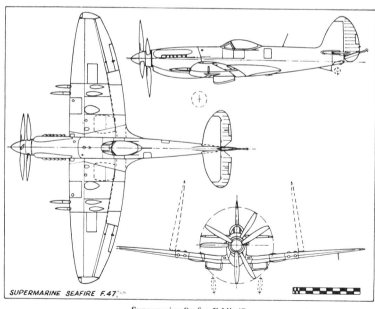

SUPERMARINE SEAFIRE F.47

Supermarine Seafire F.Mk.47

312

World Air Speed Record of 606 m.p.h. The next year, on 7th September, Gp.Capt. E. M. Donaldson raised the Record to 616 m.p.h. in EE549. Later F.Mk.4s, produced to Specification F.11/46, used the clipped wings of 37 ft. 2 in. span with consequent benefits to top speed and rate of roll.

In the course of 1944, Specification N.11/44 was evolved by the Naval Air Staff and issued on 1st January, 1945. It called for a long-range day fighter, capable of carrying a torpedo and powered by a single Rolls-Royce Eagle RH2SM engine driving two four-blade Rotol contra-propellers with two-

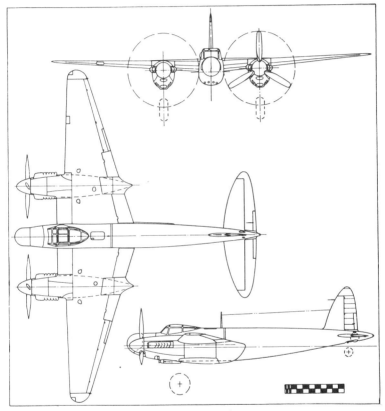

D.H. Mosquito N.F.Mk.36

speed gear as power plant A. The fuselage was to be able to take a turbine-propeller unit and, if possible, standard wings and tail unit were to be inter-changeable. The undercarriage was to be capable of withstanding 12 ft./sec. velocity but, if necessary, the attachments had to absorb 14 ft./sec. Pro-vision was to be made in the design of the units for increases in area if found necessary after tests. Class I protective treatment, power wing-folding and spreading, VHF/HF/RT, AN–ARR2(ZB), TR1501/02, I.F.F. Mk.IIIA, two or four 20 mm. Mk.V. cannon and the ability to accommodate eight rocket

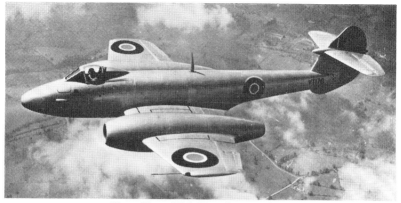

Gloster Meteor F.Mk.IV. (Rolls-Royce Photo.)

projectiles, three 1,000 lb. bombs, and an 18 in. Mk.VIII torpedo or a 1,820 lb. Mk.VI mine were specified.

The N.11/44 contender could use any power plant but a British unit would be preferred. Air combat was to be the design's primary feature, the secondary rôle being attack against shipping or land targets with the ability to carry the appropriate weapons without prejudice to the primary fighting purpose. It was desirable that the machine should not exceed 17,500 lb. for landing with one hour fuel reserve and remaining ammunition. Provision was to be made for R.A.T.O.G. and measurements were not to exceed 50 ft. span spread and 19 ft. 6 in. folded, 40 ft. length and 15 ft. 9 in. height. Maximum speed and fighting manœuvrability were to be the highest possible, with the aims of a climb rate of 15,000 ft. in 5 mins., operational height of 10,000 ft. to 20,000 ft. and a radius of action in still air of 240 n.m. at cruising speed, while spending 15 minutes at 10,000 ft.

Westland Wyvern T.F.Mk.1 fitted with Eagle 22. (Rolls-Royce Photo.)

Two firms, Westland and General Aircraft, submitted tenders to N.11/44. The General Aircraft project was the G.A.L.56 which was not selected for development but the Westland design by John Digby, the Wyvern W.34, met with favour and work proceeded on it. Subsequently, some six months after the issue of Specification N.11/44, Specification F.13/44 came forth on 17th July, 1945, from the Air Ministry, Ref.SB.61153/RDT2d, for an R.A.F. long-range escort fighter development of the Wyvern. An amendment of 28th August, 1945, reduced the range demanded from 1,500 miles to 1,000 miles. The twenty-four-cylinder Eagle R.Ea.2SM, coupled to a pair of Rotol four-

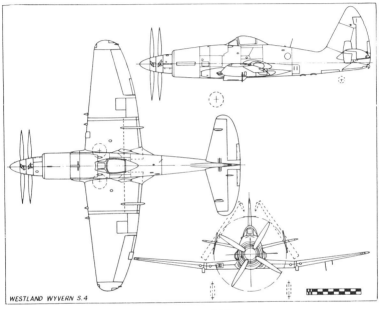

WESTLAND WYVERN S.4

Westland Wyvern S.Mk.4

blade contra-rotating propellers, was specified as power plant A installation. Multi-channel V.H.F. and lightweight I.F.F. were to be provided, together with protection for the front and the rear of the pilot, windscreen, header tank, ammunition and the oil tank against 20 mm. armour-piercing shells fired from 200 yd. range and 10° each side of the thrust line. Internal self-sealing tanks were required and the machine had to be able to take-off, climb to 20,000 ft., operate at that height on full power for combat for 15 minutes and have a still-air range of 1,000 miles at 25,000 ft. at the most economical cruising speed. Drop tanks were to provide 1,000 miles radius of action when the return journey was to be on internal tanks less 15 minutes at full combat power. Examples subsequent to the second prototype were to be regarded as production aircraft. The machine was to be structurally similar to the N.11/44 fighter and to be able to come to rest with full internal tanks within 1,000 yd.

in still air after crossing a 50 ft. screen. A saving of weight was to be effected by deletion of wing-folding, accelerating and slinging gear, arrester hook and two-speed propeller reduction gear. A 12 ft./sec. vertical velocity absorption was demanded from the undercarriage and camera space was to be provided so that a limited number of aircraft could be converted for photographic reconnaissance.

In the course of the change to pure jet fighters the F.13/44 requirement was not pursued but intensive development proceeded with the N.11/44 programme. Eagle-engined Wyvern T.F.Mk.1s TS375, TS378, TS387, VR132 and VR134 were evaluated at A.&A.E.E. Boscombe Down, Report 853/Pt.3 of 13th January, 1950, dealing with deck landing assessment and initial carrier trials carried out from April until July, 1948, with TS378 and a stand-by TS380. TS378 arrived at A.&A.E.E. in April, 1948, and was found to have smaller 5·7% elevator horn balances than those fitted during its short initial stay at the Establishment during October, 1947. As the longitudinal stability was unsatisfactory TS378 went back to Westland to have the original 8% horns re-installed. On its return to A.&A.E.E. after three deck landings had been made on H.M.S. *Implacable* from 9th June, 1948, a propeller translation unit bearing failure on the standby TS380 grounded all Wyverns. A pair of four-blade 13 ft. Rotol propellers then replaced the original pair of three-blade 13 ft. de Havilland type and, after a number of airfield dummy deck landings had been made, carrier trials were resumed, with both TS378 and TS380. On 13th July, fifteen take-offs and landings were made with TS378 and seven take-offs and landings with TS380 on 14th July, arrested decelerations being found high despite a windspeed of over 40 kt. in nearly every case. Deck-landing qualities were considered basically good and particular praise was bestowed on the excellent view during the approach. Take-off performance was thought poor and the longitudinal instability immediately after take-off and during the approach made the Wyvern unsuitable for Service deck operation in the form tested. TS375 was fitted with the Malcolm pilot ejection seat device but the arrival at A.&A.E.E. of the Wyvern W.35 T.F.Mk.2, destined as the Service version, rendered further trials with the Mk.1 unnecessary after five prototypes had been built and ten of the pre-production batch completed to Specification 17/46P. The F.Mk.1 and the T.F.Mk.1 Wyverns were the only aircraft in which the Eagle flew.

The spread of interest in the gas turbine brought a corresponding slackening in the development of high-power piston engines and plans were well under way for the continuation of the Wyvern project with propeller-turbine power. Although, in the first place, the gas turbine was put to use as a pure jet engine, parallel development was pursued to harness the new prime mover's output through gearing to a propeller. Two propeller-turbine units, the Rolls-Royce Clyde and the Armstrong Siddeley Python, were selected for powering the Wyvern T.F.Mk.2.

On 18th January, 1949, VP120, the 4,000 lb.s.t. Clyde-engined T.F.Mk.2 made its first flight, followed on 22nd March, 1949, by the Python-powered

VP109. Both versions were evolved to meet Specification N.12/45 but the Wyvern was destined to be beset with serious teething troubles for a long time before it entered the Fleet Air Arm. The Python was finally selected as the Wyvern's power plant but, in developing the machine, Westland and Armstrong Siddeley were pioneering in a new and relatively unknown field, the aircraft acting also as a testbed for the Eagle, Clyde and Python. The main trouble which arose lay in matching the great thrust developed to the contra-rotating propellers under varying conditions, especially in cutting the engine when landing on deck and again when utilizing full thrust at high speed, the last-named condition bringing on sudden surges of power which resulted in

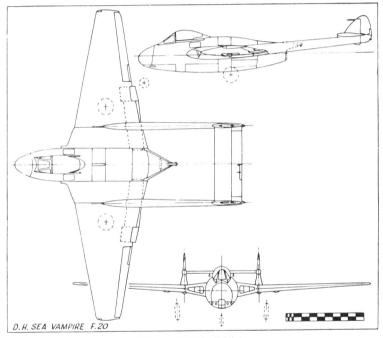

D.H. SEA VAMPIRE F.20

D.H. Sea Vampire F.Mk.20

all Wyverns under official test being grounded for a while pending a remedy being found. The answer was eventually evolved by Armstrong Siddeley and Rotol who developed an inertia controller after a long period of dangerous test flying had been undertaken by the pilots involved. Following seven years gestatory period, the Wyvern ultimately joined the Fleet in May, 1953, to vindicate the faith of its supporters.

The success of the Vampire led to its immediate adaptation as a carrier fighter for the Navy. LZ551, the third F.Mk.1 prototype, was equipped with an arrester hook at the rear of the nacelle and was notable as the first pure jet aircraft to operate from an aircraft carrier when Lt.Cdr. E. M. Brown flew it as the Sea Vampire Mk.10 from H.M.S. *Ocean* on 3rd December, 1945. The trials were eminently successful, being accomplished in two days, after which the Sea Vampire F.Mk.20 went into production for the Fleet Air Arm to Specifications 45/46 and 46/46 to cover those built by de Havilland and English Electric respectively.

During early 1949, experiments were conducted on H.M.S. *Warrior* with a strengthened version of the Sea Vampire F.Mk.21 which was landed with retracted undercarriage on a rubberized deck.

In 1946, under the designation CXP-1001, the Gloster Company was engaged at Brockworth in a project for a single-seat, mid-wing monoplane jet fighter designed by W. G. Carter to the order of the Chinese Nationalist

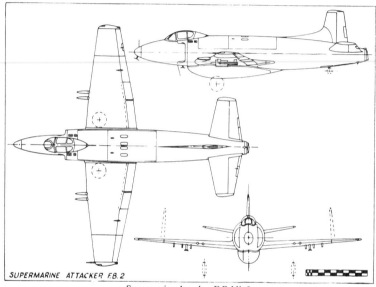

Supermarine Attacker F.B.Mk.2

Government. The layout was prepared around a single 5,000 lb.s.t. Rolls-Royce Nene engine with four 20 mm. cannon disposed in the periphery of the nose intake. A top speed of more than 600 m.p.h. at 10,000 ft. was anticipated but the whole scheme was abandoned after a year's work when the Nationalist Government collapsed.

Along with Gloster and Hawker, Supermarine soon turned attention to producing a single-seat jet fighter. The machine was based on Specification E.10/44 and appeared in 1946 to make its first flight on 27th July at Chilbolton. The Type 392 TS409 was a clean low-wing monoplane, the wings being founded on the laminar-flow planes used in the Spiteful. The choice of a tailwheel undercarriage was unusual at a time of unanimous adoption of the tricycle type, particularly for jet aircraft. Power plant was the 5,100 lb.s.t. Nene 3, aspirated by way of fuselage-mounted intakes on each side of the cockpit.

A.&A.E.E. Boscombe Down Report 846/Pt.2 of 31st May, 1949, covered trials with TS409 from 6th February until 11th March, 1948, recording at 11,000 lb. loaded weight a maximum speed at sea level of 508 m.p.h. and 456 m.p.h. at 35,000 ft., and climb rates at 11,500 lb. take-off weight at sea level of 6,350 ft./min. and 1,980 ft./min. at 35,000 ft. As TS409 was not a naval prototype, it was devoid of arrester hook and lift spoilers and was fitted with a large span tailplane and elevators allied to small fin and rudder. The engine was Nene No. 28, with boundary-layer by-pass ducts in which air passing through was discharged through louvres above and below the bifurcated intake trunks on each side.

Royal Air Force interest in the Supermarine E.10/44 died but a naval version was prepared as the Type 398 Attacker F.Mk.1 by converting TS413, the second E.10/44 prototype to Specification E.1/45, the first flight taking place on 17th June, 1947. The modifications consisted of installing a V arrester hook behind the twin tailwheels, long-stroke main undercarriage oleos, plain flaps in place of the split type fitted to TS409, and upper-surface lift spoilers in front of the flaps. For preliminary deck-landing trials, described in A.&A.E.E. Boscombe Down Report 846/Pt.3 of 17th July, 1950, and carried out from September until October, 1947, the four 20 mm. cannon ports in the wings and the engine boundary-layer by-pass ducts were faired over. Brief preliminary flights, followed by A.D.D.L.s with and without use of lift spoilers, were made to establish a suitable deck-landing technique, following which three landings were made on H.M.S. *Illustrious* on 5th October, 1947. The trials were conducted by Supermarine's Lt.Cdr. M. J. Lithgow, Lt.Cdr. E. M. Brown of R.A.E. Farnborough, and A.&A.E.E. Boscombe Down pilots, conclusions reached being that lift spoilers on the approach and in landing were not needed and that the view on the approach was not as good as was expected. After modification further trials were made with TS413 at Boscombe Down during April and June, 1948, until they were terminated by a fatal crash while flying with a 270 gallon ventral drop tank installed.

Following the loss of TS413, trials were resumed with TS409 to Attacker F.Mk.1 standard, A.&A.E.E. Report 846/Pt.1 of 25th July, 1950, covering the period from January until April, 1950, and commenting adversely on ground handling qualities and the cramped cockpit with its only fair general view, except straight ahead. The trials revealed that the 250 gallon drop tank did not adversely affect the machine's handling characteristics but, on one or two occasions, the formation of ice inside the Attacker's unheated cockpit made operation of the elevator trim wheel difficult. When Attacker F.Mk.1 TS416 joined TS409 for further carrier trials, it had been modified to incorporate a pressure cabin, wings set about 18 inches further aft, larger air intakes, long-stroke oleos and extra tankage.

Attacker F.Mk.1 WA469, the first production aircraft, was tested for handling at A.&A.E.E. during November and December, 1950, Report 846/Pt.13 of 26th February, 1951, noting that, at 40,000 ft., the machine was safe for high-altitude Service use but that, since it would not be a good gun platform above 35,000 ft. and because of extreme engine operating sensitivity at such heights, the machine would have very little operational use at over 35,000 ft.

WA469 made its first flight on 4th April, 1950, and the Attacker thereafter went into service as the F.Mk.1 and F.B.Mk.1 with the 5,100 lb.s.t. Nene 3, to be followed by the Nene 102-powered and modified F.B.Mk.2. R.A.T.O.G. was incorporated and the F.B. versions were armed also with eight 60 lb. R.P.s or two 1,000 lb. bombs.

Since 1925, when authority finally came partially to its senses to show some belated consideration for human life, aircrew had been equipped with parachutes. The great increases in speed of aircraft and the introduction of enclosed cockpits and installation of extra equipment made it steadily more difficult to leave a machine in an emergency. The jet fighter brought with it severe problems in this direction and further realization that a pilot's life was not so cheap after all and was worth saving. It is not inconceivable that the great increases in time and cost involved in aircrew training were responsible to some degree for the growth in concern over aircrew survival.

Although James Martin's outstanding brilliance as a fighter designer was not to be recognized with production orders for his creations, subsequent recognition and an undoubtedly extremely satisfying reward came his way with the development from early 1944 of his ingenious Martin-Baker ejector seats which have saved the precious lives of over 4494 aircrew, every member having reason for the profoundest gratitude to James Martin and to his team of pilots and technicians who explored the unknown field at great personal danger and with supreme courage.

The first live ejection was made successfully on 24th July, 1946, by Bernard Lynch from a Meteor F.Mk.3 EE416 travelling at 320 m.p.h. I.A.S. at 8,000 ft. and, from then on, the ejector seat principle was exploited and developed to cater for every contingency that might arise in jet-powered fighters, the sequence of operations becoming progressively less manual and more automatic.

While concentrating increasingly on the successful development of the ejector seat, James Martin prepared one more project for a single-seat fighter—the extremely advanced delta wing, tailless Martin-Baker M.B.6— which would have been powered by a single turbo-jet housed in the fuselage and aspirated through the circular nose duct. Unfortunately, the design never became reality to enable the M.B.6 to display its supremely elegant shape in the air.

The Meteor was assessed for deck landing from April until June, 1948, A.&A.E.E. Boscombe Down Report 817/f of 28th April, 1950, describing trials with EE337 and EE387. Each was a late production short nacelle F.Mk.3 fitted with Derwent 5 engines, a strengthened undercarriage to absorb 11·5 ft./sec. and a Sea Hornet V frame arrester hook about 12 ft. aft of the trailing edge. All non-essential equipment was removed to lighten the machine. Thirty-two carrier landings were made between 10th and 18th June on H.M.S. *Implacable* by two A.&A.E.E. pilots who found that the

The two-seat de Havilland D.H.103 Sea Hornet N.F.Mk.21. (de Havilland Photo.)

machine made an excellent deck-landing aircraft, with particularly good take-off characteristics and possessing better deck-landing qualities than any other jet aircraft tested at A.&A.E.E. until June, 1948. The view for deck landing was excellent, a power-on approach being made at a steady rate of descent at 85–90 knots I.A.S.

From 1949 until 1954 the de Havilland Sea Hornet N.F.Mk.21 served as the Fleet Air Arm's two-seat, carrier-borne night fighter. The prototype was developed to Specification N.21/45 by the conversion of F.Mk.1 PX230 by Heston Aircraft, a radar operator/navigator being carried behind the pilot to operate the A.S.H. equipment, the scanner of which was housed in the lengthened nose. PX230 first flew on 9th July, 1946, and PX239, the second prototype, was given folding wings and a dorsal fin extension, standardized on subsequent production N.F.Mk.21s. A combination of 2,030 h.p. Merlins 134 and 135 provided the power and four 20 mm. cannon and eight 60 lb. rockets the armament.

Specification F.19/43 dealt with a class of fighter not constructed in Britain, that of a single-seater powered by a jet and a piston engine, the design of

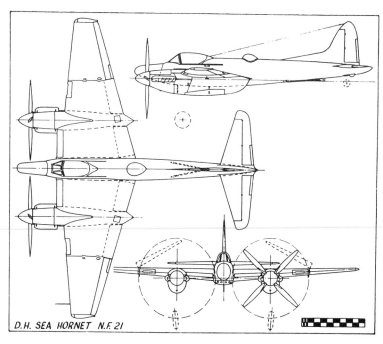

D.H. Sea Hornet N.F.Mk.21

which was to have been undertaken by Folland with construction by English Electric.

Development of the successful Vampire brought the F.Mk.3, the prototype TG275 flying for the first time on 4th November, 1946, production taking place to Specification 3/47. Internal fuel tankage was increased from 202 gallons to 326 gallons and a shapelier fin and rudder outline accompanied the lowering of the horizontal tail surfaces. To six F.Mk.3s of No. 54 Squadron fell the distinction of making the first jet crossing of the Atlantic in July, 1948. The Vampire F.Mk.3 prototype TG275, together with the pressurized VF343, was sent to A.&A.E.E. Boscombe Down for handling trials conducted from August, 1947, until February, 1948. Conclusions reached in Report 819/d/Pt.2 of 7th March, 1949, were that the F.Mk.3, both with and without its pair of 100 gallon drop tanks, did not meet the required standards of stability under certain conditions but the type was cleared to the Service provided that pilots were warned of its shortcomings and that effective modifications were evolved and incorporated as soon as possible, particularly before the F.Mk.3 was used in bad weather or at night.

Continued development of the basic design brought the ground attack Vampire F.B.Mk.5. A reduction of 2 ft. in span was effected, the tips being square cut, and other modifications were made to fit the machine for its fighter bomber rôle. The first example flew on 23rd June, 1948, the F.B.Mk.5

de Havilland D.H.100 Vampire F.Mk.III. (de Havilland Photo.)

ultimately becoming the most widely used Vampire of all. VV215, an early production F.B.Mk.5 was assessed in A.&A.E.E. Boscombe Down Report 819/e/Pt.2 of 25th October, 1949, which covered trials during August, 1948. The flying characteristics were acceptable for Service use but disappointment was expressed at the altitude performance, with and without drop tanks, as an interceptor fighter.

During 1947, a development of the Firebrand T.F.Mk.V made its appearance from Blackburn. Designed to Specification S.28/43, the B.48 Y.A.1 Firecrest was a handsome single-seat, low-wing monoplane designed by G. E. Petty and fitted with the eighteen-cylinder 2,840 h.p. Centaurus 59. Its rôle was that of a strike fighter to carry a torpedo; armament comprised two ·50 machine-guns, together with rockets or two 500 lb. bombs. The hydraulically-folding wings embodied anhedral at their roots, four high-lift flaps and dive brakes on upper and lower surfaces. The Firecrest's pilot had an excellent view in most directions. Three prototypes were built, the first of which—RT651—flew in 1947, reaching a top speed of 380 m.p.h. at 19,000 ft. The machine arrived right at the end of the piston-engine era, with

Blackburn Y.A.1 VF172. (Blackburn Photo.)

323

TG263, the first prototype Saro SR.A1. (Saro Photo.)

consequently small chance of adoption by the Navy, and no contract was awarded to the Firecrest for the Fleet Air Arm.

Sporadic efforts, unrewarded by production orders, have been made over the years to produce single-seat flying-boat fighters, one of the most striking and successful machines in this category being the jet-engine Saunders-Roe SR.A.1 of 1947, the first jet-driven flying-boat of all.

Designed by Henry Knowler, three prototypes were built to Specification E.6/44, a requirement drawn up in anticipation of the need for a long-range water-borne fighter for use in the Pacific against the Japanese. TG263, the first prototype, made its maiden flight at East Cowes during the evening of 15th July, 1947, piloted by Geoffrey Tyson. The engines were a pair of Metro-vick F.2/4A Beryl M.V.B.1 axial-flow turbines derated to 3,300 lb.s.t. each but the following two SR.A.1s were given 3,500 lb. and 3,850 lb. Beryl M.V.B.2 units respectively. Tip floats retracted underneath the lower wing surfaces and the SR.A.1's armament of four 20 mm. Hispano Mk.V cannon was installed in the decking above the oval nose intake. The design was ex-tremely manœuvrable and recorded a top speed of 516 m.p.h. in the third prototype but was destined to remain another promising type not chosen for production.

Specification E.5/42 for a single-seat jet fighter was revised as Specification E.1/44, the machine produced to meet it appearing in 1947 as the Gloster G.A.2 Ace designed by W. G. Carter. Two G.A.1 airframes—a flying shell SM801 and a prototype SM805—were under construction in 1944 but were abandoned in favour of the G.A.2. The 5,000 lb.s.t. Nene 2 was selected to power the 36 ft. span mid-wing monoplane but the first prototype G.A.2 SM809 never flew as it was wrecked in an accident during August, 1947, while on its way by road to A.&A.E.E. Boscombe Down for its initial flight. TX145, the second G.A.2—a pre-production prototype—made its first flight at Boscombe Down on 9th March, 1948, piloted by Sqn.Ldr. W. A. Waterton. During 1949 TX148, the next pre-production prototype, appeared, but differed from its predecessors in having a Meteor F.Mk.8 type of tail unit with high-set tailplane. A development of the G.A.2, the G.A.3 TX150 with the 5,000 lb.s.t. D.H. Ghost engine in place of the Nene 2, was in process of construction in 1949 but was not completed.

Specification 23/46P was issued on 15th November, 1946, to cover the Gloster E.1/44 production G.A.4. with the Nene 2 installation. Alterations to the original requirement were the installation of internal fuel tanks with a total capacity of 480 gallons, two filling points capable of operating at a rate of 100 gallons a minute, and the ability to carry two external jettisonable tanks of 100 gallons each. The span was to be reduced to 32 ft., the gun installation of nose-mounted four 20 mm. Hispano cannon was to incorporate the Martin-Baker feed system and, in addition, rocket projectiles or a bomb load of either two 500 lb. or two 1,000 lb. bombs was specified. Stainless steel was used extensively in the Ace's construction but, although it reached a top speed of 630 m.p.h. at sea level, performance was not considered to be sufficiently in advance of the Meteor to warrant production.

By 1944 Hawker, in common with other fighter manufacturers, were faced with making the inevitable complete changeover to jet propulsion. The first such project by the firm was the P.1035 of November, 1944, to embody the Rolls-Royce B.41 engine in the fuselage of the F.2/43 Fury. At the end of 1944 the P.1035 design was discarded in favour of a new layout—the P.1040—to Specification N.7/46, issued for a Fleet Air Arm interceptor after R.A.F. interest had lapsed. VP401, the P.1040 prototype, gained the distinction of being the first of many Hawker jet fighters to follow and was a design in which Sydney Camm achieved superb elegance of line. The fineness of the fuselage was gained by feeding the 4,500 lb.s.t. Nene 1 engine by way of a pair of intakes in the thick roots of the mid-wings and exhausting through bifurcated outlets

Gloster G.A.2. (Gloster Photo.)

The prototype Hawker P.1040 VP401 with modified jet outlet fairing. (Hawker Photo.)

in the rear fairings of the centre section. VP401's first flight was at Boscombe Down on 2nd September, 1947, with Sqn.Ldr. T. S. Wade at the controls. The P.1040 had been built basically to N.7/46 to prove the design but was without its armament, wing-folding and arrester hook. Minor alterations had been made by the time that VP401 arrived at A.&A.E.E. Boscombe Down for brief pre-view handling trials in June, 1948, described in Report 860/Pt.1 of 28th April, 1950. The general handling and flying qualities of the machine, fitted with Nene No. 36, were well liked and deck landing of the navalized N.7/46, with the excellent forward view and tricycle undercarriage, was expected to be relatively straightforward. Points noted were the lack of airbrakes which were

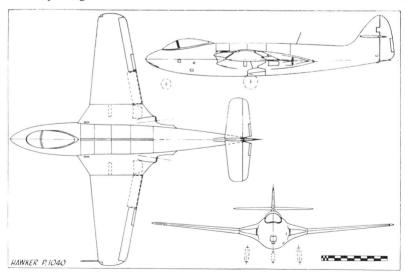

HAWKER P.1040

Hawker P.1040

thought to be vital for Service use, the stick force per "g" which was too low at low airspeeds and excessively high at high airspeeds, and the lack of an aileron trimmer—also thought absolutely necessary. As the Malcolm pilot ejection installation was found to be unsatisfactory, the intended testing programme was not completed but, during the short test period, the P.1040's take-off run was found in simulated trials to be too long for satisfactory unassisted take-off from a carrier. On 3rd September, 1948, VP413—the N.7/46 Sea Hawk F.Mk.1 prototype—made its maiden flight, the airframe incorporating folding wings, four nose-mounted 20 mm. Hispano cannon and catapulting points. Trials dictated an increase in span of 2 ft. 6 in. and this modification was built into the wings. After thirty-five F.Mk.1s had been built by Hawker, Armstrong Whitworth assumed complete responsibility for Sea Hawk production and development.

One of the most graceful of all fighters, the Hawker Sea Hawk F.Mk.1 WF144. (Dowty Photo.)

Specification 25/48P Ref. No. 7/Aircraft/4460/R.D.T.2, issued on 17th January, 1949, covered production of the Sea Hawk to N.7/46. The Nene 4 with cartridge starting was specified, together with four 20 mm. Hispano Mk.V cannon and 200 r.p.g., rocket projectiles in lieu of drop tanks, V.H.F., I.F.F., Homing Receiver and Beam Approach. Maximum speed was demanded between sea level and 15,000 ft., with internal fuel for take-off and climb to 35,000 ft., 285 n.m. radius, 15 min. combat at 35,000 ft., return to base at best speed at 35,000 ft., 20 min. loitering at sea level prior to landing and provision for drop tanks for above 490 n.m. range. Other 25/48P requirements were a pressure cabin, ejector seat, airbrakes, undercarriage absorption of 16 ft./sec., good manoeuvrability, long range at most economical height, high speed at the expense of climb rate if necessary, the ability to operate in all parts of the World, day and night landing on carriers equipped with Mk.10, 11, 12 or 13 arrester gear, provision for R.A.T.O.G., lowest possible all-up weight, maximum wing span of 40 ft. spread and 18 ft. folded, maximum folded height of 16 ft. 10·5 in., armour and shatter-proof windscreen, and good ditching qualities.

Daytime deck trials on H.M.S. *Eagle* with early production F.Mk.1s WF144 and WF145, equipped with Nene 4s, were summarized in A.&A.E.E. Boscombe Down Report 860/2/Pt.1 of 26th August, 1952, in which catapulting was assessed as straightforward and deck-landing characteristics as excellent. The arrester hook, which hung rather low, called for modification to avoid trouble in service. The primary capability required in N.7/46 was that of a day interceptor fighter, with its supplementary rôles of long-range strike support fighter, fighter reconnaissance, bombardment spotting and limited ground attack. The basic Sea Hawk design underwent considerable development through the F.Mk.1, F.Mk.2, F.B.Mk.3, F.G.A.Mk.4, F.B.Mk.5, F.G.A.Mk.6, and several versions for foreign air arms, proving to be a most successful aircraft as well as being one of the sleekest and best looking fighters ever designed.

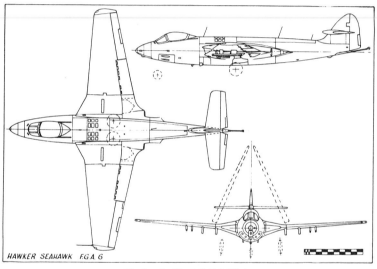

HAWKER SEAHAWK F.G.A. 6

Hawker Sea Hawk F.G.A.Mk.6

12th October, 1948, witnessed the first flight of VT150, the prototype Gloster G.41P Meteor F.Mk.8. A development of the F.Mk.4, the newcomer was powered by a pair of 3,600 lb.s.t. Rolls-Royce Derwent 8 engines and incorporated a longer fuselage to provide extra internal tankage, a feature tested beforehand on RA382, a modified F.Mk.4. A square-cut tail was used and the combined underfin and bumper beneath the rear fuselage was discarded. Other improvements included a new clear-view canopy and an ejector seat. Top speed was boosted to 590 m.p.h., accompanied by better handling qualities. The F.Mk.8 entered R.A.F. service on 10th December, 1949, with No. 245 Squadron receiving its first aircraft on 29th June, 1950. Later F.Mk.8s produced were given engine intakes with greater diameter, a revised cockpit canopy and spring tabs on the ailerons. Meteor F.Mk.8s of No. 245

Gloster Meteor F.Mk.8 of No. 245 Squadron fitted with flight refuelling probe. (Flight Refuelling Photo.)

Squadron were equipped with nose probes for refuelling in flight using the probe and drogue system developed by Sir Alan Cobham's company Flight Refuelling Limited, experiments during 1951 proving that six Meteors could be kept flying for three to four hours at a stretch. The object of these trials, which were very successful, was to increase endurance to enable standing patrols of fighters to be kept airborne for extended periods.

Among the various specifications issued just after the Second World War to stimulate single-seat jet fighter evolution was E.38/46 to cover the Hawker P.1052. The design superseded two proposed derivatives of the P.1040, the P.1046 and P.1047, both of which would have had tail-mounted rocket engines. The P.1047 was schemed to use swept-back wings and this feature

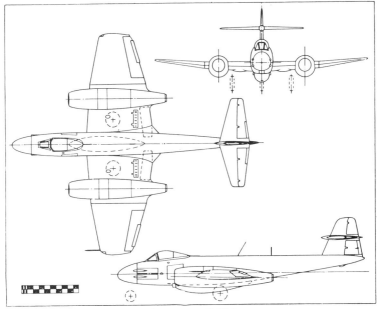

Gloster Meteor F.Mk.8

The first prototype Hawker P.1052 VX272. (Hawker Photo.)

was carried on in the two P.1052 prototypes, VX272 and VX279. The rocket engine idea was dropped temporarily, the sole power plant being the 5,000 lb.s.t. Nene R.N.2. Sqn.Ldr. T. S. Wade made the first flight of VX272 at A.&A.E.E. Boscombe Down on 19th November, 1948. VX279, the second prototype, underwent pre-view handling trials at A.&A.E.E. during July, 1949, following its first flight on the previous 13th April. The object of the trials was to assess the type as a potential interceptor fighter as, although designed originally as a research aircraft to investigate the properties of swept-back wings, considerable interest had been shown in promoting it as a Service fighter.

Report 856/Pt.1 of 23rd July, 1949, dealt with the evaluation of VX279, the wings of which were swept back on the quarter-chord line at 35°; Hawker

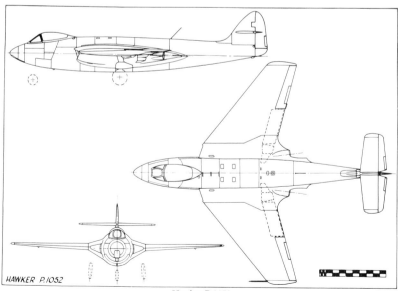

Hawker P.1052

330

H10% symmetrical was the wing section used. To assess fairly the P.1052's qualities as a fighter it was flown in the attacking rôle in mock combat with a Meteor F.Mk.4 between 12,000 ft. and 25,000 ft. Under such conditions, the elevator control stood out as too heavy for a fighter, with movements too large, response poor and insufficient effectiveness. This was very tiring for the pilot. In contrast, the ailerons on VX279 were assessed as delightfully quick throughout the speed range and the rate of roll was good. The P.1052 was liked by all pilots and was considered pleasant to fly. The swept-back wings produced the required effect of giving the high usable Mach number of 0·9 but introduced the phenomenon of Dutch rolling. Report 856/Pt.2 of 29th July, 1949, dealt with brief performance trials of VX279, carried out also in July, 1949, and Report 856/Pt.5 of 26th August, 1949, was concerned with a preliminary deck landing assessment of VX279 conducted in July, 1949, under A.D.D.L. conditions. The general opinion was that the P.1052 was a very pleasant machine in which to make A.D.D.L.s and that its slow-speed handling characteristics were superior to those of the P.1040. Further experimental flying was carried out, VX272 suffering several forced landings in the next three years.

While the P.1052 was providing Hawker with swept-wing experience, Supermarine evolved the Type 510 Swift VV106 as a research vehicle to Specification E.41/46. Basically, the machine consisted of the Attacker's fuselage to which were mated new wing and tail surfaces, all swept back at an angle of 40° on the quarter-chord line. A laminar-flow section was employed for the wings and the engine installed was the 5,000 lb.s.t. Nene R.N.2 No. 24. Despite the increasingly universal adoption of the tricycle undercarriage, the Type 510 adhered to the tailwheel formula. VV106's maiden flight took place on 29th December, 1948, handling trials being carried out at A.&A.E.E. Boscombe Down from January until March, 1950. These were recorded in Report 859/Pt.2 of 31st May, 1950, and noted that, following its arrival at A.&A.E.E. in October, 1949, the machine had to be returned to Supermarine in the following month for investigation of severe vibration encountered on throttling back to low engine speeds. With modifications made to eradicate the fault the Swift arrived back at A.&A.E.E. in January, 1950, for continuation of its assessment as potential fighter equipment. During its return to Supermarine between November, 1949, and January, 1950, the Swift's needle nose was replaced by the original Attacker type, air intake boundary layer suction was increased by raising the exit louvres proud of the fuselage skin, the cabin ventilator was removed, and the cooling air gap at the rear of the plenum chamber was enlarged. Split trailing-edge flaps and small underwing dive recovery flaps were installed but no airbrakes.

Ground manœuvring was thought poor and would have gained greatly by the fitting of a tricycle undercarriage. The tailwheel landing gear restricted also the view while taxiing owing to the sharp ground angle. Generally, opinion was that the Swift was fairly easy and pleasant to fly and was free from troubles expected in an aircraft with sharp sweepback. The usable Mach number of about 0·93 was a considerable advance over contemporary Service equipment and no serious tendencies towards Dutch rolling or snaking

de Havilland D.H.113 Vampire N.F.Mk.10 prototype G–5–2. (de Havilland Photo.)

were encountered. The delightfully light and crisp ailerons conferred a good rate of roll but the elevators were too heavy for a fighter. With a tricycle undercarriage and better elevator control the Swift was thought to have the makings of a good fighter.

The Swift VV106, flown by Lt. Parker, R.N., gained the distinction on 8th November, 1950, of making the first four carrier landings by a swept-wing aeroplane and A.&A.E.E. Report 859/Pt.4 of 15th August, 1951, covered deck landing assessment and initial carrier trials, conducted as a result of the A.& A.E.E.'s earlier recommendation that the Swift should be equipped for experimental deck landings. The subsequent trials were made during November, 1950, from H.M.S. *Illustrious* by Lt. Elliott, R.N., from Farnborough,

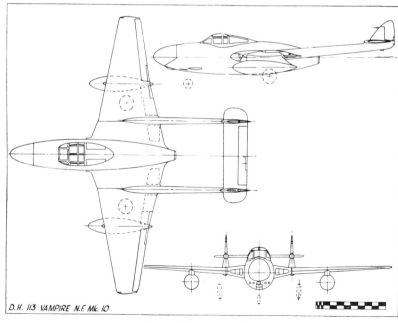

D.H. 113 VAMPIRE N.F. Mk. 10

D.H. Vampire N.F.Mk.10

332

Lt.Cdr. M. J. Lithgow of Supermarine and Lt. Parker of the A.&A.E.E. Boscombe Down. R.A.T.O. units were fitted to VV106 for use during the trials. In general, deck landing and deck handling characteristics of the Swift were superior to those of the Attacker but take-off performance was poor and had to be rocket-assisted in every case, even in the 50 knot windspeed used for the tests. The adverse criticisms applied to the cockpit of the Attacker were even stronger in the case of the Swift, the cockpit being considered even more cramped and badly laid out than that of the Attacker.

The night fighter Mosquitoes of the R.A.F. were scheduled to be succeeded by the Meteor N.F.Mk.11 and Venom N.F.Mk.2 but, when the embargo on arms to Egypt was imposed, the D.H.113 Vampires ordered by that country were directed into the R.A.F. as Vampire N.F.Mk.10 interim two-seat jet night fighters. The first flight of the D.H.113 took place with G. H. Pike on 28th August, 1949, and the N.F.Mk.10 joined the R.A.F. in 1951 when No. 25 Squadron re-equipped with it. The engine was the 3,350 lb.s.t. Goblin 3 and the armament of four 20 mm. cannon was housed in the belly of the nacelle in which the pilot and his radar navigator sat side by side.

Following its first flight in August, 1949, G-5-2—the Private Venture first D.H.113 prototype—was sent to Boscombe Down for assessment from December, 1949, until March, 1950. Handling trials were reported in A.& A.E.E. Report 819/h/Pt.1 of 16th August, 1950, the machine being powered by Goblin 3 No. 8032. Conclusions drawn were that the D.H.113 possessed handling qualities similar to those of the Vampire F.B.Mk.5 and that, following the incorporation of minor modifications, the type would make a good interim night fighter. Level speed tests conducted in February and March, 1950, were curtailed when G-5-2 sustained severe damage on losing its nose section during a handling flight. Cockpit appraisal and night-flying assessment of WP232, the second production N.F.Mk.10, were recorded in A.&A.E.E. Report 819/h/Pt.8 of 29th June, 1951, the machine being evaluated in April, 1951. The aircraft was pleasant to fly at night but the facilities for escape of the crew during flight were condemned as grossly inadequate, with twin ejector seats suggested as the only acceptable solution.

As a successor to the Vampire, de Havilland designed the D.H.112 to Specification 15/49. First intention was to designate the machine Vampire F.B.Mk.8 but it was ultimately called the Venom F.B.1. The new single-seat interceptor was intended to undertake also the rôle of ground-attack fighter-bomber and retained the same layout as that of the Vampire but the nacelle accommodated the more powerful 4,850 lb.s.t. D.H. Ghost 103 engine. A higher Mach number was aimed at by sweeping back the wings' leading edge at $17°6'$ angle and reducing the thickness/chord ratio to 10% compared with the Vampire's 14%. VV612, the prototype Venom F.B.Mk.1, made its initial flight on 2nd September, 1949, and was sent to Boscombe Down for trials during May, 1950. Tests at high Mach numbers were detailed in A.&A.E.E. Report 868/Pt.1 of 25th August, 1950, which concluded that characteristics were reasonably satisfactory but that further development was

de Havilland D.H.112 Venom F.B.Mk.1. (de Havilland Photo.)

needed. Report 868/Pt.2 of 31st October, 1950, concluded from pre-view handling trials with VV612 during the period May until September, 1950, that—apart from certain faults which needed correction—the Venom F.B. Mk.1 showed a noticeable advantage in mock combat with two current fighters. A.&A.E.E. Report 868/Gen/Pt.1 of 8th November, 1951, summarized trials with VV612, VV613 and WE255. VV613 was the second prototype

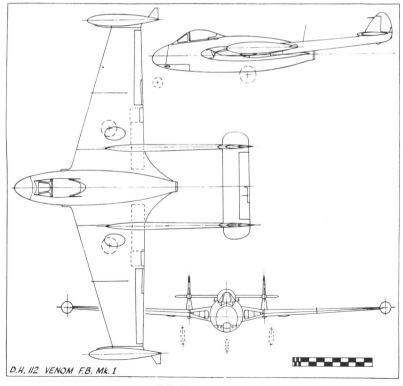

D.H. 112 VENOM F.B. Mk. 1

D.H. Venom F.B.Mk.1

and drew the comment that, while its rate of roll without tip tanks was poor, with them the rate of roll was deplorable. WE255 was the first production Venom and demonstrated a recurrence of the nose-up pitch at medium and high altitudes—first noticed on VV612 and thought to be cured—following deterioration of the wing surface. Regret was expressed at the absence of an ejector seat in the prototype Venom. However, the aircraft had been flown at 51,000 ft. with reasonably satisfactory control characteristics. Armament of the Venom consisted of four nose-mounted 20 mm. Hispano Mk5. cannon.

The same procedure in producing the two-seat Venom N.F.Mk.2 was

de Havilland D.H.112 Venom N.F.Mk.2 prototype. (de Havilland Photo.)

adopted as that resorted to in evolving the Vampire night fighter by seating the radar-navigator beside the pilot in a wider nacelle. The Private Venture prototype Venom N.F.Mk.2 G–5–3 took off for the first time on 22nd August, 1950, at Hatfield. The nose was lengthened to house the A.I. radar. A.&A.E.E. trials of G–5–3 were conducted with the machine carrying the serial WP227 during the period April until September, 1951, and were assessed in Report 868/2 which noted that, in preliminary handling trials, the rate of roll was barely adequate for a night fighter and would have been insufficient were the machine to be employed alternatively as an all-weather fighter. Great regret was expressed at the lack of any intention to provide ejector seats for the crew. Similar regret was recorded in the case of WK376 which, together with WP227, was used for deck-landing assessment. For carrier service the Venom N.F.Mk.2 was considered to have potentially very good deck-landing characteristics. Praise was elicited by the good all-round view and by the

The prototype Gloster Meteor F.R.Mk.9. (Gloster Photo.)

roominess of the cockpit. The Venom N.F.Mk.2 eventually joined the R.A.F. in 1953, several different marks subsequently serving with success for several years.

The potentialities of the Meteor were exploited in the fighter reconnaissance rôle with the introduction of the F.R.Mk.9, the prototype of which, VW360, was flown for the first time on 23rd March, 1950. In addition to its armament of four 20 mm. cannon, the F.R.Mk.9 was equipped with a camera in a specially developed nose mounting and was powered by a pair of 3,500 lb.s.t. Derwent 8 engines.

Some nine weeks after the Meteor F.R.Mk.9's initial flight, the two-seat Meteor N.F.Mk.11 prototype WA546 to Specification F.24/48 flew for the first time on 31st May, 1950. F.24/48, issued on 12th February, 1949, called for a night fighter version of the Meteor evolved from the T.1/47 T.Mk.7 and to carry a tandem-seated pilot and navigator-radar operator. The machine was to be suitable for economic production of two hundred aircraft at the rate of fifteen a month. Two Derwent 8s were specified with armament to comprise four 20 mm. Hispano Mk.5 cannon backed by 640 r.p.g. and installed in the wings outboard of the engines. A gyro gunsight was to be fitted, together with V.H.F. of minimum sixteen channels, A.I.Mk.10 in an extended nose, I.F.F. Mk.3GR and AYF radio altimeter. An alternative design to incorporate A.I.Mk.17 was to be prepared. Duration was to be at least 2 hrs.

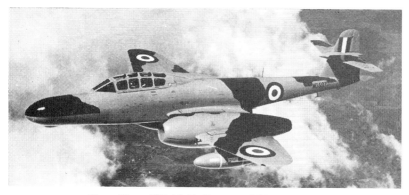

Gloster Meteor N.F. Mk.11. (Armstrong Whitworth Photo.)

at 30,000 ft. and an appreciable increase in longitudinal stability over that of the T.7 was demanded. The machine was required as soon as possible to span the interim period prior to production of the Gloster Javelin to Specification F.4/48. Responsibility for design and production of the N.F.Mk.11 was assumed by Armstrong Whitworth, the first production machines entering service during 1951.

Interest shown by the Australian Government encouraged Hawker to prepare a proposal during January, 1950, for a modified version of the P.1052 equipped with the Rolls-Royce Tay. Delays encountered in development of

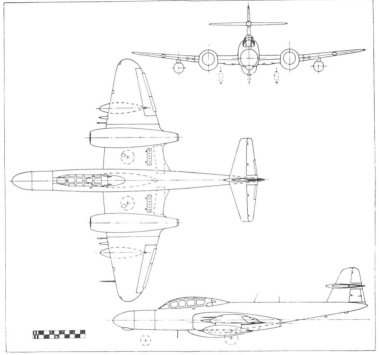

Gloster Meteor N.F.Mk.11

the new engine led Hawker to proceed to design the P.1081 around the 5,000 lb.s.t. Nene RN2 exhausting through a straight pipe. VX279, the second prototype P.1052, was selected for transformation into the P.1081 and was provided with a revised swept tail unit mounted above the rear jet outlet. VX279's first flight was made by Sqn.Ldr. T. S. Wade on 19th June, 1950, the machine eventually recording a speed of Mach 0·89 at 36,000 ft. For the ensuing five months various revisions were made to the machine as a result of flight trials until, following the end of Australian interest in the design, the P.1081 was transferred to R.A.E. Farnborough for further trials. The machine's end came suddenly when, on 3rd April, 1951, it crashed while Wade was flying it, killing the pilot and leaving no clue to the cause of its demise.

Hawker P.1081 VX279. (Hawker Photo.)

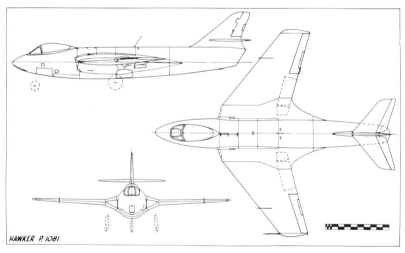

HAWKER P.1081

Hawker P.1081

The advent of the 2,000 lb. thrust Armstrong Siddeley Snarler ASSn1 rocket engine revived the interest shown at Hawker during October, 1945, which had lapsed later owing to the lack of a rocket unit. Under the designation P.1072, VP401—the P.1040 prototype used for N.7/46 trials—was modified to carry the Snarler in its rear fuselage, the jet engine being the 5,000 lb.s.t. Nene RN2. The rocket installation ran for 2·75 minutes and VP401 made use of this form of power for the first time on 20th November, 1950, flying from Bitteswell. Some half a dozen test flights were carried out utilizing the Snarler's thrust but ceased when the Air Ministry indicated a

338

Hawker P.1072. (Hawker Photo.)

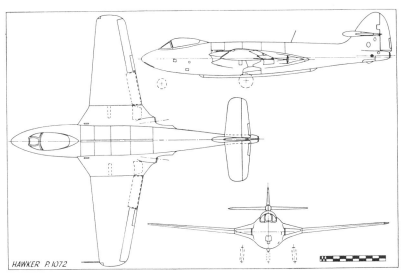

HAWKER P.1072

Hawker P.1072

lack of interest resulting from a preference to sponsor the development of after-burning to provide extra thrust when needed.

To follow the Type 510 Swift, Supermarine constructed a later prototype—the Type 517—with an after-burner incorporated in the Nene installation. The Type 517 prototype was then revised with a longer nose and a tricycle undercarriage and redesignated Type 535, making its first flight on 23rd August, 1950.

By the time that five years had elapsed after the end of the Second World War, the pattern of British fighter evolution was reasonably clear. The piston engine had ceased to play any further part in the fighter's development and, after a brief spell in the limelight as the power plant of the Wyvern, the propeller turbine slipped from the fighter scene, yielding the field to the pure jet engine. Between the two main turbine types—centrifugal and axial flow—the slimmer axial-flow engine was already making its attractions felt by the aircraft designer, who, using it, could more nearly approach his ideal form in airframe design. The concept of the jet fighter had brought with it a number of new and urgent problems, among them crew survival, compressibility, revised forms of armament and new operational techniques, each of which demanded a solution so that the aircraft being evolved could operate at maximum efficiency under all conditions.

de Havilland D.H.112 Sea Venom F.A.W.Mk.22. (de Havilland Photo.)

CHAPTER NINE

MACH ONE PLUS

The period of well-deserved peace which succeeded the terrible, destructive years of the Second World War were not long destined to be without fears of another holocaust or without actual conflict. At an appalling cost in good British and Allied lives, the criminal war machine of Germany and that of her allies had been destroyed but, almost immediately, Germany and its people had again become a danger to the hard-won peace. As a natural aftermath of the War, aircraft production lines had rapidly slowed down as contracts were cut back and cancelled. Before the conflict ended plans were prepared for the change over to civil aircraft of vastly improved new type to take over from those long overdue for replacement.

Hardly had Britain's fighting strength been reduced to the dangerously low level considered by authority as sufficient to enable the United Kingdom to hold up its head among other nations and to maintain its position in the World, than a speedy build-up was demanded to meet the needs thrust urgently on the Services.

Trouble in Europe was accompanied by the outbreak of war in Korea and these events, together with minor emergencies elsewhere, brought a swift return to a closing of the ranks and rearmament. Automatically, research and development swept forward at a greatly accelerated pace, no less in fighter design than in any other sphere of aeronautics.

At the start of the 1950s basic existing fighter types continued to receive attention to improve their qualities while new designs were evolved. The Vampire continued in production as the F.B.Mk.9 and the Venom was adopted by the Royal Navy as its first two-seat all-weather fighter, fulfilling also the rôle of strike fighter. The R.A.F. Venom N.F.Mk.2 prototype G–5–3

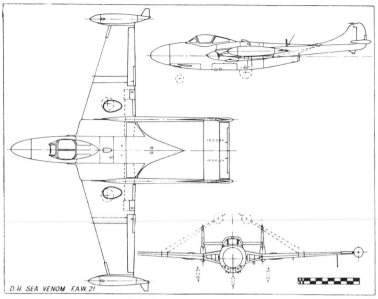

D.H. Sea Venom F.A.W.Mk.21

was used for initial naval trials as WP227, followed by the first prototype Sea Venom N.F.Mk.20 WK376 which undertook its first carrier take-off on 9th July, 1951, from H.M.S. *Illustrious*. WK385, the third prototype, received folding wings. The Sea Venom passed into production as the F.A.W.Mk.20, the first of which—WM500—took to the air for the first time on 27th March, 1953. A.&A.E.E. Boscombe Down Report 868/1/Pt.5 of 15th September, 1952, referred to daytime carrier trials with WK376 on H.M.S. *Eagle* in May and June, 1952, and accorded the aircraft excellent deck take-off and landing characteristics with the exception of poor hook damping. The second prototype N.F.Mk.20, WK379, was employed also in the A.&A.E.E. evaluation.

WM504, a production Sea Venom F.A.W.Mk.20, underwent deck landing assessment and day and night deck trials during October and November, 1953, with conclusions recorded in A.&A.E.E. Report 868/1/Pt.11 of 3rd December, 1954. WM504 differed from the prototypes in possessing increased fin area, giving altered fin and rudder outline, folding wings incorporating non-jettisonable tip tanks, boundary layer fences, a camera gun on a faired pylon under the port wing root, symmetrical cast perspex cockpit canopy and a Venom F.B.Mk.1 elevator. Provision of a windscreen wiper was considered essential and a warning was sounded against unduly high stalling speeds in production aircraft. Lateral and directional characteristics were thought unsuitable for deck landings employing standard techniques but use of a mirror sight, following A.D.D.L.s, seemed more promising. Further tests with Sea Venom F.A.W.Mk.20s WM501 and WM502, carried out from March until

342

October, 1954, and assessed in A.&A.E.E. Boscombe Down Report 868/1/Pt.15 of 28th January, 1955, confirmed the poor lateral and directional control criticized previously but noted that a considerable improvement in this respect had been effected in the Sea Venom F.A.W.Mk.21.

Powered ailerons and Maxaret brakes were introduced in the Sea Venom F.A.W.Mk.21 which was powered by the 4,950 lb.s.t. Ghost 104. XA539 was used for deck landing trials during August and September, 1954, A.&A.E.E. Boscombe Down Report 868/3/Pt.1 of 4th July, 1955, assessing the F.A.W. Mk.21 as suitable for day and night deck landing subject to the provision of a suitable twin pointer, open scale A.S.I. Four pilots were responsible for XA539's trials on H.M.S. *Albion* which consisted of twenty catapult take-offs and twenty landings by day, including the transit flights. The carrier was fitted with an interim 5° angled deck and all of the landings were made using the mirror aid. Martin-Baker Mk.4 ejection seats were fitted later to the Sea Venom F.A.W.Mk.21 and the final production version was the F.A.W.Mk.22 with the Ghost 105.

During the year following the end of the Second World War the question of ultimately providing a replacement for the first generation of jet fighters was receiving attention and on 24th January, 1947, an important step to provide the R.A.F. with a new fighter to replace the Meteor was taken with the issue of Specification F.43/46 Ref.7/Aircraft/1514/R.D.T.2(d). The requirement called for a prototype single-seat interceptor fighter for the destruction in daylight of high-speed, high-altitude enemy bombers. Armament was to consist of two 30 mm. cannon with 200 r.p.g. or a single recoilless 4·5 in. gun with six or possibly ten rounds of ammunition. No muzzle flash was to be visible at night and the machine was to be equipped with a gyro gunsight and nose-mounted scanner, V.H.F., I.F.F. and Rebecca. Required maximum speed was to be approximately 547 kt. at 45,000 ft. If production were to be delayed by the use of swept wings to meet this speed demand, the Air Staff would consider a top speed of 500 kt. at 45,000 ft. on the understanding that the wing design could be changed later to give the requested higher speed. A height of 45,000 ft. was to be attained in not more than 6 min.—excluding taxi time—from pressing the engines' starter button, and service ceiling was to be 50,000 ft. The use of drop tanks was envisaged to increase range but the built-in endurance of not less than one hour from take-off until landing was to include climb to 45,000 ft., 10 min. combat at that height with the remaining time to be spent at an economical cruising speed. The greatest possible acceleration was demanded, together with highest possible climbing speed. Interception was to be visual after radar ground control to within one mile or so of the target. The F.43/46 contender was to be designed for economic production of six hundred aircraft at a maximum rate of twenty a month. Very rapid starting was required without external assistance and with engines idling within 10 secs. for take-off but preferably in 5 secs. The cockpit interior was required to be in matt black with red as the only other colour for use on emergency controls and exits. Measures were to be taken to prevent mud, stones and other matter from damaging the flaps and any vulnerable parts.

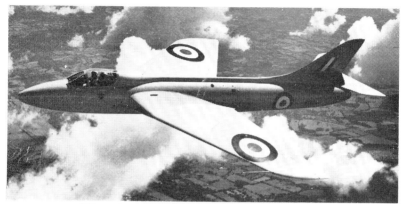

WB188, the Hawker Hunter P.1067 prototype. (Hawker Photo.)

Hawker Hunter F.Mk.1 WT594 with dive-brake lowered. (Hawker Photo.)

Hawker Hunter F.Mk.5 WN958 with external stores. (Hawker Photo.)

The machine's airbrakes were to be operable within 4 sec. at all speeds from stalling to maximum without a large trim change taking place. F.43/46 required a take-off and landing distance not exceeding 1,200 yd. in still air after crossing a 50 ft. screen in each case.

The aircraft was to be capable of the best possible manœuvrability at high altitude and was to be stressed to withstand 4g at maximum speed at sea level.

When in use the airbrakes were not to cause vibration which would limit the use of the gunsight. At a height of 50,000 ft. the cabin was to be capable of maintaining a pressure at 25,000 ft., the cabin either being completely jettisonable or containing an ejector seat. A bullet-proof cockpit was not required but the cabin had to be able to resist "window" from attacked aircraft. Although the fuel tanks were not necessarily self-sealing, after one hit they were not to lose more than 50% of the remaining fuel. Other qualities, obviously essential in a fighter, were to be a quick turn-around and rapid and simple servicing.

At the same time as F.43/46 was evolved, Specification F.44/46 was drawn up for a two-seat night fighter and both requirements were considered by Hawker as possible projects. Each specification was found by Hawker to fall short of producing the right type of aircraft, and in 1947 the firm started work on a Private Venture fighter based on a single Rolls-Royce A.J.65 axial turbine which would give greatly increased power compared with previous engines available. Eventually, after submission in January, 1948, Specification F.3/48 was prepared and issued in March, 1948, to envelop the Hawker design designated P.1067.

As first envisaged, the machine was somewhat different in appearance from that of its ultimate layout. A nose intake and a tailplane set on top of the fin and rudder were proposed originally, together with armament of a pair of 30 mm. Aden guns.

Several revisions had taken place in the P.1067 by the time that WB188, the first prototype P.1067, made its first flight at Boscombe Down on 20th July, 1951, piloted by Sqn.Ldr. N. F. Duke. Once again, Sydney Camm had evolved a single-seat fighter of superlative appearance, matched by excellent performance. The sleek swept-back, mid-wing monoplane looked a thoroughbred, was christened appropriately Hunter and soon set for an auspicious service career. Its 7,500 lb.s.t. Avon—as the Rolls-Royce A.J.65 engine had become—was aspirated by wing-root intakes and the tailplane had been moved to a new position lower on the fin. WB188 was not fitted with its armament but the second prototype WB195—also Avon-engined—received the special completely removable pack, consisting of four 30 mm. Aden guns, which had been developed by Hawker. To facilitate speedy rearming the entire gun installation, complete with magazines, could be unloaded from the nose and replaced immediately by a similar new unit. As specified in the contract for three prototype P.1067s, one was to be fitted with the Armstrong Siddeley Sapphire and the machine chosen was the third prototype WB202.

The Hunter's gracefully shaped wings were of 8·5% thickness/chord ratio and were swept back 40°. Minor modifications made early in trials included the addition of a bullet-shaped fairing to the rear of the point at which the fin and tailplane met and the incorporation of a ventral airbrake to replace the original perforated flaps.

Three Hunter F.Mk.1s, the first production example WT555, WT573 and WT576, were sent to Boscombe Down for C(A) release appraisal from

November, 1953, until June, 1954. The A.&A.E.E. findings were recorded in Report 890/Pt.4 of 6th April, 1955. WT555 had made its first flight on 16th May, 1953, and the remaining two F.Mk.1s for assessment came also from the first production batch. WT555 arrived on 30th October, 1953, and differed little in its handling qualities from the second prototype WB195 on which brief A.&A.E.E. tests had been terminated by severe vibration.

In December, 1953, as a result of renewed criticism of the aileron forces at high Indicated Air Speed, and high Indicated Mach Number, the 14:1 power assistance of the aileron power control system was altered to full power. In January, 1954, it was decided that Service release could not be granted to the Hunter until it was fitted with an airbrake assuring greater safety than that provided by the flaps. The under-fuselage airbrake evolved by Hawker could not conveniently be fitted to WT555 but was assessed on its companion F.Mk.1s WT573 and WT576. As WT555 arrived at A.&A.E.E. without a tail parachute it was decided in December, 1953, that one should be fitted. Successive difficulties with design, installation and approval delayed the first flight with the tail parachute until mid-May, 1954. The first engine fitted to WT555 was the 7,500 lb.s.t. Avon RA7 104 which was changed later to a Mk.113; WT573 and WT576 both received the 7,500 lb.s.t. Avon RA7 107. Made in small numbers only, the Mk.104 was superseded by the Mk.107 which was fitted for intake anti-icing. Neither the Mk.104 nor the Mk.107 was satisfactory and were replaced by the RA.21 113 of 7,600 lb.s.t. with increased nozzle guide vane area. Nominal RA.21 thrust rating was 8,000 lb. and it was hoped that the Mk.115, achieving 8,000 lb.s.t., would replace the Mk.113 which had been fitted at an interim stage of development owing to the RA7's unsatisfactory characteristics.

At maximum take-off weight the wing loading was 48 lb./sq.ft. and the Hunter F.Mk.1 made a generally favourable impression, representing a considerable advance on previous British service fighters with its rate of climb from wheels rolling of about 7 min. to reach 40,000 ft., level speed of 0·93 True Mach Number, and maximum practicable fighting altitude of about 45,000 ft. Transonic handling characteristics were found to be docile with no limit on Mach number and aileron control in power was thought excellent. The cockpit's comfort, roominess, simple and logical layout, and general view—apart from some limitation to the rear caused by the height of the ejector seat—drew praise. In the A.&A.E.E. assessment it was felt that the Hunter's advance over current operational types was sufficient to justify its release in the state tested, even though operational handicaps would be entailed until certain deficiencies were resolved. Points which called for rectification before the Hunter's full potential could be realized in service included the rapid pitch-up in some manœuvres at the higher subsonic Mach numbers, which occurred without adequate warning, thereby restricting manœuvring for aiming and also, at moderate altitudes, introduced structural hazards.

Another troublesome condition was that of engine surge which occurred particularly in the Avon 104 in WT555 but to a lesser degree in the Mk.113

engines, causing the Mk.113 to be stipulated for C(A) release. Subsequently, gun firing was found seriously to increase the occurrence of engine surging and further development was called for to eliminate it. Diving to increase airspeed and to reduce altitude normally brought recovery from the surge but could induce flame-outs. Other points which needed attention were a reduction in the heaviness of the elevator control at high I.A.S., an increase in the drag of the airbrake and the early introduction of Maxaret brakes. The Hunter F.Mk.1 was found to achieve supersonic flight readily in shallow dives of about 25° with transition to supersonic flight taking place at about 0·98 I.M.N. when supersonic bangs were heard. In these conditions, the control column could be moved forwards and backwards through 1 in. to 2 in. without any effect on the flight path and, if a sufficiently steep dive were established at high altitude, 1·15 I.M.N. could readily be achieved.

The Hunter began its praiseworthy service career when No. 43 Squadron at Leuchars received its F.Mk.1s in July, 1954. The basic Hunter F.Mk.1 was used to test numerous trial installations, including alternative styles of air-brake, an area-ruled fuselage on WT571 and blown flaps on WT656.

Fitted with the 8,000 lb.s.t. Sapphire ASSa6 101 engine, WN888, the first of the Armstrong Whitworth-built Hunter F.Mk.2s, made its initial take-off on 14th October, 1953. WB188, the all-red sole Hunter Mk.3, brought the World Air Speed Record to Hawker on 7th September, 1953, when Sqn.Ldr. N. F. Duke flew it at 727·6 m.p.h. powered by the 7,130 lb.s.t. Avon RA7R which developed an after-burning thrust of 9,600 lb.

The next production Hunter was the F.Mk.4, the first of which—WT701— flew on 20th October, 1954, being basically a Mk.1 with greater fuel capacity and the Avon RA21 113; this mark of Avon was superseded later by the Mk.115, embodying modifications to remedy the onset of surging experienced when the guns were fired. Equipped with radar and powered controls, and in production on a large scale, the Hunter soon became a familiar sight in Britain and on the Continent where it served with the 2nd Tactical Air Force. The F.Mk.4 was adapted to carry combinations of external stores, drop tanks, 1,000 lb. bombs and rockets, and tests were carried out also on Hunters with D.H. Firestreak and Fairey Fireflash air-to-air missiles. The F.Mk.5, built by Armstrong Whitworth, used the 8,000 lb.s.t. Sapphire 101, the first example—WN954—making its initial flight on 19th October, 1954, and incorporating greater fuel capacity than the F.Mk.2 and pylons for external stores.

The Hunter had the ability to exceed Mach 1 in a shallow dive but the advent of more powerful engines would obviously shortly bring this capability to fighters in normal level flight. As far back as 1943 plans were laid to prepare for this eventuality by the issue of Specification E.24/43 for an experimental research aircraft to explore the high-speed field. Several important aspects of the science of flight at such greatly increased speeds needed urgent investigation, including the problems of a completely fresh approach in aerodynamics, the evolution of new forms of construction, the provision of

Hawker Hunter F.Mk.6. (Hawker Photo.)

specially developed control systems and a method of enabling the pilot to escape from an aircraft at ultra-high speeds.

Miles prepared the M.52 design as an extremely advanced mid-wing monoplane, with the pilot seated in the pointed nose cone, and expected to reach 1,000 m.p.h. The project progressed over three years as far as constructing a full-scale mock-up of the machine and flight-testing wooden versions of the

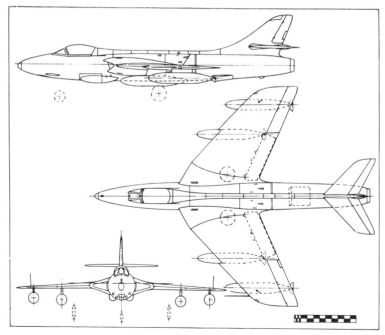

Hawker Hunter F.Mk.6

M.52's thin wings and horizontal tail surfaces on L9705, a modified Miles M.3B Falcon known as the Gillette.

All of the progress made by Miles came to an abrupt halt during 1946 when, in an extraordinary and unprecedented show of concern over the risks involved in flying the M.52 by the pilot, the Ministry of Supply cancelled the project and decided instead to try to obtain information concerning high-speed flight by telemetred data from unmanned missiles. The decision came among others made after a catastrophic war in which Great Britain was victorious at a cost of many fine, brave lives but, for no good reason at all, stepped forth into a humiliating and inglorious era of self-liquidation and of squandering her wealth.

The lead in high-speed flight research and development which would have been firmly in the hands of Great Britain's aeronautical technicians was thus blithely thrown to the winds, to be snatched swiftly by her more businesslike and less timorous rivals. This scandalous and ill-starred decision stands at the head of a long and ever-growing list of similar examples over the ensuing years involving enormous sums of the long-suffering, mute taxpayer's money, the Industry's effort and test pilots' lives, all to be eventually wasted by lack of positive decision and by vacillations in policy.

Despite the sordid business of the cancellation of the M.52, the relentless pressure of progress brought up again the question of supersonics which had to be faced and resolved if Great Britain were not to give up fighter design altogether. Other countries showed no such timidity and reluctance to pursue the course of ever-increasing performance and were certainly not going to hold back in deference to the faintness of heart displayed by the policy-makers of the United Kingdom.

The revival of interest in supersonic flight in Great Britain manifested itself at Hawker in November, 1951, when the design was started of the P.1083, a revision of the Hunter fitted with wings swept back 50° and an Avon RA14R engine equipped with after-burning. Construction of WN470, the prototype P.1083, was well under way when, in June, 1953, the Air Staff withdrew support for the design, expressing a preference for a fighter using an engine of greater inherent power output than one capable of producing increased power for short periods by after-burning. Consequently, Hawker ceased work on the P.1083 and directed attention to the P.1099, a new version of the basic Hunter to use the 10,000 lb.s.t. Avon 200-series engine. Designated Hunter F.Mk.6, the prototype XF833 made its first take-off on 22nd January, 1954. Early in its trials, engine failures brought delays but WW592, the first production F.Mk.6, made its maiden flight on 25th March, 1955. XG833 was of note in being used to test the Rolls-Royce thrust reversing device and the production F.Mk.6s incorporated several modifications, including extensions to the outer leading edge to eradicate a propensity to pitch up.

A general appreciation of the F.Mk.6 with the Avon 203 was contained in A.&A.E.E. Boscombe Down Report 890/5/Pt.11 of 5th July, 1957, which stated that good overall handling characteristics and level of performance in conjunction with heavy fire-power and facilities for a wide variety of bombs, rockets and drop tanks made the aircraft well suited to the rôles of air superiority and ground attack. The F.Mk.6 took-off in 550 yd., climbed from wheels rolling to 40,000 ft. in 6 min. and to 45,000 ft. in 7·7 min., reached a level speed of 620 kt. at sea level, M. 0·95 up to the tropopause and M. 0·93 at 45,000 ft., and had a turning radius of 4 n.m. at 45,000 ft. height and speed constant, or 2 n.m. otherwise. All-up weight was 17,800 lb., and fuel contents 388 gallons. R.P. posts and four pylons were fitted, longitudinal control was by full-powered elevator with electric follow-up tailplane, lateral control was with full-powered aileron system, the under-fuselage airbrake had 67° travel, the Mk.2 Maxaret brake units were hand operated and the four 30 mm. Aden Mk.1 guns were equipped with deflectors on blast tubes. Arming time was between five and seven minutes and the F.Mk.6 was cleared to carry combinations of up to two 1,000 lb. bombs, up to four 100 gallon drop tanks, up to twenty-four air-to-ground rocket projectiles and up to two thirty-seven-tube 2 in. air-to-air rocket pods. The fully developed F.Mk.6 was thought, in relation to contemporary subsonic day fighters, to have take-off and climb performance and manœuvring capability at high altitude that were very creditable indeed.

Parallel with the Hunter, and designed by J. Smith, the Type 541 Swift F.Mk.1 and its successive variants were under development by Supermarine from the Type 535. WJ960, the first prototype F.Mk.1, was taken on its maiden flight on 1st August, 1951, and was fitted with the axial-flow 7,000 lb.s.t. Avon RA7. The F.Mk.1's armament comprised two 30 mm. Aden cannon mounted in the fuselage beneath the cockpit and the machine retained the comparatively plump fuselage of the Types 510 and 535, which originally housed the greater diameter centrifugal Nene engine, advantage being taken of the resulting extra space by fitting additional internal fuel tankage. The Swift's low-set wings were of H.S.A.1 section and were swept back 40° at quarter chord.

In view of the need to introduce the Swift F.Mk.1 into service at the earliest practicable opportunity, very urgent tests were required on representative aircraft to ensure adequate flying safety and satisfactory handling qualities for release to the Service. WK201 and WK202, each fitted with the 7,500 lb.s.t. Avon RA7 105, were therefore sent to A.&A.E.E. Boscombe Down for assessment between January and May, 1954, results being recorded in Report 859/Gen/Pt.1. At an early stage in the evaluation a restricted release to the R.A.F. was given to the limits of 550 kt. I.A.S. between sea level and 5,000 ft., and Mach 0·91—0·9 indicated—between 5,000 ft. and 25,000 ft., with a height limitation of 25,000 ft. These limitations were imposed after the handling trials with the F.Mk.1 had shown the machine to have several major deficiencies which made it unacceptable for full service use. The major adverse criticisms were severe pitch-up at high Mach numbers above 25,000 ft. at low g values which seriously impaired the usable turning performance, a marked loss of elevator control above Mach 0·91, heavy elevator control forces at high I.M.N., a marked nose-down trim change with extension of the airbrakes above Mach 0·96—0·94 indicated—and a marked wing drop between Mach 0·93 and 0·96—0·92 and 0·94 indicated. In addition, engine surge with or without gun firing was present and turning performance at altitude was limited to a low value by the onset of buffet. Stalling and spinning tests showed that, when the stall was advanced, dangerously high rates of descent and very strong pro-spin tendencies existed. WK202 was used for the majority of the handling trials and WK201, the only machine of the two to be fitted with an anti-spin parachute, was employed for the stalling and spinning tests. Other limitations imposed on the F.Mk.1 included 600 kt. I.A.S., maximum take-off weight 17,200 lb., maximum landing weight 16,000 lb., maximum permissible normal acceleration 6g, spinning prohibited and negative g not to exceed 5 seconds.

The Swift F.Mk.1 joined No. 56 Squadron during February, 1954, thus wresting from the Hunter by a few months the distinction of being the first British swept-wing jet fighter in service.

Immediately following the restricted release to the R.A.F. of the Swift F.Mk.1 early in 1954, urgent trials were required on the F.Mk.2 to determine its suitability for service. A.&A.E.E. Report 859/Gen/Pt.2 covered these tests, the first machine to arrive being WK214 which was tested from 5th March until 30th April, 1954, and differed from the F.Mk.1 in having an extended wing leading edge near the root which housed an extra 30 mm. Aden gun on each side, making four in all, and an increase in weight of about 1,000 lb. caused mainly by the extra armament.

It was quickly established that the alterations in the F.Mk.2 caused a considerable worsening of the pitch-up characteristics and, as the longitudinal qualities were considered to fall far below the standard required to ensure an adequate service safety margin, and were certainly unacceptable by operational standards, WK214 was therefore returned to Supermarine. Eventually, A.&A.E.E. pilots were invited to assess WK216, an improved F.Mk.2 at the firm from 29th May until 12th August, 1954. During this period modifications were carried out over five successive stages but with disappointing results.

The F.Mk.2 was considered to be an interim variant in the line of development and the deficiencies imposed by its obsolescent form of longitudinal control and the absence of after-burning made it impossible to regard it as an operational fighter, the deficiencies found being considered confirmation that the machine was quite unsuitable and unsafe for such a rôle. It was therefore judged for its suitability in a non-operational capacity, the main purpose of which was to be to enable flying and servicing experience to be obtained.

The culmination of deficiencies in the F.Mk.2 rendered the aircraft far below the standard required from an operational interceptor and C(A) release was therefore given only for a non-operational rôle, subject to limitations of 550 kt. I.A.S. between sea level and 5,000 ft., 0·90 I.M.N. and an altitude of 25,000 ft. Intentional spinning, use of the aircraft for ground attack and the carrying of ammunition or ballast in lieu were all prohibited

Supermarine Type 535. (Supermarine Photo.)

and in August, 1954, the Swift F.Mk.2 began to join No. 56 Squadron, the unit becoming the sole one to fly the F.Mks.1 and 2.

Development of the Swift proceeded in the shape of eliminating its unfortunate faults and, following the limited R.A.F. release of the F.Mks. 1 and 2, full C(A) release handling trials were undertaken at A.&A.E.E. on the F.Mk.3, the aircraft used being WK248, a production version fitted with an Avon RA7R 108 equipped with after-burning to give 9,500 lb.s.t. Report 859/Gen/Pt.3 covered the trials carried out from 3rd until 27th November, 1954, and from 9th December, 1954, until 13th January, 1955. Minor changes

Supermarine Swift F.Mk.4 WK198 which set a new World Air Speed Record in 1953. (Dowty Photo.)

352

Supermarine Swift F.R.Mk.5 XD903. (Supermarine Photo.)

were made to WK248 between the two test periods, early curtailment of the first resulting from inadequate longitudinal control.

The main differences in the F.Mk.3 compared with the F.Mk.2 were, apart from the addition of the after-burner, the extension of the leading edges towards the tips—to alleviate the severe pitch-up experienced—thereby increasing the local chord by 10%, and the slightly drooped section of the extensions. Considerable improvements had been effected with the F.Mk.3; among them the pitch-up at high Mach numbers was now controllable, approach and landing characteristics were greatly improved and the general level of elevator forces had been reduced. Climb performance of 40,000 ft.

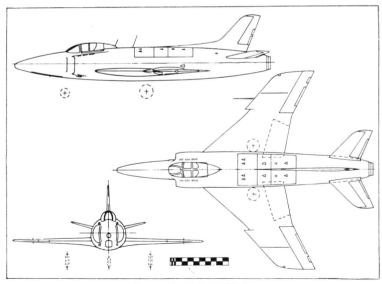

Supermarine Swift F.R.Mk.5

353

in about 6 min. was, by a small margin, the best of current British interceptors but fuel consumption using after-burning to give intended combat
performance was extremely high and resulted in very short sortie times.
Another drawback was that the engine, with or without gun firing, was still
liable to surge. Despite the general improvement, however, unlimited operational release could still not be given.

During November, 1954, the Swift F.Mk.4, the first version intended for
quantity production, was submitted to A.& A.E.E. for assessment, the trials
carried out until February, 1955, being recorded in Report 859/Gen/Pt.4.
WK272 was not a production example but was representative in most respects and was fitted with the 9,500 lb.s.t. Avon 114 with after-burning. Unacceptable longitudinal control and engine characteristics dictated the return
of the machine to Supermarine for nearly two months for modification. A
variable incidence tailplane was installed and the fin had been increased
by approximately one foot in height, the larger fin being intended
to provide sufficient directional stability when a ventral fuel tank was
carried.

Despite the improvements made during development of the various marks
of Swift, the F.Mk.4, in view of its low manœuvrability, could be regarded
only as effective for interceptor duties up to 38,000 ft. to 40,000 ft. and was
likely to be outclassed in manœuvres by other fighters at all heights above
about 15,000 ft. Also, its endurance appeared to be marginal.

The Swift F.Mk.4 prototype WK198 enjoyed a brief burst of glory when
it succeeded in setting a new World Air Speed Record with Lt.Cdr. M. J.
Lithgow on 25th September, 1953, of 737·7 m.p.h. and also broke several
other records during its career.

In spite of its extremely unfortunate failure as an interceptor fighter, the
Swift reached two squadrons, Nos. 2 and 79, in 1956 as the Type 549
F.R.Mk.5, developed for fighter-reconnaissance duties to succeed the Meteor
F.R.Mk.9. A one-piece sliding cockpit canopy was fitted, a lengthened nose
housed three cameras and armament consisted of two 30 mm. Aden cannon
augmented by rockets or bombs.

Every possible endeavour was made by Supermarine and by the A.&A.E.E.
pilots to overcome the Swift's misfortunes but, finally, hopes of developing it
into a satisfactory interceptor fighter had to be abandoned and its contemporary from Hawker, the Hunter, flashed on in its increasingly illustrious
career.

Nevertheless, another Supermarine single-seat fighter was destined to join
the Fleet Air Arm. While the intensive and hopeful development programme
for the Swift had been under way, a Royal Navy requirement was also receiving attention. During 1945 the possibility of using a carrier fighter without
landing gear was investigated, launching being by catapult with the landing
proposed to be accomplished on a rubber-clad deck. The Type 505 was drawn
up to meet the case, using a pair of fuselage-mounted 6,560 lb.s.t. Rolls-Royce
A.J.65 engines installed alongside each other, unswept wings of 7% thickness/
chord ratio and an unusual butterfly style of tail surfaces. During 1964 an

The first production Supermarine Scimitar F.Mk.1 XD212. (Supermarine Photo.)

order was received by Supermarine for six Type 505 prototypes but, at the beginning of 1947, it was cancelled on the decision not to use the machine for flying without an undercarriage. The design itself was not abandoned and emerged in revised form as the Type 508 with wings of increased area and 9% thickness/chord ratio and equipped with a nosewheel undercarriage. The butterfly tail and straight wings were at first retained for three examples to be constructed to Specification N.9/47 and VX133, the first prototype, made its maiden flight powered by two 6,500 lb.s.t. Avon RA3s on 31st August, 1951, at A.&A.E.E. Boscombe Down with Lt.Cdr. M. J. Lithgow at the controls. The Hawker P.1063 and Westland projects to N.9/47 were not pursued.

Revisions in the second prototype—VX136—which flew just under a year later, resulted in the new designation Type 529. Both machines were armed with four 30 mm. Aden guns firing from the bases of the engine intakes and,

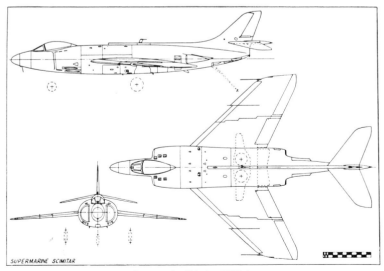

Supermarine Scimitar F.Mk.1

355

although such powerful aircraft, were remarkably elegant in appearance. Handling performance for carrier operations was kept within the necessary limits by the provision of generous flaps and drooping leading edges to the wings, and the bulky engine bays were beautifully blended into the central portion of the finely contoured fuselage. By February, 1950, the decision had been taken to revise considerably the third prototype on order so that, as Type 525 VX138, it was completed with new wings incorporating 45° sweepback at quarter chord and a tail unit including a normal single fin and rudder, undergoing its first flight on 27th April, 1954. By that time the issue of Specification N.113D in 1951 had brought an additional three prototype Type 525s towards completion and production had been under way since December, 1952, to Specification N.113P. WT854, the first prototype Type 544, as the design had been redesignated and was later to be named Scimitar, flew for the first time on 20th January, 1956. The Type 544 possessed an extremely purposeful and elegant appearance as a large single-seat strike fighter and, in comparison with the Type 525, embodied several modifications. The nose had been lengthened, area rule had been applied to the cross-section of the fuselage and the upper surface of the fuselage was surmounted by a slim dorsal spine which was faired into the fin and housed at its front end an air intake. The Type 525 VX138 had tested flap-blowing and this system was retained in the Type 544, accompanied by the introduction of an all-moving, anhedralled slab tailplane and extended outer leading edges to the wings. A pair of 11,250 lb.s.t. Avon 202 engines powered the production Type 544 Scimitar F.Mk.1 which, through steady, progressive and successful development, provided the Fleet Air Arm with its first swept-wing fighter which could carry a useful combination of weapons, including an atomic bomb and Sidewinder air-to-air missiles, and was equipped with a nose-probe for in-flight refuelling.

The requirements of Specifications N.40/46 and N.14/49 from the Admiralty and F.44/46 and F.4/48 from the Air Ministry for a two-seat, all-weather fighter were responsible for the eventual appearance in 1951 of the massive D.H.110.

F.44/46 Ref. No. 7/Aircraft/1513/R.D.T.2(d) was issued on 24th January, 1947, for a prototype R.A.F. night-fighter for early production and to be capable of intercepting enemy aircraft at 40,000 ft. A crew of two—pilot and radar operator—was specified, the machine was to carry multi-channel V.H.F., A.I., Rebecca, I.F.F. and possibly blind-landing equipment, with armament to comprise four forward-firing 30 mm. guns backed by sufficient ammunition for 15 sec. firing per gun, together with gyro gunsight and radar presentation. Maximum speed was to be not less than 525 kt. at 25,000 ft. and other performance demands were a climb to 45,000 ft. in a maximum of 10 mins. from pressing the starter button of the first engine and excluding taxiing time, a service ceiling of 45,000 ft., and a minimum endurance of 2 hours from take-off to landing including taxiing, climb to 25,000 ft., 15 min. combat at that height with the remainder of the time spent in cruising at 25,000 ft. If possible, range was to be increased by the fitting of drop tanks.

de Havilland D.H.110 Sea Vixen F.A.W.Mk.1 with refuelling probe. (de Havilland Photo.)

The machine was to be suitable for economic production of one hundred and fifty aircraft at a maximum rate of ten a month. Very rapid take-off in 10 sec., but preferably in 5 sec., was called for without external assistance. Airbrakes were to operate in 4 sec., take-off was to be in 1,500 yd. and landing in 1,200 yd. over a 50 ft. barrier, 4g manœuvres were to be possible at top speed at sea level and the pressure cabin was to be able to reproduce the pressure at 25,000 ft. at 45,000 ft. actual aircraft height. The cockpit interiors were to be matt black with emergency controls marked in red and the cabin was to be jettisonable or to accommodate the crew in ejector seats side-by-side or in tandem. Although not required to be bullet-proof, the cabin had to be able to

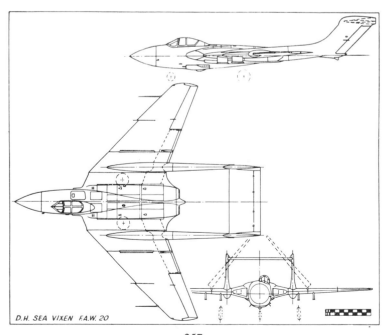

D.H. SEA VIXEN F.A.W. 20

357

Gloster Javelin F.A.W.Mk.4. (Gloster Photo.)

resist "window". Self-sealing tanks were not mandatory but, if hit, they were not to lose more than 50% fuel from one strike. Good control was demanded at height and also at low speed and low altitude for bad weather landing. Full night-flying equipment was required and the crew were to be provided with oxygen for 2·5 hrs. at 25,000 ft., two K-type dinghies and parachutes. Simple and rapid servicing was a requirement to ensure swift turn-around.

Two prototype de Havilland D.H.110s were ordered during 1949 to Specification F.4/48 for the R.A.F. requirement, following designs drawn up to

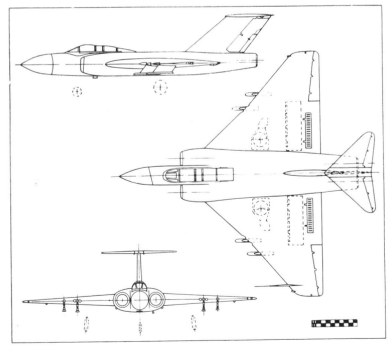

Gloster Javelin F.A.W.Mk.7

cater for both Air Ministry and Admiralty needs. Eventually, R.A.F. interest lapsed following the decision to proceed with development of the Gloster Javelin as the Service's new all-weather fighter and the D.H.110 instead found itself being prepared to take the place of the Navy's Venom.

In designing the D.H.110, the same layout was retained as that exploited so successfully in the Vampire and Venom series but on a considerably increased scale. The central nacelle housed the pilot in a cockpit off-set to port in the nose, with the radar operator stationed slightly to his rear and to starboard in the interior, and a pair of 7,500 lb.s.t. Avons installed side-by-side ejecting between the twin booms which carried the tail unit. The 50 ft. span wings were swept back and incorporated the engine intakes at the leading edge roots. The result was an exceedingly impressive looking aircraft when WG236 took off for its first flight on 26th September, 1951, flown by Gp.Capt. J. Cunningham and WG240—the second prototype—followed in July, 1952. Misfortune hit WG236 when it disintegrated at the 1952 S.B.A.C. Display at Farnborough in September. Development continued and the machine passed into production for the Fleet Air Arm as the Sea Vixen F.A.W.Mk.1 to Specification N.139P with two Avon 208s for power. The scheduled armament of four 30 mm. Aden cannon was replaced by four wing-mounted D.H. Firestreak air-to-air missiles and fifty-six rocket projectiles carried in extending launchers in the belly. The Sea Vixen's range was extended by in-flight refuelling through a probe in the port wing.

Before the Gloster Javelin arrived, the R.A.F.'s all-weather fighters had been adapted from day interceptors but the G.A.5 was designed by R. W. Walker for the rôle from the start. Thick mid-wings of delta plan-form were adopted for the Javelin which carried its pair of Sapphire engines in nacelles blended into each side of the fuselage. The pilot and radar operator were seated in tandem and delta horizontal tail surfaces surmounted the large sweptback fin and rudder. Provision of the tailplane enabled use to be made of flaps and also eliminated the need for the usual form of high-angle touchdown used with delta-wing aircraft—a great advantage for operations during darkness.

The Javelin was evolved by way of Specifications F.43/46 for a day fighter and F.44/46 for a night fighter, to embrace which Gloster prepared designs early in 1947. In February, 1948, these requirements were superseded by Specifications F.3/48 for a day fighter and F.4/48 for a night fighter. From the beginning the idea had been to use one basic design adapted for each rôle but, finally, the decision was reached to work on towards the F.4/48 night fighter requirement, with armament subsequently settled as four 30 mm. Aden guns carried two in each wing.

WD804, the first prototype, took off at Moreton Valance on 26th November, 1951, for its maiden flight flown by Sqn.Ldr. W. A. Waterton under the power of two 7,000 lb.s.t. Sapphire ASSa3s. On the second prototype, WD808, new wings were later fitted with increased chord on the outer panels, thus producing a kink mid-way along the leading edge. The smooth progress

Gloster Javelin F.A.W.Mk.5. (Gloster Photo.)

Gloster Javelin F.A.W.Mk.9. (Gloster Photo.)

of development was marred by accidents to prototypes but the first production Javelins eventually reached No. 46 Squadron in February, 1956, becoming the first delta-wing aircraft to enter the R.A.F. and representing a great advance in fighter equipment.

Subsequent development produced progressively improved variants with an all-moving tailplane appearing on the F.A.W.Mk.4. Engine power was increased and armament was modified to include Firestreak air-to-air missiles, rockets and bombs.

After the first Javelin prototype had flown, a revised version was prepared to Specification F.153D in 1952. The new Javelin was to be considerably higher powered with a pair of 16,000 lb.s.t. Bristol Olympus engines in the first prototype, succeeded by the 17,160 lb.s.t. Olympus in the third production machine and subsequent examples. Of particular importance were the increase in wing area and the reduction in thickness/chord ratio to 7% at the roots and 5% at the wingtips. Red Dean or Blue Jay missiles were to have been carried but the thin-wing Javelin never flew as the contract for a batch ordered during 1955 was cancelled in 1957. Main external differences from the Javelin were the omission of a tailplane, sharp leading edge sweepback combined with a swept-back trailing edge, and fairings on each side of the rear jet nozzles. Supersonic level flight was expected to be possible with a later area-ruled variant which also was discontinued.

Another interesting project which was abandoned was the Hawker P.1091, a drastically revised version of the Hunter with delta wings drawn up during 1951.

While the Javelin was under development, further versions of the Meteor N.F.Mk.11 were evolved and entered service. They were the N.F.Mk.12 which was equipped with better radar, the N.F.Mk.13 prepared for use in the Middle East and the N.F.Mk.14 which ended the line and was rather longer and received a one-piece cockpit canopy.

During the early 1950s a considerable amount of research was carried out on the concept of the mixed power plant interceptor which offered the attractions of the short bursts of high speed obtainable from the liquid fuel rocket engine, combined with longer periods of flight under the gas turbine engine. In competition with after-burning the rocket engine—with its attendant difficulties of handling very volatile fuels—was a less attractive proposition but the mixed power plant formed the basis of the single-seat, delta-wing Avro 720 designed during 1953, by S. D. Davis to Specification F.137D. The

Gloster Meteor N.F. Mk.12 of No. 25 Squadron. (Armstrong Whitworth Photo.)

Armstrong Whitworth-built Gloster Meteor N.F.Mk.14 of No. 25 Squadron. (Rolls-Royce Photo.)

Avro 720. (Avro Photo.)

wings were set mid-way in the fuselage depth with the Armstrong Siddeley Viper forming the turbine power plant and the Armstrong Siddeley Screamer the rocket unit above it. Apart from its type of power installation, the Avro 720 was of particular note as approximately 85% of its total structure utilized metal honeycomb sandwich, the fuselage being formed as a monocoque cylindrical shell of honeycomb 1 in. in thickness. The wings, of 27 ft. 3·5 in. span, were formed with a structure of light shear webs running across the span and covered with strips of ·5 in. thick honeycomb sandwich laid in the same direction, the normal spars being omitted.

XD696, the prototype, was nearly complete in 1956 when the whole project was cancelled owing to doubts arising over the advisibility of employing liquid oxygen as the oxidizer in manned aircraft, with the result that work on the Screamer was terminated. A speed of Mach 2 was expected at over 40,000 ft. but the Avro 720 was never completed and flown.

While Hawker had been working on the subsequently cancelled supersonic P.1083, Specification F.105D2 was responsible for another supersonic single-seat fighter, the Type 545 of Supermarine. In a number of respects redolent of the Type 541 Swift, the Type 545 was a low-wing monoplane, the wings of which possessed a straight sweptback trailing edge while the leading edge introduced compound taper with the inner section swept 50°, the middle section swept 40° and the outer sections swept 30°. The thickness/chord ratio at the roots of 8% tapered to 5·67% at the tips. The 9,500 lb.s.t. Avon RA14 received its air through twin intakes set side-by-side in the nose.

Cancellation came during 1955 when the Type 545 prototype XA181 was near completion and the same fate was suffered in the drawing-office by an improved version of the Type 545 scheduled to attain Mach 2 with an afterburning Rolls-Royce R.B.106 installed inside a new fuselage.

Designed by W. E. W. Petter, the English Electric Canberra had proved itself an excellent and capable aircraft in several rôles, making the addition in 1954 of two-seat night intruder as the B.(I).Mk.8. The main alterations to produce the intruder Canberra were the housing of the pilot to port in the nose under an off-set clear-view fighter style canopy and the installation under the rear portion of the bomb-bay of a Boulton Paul-designed external pack of four 20 mm. guns. The B.(I).Mk.8 could carry also bombs or rockets beneath its wings and bombs inside the fuselage.

The damage suffered by British technology through the ill-considered and disastrous cancellation of the Miles M.52 supersonic research aircraft in 1946 soon became painfully evident. The denial to the Industry of much invaluable experience brought enormous problems when the inevitable question of providing new fighters for the Services arose. Instead of being able to draw upon aerodynamic, structural and handling knowledge accumulated steadily, objectively and in a manner best understood by its own experienced and dedicated designers, engineers and pilots, any firm attempting to design a fighter which would be worth delivering to the squadrons after the ever-lengthening gestatory period was over was faced with a programme of research of immeasurably increased magnitude to enable it to make up the lost ground.

This unpalatable and costly situation—one which should never have been allowed to develop—was brought home sharply in 1948 when it was obvious that the task of forging ahead and producing a manned supersonic aircraft had to be faced in competition with other nations. The lead which could have been Great Britain's had, as in so many other instances, been blandly thrown away but, towards the end of 1947, the Ministry of Supply engaged in talks with aircraft firms with a view to planning the United Kingdom's belated entry into the supersonic field. Specification E.R.103 was issued for a research aircraft and Fairey and English Electric set to work to produce their ideas in concrete form.

The Fairey project subsequently appeared as the F.D.2 for high-speed research but English Electric combined the high-speed requirements with the concept of a fighter designated P.1 and designed under the direction of

English Electric Canberra B.(I).Mk.8. (Air Ministry Photo.)

363

W. E. W. Petter. Two prototype P.1s were ordered, together with another airframe for static test, to E.R.103. During mid-1949 Specification F.23/49 was issued for a supersonic day fighter and English Electric pressed ahead with their P.1 to meet it. In evolving the basic design which was to become the Lightning—a superb product later to be claimed to be the best fighter in the World—English Electric showed a most commendable determination not to be bound by convention in tackling the project.

The great challenge facing English Electric lay in producing in virtually one stage a supersonic aircraft containing all the ingredients of a first-class operational fighter without the facilities for direct research and experience afforded by previous experimental research vehicles of comparable performance. However, great assistance was rendered by the Short S.B.5, which reproduced on a smaller scale the features of the P.1, in proving the radical layout with particular emphasis on the alleviation of pitch-up—the evil phenomenon which beset in greater or smaller degree most high-speed, swept-wing aircraft. Approximately treble the amount of engineering man-hours in design and development is absorbed by a supersonic operational aircraft as is consumed by a comparable subsonic high-speed machine and the additional amount of flight testing involved in the far more complex supersonic aircraft increases the entire programme time to a substantial extent. Further assistance with the programme was given by the installation at Warton of both water and wind tunnels, including equipment capable of operating at Mach 4 and Mach 6. With other advanced engineering and electronic equipment at its elbow, the firm was in a good position to be able to produce a successful aircraft in the P.1 despite the manifold complexities involved in transforming the machine into the carrier of a fully-integrated weapons system including armament, fire control, navigation and radar equipment far in advance of any previous R.A.F. equipment.

The fact that less fuel would be consumed by two engines of similar size than by a single large unit combined with after-burning was instrumental in the decision to use a pair of power plants. By astute and careful positioning of one engine above and behind the other in the fuselage, double the thrust of one engine was available at the expense of but 50% increase in frontal area over that of a single unit. The result was a fuselage slim in width but of fairly constant depth along its length. Sharp sweepback of 60° was built into the wings which, had the trailing edge been continuous, would have been of delta form. The delta wing, however, was rejected as possessing insufficient control during certain flight contingencies and the positive control provided by a tailplane was preferred for the P.1. A deep notch was cut into the trailing edge of the shoulder wings at about 50% of each half-span, with the ailerons being carried along the outer transverse trailing edge to the tips. The sharply swept-back tailplane was mounted low on the fuselage beneath the front engine's tailpipe in an endeavour to avoid pitch-up difficulties and a remarkable feat in the design was the retraction of the main wheels of the undercarriage into the thin wings.

With W. E. W. Petter's departure from English Electric during 1950 to join Folland Aircraft, the responsibility for design and subsequent development of the P.1 was taken over by F. W. Page.

WG760, the first prototype P.1, was fitted with two 7,500 lb.s.t. Sapphires fed through the single nose intake which was bifurcated internally to each engine, the tailpipes of which exhausted one above the other at the extreme tail. The machine was finished during the Spring of 1954 and made its first take-off on 4th August, 1954, at A.&A.E.E. Boscombe Down, flown by Wg.Cdr. R. P. Beamont, reaching Mach 0·85 on the first flight. In the course of its third flight a few days later, on 11th August, from Boscombe Down, WG760 exceeded Mach 1, becoming the first aircraft to fly supersonically in Great Britain in level flight.

In the course of the development of the P.1 into the anticipated fighter, the

An outstanding achievement in British fighter design, the English Electric Lightning F.Mk.1, represented by a pre-production P.1B with fin of increased size. (English Electric Photo.)

two flying research prototypes WG760 and WG763 were redesignated P.1A, the fighter project becoming P.1B. WG763 was armed with a pair of 30 mm. Aden cannon fitted in the upper nose decking and flew with the leading edge flaps fixed in place as they had been found to be superfluous.

The decision to order three more prototypes and a pre-production batch of twenty P.1Bs brought about a virtually complete redesign of the machine although the general aerodynamic layout and concept were retained. The work was done extremely swiftly and XA847, the first prototype P.1B, was flown from Warton for the first time on 4th April, 1957, with Beamont at the controls. The change to Avon 200-series engines with after-burning had nearly doubled the thrust available and XA847 exceeded Mach 1 on its maiden flight, subsequent development enabling it to better Mach 2 on 6th January, 1959. Handling trials had indicated a need for larger fin area and this was increased later by 30%. On 23rd October, 1958, the P.1B received at Farnborough the name of Lightning, the first F.Mk.1 production example flying just over a year later. Ferranti Airpass 1 radar was housed inside the nose shock cone and the F.Mk.1's armament comprised two 30 mm. Aden guns in the upper nose, supplemented by two additional 30 mm. Adens in the lower fuselage, a pair of side-by-side retractable packs each containing twenty-four 2 in. rockets, and a pair of Firestreak missiles mounted one on each side of the fuselage.

By 1960 the stage was set for the Royal Air Force to receive the Lightning as its magnificent new operational equipment and No. 74 Squadron at Coltishall was chosen to re-equip with the F.Mk.1 in July. The F.Mk.1 and the F.Mk.1A which followed it into service within a year were fitted with two 11,250 lb.s.t. Avon RA.24R engines which developed each 14,430 lb.s.t. with two-position after-burning operating. On 11th July, 1961, the Lightning F.Mk.2 prototype XN723 took to the air as an improved version with a number of refinements including fully-variable after-burning and improved all-weather navigational equipment.

The vast effort injected into every facet of the Lightning programme brought to the R.A.F. a superlative fighter worthy of its pilots and an aircraft of which everyone connected with it could be immensely proud as a product in the highest traditions of British fighter development.

The designer originally responsible for the conception of the Lightning, W. E. W. Petter, was at work on a new project for Folland soon after his arrival there. His new interest involved switching from one end of the fighter scale, represented by the advanced and complex Lightning, to the other extreme—the simplified, lightweight fighter.

Petter was well acquainted with the phenomenal rise in production man-hours, weight, complexity and, ultimately, the cost of aircraft. No positive attempt had been made to arrest the steep upward spiral which had progressed unchecked for years and Petter was fully convinced that there was plenty of scope for investigation of the idea of producing a lightweight, single-seat fighter.

For some two years various widely different layouts were studied but each retained the same common features of low cost and weight, simplicity and advanced performance. Thought was given to a prone-pilot project, the use of two 2,000 lb.s.t. short-life jet engines in various locations, a twin-boom layout with an inverted V tail and one in the Autumn of 1951 using a pair of short-life Rolls-Royce RB.93 engines alongside each other in the rear of the fuselage. Eventually, the project crystallized during January, 1952, in the FO.140/1 with a 3,750 lb.s.t. Bristol BE.22 Saturn engine and, simultaneously, as the FO.140/2 scheduled to use the Derwent for power. Cancellation of development of the Saturn in the Autumn of 1952 and the realization of the unsuitability of the Derwent brought both designs to a halt but the resumption of interest during 1953 at Bristol in producing a new small engine—eventually to emerge as the Orpheus—resulted in the revival of the Folland design in a revised form designated FO.139 and named Midge. As the development of the Orpheus was expected to take longer than that of the

The diminutive Folland Fo.141 Gnat F.Mk.1 XK740, one of the development batch. (Folland Photo.)

Midge, the aircraft was evolved to take first of all the 1,640 lb.s.t. Armstrong Siddeley ASV5 Viper 101.

In every aspect of its layout, the tiny 20 ft. 8 in. span Midge conformed to the latest design practice, incorporating wings swept back 40° at quarter chord and set at shoulder level, sweptback tail surfaces and a low-set tailplane. Registered G-39-1, the Midge made its first flight on 11th August, 1954, flown by Sqn.Ldr. E. A. Tennant and later exceeded Mach 1 in a dive.

The Midge was sent to A.&A.E.E. Boscombe Down at the manufacturer's invitation for pre-view handling assessment from 13th until 16th September, 1954, Report 907/Pt.2 of 8th February, 1955, noting that after amassing 17 hours flying in the five weeks following the first flight, fourteen flights were made at A.&A.E.E. in three days by eight different pilots, all of whom were most enthusiastic about its handling qualities within the prescribed limits of 0·95 I.M.N. and 450 kt. I.A.S. Ten of the test flights were made by A.& A.E.E. pilots—three R.A.F. and two R.N.—the others being from R.A.E. and C.F.E. Longitudinal characteristics in particular were thought excellent for use in interception and ground attack but major criticisms were made of the approach qualities, which included lateral rocking in bumpy air, a somewhat high approach speed, and a high attitude and low drag on the approach. Considering the developments of the Orpheus engine and of the airframe known to be in progress, the forthcoming Gnat was thought to have every prospect of being a good fighter, provided that it could be made available in reasonable time and could carry adequate operational equipment. Naval pilots shared the enthusiasm for the Midge's handling qualities, its simple and compact design recommending it for use at sea but, for such employment, ample endurance would be needed. The A.&A.E.E. pilots were very impressed with the Midge's general behaviour throughout the range covered and, with the exception of the approach characteristics and minor points, the general handling qualities were considered to be superior to those of any existing aircraft in service. Serviceability also was excellent during the period at A.&A.E.E.

After just over a year's successful flying, the Midge was wrecked in an accident on 26th September, 1955, but by then the FO.141 Gnat G-39-2 was flying, having made its maiden flight on 18th July, 1955. The Gnat prototype was powered by the 3,285 lb.s.t. Orpheus BOr1 and work was soon under way to complete the Air Ministry contract for a development batch of six Gnats, the sixth example finding itself taken for use in connection with an order received from India. XK724, the first of the Air Ministry Gnats, carried two 30 mm. Aden cannon, one being housed in the air intake on each side of the fuselage. The Air Ministry aircraft were used for evaluation of various items, including the 4,520 lb.s.t. Orpheus BOr2, the slab tailplane, and external stores of rockets, bombs and tanks. Despite its many attractive and successful features, the Gnat was not adopted by the R.A.F. as a fighter but was purchased as a two-seat trainer, the FO.144. Petter's cost-saving Gnat did, however, recommend itself to Finland and India, the air forces of both countries buying it.

XK739, the second of the five Air Ministry development Gnats, spent the period from 12th until 19th January, 1957, at A.&A.E.E. Boscombe Down for limited pre-view handling trials. Report 926/Pt.1 of 21st June, 1957, covered the assessment which was carried out before the introduction of the flying tailplane and the Orpheus 2 engine. It was intended to carry out about ten hours flying in fairly comprehensive trials but progress was slow owing to adverse weather and the limited endurance of XK739. Only about one third of the programme had been completed before the machine had to return to Folland. Limitations imposed during the tests were 500 kt. I.A.S. up to 9,000 ft., 1·05 I.M.N. above 26,000 ft., two turns of a spin and 200°/sec. rate of roll which was not to be maintained for more than 180° of roll. XK739 was airborne at 125 kt. and the build up of speed was extremely fast. Handling characteristics were found to be generally satisfactory.

The Folland Gnat vindicated fully its designer's contentions and became the first true light fighter to achieve normal production status out of the number of prototypes constructed hopefully over the years with the same object in mind.

Compared with the fairly intensive and widespread activity in fighter design during the first decade after the 1939–45 War, the later years of the 1950s displayed a marked reduction in the number of projects under active pursuit, astronomical cost of development—allied to prognostications of the imminent demise of the manned fighter—bringing with it a very different aspect to the fighter scene.

Saro SR.53. (Saro Photo.)

CHAPTER TEN
THE FIRST HALF CENTURY

The arrival in service of the incomparable English Electric Lightning was accompanied by a regrouping of Britain's aircraft industry. To cope with the threat of the fast, high-flying bomber with its all-destroying nuclear load, the defending fighter had forced its designer into a thicket of ever-increasing complexity. One major effect of the new order was that the sharing of design, research and production facilities within the newly constituted groups brought a vast potential of assistance to each section concerned in the design and development of any new aircraft.

Enthusiasm in general for the mixed power plant fighter—using turbo-jet and liquid-fuel rocket—seemed fated not to progress beyond the lukewarm despite the intensive effort put into such projects by the technicians and pilots concerned. Specification F.138D produced the Saro SR.53, designed by M. J. Brennan and completed in 1957. Primary power for the S.R.53 was provided by the D.H. Spectre variable-thrust rocket engine housed in the lower section of the fuselage and using highly concentrated hydrogen peroxide as its oxidant. An Armstrong Siddeley Viper provided a secondary source of power and was installed to exhaust under the tail assembly and above the Spectre's outlet. The superimposed installation of the engines resulted in a slim, comparatively deep fuselage, borne on square-tipped, mid-set delta wings, together with a delta tailplane surmounting the swept-back fin and rudder. The SR.53's two Firestreak missiles were mounted one on each tip of the 25 ft. 1·25 in. span wings.

Two prototypes were ordered, XD145 and XD151, XD145 taking to the air for the first time on 16th May, 1957, at A.&A.E.E. Boscombe Down with

Sqn.Ldr. J. S. Booth piloting. Performance of the SR.53 was expected to include a top speed of Mach 2·2 at over 45,000 ft., a climb rate of 52,800 ft./min. and a service ceiling of 60,000 ft. During trials the machine attained Mach 1·33 and a height of 50,000 ft. in 2 mins. XD151, the second SR.53, crashed on 5th June, 1958, while taking-off at Boscombe Down and the pilot, Sqn.Ldr. Booth, was killed.

A proposal for a version of the S.R.53 equipped with the sole power of the Armstrong Siddeley PR9 rocket engine and launched from the top of an Avro Vulcan in flight was studied but abandoned.

Shortly after design work on the Saro SR.53 commenced, Saunders-Roe initiated the design of the SR.177, a development of the SR.53 some 10% larger overall and intended for the R.A.F. The new project was destined for the rôle of a long-range, single-seat strike fighter, able to undertake also the work of reconnaissance, ground attack and support. Admiralty interest by March, 1955, was sufficient to gain in 1956 a contract for six pre-production prototypes of a navalized SR.177 to have a stronger airframe, deck arrester hook and catapulting points. The mixed power plant concept was retained, employing the 8,000 lb.s.t. D.H. Gyron Junior turbo-jet, aspirated through a nose intake, and the 8,000 lb.s.t. D.H. Spectre 5A liquid fuel rocket. The mid-set delta wings and delta horizontal tail surfaces formula of the SR.53 was retained in the SR.177 and the machine was scheduled to be equipped with A.I. radar and facilities for refuelling in flight. Each wingtip was to carry a Firestreak air-to-air missile in a similar manner to the SR.53.

The SR.177 was one of the unfortunate projects to suffer in the repercussions of the notorious 1957 White Paper but hope was entertained by Saunders-Roe that West German inquiries might result in a production order. Prototypes were nearing completion but termination of the foreign interest brought the entire project to an end and the demise of a fighter which was expected to be able to reach Mach 2·35.

Among projects studied at Hawker was one for a Mach 2 missile-armed interceptor to Operational Requirement 329 of March, 1954, to meet which the firm prepared the two-seat P.1103. Official support ceased in the Summer of 1956 but Operational Requirement 339, issued in 1957, was responsible for the revival of the P.1103 and its adaptation as the P.1121 single-seat fighter.

Operational Requirement 339 was subsequently revised to produce a two-seater with greater range than the P.1121 would have possessed but Hawker made the decision to carry on with the P.1121 as a Private Venture for high-altitude interceptions and low-level strikes. Various engines assessed for use in the P.1121 included the Bristol Olympus B.Ol.2R of 29,000 lb.s.t. with after-burning, the Rolls-Royce Conway R.CO.11R which developed 15,800 lb.s.t. and 25,700 lb.s.t. using after-burning, and the 20,000 lb.s.t. D.H. Gyron P.S.26–3 which produced 27,000 lb.s.t. with after-burning in operation. Eventually, the 17,400 lb. Gyron P.S.26–6, which offered 23,800 lb.s.t. with after-burning was selected with its wedge-shaped intake installed beneath the fuselage.

The mock-up of the Hawker P.1121. (Hawker Photo.)

The P.1121 was an exceedingly impressive machine in appearance and would have been armed with fifty 2 in. rockets in a pair of retractable fuselage packs, together with two Firestreak missiles or strike weapons weighing up to 2,000 lb. At 36,000 ft. the P.1121 was expected to attain Mach 2·35 but, owing to lack of official backing, was destined to be abandoned in December, 1958, when the prototype was approaching completion.

During 1959, conversion of the first Javelin F.A.W.Mk.7 to F.A.W.Mk.9 standard was completed, first flight of the new variant taking place on 6th May. The F.A.W.Mk.9 programme of conversion from F.A.W.Mk.7s was undertaken during 1960 and consisted primarily of fitting after-burners, a drooping leading edge to the outer panels of the wings and a fuselage probe for in-flight refuelling. Improvements were made also in the systems of the flying controls. As far as is known, no successor to the two-seat, all-weather Javelin has been proposed as an R.A.F. requirement, all-weather fighter duties being considered the province of the Lightning F.A.W.Mk.6.

Throughout the whole of the history of the fixed-wing operational aircraft weight and, consequently, the wing loading have increased inexorably as greater overall performance was demanded. As a direct result field performance suffered, the length of take-off and landing runs stretching steadily. To a degree, this disadvantage could be mitigated on home-based airfields by lengthening the runways but tactical mobility, however, worsened increasingly as the point was reached where an aircraft found itself restricted in the number of airfields which could be used in a possible campaign. With the enormous thrust becoming available from the jet engine, the possibility grew late in the 1950s of installing sufficient power in a fighter to exceed the all-up weight and thus open the way to vertical take-off and landing.

Following the cancellation of the P.1121, the Hawker design staff led by Sir Sydney Camm became absorbed by the possibility of producing a VTOL successor to the Hunter, particularly as a tactical ground attack fighter. Assessment of the number of forms which could be adopted to provide the vertical lift component resulted in the decision to use the technique of rising with the airframe horizontal. Having decided on the flat-riser the next main

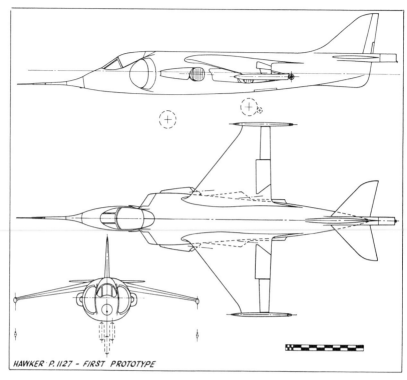

HAWKER P.1127 - FIRST PROTOTYPE

Hawker P.1127

point to be resolved was the type of power plant, the choice lying primarily between the installation of a separate battery of small engines to provide vertical lift when required, or designing the aircraft around an engine capable of providing both vertical and horizontal thrust in a single unit.

In conjunction with Bristol Aero-Engines during July, 1957, the vectored-thrust engine layout was agreed, together with the basic design of the P.1127 to use it. No time was lost in preparing and submitting the brochure which outlined a single-seat fighter with the emphasis on strike and reconnaissance rôles and able to operate from rudimentary landing grounds. Simplicity and strength were also keynotes of the design to afford maximum serviceability for long periods far away from well-equipped base airfields. To achieve adequate success with the P.1127 on the 13,000 lb.s.t. to 14,000 lb.s.t. expected from the Bristol engine, it was essential for the design to be kept ultra-light in weight, thereby resulting in a subsonic aircraft rather than one capable of supersonic speed.

By the early part of 1959, it had been decided at Hawker to construct a single prototype P.1127 as a Private Venture, and in March of that year the Experimental Department received the first drawings. The commencement of construction during May, 1959, was followed in June, 1960, by a contract from the Ministry of Aviation for a total of six prototypes.

Concurrently with the aircraft which it was to power, the all-important Bristol Siddeley B.S.53 engine progressed steadily through its development stages, making its first run during September, 1959. An exceedingly ingenious turbo-fan design, it discharged the major part of the low-pressure air delivered by the fan through the front pair of rotating nozzles, the rest of the air supply passing through the high-pressure compressor and combustion stages for exit by way of the rear pair of similar rotating nozzles. The B.S.53, later christened Pegasus, was designed for supersonic operation, being limited to Mach 1 at sea level but able to fly at nearly Mach 2 at altitude. To enable supersonic thrust to be generated a system of plenum chamber burning was evolved for introduction in the front ducts carrying the by-pass air, giving an increase of some 30% static thrust. The PCB system was found to produce greater thrust than after-burning.

The first prototype P.1127—XP831—was completed in July, 1960, and taken to the Hawker airfield at Dunsfold. The 24 ft. 4 in. span machine was of singularly striking appearance. The square-tipped, anhedralled wings were swept back sharply on the leading edge and mounted at shoulder position above the Pegasus in the broad fuselage. The cockpit in the nose was flanked by side intakes of generous area, the edges of which were of inflatable rubber to give sharp lips for high-speed flight and large-radius lips for low-speed flight and hovering. A zero-track main undercarriage was fitted and small wheels on wingtip outriggers supported the P.1127 on the ground. Engine runs were conducted during September, 1960, and XP831 performed its first tethered hovering flight the following month on 21st October with A. W. Bedford piloting. On 19th November two untethered hovering tests were made.

Rotation of the nozzles of the B.S.53 engine in the P.1127 could be made

A new concept in fighters, the VTOL Hawker P.1127. XP972, the third prototype, in forward flight. (Hawker Photo.)

373

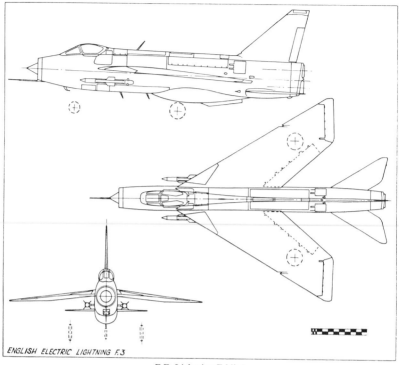

E.E. Lightning F.Mk.3

extremely quickly through 100° in under one second, the movement being governed by the nozzle selector lever alongside the throttles, this lever being the sole additional control in an otherwise conventional cockpit. The jet reaction control valves at the nose, tail and each wingtip were operated direct by the control column and rudder pedals, their air supply during vertical and hovering flight being obtained from the high-pressure compressor of the engine.

After transport to R.A.E. Bedford, XP831 made its first orthodox take-off, flight and landing on 13th March, 1961, with A. W. Bedford in control. The machine then returned to Dunsfold and tests were resumed in company with XP836, the second P.1127 prototype. In September, 1961, XP831 finally demonstrated that it could do all that was expected of it when it performed the complete routine of vertical take-off and transition to horizontal flight, ending with vertical landing.

Minor alterations were made in the successive P.1127s of the prototype batch and on 8th February, 1963, H.M.S. *Ark Royal* was the scene of the first tests carried out with a fixed-wing VTOL aircraft at sea when the P.1127 demonstrated its outstanding capabilities successfully on the carrier off Lyme Regis. XP831 was the aircraft used and was flown by A. W. Bedford and H. C. H. Merewether.

XP697, the fifth production Lightning F.Mk.3. (English Electric Photo.)

Having fully vindicated its designer's theories in practical form, the P.1127 was responsible for the preparations of the design of the Hawker P.1154 to use the much more powerful Bristol Siddeley B.S.100 vectored-thrust turbo-fan engine, designed to fly at Mach 1·2 at sea level and Mach 2 at altitude and using plenum chamber burning. Development of the P.1154 was aimed at providing a replacement for the R.A.F.'s Hunter and, possibly, also for the Navy's Sea Vixen, the intention being to attempt to reconcile conflicting requirements in one basic aircraft. It was hoped too that the P.1154 might meet the NATO requirement for a new tactical strike fighter.

On 1st January, 1964, the first Lightning F.Mk.3 was delivered to the Air Development Squadron of the Central Fighter Establishment. The latest mark of Lightning incorporated a square-tipped, larger fin and jettisonable fuel tanks mounted on the upper surfaces of the wings, and was powered by a pair of Avon 300-series engines producing well over 16,000 lb.s.t. each. In comparison with earlier versions of the Lightning, the F.Mk.3 was considerably revised and improved, carrying more fuel, new weapons and improved radar, navigation, flight and fire-control systems. Two D.H. Red Top missiles or forty-eight 2 in. unguided rockets could be carried as armament.

Towards the end of 1964 No. 74 Squadron became the first operational unit to equip with the F.Mk.3 but further changes became evident on later production F.Mk.3s. These included revised wings embodying an extension of the outer leading edge and the incorporation of camber, together with a considerable increase in the capacity of the ventral fuel tank. These modifications were applied retrospectively to serving early F.Mk.3s. Power for the

375

English Electric Lightning F.Mk.6 XR754. (English Electric Photo.)

Lightning F.Mk.3 was provided by a pair of Avon 301s, each delivering 12,690 lb.s.t. and boosted to 16,360 lb.s.t. each with after-burners in operation.

The excellent basic design of the Lightning has been amply demonstrated by its continued development, and the latest version to enter Royal Air Force service is that of the F.Mk.6, its first flight taking place on 16th June, 1965. No. 5 Squadron accepted the first F.Mk.6 examples during October 1965, and F.Mk.3s in the U.K. were converted eventually to F.Mk.6 standard. This refinement increased range by approximately 20%, thus imbuing the Lightning with much enhanced overall performance—increased afterburning acceleration capacity, a considerably longer patrol period and improved supersonic endurance while intercepting and attacking—in its prescribed rôles. Refuelling in flight is by means of a probe carried beneath the port wing close to the fuselage. Armament of the Lightning F.Mk.6 comprises either two de Havilland Red Top missiles—developed from the Firestreak—or forty-eight 2 in. rockets.

In spite of the dramatic lead in fighter evolution attained by Hawker with the remarkable P.1127, the hopes entertained for its developed successor—

the P.1154—were not subsequently realized as the project was cancelled during 1965. Trials with the P.1127 proceeded, however, and led ultimately to the placing of an order for the R.A.F. The first and second prototype P.1127s were followed by four more—XP972, XP976, XP980 and XP984— each embodying modifications. XP984 was the first to introduce sweepback on the wings' trailing edge, together with an increase in length, a mainwheel door-cum-airbrake and ventral strakes. This version was basically the ultimate design 'which was used to provide the nine Kestrel F.(G.A.)Mk.1s— XS688–XS696—constituting the equipment of the tripartite trials squadron which evaluated the concept at West Raynham during 1964 and 1965.

Still further revision of the P.1127 was evident with the appearance of XV276, the first of the pre-production batch of the R.A.F. version, which made its first maiden flight on 31st August, 1966, using the 15,200 lb.s.t. B.S.53 Pegasus B.Pg.5 as its power. Further trials at sea were conducted successfully with XP984 during 1966 from the aircraft carrier H.M.S. *Bulwark*. Designated ultimately Harrier G.R.Mk.1, the all-metal, stressed-skin production model P.1127/7 was an aircraft redesigned throughout to the Ministry of Defence Operational Requirement 356 under the direction of J. W. Fozard, appointed Chief Designer Harrier in 1965 following his period as Chief Designer P.1154 during 1963–65. The Harrier's developed Pegasus 101 engine of 19,200 lb.s.t. was capable of producing about twice the output of the original B.E.53 of 1960, and the type's armament comprised twin 30 mm. Aden guns installed in under-fuselage pods, augmented by combinations of Sidewinder missiles, 68 mm. SNEB rockets on Matra rocket-launchers, or bombs—to a total weapon load of 8,000 lb. The first definitive production G.R.Mk.1—XV738—was flown initially by D. M. S. Simpson on 28th December, 1967, at Dunsfold, and the inceptive contract for 60 Harrier G.R.Mk.1s was increased subsequently to 77 examples.

By the time that the Harrier entered service some nine years had elapsed since the first flight of the revolutionary new aircraft; nevertheless, the Royal Air Force was still the inaugural air arm to operate a fighter with VTOL capability and this ultra-significant distinction was achieved on 1st April,

Impression of Hawker P.1154 two-seat Royal Navy variant with wing fairings for the main under-carriage units; development of both Royal Air Force and Royal Navy versions was cancelled during 1965. (British Aerospace Photo.)

1969, when No. 1 Squadron at Wittering relinquished its Hunter F.G.A.Mk.9s in favour of the Harrier G.R.Mk.1. In June, 1970, No. 4 Squadron at Wildenrath became the second unit to receive the Harrier, and was followed, also in Germany, by both No. 20 Squadron on 1st October, 1970, and No. 3 Squadron on 1st January, 1972. Subsequently, all of the G.R.Mk.1s were converted with uprated 20,000 lb.s.t. Pegasus 102 engines to G.R.Mk.1As, then—finally—to G.R.Mk.3 standard by installation of the 21,500 lb.s.t. Pegasus 103; additional Harriers appeared direct from the production line as G.R.Mk.3s. In February, 1977, No. 20 Squadron's Harriers were transferred to augment Nos. 3 and 4 Squadrons at Gütersloh. Intensive development of the basic concept over a considerable period has resulted in the embodiment of numerous modifications in the Harrier, one of the most conspicuous to its exterior being the incorporation of the Ferranti laser

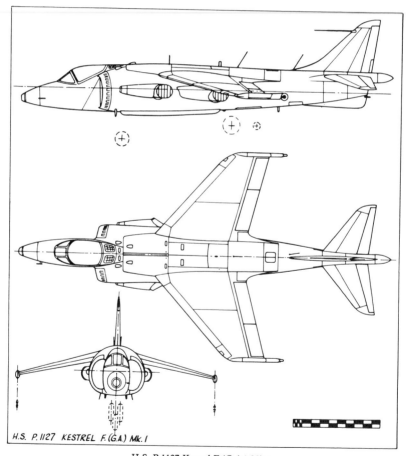

H.S. P.1127 KESTREL F.(G.A.) Mk.1

H.S. P.1127 Kestrel F.(G.A.) Mk.1

378

XV276, first of six pre-production Hawker P.1127s ordered for the R.A.F. (Hawker Photo.)

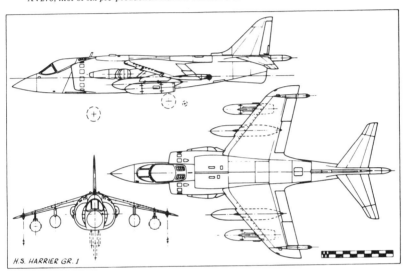

H.S. Harrier G.R. Mk.1

Hawker Siddeley Harrier G.R. Mk. 1. (Hawker Siddeley Photo.)

In roughly-applied Winter camouflage and equipped with Matra rocket-launchers, 100 gallon external combat tanks, 30 mm. Aden cannon pods and centre-pylon bomb-load, a Hawker Siddeley Harrier G.R.Mk.1 of No. 1 Squadron emerges from its snow-surrounded, net-covering hide. (British Aerospace Photo.)

Hawker Siddeley Harrier G.R.Mk.1 equipped with a pair of 330 gallon external ferry tanks and flight-refuelling probe installed on port air intake in ferry position. (British Aerospace Photo.)

The fourth production Hawker Siddeley Harrier G.R.Mk.1 XV741 of No. 1 Squadron making a vertical take-off from Somerstown Coalyard, St. Pancras, London, in May, 1969, while participating in the *Daily Mail* Transatlantic Air Race. (British Aerospace Photo.)

ranger nose; marked target seeker equipment has been fitted in addition.

Evolution of flying techniques has produced the operational practice of VIFF—thrust vectoring in forward flight—to endow the Harrier with a unique form of extra combat manoeuvrability, and successful flight trials at sea during August, 1969, from a small platform aft on the cruiser H.M.S. *Blake*, on board the aircraft carrier H.M.S. *Eagle* in 1970, and with the aircraft carrier H.M.S. *Ark Royal* in May, 1971, were instrumental in inducing the decision of May, 1975, to proceed with development of the Sea Harrier F.R.S.Mk.1 by adapting the basic G.R.Mk.3 to the new rôle. Evolved to embrace fighter, reconnaissance and strike duties, the Sea Harrier is powered by the 21,500 lb.s.t. Pegasus 104 turbo-fan and incorporates—among other changes—a revised fore-fuselage, a cockpit raised by 11 inches, new avionics,

Carrying two 100 gallon external combat tanks and embodying a laser nose, a Hawker Siddeley Harrier G.R.Mk.3 hovers with airbrake and undercarriage units lowered. (British Aerospace Photo.)

Ferranti Blue Fox multi-mode radar utilising a 20 in. diameter dish aerial, new Doppler navaid, the elimination of seven magnesium airframe components and two in the Pegasus 104 engine, nose-leg tie-down lugs, and an emergency brake system. In addition, the Martin-Baker Type 10 zero-zero ejector seat replaces the Type 9 installed in the R.A.F. G.R.Mk.3. During May, 1975, the Royal Navy ordered 24 Sea Harrier F.R.S.Mk.1s, commencing with XZ438, and in May, 1978, placed a contract for a further ten of the same version. At Dunsfold on 20th August, 1978, J. Farley accomplished the 35-minute initial flight of XZ450, the first production F.R.S.Mk.1. With a span of 25 ft. 3 in., length 47 ft. 7 in., and height 12 ft. 2 in., empty weight of 12,500 lb. and loaded weight of 25,000 lb., the Sea Harrier achieved a top speed of 740 m.p.h., and a service ceiling in excess of 50,000 ft.

In Royal Navy service, apart from its normal intrinsic vertical take-off faculty, the Sea Harrier will be able to utilise the newly-developed ski-jump launching technique conceived in 1969 by Lt.Cdr. D. R. Taylor, R.N., later of the Future Projects (Aircraft) Section of Aircraft Department (Navy) M.O.D.(N) London, to endow an aircraft with a considerable gain in per-

The prototype Hawker Siddeley Sea Harrier F.R.S.Mk.1 XZ450 hovering by using vectored thrust. (British Aerospace Photo.)

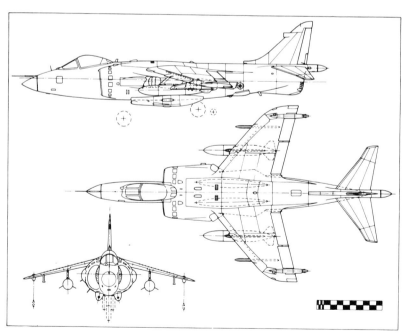

Hawker Siddeley Sea Harrier F.R.S.Mk.1

formance at take-off by increasing its payload or reducing its deck run. This benefit is achieved by launching the machine in a ballistic trajectory from an upwards-curved ramp installed at the front of the flight deck, thereby enabling the aircraft to become airborne at a lower speed than would be the case from a flat surface. On 13th November, 1978, XZ450 commenced its initial deck trials aboard the aircraft carrier H.M.S. *Hermes* in the Moray Firth and had completed ten sorties by 18th November, 1978. The Sea Harrier Intensive Flying Trials Unit—later in 1979 to commission as No.

Hawker Siddeley Sea Harrier F.R.S.Mk.1 XZ450 prototype takes off from the ski-jump ramp at R.A.E. Farnborough. (British Aerospace Photo.)

700A Squadron—formed on 26th June, 1979, at Yeovilton and the same base was scheduled to be used for the formation of the three operational Sea Harrier F.R.S.Mk.1 squadrons—Nos. 800 and 801 early in 1980, and No. 802 early in 1981. No. 800 Squadron was due to become operational at sea during mid-1980 aboard H.M.S. *Invincible* of 19,500 tons displacement launched on 3rd May, 1977, as the first of three new anti-submarine command cruisers equipped each with a bow-mounted ski-jump ramp; H.M.S. *Hermes* refitted during 1980 was to receive No. 801 Squadron early in 1981, the 16,000 tons displacement H.M.S. *Illustrious* launched on 1st December, 1978, was to embark No. 802 Squadron at the end of 1982, and H.M.S. *Ark Royal*—formerly to be named H.M.S. *Indomitable*—would commission last. Initially, the strength of each squadron was to be eight aircraft. The Sea Harrier F.R.S.Mk.1's weapon-load was designed to include five 1,000 lb. bombs or six 36-tube rocket-launchers, together with Martel or Sidewinder AIM-9L air-to-air missiles, 30 mm. Aden gun pods and two British Aero-

Second Hawker Siddeley Harrier Mk.50 AV–8A supplied to the United States Marine Corps. (British Aerospace Photo.)

space P3T sea-skimming anti-ship missiles. Yet another radical feature developed specifically for the Sea Harrier is a trim system for adjusting speed during the landing approach to a ship's deck by changing the angle of the engine's nozzle setting instead of altering the pitch of the aircraft, thus avoiding the danger of the pilot being unable to see the ship. The change of 11 deg. in nozzle angle from the datum in either direction is accomplished in conjunction with the airbrake switch on the throttle lever.

The outstanding qualities inherent in the Harrier aroused intense interest in the aircraft universally but, apart from its service in the Royal Air Force since 1969 and its scheduled Royal Navy début ten years later, only two other services—the United States Marine Corps in using it as the Mk.50 AV–8A

Hawker Siddeley Harrier Mk.55, one of six ordered through the United States Navy and operated as the Matador by one squadron of the Armada Espanola. (British Aerospace Photo.)

384

and the Spanish Navy with the Mk.55 Matador for operation exclusively at sea—have adopted the unique design. In America prolonged development by McDonnell Douglas in conjunction with Hawker Siddeley brought about the appearance—by way of the AV–16A Advanced Harrier and the AV–8A— of the AV–8B light attack version intended for the United States Marine Corps. Embodying not only new wings of graphite epoxy composite construction for reduced weight and longer life and which incorporated a supercritical aerofoil, but also revised intakes, under-fuselage lift-improvement devices, and redesigned forward engine nozzles, the McDonnell Douglas/ British Aerospace prototype YAV–8B Advanced Harrier 158394 made its successful first flight at the Lambert–St. Louis International Airport on 9th November, 1978, with Charles A. Plummer at the controls.

First prototype McDonnell Douglas YAV–8B Advanced Harrier 158394, one of two modified from United Kingdom-built AV–8As, which—piloted by Charles A. Plummer—made its initial flight on 9th November, 1978, at Lambert–St. Louis International Airport. (British Aerospace Photo.)

Concurrently with development of the Harrier, British capacity was involved in design and production of the S.E.P.E.C.A.T. Jaguar supersonic tactical fighter by the British Aircraft Corporation in collaboration with Avions Marcel Dassault/Breguet Aviation in France. A single-seater, the Royal Air Force's G.R.Mk.1 is a shoulder-wing monoplane of 28 ft. 6 in. span and is powered by two 4,620 lb.s.t. Rolls-Royce Turboméca RT.172 Adour 102 turbo-fans installed side-by-side in the rear fuselage. Armament comprises two 30 mm. Aden guns and the Jaguar is able to carry a weapon-load of 10,000 lb. externally on five strong-points and in a variety of combinations.

Piloted by Wg.Cdr. J. L. Dell, the first British-built Jaguar S.06—XW560 —made its initial flight at Warton on 12th October, 1969, and the type commenced its Royal Air Force service on 13th September, 1973, with No. 54 Squadron at Leuchars becoming the first operational unit to fly the Jaguar, receiving the G.R.Mk.1 as a strike fighter on 21st March, 1974, and moving eventually to Coltishall. Subsequently, seven additional squadrons re-equipped with the Jaguar G.R.Mk.1 and these were No. 6 in the Autumn of 1974, also at Coltishall as a strike fighter unit; No. 14 at Brüggen in the Spring, 1975, strike fighter; No. 17 at Brüggen in July, 1975, strike fighter; No. 2 at Laarbruch in February, 1976, tactical reconnaissance; No. 41 at

B.A.C. Jaguar S.07. (B.A.C. Photo.)

The second aircraft of the initial B.A.C. Jaguar G.R.Mk.1 production batch—XX109—taking off with reconnaissance pod on its centre pylon and a pair of 264 gallon external fuel tanks. (British Aerospace Photo.)

B.A.C. Jaguar G.R.Mk.1 of No. 54 Squadron based at Coltishall, piloted by the Commanding Officer Wg.Cdr. R. J. Kemball and carrying two 264 gallon external fuel tanks and four 1,000 lb. bombs. (British Aerospace Photo.)

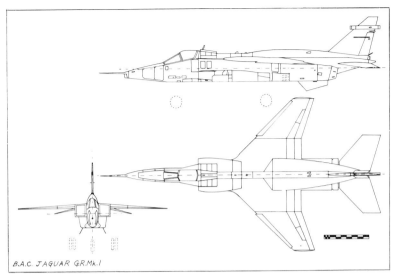

B.A.C. Jaguar G.R.Mk.1

Coltishall on 27th April, 1976, tactical strike and reconnaissance; No. 31 at Brüggen on 1st July, 1976, strike fighter; and No. 20 at Brüggen on 4th February, 1977, strike fighter. During 1978 work was in progress to uprate the Jaguar's Adour 102 engines to RT.172–26 standard as Adour 104s, thereby increasing take-off thrust by about 10% and producing an extra 27% for low-level high-speed cruising flight. In addition the G.R.Mk.1 was to be

The five German-based B.A.C. Jaguar G.R.Mk.1 squadrons represented by—front to rear—No. 2 XZ109, No. 14 XX960, No. 17 XX768, No. 20 XZ374 and No. 31 XZ391. (British Aerospace Photo.)

fitted with active ECM equipment and there was the possibility that this would be installed in the Harrier as well.

Coincidentally with the Jaguar, the British Aircraft Corporation has been engaged in design and production of the Panavia 200 Tornado, evolved collaboratively with Messerschmitt–Bölkow–Blohm in West Germany and Aeritalia in Italy as a multi-rôle combat aircraft. The entire project stemmed from the original realization in 1967 that several countries had future requirements for a similar combat aircraft so that, during 1968, Great Britain, West Germany, Italy, Belgium, Holland and Canada engaged in joint discussion on the proposed MRCA–75. Although, by the end of that year, agreement had been reached on the technical requirements for a combined feasibility

Panavia 200 Tornado G.R.Mk.1 taking off with eight bombs, two 330 gallon external fuel tanks and two ECM pods. (British Aerospace Photo.)

study, Belgium and Canada withdrew and Holland took the same action in 1969. Nevertheless, on 26th March, 1969, Panavia Aircraft GmbH was constituted to undertake a feasibility study which terminated on 1st May, 1969, the concept passing on 16th May, 1969, into the project definition phase, to be approved subsequently by the three governments concerned. On 20th July, 1970, the development phase leading to the flight of the first prototype was instituted by Great Britain and West Germany, with Italy signing on 30th September, 1970: during September, 1971, a second tri-national programme review was completed and, at the end of the next review in March, 1973, joint development of the project as planned was announced, together with authorization for production preparation. A further review in 1974 sanctioned continuation of the programme.

During September, 1969, the engine consortium Turbo-Union—with Rolls-Royce, Motoren und Turbinen Union, and Fiat as component companies—was constituted to produce the aircraft's 8,500 lb.s.t. RB.199–34R–4 Mk.101 re-heated turbo-fan, a small but powerful unit with the benefit of outstandingly low specific fuel consumption conferred by the three-spool layout, and of small size which has enabled the fuselage dimensions to be kept to the minimum. The first engine ran in September, 1971, and the Tornado evolved ultimately as a two-seat supersonic monoplane with variable-geometry mainplanes set at the shoulder-wing position and reaching a fully-

The prototype Panavia 200 Tornado F.Mk.2 Air Defence Variant with four Sky Flash missiles under the fuselage. (British Aerospace Photo.)

swept angle of 65 deg. Extended span is 45 ft. 8 in., span in the swept position 28 ft. 3 in., length 54 ft. 9·5 in. and height 18 ft. 8·5 in. Aluminium alloy is employed as the main structural material, augmented by a limited amount of steel and titanium.

The maiden flight of the first prototype Tornado P–01 D–9591 took place at Manching on 14th August, 1974, with Paul Millett of British Aircraft Corporation in control, and he was accompanied by Messerschmitt–Bölkow–Blohm pilot Nils Meister in the second seat. On 30th October, 1974, Paul Millett was in charge also of the second prototype Tornado P–02 XX946 initial flight at Warton, with Pietro Trevisan of Aeritalia as crew member. The fifth tri-national government review of the programme began in May, 1975, and was followed at the end of that year by the announcement of production requirements.

For the Royal Air Force, in addition to procuring 220 Tornado G.R.Mk.1s for the interdictor strike rôle, it was decided to order 165 Tornado F.Mk.2s

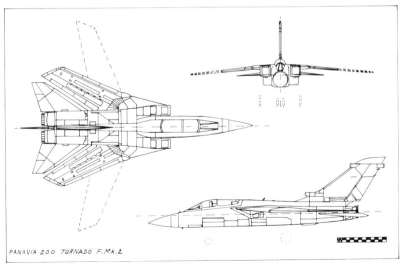

PANAVIA 200 TORNADO F.MK.2

Panavia 200 Tornado F.Mk.2

for air defence interceptor duties for which they were scheduled to commence replacing Lightnings and Phantoms during the mid-1980s. For this purpose the F.Mk.2 was to be equipped with Marconi-Elliott air-interception radar housed in a longer nose and to have increased fuel capacity in a lengthened centre fuselage. Scheduled fixed armament consisted of a single 27 mm. high-velocity cannon designed and developed by I.W.K.A.-Mauser and able to attain an express rate of fire; a semi-recessed under-fuselage installation accommodated four Sky Flash medium-range air-to-air missiles, and the aircraft was designed to carry also two AIM-9L Sidewinder short-range air-to-air missiles. Improved combat manoeuvrability for the F.Mk.2 was to be achieved by extensions to the wing-roots and the flight-refuelling probe was to be made retractable. First flight of the Tornado F.Mk.2 ADV—Air Defence Variant developed specifically for the Royal Air Force to meet its future air defence commitments—was planned to take place at Warton towards the end of 1979, and it was designed to be able to patrol at 300–400 miles from its home territory for over two hours without in-flight refuelling and to carry out an interception including air combat for ten minutes. The aircraft's equipment was to provide air-to-air refuelling during combat air patrol so as to augment its endurance very considerably. Royal Air Force air defence units designated to re-equip with the Tornado F.Mk.2 include Nos. 5, 11, 19, 23, 29, 43, 56, 92 and 111 Squadrons.

Although, initially, the Hawker Siddeley HS.1182 Hawk was evolved for the Royal Air Force as a small, single-jet, two-seat, low-wing monoplane in both the flying-training and weapon-training rôles, its significant potential for combat use was recognised immediately by interested air forces abroad and, particularly, by those impelled by cost considerations to purchase aircraft able to undertake multiple duties. Consequently, the Hawk is offered for export fitted with the uprated 5,700 lb.s.t. Rolls-Royce Turboméca RT.172–56

Hawker Siddeley HS.1182 Ground Attack/Trainer equipped with one 30 mm. Aden cannon, two Sidewinder air-to-air missiles and two external fuel tanks. (British Aerospace Photo.)

turbo-fan in its ground-attack fighter version and, additionally, has been developed into an advanced single-seat variant.

Revelation of Air Staff Target 403 disclosed that studies were being undertaken to evolve a single aircraft type combining air combat and battlefield rôles in a fighter-bomber to replace both the Harrier and the Jaguar by entering Royal Air Force service in 1987. Early in 1977 British Aircraft Corporation and Hawker Siddeley submitted just over 30 designs to the Ministry of Defence for appraisal and, by the Autumn of 1977, the choice had been reduced to four or five of the proposals. Although Air Staff Target 403 had not specified V/STOL capability, the vulnerability of European airfields was considered as rendering such an attribute mandatory and this assessment, combined with Air Staff Target 403's requirement for a Mach 1·6 single-seater equipped with radar—together with electro-optical and other advanced navigation/attack systems, may produce eventually another vectored-thrust design. Subsequently, however, the Royal Air Force's Harrier replacement specification was separated from Air Staff Target 403.

During January, 1979, an announcement came from British Aerospace that consideration was being given to development of the Super Harrier or Harrier Mk.5, an advanced version of the successful basic design to incorporate probably larger wings with increased performance and weapons capability, together with modifications to improve lift and handling.

In every instance since their inception, Great Britain's fighter aircraft have had to be devised in each respect to meet foreseeable contingencies, and constantly changing conditions in the World—coupled with unceasing progress in the absorbing and challenging science of aviation both at home and abroad—have influenced the performance, appearance and the intended rôles of the combat designs evolved over a period of approaching seventy years.

In the light of the continued and intensive development proceeding universally, the exceedingly dangerous and pathetically naïve supposition that the demise of the manned fighter was imminent—current in United Kingdom defence planning towards the close of the 1950s—has been exposed demonstrably as completely unfounded and to be a discreditable and flagrant misconception.

Despite startling and dramatic advances in the field of missiles, the indisputable fundamental reality—proven in innumerable instances—is that the fighter is required to fulfil its indispensable and long-standing duties with the Royal Air Force and the Fleet Air Arm for an indeterminate period in the future.

DATA

Manufacturer/ Designer	Type No.	Name	Engine(s) h.p./lb.s.t.
A. D.		Sparrow	1 × 80 Gnome
Alcock	A.1	Scout	1 × 100 Mono. Gnome
Armstrong Whitworth	F.K.1	Sissit	1 × 50 Gnome
,, ,,	F.K.6		1 × 250 Eagle
,, ,,	F.K.10		1 × 130 Clerget
,, ,,	F.M.4	Armadillo	1 × 230 B.R.2
,, ,,		Ara	1 × 320 Dragonfly
,, ,,	S.R.2	Siddeley Siskin	1 × 320 Dragonfly
,, ,,		Siskin Mk.III	1 × 325 Jaguar III
,, ,,		Siskin Mk.IIIA	1 × 420 Jaguar IVS
,, ,,	A.W.14	Starling Mk.I	1 × 385 Jaguar VII
,, ,,	A.W.14	Starling Mk.II	1 × 540 Panther IIIA
,, ,,	A.W.16		1 × 540 Panther VII
,, ,,	A.W.35	Scimitar	1 × 624 Panther IXA
Austin	A.F.T.3	Osprey	1 × 230 B.R.2
,,		Greyhound	1 × 320 Dragonfly 1
Austin-Ball	A.F.B.1		1 × 200 Hispano-Suiza
Avro	504K N.F.		1 × 110 le Rhône
,,	508		1 × 80 Gnome
,,	511	Arrowscout	1 × 80 Gnome
,,	521		1 × 110 Clerget
,,	530		1 × 200 Hispano-Suiza
,,	531	Spider	1 × 130 Clerget
,,	566	Avenger	1 × 525 Lion VIII
,,	584	Avocet	1 × 230 Lynx IV
,,	720		1 × 1750 Viper/
			1 × 8000 Screamer
B.A.T.	F.K.22	Bat	1 × 120 Mosquito
,,	F.K.22	Bantam Mk.II	1 × 100 Mono. Gnome
,,	F.K.23	Bantam Mk.I	1 × 170 Wasp I
,,	F.K.25	Basilisk	1 × 320 Dragonfly
Beardmore	W.B.III		1 × 80 le Rhône
,,	W.B.IV		1 × 200 Hispano-Suiza
,,	W.B.V		1 × 200 Hispano-Suiza
,,	W.B.26		1 × 360 Eagle IX
Blackburn		Triplane	1 × 100 Mono. Gnome
,,		N.1B	1 × 200 Hispano-Suiza
,,		Nautilus	1 × 520 Kestrel F.XII
,,	F.2	Lincock Mk.I	1 × 235 Lynx IV
,,	F.1	Turcock	1 × 490 Jaguar VI
,,	F.3	F.7/30	1 × 660 Goshawk III
,,	B.24	Skua	1 × 905 Perseus XII
,,	B.25	Roc	1 × 905 Perseus XII
,,	B.45	Firebrand T.F.Mk.V	1 × 2305 Sabre III
,,	B.48	Firecrest Y.A.1	1 × 2840 Centaurus 59
Boulton & Paul	P.3	Bobolink	1 × 230 B.R.2
,, ,,	P.31	Bittern	2 × 230 Lynx
,, ,,	P.33	Partridge	1 × 440 Jupiter VII
Boulton Paul	P.82	Defiant F.Mk.I	1 × 1030 Merlin III

TABLES

Max. Speed m.p.h.	Wt.(E) lb.	Wt.(L) lb.	Span	Length	Prototype
84			33'5" app. 24'3"	24'9" app. 19'1"	1452
75					
			62'	37'0·75"	7838
94	1236	2019	27'10"	22'3"	N511
125	1250	1860	27'9"	18'10"	X19
150	1320	1930	27'5"	20'3"	F4971
145	1463	2181	27'6"	21'3"	C4541
134	1830	2735	33'1"	23'	J6583
156	2061	3012	33'2"	25'4"	J8048
177·5	2060	3095	31'4"	25'2"	J8027
183·5		3225	34'3"	24'8·5"	J8028
217	2795	4054	33'	25'	A–2
217	2989	4133	33'	25'	G–ACCD
118·5	1106	1888	23'	17'7"	X15
129	1838	3032	39'	26'8·5"	H4317
138	1525	2077	30'	21'6"	B9909
95	1531	1660	36'	29'5"	
65	1000	1800	44'	26'9"	
100	675	1165	26'	22'9"	
90	1150	1995	30'	28'2"	1811
114	1695	2680	36'	28'6"	B9431
120	963	1517	28'6"	20'6"	B3952
180	2368	3414	28'	25'6"	G–EBND
133	1678	2495	29'	24'6"	N209
M.2·0	7812	17575	27'3·5"	43'2·75"	XD696
			24'8"	20'8"	B9945
100	866	1260	24'8"	20'8"	B9945
138	833	1321	25'	18'5"	B9947
142·5	1454	2182	25'4"	20'5"	F2906
103	890	1289	25'	20'2·5"	9950
110	2055	2595	35'10"	26'6"	N38
112	1860	2500	35'10"	26'7"	N41
145	2555	3980	37'		
115	1011	1500	24'	21'5·25"	N502
114	1721	2390	34'10"	28'	N56
154	3223	4750	37'	31'8"	N234
160	1240	2000	22'6"	18'1"	G–EBVO
181	2282	2720	31'	24'4"	G–EBVP
190	2500	4003	36'10·8"	27'	K2892
225	5490	8228	46'2"	35'7"	K5178
223	6121	8800	46'	35'7"	L3057
350	11835	17500	51'3·5"	38'11"	EK741
380	10500	15280	44'11·5"	39'3·5"	RT651
125	1226	1992	29'	20'	C8655
145		4500	41'	32'	J7936
167	2021	3100	35'	23'1"	J8459
303·5	6078	8350	39'4"	35'4"	K8310

Manufacturer/ Designer	Type No.	Name	Engine(s) h.p./lb.s.t.
Bristol		P.B.8	1 × 80 Gnome
,,		S.B.5	1 × 80 Gnome
,,		S.S.A.	1 × 80 Clerget
,,		Scout A	1 × 80 Gnome
,,	6	T.T.A.	2 × 120 Beardmore
,,	8	S.2A	1 × 110 Clerget
,,	10	M.1A	1 × 110 Clerget
,,	12	F.2A	1 × 280 Falcon I
,,	13	M.R.1	1 × 150 Hispano-Suiza
,,	14	F.2B	1 × 280 Falcon I
,,	21	Scout F	1 × 220 Arab
,,	23	F.2C Badger Mk.I	1 × 320 Dragonfly
,,	23	F.2C Badger Mk.II	1 × 450 Jupiter I
,,	52 M.F.A.	Bullfinch Monoplane	1 × 450 Jupiter III
,,	53 M.F.B.	Bullfinch Biplane	1 × 450 Jupiter III
,,	76	Jupiter-Fighter	1 × 425 Jupiter IV
,,	84	Bloodhound	1 × 436 Jupiter V
,,	95	Bagshot	2 × 515 Jupiter VI
,,	101		1 × 450 Jupiter VII
,,	105	Bulldog Mk.II	1 × 490 Jupiter VII
,,	107	Bullpup	1 × 450 Mercury IIA
,,	123		1 × 600 Goshawk III
,,	133		1 × 620 Mercury VIS4
,,	142	Blenheim Mk.IF	2 × 840 Mercury VIII
,,	142	Blenheim Mk.IVF	2 × 840 Mercury XV
,,	146		1 × 840 Mercury VIII
,,	156	Beaufighter Mk.IF	2 × 1590 Hercules XI
,,	156	Beaufighter Mk.IIF	2 × 1280 Merlin XX
,,	156	Beaufighter Mk.VIC	2 × 1670 Hercules VI
de Havilland	D.H.1A		1 × 120 Beardmore
,, ,,	D.H.2		1 × 110 le Rhône
,, ,,	D.H.5		1 × 110 le Rhône
,, ,,	D.H.77		1 × 301 Rapier I
,, ,,	D.H.98	Mosquito N.F.Mk.II	2 × 1460 Merlin 23
,, ,,	D.H.98	Mosquito F.B.Mk.VI	2 × 1635 Merlin 25
,, ,,	D.H.98	Mosquito N.F.Mk.30	2 × 1710 Merlin 76
,, ,,	D.H.100	Vampire F.Mk.I	1 × 2700 Goblin I
,, ,,	D.H.100	Vampire F.Mk.III	1 × 3100 Goblin II
,, ,,	D.H.100	Sea Vampire F.Mk.20	1 × 3100 Goblin II
,, ,,	D.H.103	Hornet F.Mk.3	2 × 2030 Merlin 130/131
,, ,,	D.H.103	Sea Hornet F.Mk.20	2 × 2030 Merlin 133/134
,, ,,	D.H.103	Sea Hornet N.F.Mk.21	2 × 2030 Merlin 134/135
,, ,,	D.H.110	Sea Vixen F.A.W.Mk.1	2 × 1000 Avon 208
,, ,,	D.H.112	Venom F.B.Mk.1	1 × 4850 Ghost 103
,, ,,	D.H.112	Sea Venom F.A.W.Mk.21	1 × 4850 Ghost 104
,, ,,	D.H.113	Vampire N.F.Mk.10	1 × 3350 Goblin 3
English Electric		Canberra B.(I).Mk.8	2 × 7500 Avon RA7
,, ,,		Lightning F.Mk.1	2 × 11250 Avon RA24R

Max. Speed m.p.h.	Wt.(E) lb.	Wt.(L) lb.	Span	Length	Prototype
			27'6"	27'6"	199
					183
106	913	1200	26'3"	18'9"	219
95	617	957	22'	19'9"	206
86·7	3820	5100	53'6"	39'2"	7750
95		1400	28'2"	21'3"	7836
128	913	1326	30'9"	20'3"	A3158
110	1727	2753	39'2·5"	25'9"	A3303
110	1700	2810	42'2"	27'	A5177
111·5	1700	2650	39'3"	25'10"	A7101
138	1300	2100	29'7"	20'10"	B3989
135	1948	3150	36'9"	23'8"	F3495
142	1950	3150	36'9"	23'8"	J6492
137	2175	3205	38'5"	24'5"	J6901
120	2495	4088	38'5"	24'5"	J6903
134	2190	3079	39'3"	25'	G–EBGF
122	2515	4236	40'4"	26'6"	G–EBGG
125	5100	8195	70'	44'11"	J7767
150	2100	3540	33'7"	27'4"	G–EBOW
174	2412	3503	33'11"	25'	J9480
190	1910	2850	30'	23'2"	J9051
235	3300	4737	29'6"	25'2"	R–9
260	3322	4738	39'	28'	R–10
260	8100	12500	56'4"	39'9"	L1424
260	9200	13800	56'4"	42'7"	
287	3283	4600	39'	27'	K5119
323	14069	20800	57'10"	41'4"	R2052
330	13600	20290	57'10"	41'8"	R2058
333	14600	21600	57'10"	41'8"	X7542
90	1610	2340	41'	28'11·25"	4606
92	1004	1547	28'3"	25'2·5"	4732
102	1010	1492	25'8"	22'	A5172
204	1655	2279	32'2"	24'4·75"	J9771
370	14300	18100	54'2"	40'10·75"	W4052
380	14300	19500	54'2"	40'10·75"	HJ662
407	15400	21600	54'2"	41'9"	MM686
531	6372	8578	40'	30'9"	TG274
531	7134	11970	40'	30'9"	TG275
526	7623	12660	38'	30'9"	LZ551
472	12880	20900	45'	36'8"	PX312
467	13300	18250	45'	36'8"	PX212
430	14230	19530	45'	37'	PX230
645	27952	35000	51'	55'7"	WG236
640	8468	15400	41'8"	31'10"	VV612
630	10853	16220	42'10"	36'7·25"	WK376
550	6984	11350	38'	34'7"	G–5–2
541	27950	54950	63'11·5"	65'6"	VX185
1500	25753	40000	34'10"	55'3"	XM134

Manufacturer/ Designer	Type No.	Name	Engine(s) h.p./lb.s.t.
English Electric		Lightning F.Mk.1A	2 × 11250 Avon 210
,, ,,		Lightning F.Mk.3	2 × 13220 Avon 301
,, ,,		Lightning F.Mk.6	2 × 13220 Avon 301
Fairey		Hamble Baby	1 × 110 Clerget
,,	F.2		2 × 190 Falcon
,,	21	Pintail Mk.I	1 × 450 Lion V
,,		Flycatcher Mk.I	1 × 400 Jaguar III
,,		Flycatcher Mk.II	1 × 480 Mercury IIA
,,		Fleetwing	1 × 480 Kestrel F.XII
,,		Firefly Mk.I	1 × 430 Felix
,,		Firefly Mk.II	1 × 480 Kestrel IIS
,,		Firefly Mk.III	1 × 480 Kestrel IIS
,,		Fantôme	1 × 925 Hispano-Suiza 12 Ycrs
,,		Fox Mk.VII	1 × 860 Hispano-Suiza 12Y
,,		Fulmar Mk.I	1 × 1060 Merlin RM3M
,,		Firefly F.R.Mk.I	1 × 1730 Griffon IIB
,,		Firefly F.R.Mk.4	1 × 2245 Griffon 74
Folland	Fo.139	Midge	1 × 1640 Viper
,,	Fo.145	Gnat F.Mk.1	1 × 4500 Orpheus BOr701
Gloster		Mars Mk.VI	1 × 325 Jaguar II
,,		Grouse Mk.I	1 × 230 B.R.2
,,		Grebe Mk.I	1 × 400 Jupiter IV
,,	G.16	Gorcock Mk.I	1 × 450 Lion IV
,,	G.19	Guan	1 × 450 Lion IV
,,	G.30	Goldfinch	1 × 450 Jupiter VIIF
,,		Gambet	1 × 420 Jupiter VI
,,		Gamecock Mk.I	1 × 425 Jupiter VI
,,	G.28	Gnatsnapper Mk.I	1 × 480 Mercury IIA
,,	S.S.18B		1 × 450 Jupiter VIIF
,,	S.S.19B		1 × 530 Mercury IV
,,	S.S.19B	Gauntlet Mk.I	1 × 645 Mercury VIS2
,,	S.S.35	Gnatsnapper Mk.III	1 × 600 Kestrel IIS
,,	S.S.37	Gladiator Mk.I	1 × 840 Mercury IX
,,	G.38	F.5/34	1 × 840 Mercury IX
,,	G.39	F.9/37	2 × 1050 Taurus TE/1
,,	G.39	F.9/37	2 × 885 Peregrine VIIIA
,,		Sea Gladiator	1 × 840 Mercury VIIIA
,,	G.41A	Meteor F.Mk.I	2 × 1700 Welland I
,,	G.41C	Meteor F.Mk.III	2 × 2000 Welland
,,	G.41F	Meteor F.Mk.IV	2 × 3500 Derwent 5
,,	G.41P	Meteor F.Mk.8	2 × 3600 Derwent 8
,,	G.41L	Meteor F.R.Mk.9	2 × 3500 Derwent 8
,,	G.47	Meteor N.F.Mk.11	2 × 3600 Derwent 8
,,	G.47	Meteor N.F.Mk.12	2 × 3800 Derwent 9
,,	G.47	Meteor N.F.Mk.13	2 × 3700 Derwent 8
,,	G.47	Meteor N.F.Mk.14	2 × 3700 Derwent 8
,,	G.A.2	E.1/44 Ace	1 × 5000 Nene II
,,	G.A.5	Javelin F.A.W.Mk.1	2 × 8150 Sapphire ASSa6
,,	G.A.5	Javelin F.A.W.Mk.2	2 × 8500 Sapphire ASSa6
,,	G.A.5	Javelin F.A.W.Mk.4	2 × 11000 Sapphire ASSa7
,,	G.A.5	Javelin F.A.W.Mk.7	2 × 11000 Sapphire ASSa7 203/204
,,	G.A.5	Javelin F.A.W.Mk.8	2 × 11000 Sapphire ASSa7

Max. Speed m.p.h.	Wt.(E) lb.	Wt.(L) lb.	Span	Length	Prototype
1500	25737	40000	34'10"	55'3"	XM169
1500	26905	42000	34'10"	55'3"	XP693
1500	28041	42000	34'10"	55'3"	XP697
90	1386	1946	27'9·25"	23'4"	8134
93		4880	77'	40'6·5"	3704
125		4700	40'	30'	N133
133	2039	3028	29'	23'	N163
164		3150	35'	24'9"	N216
169		4380	37'	28'6"	N235
188		3616	31'6"	24'10"	
212	2387	3202	30'8"	24'8"	
172		3740	33'6"	25'4"	G–ABFH/S1592
270	2500	4120	34'6"	27'6"	G–ADIF/F–6
232			38'	29'8"	A.F.6134
272	7384	9804	46'	40'2"	N1854
316	9750	14020	44'6"	37'7·25"	Z1826
386	9674	13500	41'2"	37'11"	Z2118
575		4500	20'8"	28'9"	G–39–1
M.0·98	3967	6191	22'1"	29'8"	G–39–2
150	1816	2550	28'	18'	J6925
128	1357	2106	28'	19'	G–EAYN
153	1720	2622	29'4"	20'3"	J7283
168	2364	3179	28'6"	26'1"	J7501
155	2859	3660	32'	22'	J7722
157	2058	3102	30'	22'3"	J7940
148	1944	3028	31'10"	21'3·5"	J–AAMB
155	1930	2863	29'9·5"	20'7"	J7497
165	2970	3625	33'6"	24'7"	N215
195		3510	32'9·5"	25'9"	J9125
193·5		3468	32'9·5"	26'2"	J9125
230	2775	3970	32'9·5"	26'2"	J9125
191	3391	3996	35'	31'3"	N227
253	3476	4750	32'3"	27'5"	K5200
315	4243	5400	38'2"	32'	K5604
360	8828	11653	50'	37'	L7999
330	9222	12108	50'	37'	L8002
245	3745	5420	32'3"	27'5"	N2265
410	8140	13800	43'	41'4"	DG202
460	8810	13300	43'	41'	EE230
585	9980	15175	37'2"	41'4"	EE360
590	10626	19100	37'2"	44'7"	VT150
595	10790	15660	37'2"	43'6"	VW360
554	12019	22000	43'	48'6"	WA546
554	12292	20380	43'	49'11"	WS590
576	12347	20490	43'	48'6"	WM308
578	12620	20444	43'	51'4"	WS722
630	8260	11400	36'	38'	SM809
M.0·94		31580	52'	56'3"	WD804
M.0·94		32100	52'	56'3"	XA773
M.0·96		32800	52'	56'3"	XA629
M.0·95		40000	52'	56'3"	XH704
M.0·95		37410	52'	56'3"	XH966

Manufacturer/ Designer	Type No.	Name	Engine(s) h.p./lb.s.t.
Gloster	G.A.5	Javelin F.A.W.Mk.9	2 × 11000 Sapphire ASSa7
Grahame-White	6	Warplane	1 × 90 Austro-Daimler
„ „	11	Warplane	1 × 100 Mono. Gnome
„ „	13	Scout	1 × 100 Mono. Gnome
„ „	20		1 × 80 le Rhône 9C
„ „	21		1 × 80 le Rhône 9C
Handley Page	H.P.21	S-1	1 × 230 B.R.2
Hawker		Woodcock Mk.I	1 × 358 Jaguar II
„		Woodcock Mk.II	1 × 380 Jupiter IV
„		Danecock	1 × 385 Jaguar IV
„		Heron	1 × 455 Jupiter VI
„		Hornbill	1 × 698 Condor IV
„		Hoopoe	1 × 560 Panther III
„		Hawfinch	1 × 450 Jupiter VI
„		F.20/27	1 × 520 Mercury VI
„		Hornet	1 × 480 R.-R.F.XIA
„		Fury Mk.I	1 × 525 Kestrel IIS
„		P.V.3	1 × 700 Goshawk B.43
„		Nimrod Mk.I	1 × 477 Kestrel IIS
„		Osprey	1 × 630 Kestrel IIMS
„		Demon	1 × 485 Kestrel IIS
„		Hurricane	1 × 1025 Merlin C
„		Hurricane F.Mk.I	1 × 1030 Merlin II
„		Hurricane F.Mk.IIA	1 × 1260 Merlin XX
„		Hurricane F.Mk.IIB	1 × 1260 Merlin XX
„		Hurricane F.Mk.IIC	1 × 1260 Merlin XX
„		Hurricane F.Mk.IID	1 × 1260 Merlin XX
„		Hurricane F.Mk.IV	1 × 1620 Merlin 24
„		Hotspur	1 × 1025 Merlin II
„		Fury Mk.II	1 × 640 Kestrel VI
„		Tornado	1 × 1760 Vulture II
„		Typhoon F.Mk.IB	1 × 2200 Sabre IIB
„		Sea Hurricane F.Mk.IIC	1 × 1260 Merlin XX
„		Tempest F.Mk.V	1 × 2180 Sabre IIA
„		Tempest F.Mk.II	1 × 2520 Centaurus IV
„		Tempest F.Mk.VI	1 × 2300 Sabre V
„		Sea Fury F.B.Mk.11	1 × 2550 Centaurus 18
„	P.1040		1 × 4500 Nene I
„	P.1040	Sea Hawk F.G.A.Mk.6	1 × 5200 Nene 103
„	P.1052		1 × 5000 Nene RN2
„	P.1067	Hunter F.Mk.1	1 × 7500 Avon RA7
„	P.1067	Hunter F.Mk.2	1 × 8000 Sapphire ASSa6
„	P.1067	Hunter F.Mk.4	1 × 7500 Avon RA21
„	P.1067	Hunter F.Mk.5	1 × 8000 Sapphire ASSa6 101
„	P.1099	Hunter F.Mk.6	1 × 10500 Avon 200
„	P.1099	Hunter F.G.A.Mk.9	1 × 10000 Avon 203
„	P.1099	Hunter F.R.Mk.10	1 × 10000 Avon 203
„	P.1072		1 × 5000 Nene RN2/ 1 × 2000 Snarler ASSn1
„	P.1081		1 × 5000 Nene RN2
„	P.1083		1 × 14500 Avon RA14R
„	P.1121		1 × 17000 Gyron P.S.26.6
„	P.1127		1 × 13500 Pegasus B.S.53
„ Siddeley	P.1127	Kestrel F.G.A.Mk.1	1 × 15500 Pegasus 5
„ „	P.1127/7	Harrier G.R.Mk.1	1 × 19200 Pegasus 10

Max. Speed m.p.h.	Wt.(E) lb.	Wt.(L) lb.	Span	Length	Prototype
M.0·95		40000	52'	56'4"	XH871
70	2200	2950	42'6"	33'9"	
80	1000	1550	37'		
85	1040	1800	27'10"	26'6"	
100					
107					
145	1410	1920	29'2"	21'5"	A–6402
143	2083	3023	34'8"	25'7"	J6987
141	2014	2979	32'6"	26'2"	J6988
145	2128	3045	32'7"	26'1·25"	151
156	2120	3126	31'10"	22'3"	J6989
187	2975	3769	31'	26'7·25"	J7782
196·5	2785	3910	33'2"	24'6"	N237
171	1925	2910	33'6"	23'8"	J8776
202	2155	3150	30'	22'9"	J9123
205	2409	3232	30'	26'3"	J9682
207	2623	3490	30'	26'8"	J9682
224	3530	4670	34'	28'2"	I–PV3
181	2901	3867	33'6·75"	26'6·5"	S1577
176	3045	4970	37'	29'4"	J9052
182	3067	4464	37'3"	29'7"	J9933
315	4129	5672	40'	31'6"	K5083
318	4670	6600	40'	31'4"	L1547
342	5150	8050	40'	32'2·5"	P3269
340	5640	8250	40'	32'2·5"	Z2326
336	5800	8100	40'	32'2·5"	V2461
322	5550	7850	40'	32'2·5"	Z2326
330	6150	8450	40'	32'2·5"	KX405
316	5800	7650	47'10·25"	36'1·5"	K8309
223	2743	3609	30'	26'8·75"	K1935
398	8377	10668	41'11"	32'10"	P5219
412	8840	13250	41'7"	31'11·5"	P5212
342	5788	7618	40'	32'3"	BD787
426	9000	11500	41'	33'8"	HM595
442	8900	11590	41'	34'5"	LA602
438	9394	12192	41'	33'10·5"	HM595
460	9240	12500	38'4·75"	34'8"	SR661
			36'6"	39'8"	VP401
630	9200	15200	39'	39'8"	VP413
593	9450	13488	31'6"	39'7"	VX272
M.0·93	12128	16200	33'8"	45'10·5"	WB188
M.0·94	11973	16200	33'8"	45'10·5"	WB202
M.0·94	12543	17100	33'8"	45'10·5"	WT701
M.0·94	12543	17100	33'8"	45'10·5"	WN954
M.0·95	12760	17750	33'8"	45'10·5"	XF833
M.0·95	13010	18000	33'8"	45'10·5"	XE617
M.0·95	13100	18090	33'8"	45'10·5"	XF429
M.0·82	11050	14050	36'6"	37'7"	VP401
M.0·89	11200	14480	31'6"	37'4"	VX279
M.1·2		20000	34'4"	45'10·5"	WN470
M.2·35			37'	66'6"	
720	8900	11800	24'4"	49'	XP831
710	9800	14500	22'11"	42'6"	XS688
730	14500	19500	25'3"	45'8"	XV276

Manufacturer/Designer	Type No.	Name	Engine(s) h.p./lb.s.t.
Hawker	P.1154		1 × 35600 B.S.100/8
Mann Egerton	H.1		1 × 200 Hispano-Suiza
,, ,,	H.2		1 × 200 Hispano-Suiza
Martin-Baker	M.B.2		1 × 1000 Dagger III
,, ,,	M.B.3		1 × 2020 Sabre II
,, ,,	M.B.5		1 × 2340 Griffon 83
Martinsyde	S.1		1 × 80 Gnome
,,	G.100	Elephant	1 × 120 Beardmore
,,	G.102	Elephant	1 × 160 Beardmore
,,	R.G.		1 × 275 Falcon III
,,	F.1		1 × 250 R.–R. Mk.III
,,	F.2		1 × 200 Hispano-Suiza
,,	F.3		1 × 275 Falcon III
,,	F.4	Buzzard	1 × 300 Hispano-Suiza
Miles	M.20	Mk.I	1 × 1260 Merlin XX
,,	M.20	Mk.II	1 × 1260 Merlin XX
,,	M.24	Master Mk.I	1 × 715 Kestrel XXX
Nestler		Scout	1 × 100 Mono. Gnome
Nieuport	B.N.1		1 × 230 B.R.2
,,		Nighthawk / Mars VI	1 × 385 Jupiter II
,,		Nightjar/Mars X	1 × 230 B.R.2
Parnall		Scout	1 × 260 Sunbeam Maori
,,		Plover	1 × 436 Jupiter IV
,,		Pipit	1 × 495 R.–R.F.XI
Pemberton Billing	P.B.9		1 × 50 Gnome
,, ,,	P.B.23E		1 × 80 le Rhône
,, ,,	P.B.25	Scout	1 × 100 Mono. Gnome
,, ,,	P.B.29E		2 × 90 Austro-Daimler
Port Victoria	P.V.1		1 × 100 Mono. Gnome
,, ,,	P.V.2		1 × 100 Mono. Gnome
,, ,,	P.V.2bis		1 × 100 Mono. Gnome
,, ,,	P.V.4		1 × 110 Clerget
,, ,,	P.V.5		1 × 150 Hispano-Suiza
,, ,,	P.V.5a		1 × 200 Hispano-Suiza
,, ,,	P.V.7	Grain Kitten	1 × 35 Gnat
,, ,,	P.V.8	Eastchurch Kitten	1 × 35 Gnat
,, ,,	P.V.9		1 × B.R.1
Robey-Peters		Pusher Scout	1 × 80 Gnome
,, ,,		Tractor Scout	1 × rotary
,, ,,		Three-seater	1 × 250 Eagle
Royal Aircraft Factory	A.E.3	R.A.E. Ram Mk.I	1 × 200 Arab
,, ,, ,,	B.E.2c	N.F.	1 × 70 Renault
,, ,, ,,	B.E.12		1 × 150 R.A.F.4a
,, ,, ,,	B.E.12a		1 × 150 R.A.F.4a
,, ,, ,,	B.E.12b		1 × 200 Hispano-Suiza
,, ,, ,,	B.S.1		1 × 100 Gnome
,, ,, ,,	F.E.2	(1911)	1 × 50 Gnome
,, ,, ,,	F.E.2	(1913)	1 × 70 Renault
,, ,, ,,	F.E.2a		1 × 100 Green
,, ,, ,,	F.E.2b		1 × 120 Beardmore
,, ,, ,,	F.E.2c		1 × 160 Beardmore
,, ,, ,,	F.E.2d		1 × 225 Eagle I
,, ,, ,,	F.E.3/A.E.1		1 × 80 Chenu
,, ,, ,,	F.E.4		2 × 150 R.A.F.5
,, ,, ,,	F.E.6		1 × 120 Austro-Daimler
,, ,, ,,	F.E.8		1 × 100 Mono. Gnome

Max. Speed m.p.h.	Wt.(E) lb.	Wt.(L) lb.	Span	Length	Prototype
M.1·93		30970	28'	58'	
100	1838	2404	30'9"	21'11"	N44
113	1760	2326	30'9"	21'11"	N45
350		5537	34'	34'2"	P9594
415		11497	35'	35'4"	R2492
460	9233	11500	35'	37'9"	R2496
87			27'8"	21'	702
95	1759	2424	38'	26'6"	4735
104	1793	2458	38'	27'	A1561
132	1740	2261	32'	25'10"	
109·5	2198	3260	44'6"	29'1"	A3933
120	1547	2355	32'	25'	
129·5	1859	2446	32'10"	25'6"	B1490
145	1710	2289	32'9·25"	25'5·75"	D4211
345	5884	7800	34'5"	30'9"	AX834/U-9
333	5870	7566	34'5"	30'9"	DR616/U-0228
226	4370	5573	39'	30'5"	N7412
127		2030	28'	18'6"	C3484
148	1818	2270	28'	18'	J2405
120	1870	2165	28'	19'2"	H8535
113·5			44'		N505
142	2035	2984	29'	23'	N160
173	3050	3980	35'	26'	N232
78	560	750	26'	20'	
89	1030	1576	33'	24'1"	9001
77		2130			
95·5	1087	1590	27'	22'	N1
93	1211	1702	29'	22'	N1
80·5		2400	32'		N8
94·5	1788	2456	32'	25'6"	N53
102·5	1972	2518	33'1"	26'9"	N54
89	284	491	18'	14'11"	N539
94·5	340	586	19'	15'7·5"	N540
110·5	1404	1965	30'11"	25'2"	N55
82	760	1150	32'5"	23'3·5"	
			54'6"	29'6"	9498
95			47'10·5"	27'8·5"	B8781
75			37'	27'3"	2028
102	1635	2352	37'	27'3"	1697
105	1610	2327	40'9"	27'3"	A562
			37'		
91·4		1200	27'6"	22'	
47·5		1200	33'	28'	
67		1865	42'	30'	
75		2680	47'9"	32'3"	2864
80·5	1993	2967	47'9"	32'3"	4256
			47'9"	32'3"	6370
92	2401	3549	47'9"	32'3"	7995
75		2100	48'	33'	
84·3	3754	7825	75'2"	38'2·5"	7993
	2000	2650	49'4"	29'6"	
94	895	1346	13'6"	23'8"	7456

Manufacturer/ Designer	Type No.	Name	Enngie(s) h.p./lb.s.t.
Royal Aircraft Factory	F.E.9		1 × 200 Hispano-Suiza
,, ,, ,,	N.E.1		1 × 200 Hispano-Suiza
,, ,, ,,	S.E.2		1 × 80 Gnome
,, ,, ,,	S.E.2a		1 × 80 Gnome
,, ,, ,,	S.E.4		1 × 160 Gnome
,, ,, ,,	S.E.4a		1 × 80 Gnome
,, ,, ,,	S.E.5		1 × 150 Hispano-Suiza
,, ,, ,,	S.E.5a		1 × 200 Hispano-Suiza
,, ,, ,,	S.E.5b		1 × 200 Hispano-Suiza
Sage	2		1 × 100 Mono. Gnome
Saro	A.10		1 × 490 R.–R.F.XIS
,,	SR.A.1		2 × 4000 Beryl
,,	SR.53		1 × 1750 Viper/ 1 × 8000 Spectre
Short	S.81	Gun-carrier	1 × 160 Gnome
,,	S.311	North Sea Scout B	1 × 310 Cossack
,,	S.364	Scout No. 3 N.2A	1 × 200 Afridi
,,	S.586	Springbok Mk.I	1 × 400 Jupiter
,,	S.744	Gurnard	1 × 540 Jupiter X
Sopwith		Tabloid	1 × 80 Gnome
,,	806	Gunbus	1 × 100 Mono. Gnome
,,		Two-seat Scout	1 × 80 Gnome
,,		Schneider Baby	1 × 130 Clerget
,,		Pup	1 × 80 le Rhône
,,		L.R.T.Tr.	1 × 250 R.–R.Mk.I
,,		1½-Strutter	1 × 110 Clerget
,,		Triplane	1 × 130 Clerget
,,	5F.1	Dolphin Mk.II	1 × 200 Hispano-Suiza
,,	2FR.2	Bulldog Mk.I	1 × 230 Clerget 11EB
,,	F.1	Camel	1 × 130 Clerget
,,	2F.1	Camel	1 × 130 Clerget
,,		Bee	1 × 50 Gnome
,,	7F.1	Snipe Mk.I	1 × 230 B.R.2
,,	T.F.2	Salamander	1 × 230 B.R.2
,,		Dragon	1 × 360 Dragonfly 1A
,,	3F.2	Hippo	1 × 200 Clerget 11EB
,,		Snark	1 × 360 Dragonfly 1A
,,		Snapper	1 × 360 Dragonfly 1A
,,		Swallow	1 × 110 le Rhône
,,	8F.1	Snail	1 × 170 Wasp I
Supermarine	P.B.31E	Nighthawk	2 × 100 Anzani
,,		N.1B Baby	1 × 200 Hispano-Suiza
,,		Seaking Mk.I	1 × 160 Beardmore
,,	224	F.7/30	1 × 660 Goshawk III
,,	300	Spitfire	1 × 1045 Merlin C
,,	300	Spitfire F.Mk.IA	1 × 1030 Merlin III
,,	329	Spitfire F.Mk.IIA	1 × 1175 Merlin XII
,,	349	Spitfire F.Mk.VC	1 × 1470 Merlin 45
,,	366	Spitfire F.Mk.XII	1 × 1735 Griffon III
,,	356	Spitfire F.Mk.21	1 × 2050 Griffon 61
,,	358	Seafire F.Mk.III	1 × 1470 Merlin 55
,,	371	Spiteful F.Mk.XIV	1 × 2375 Griffon 65
,,		Seafang F.Mk.31	1 × 2035 Griffon 61
,,	398	Attacker F.Mk.1	1 × 5100 Nene 3
,,	508		2 × 6500 Avon RA3
,,	510	Swift	1 × 5000 Nene

Max. Speed m.p.h.	Wt.(E) lb.	Wt.(L) lb.	Span	Length	Prototype
105		2480	37'9·5"	28'3"	A4818
95	2071	2946	47'10"	30'2"	B3971
85		1232	27'6"	22'	
96		1200	27'6"	22'	609
135			27'6"	21'4"	628
			27'5·2"	20'10·5"	5609
119	1399	1930	28'	21'4"	A4561
121	1400	1953	26'7·5"	20'11"	A4563
		1950	30'7"	20'10"	A8947
112	946	1546	22'2·5"	21'1·75"	
		3276	32'	24'5"	K1949/L2
516	11262	16255	46'	50'	TG263
M.2·2		12780	25'1·25"	45'10"	XD145
60	2200	3600	67'	33'9"	126
72	4900	7020	68'6"	45'9"	8319
			39'	28'	
121		4080	42'	26'11"	J6974
166·5	3086	4785	37'	28'7"	N228
92	670	1060	25'6"	20'	169
80			50'	32'6"	801
69			36'		1051
100	1226	1715	25'8"	23'	8123
111·5	787	1225	26'6"	19'3·75"	3691
			52'9"	35'3"	
106	1259	2149	33'6"	25'3"	3686
117	1101	1541	26'6"	18'10"	N500
140	1566	2358	32'6"	22'3"	D3615
109	1441	2495	33'9"	23'	X3
115	929	1453	28'	18'9"	
114	956	1523	26'11"	18'6"	N5
			16'3"	14'3"	
121	1312	2020	30'1"	19'9"	B9963
125	1844	2512	30'1·5"	18'9"	E5429
150		2132	31'1"	21'9"	E7990
115·5	1481	2590	38'9"	24'6"	X11
130		2283	26'6"	20'9"	F4068
140	1462	2190	28'	20'7"	F7031
113·5	889	1420	28'10"	18'9"	B9276
127		1478	25'9"	18'9"	
75	3677	6146	60'	37'	1388
117	1699	2326	30'5·5"	26'3·5"	N59
110			32'		
230		4950	45'10"	29'10"	K2890
346			36'10"	30'2·5"	K5054
365	4810	5784	36'10"	29'11"	K9787
357	4900	5900	36'10"	29'11"	K9788
374	5100	6785	36'10"	29'11"	N3053
393	5600	7400	32'7"	31'10"	EN221
420	6900	9200	36'11"	32'8"	DP851
352	5400	7100	36'10"	30'2·5"	MA970
494	7350	9950	35'6"	32'4"	NN664
475	7550	10574	35'	34'1"	VG471
590	8434	11500	36'11"	37'6"	TS409
			41'	50'	VX133
650	9434	12177	31'8·5"	38'1"	VV106

Manufacturer/ Designer	Type No.	Name	Engine(s) h.p./lb.s.t.
Supermarine	525		2 × 7175 Avon 114
,,	529		2 × 6500 Avon RA3
,,	535		1 × 5000 Nene
,,	541	Swift F.Mk.1	1 × 7000 Avon RA7
,,	544	Scimitar F.Mk.1	2 × 11250 Avon 202
,,	545		1 × 9500 Avon RA14
,,	549	Swift F.R.Mk.5	1 × 7175 Avon 114
Vickers	E.F.B.1	Destroyer	1 × 80 Wolseley
,,	E.F.B.2	Gunbus	1 × 100 Mono. Gnome
,,	E.F.B.3		1 × 100 Mono. Gnome
,,	E.F.B.4		1 × 100 Mono. Gnome
,,	E.F.B.5		1 × 100 Mono. Gnome
,,	F.B.5	Gunbus	1 × 100 Mono. Gnome
,,	F.B.6		1 × 100 Mono. Gnome
,,	F.B.7		2 × 100 Mono. Gnome
,,	F.B.7A		2 × 80 Renault
,,		Scout	1 × 100 Mono. Gnome
,,	F.B.8		2 × 100 Mono. Gnome
,,	F.B.9	Streamline Gunbus	1 × 100 Mono. Gnome
,,	E.S.1		1 × 100 Mono. Gnome
,,	E.S.2		1 × 110 Clerget
,,	F.B.11		1 × 250 R.-R.Mk.I
,,	F.B.12		1 × 80 le Rhône
,,	F.B.14		1 × 160 Beardmore
,,	F.B.16A		1 × 150 Hispano-Suiza
,,	F.B.19	Mk.I	1 × 100 Mono. Gnome
,,	F.B.24		1 × 200 Hispano-Suiza
,,	F.B.25		1 × 150 Hispano-Suiza
,,	F.B.26	Vampire Mk.I	1 × 200 Hispano-Suiza
,,	121	7.C1	1 × 455 Jupiter VI
,,	123		1 × 400 Hispano-Suiza 52
,,	141		1 × 510 R.-R.F.XI
,,	143		1 × 450 Jupiter VIA
,,	151	Jockey Mk.I	1 × 500 Mercury IIA
,,	151	Jockey F.7/30	1 × 450 Jupiter VIIF
,,	161	C.O.W. F.29/27	1 × 450 Jupiter VIIF
,,	177	F.21/26	1 × 540 Jupiter XFA
,,	125	Vireo	1 × 230 Lynx IV
,,	279	Venom	1 × 625 Aquila AE-3S
,,	432	F.7/41	2 × 1565 Merlin 61
Westland		N.1B	1 × 150 B.R.1
,,		N.1B	1 × 150 B.R.1
,,		Wagtail	1 × 170 Wasp
,,		Weasel	1 × 320 Dragonfly I
,,		Westbury	2 × 450 Jupiter VI
,,		Wizard	1 × 490 R.-R.F.XIS
,,		F.20/27	1 × 440 Mercury IIA
,,		C.O.W. F.29/27	1 × 485 Mercury IIIA
,,		P.V.4 F.7/30	1 × 600 Goshawk VIII
,,		Pterodactyl Mk.V	1 × 600 Goshawk
,,	P.9	Whirlwind	2 × 885 Peregrine I
,,	P.14	Welkin F.Mk.I	2 × 1650 Merlin 72/73
,,	W.35	Wyvern S.Mk.4	1 × 4110 Python ASP3
Whitehead		Comet	1 × 80 le Rhône
Wight		Quadruplane Scout	1 × 110 Clerget
,,		Baby	1 × 100 Mono. Gnome

Max. Speed m.p.h.	Wt.(E) lb.	Wt.(L) lb.	Span	Length	Prototype
	23333	28169	38'6"	55'	VX138
M.0·92	18460	22584	41'	50'	VX136
			32'4"		VV119
	12541	15591	32'4"	41'5·5"	WJ960
M.0·97	23474	34200	37'2"	55'4"	WT854
750	16548	20147	39'	47'	XA181
685	14766	21400	32'4"	43'	WN124
70	1760	2660	40'	27'6"	18
60	1050	1760	38'7"	29'2"	18/18A
60	1050	1680	37'4"	27'6"	18B
			36'6"		
70	1220	2050	36'6"	27'2"	664
70	1220	2050	36'6"	27'2"	1616
75	2136	3196	59'6"	36'	
			59'6"	36'	5717
100	600	1200	25'	20'7"	
98	1840	2700	38'4"	28'2"	
82·6	1029	1892	33'9"	28'5·5"	5271
114	843	1295	24'4·5"	20'3"	7509
112·2	981	1502	24'5·5"	20'3"	7759
96	3340	4934	51'	43'	A4814
92·4	845	1275	26'	21'6"	
99·5	1662	2603	39'6"	28'5"	
120	1170	1674	25'	19'	A8963
102	900	1485	24'	18'2"	
122	1630	2610	35'	26'	
86	1608	2454	41'6"	28'1"	
121	1470	2030	31'6"	23'5"	B1484
144	1920	2970	36'1"	23'8"	F-AHFH
149	2278	3300	34'	28'6"	G-EBNQ
177	2650	3700	34'	27'	G-EBNQ
150	2357	3170	34'	27'6"	
	3236		32'6"	23'	J9122
218	2268	3161	32'6"	23'	J9122
185	2381	3350	32'	23'6"	J9566
190	2835	4050	34'3"	27'6"	
120	1951	2550	35'	27'8"	N211
312		4156	32'9"	24'2"	PVO-10
440	16373	20168	56'10·5"	40'7·5"	DZ217
108·5	1504	1978	31'3·5"	26'5·5"	N16
107	1513	1987	31'3·5"	26'5·5"	N17
125	746	1330	23'2"	18'11"	C4291
130·5	1867	3071	35'6"	24'10"	F2912
125	4845	7877	68'	43'5"	J7765
188	2352	3275	39'6"	26'10"	J9252
	2350	3325	38'	25'4·25"	J9124
184·5	2615	3885	40'10"	29'10"	J9565
185	3687	5207	38'6"	29'6"	K2891
190	3534	5100	46'8"	20'6"	P8/K2770
360	7840	10270	45'	31'6"	L6844
387	14420	19840	70'	41'7"	DG558/G
550	15608	21200	44'	42'3"	VW880
103·5	872	1283	22'	21'	N546
86·5	1277	1864	30'8"	26'8"	9097

INDEX